Competition, Data and Privacy in the Digital Economy

International Competition Law Series

VOLUME 86

Editor

In its series editor, Alastair Sutton, Kluwer is fortunate to engage and benefit from the experience and expertise of one of the world's outstanding authorities on European Union and international economic law.

Introduction

In their efforts to regulate competition in an increasingly complex business environment, competition authorities face a daunting task. The European Commission and Courts, as well as national courts and legislatures, policymakers, and regulators, are constantly proposing, enacting, reviewing, and enforcing new legal measures, often addressing novel situations. Every industry and service is affected.

Contents/Subjects

With many titles currently available and new ones appearing regularly, the series' coverage includes detailed analyses of relevant legislation and case law in major global trading jurisdictions, defences used in cases involving the digital network economy, state aid cases, enforcement methodologies and a great deal more.

Objective & Readership

The purpose of Kluwer's International Competition Law Series is to follow the ever-changing contours of this dynamic area of the law, keeping the practice in sharp focus so that practising lawyers (including in-house counsel) and academics can be assured of the most up-to-date guidance and sources, in the widest possible range of applications.

The titles published in this series are listed at the end of this volume.

Competition, Data and Privacy in the Digital Economy

Towards a Privacy Dimension in Competition Policy?

Maria Wasastjerna

Wolters Kluwer

Published by:
Kluwer Law International B.V.
PO Box 316
2400 AH Alphen aan den Rijn
The Netherlands
E-mail: international-sales@wolterskluwer.com
Website: lrus.wolterskluwer.com

Sold and distributed in North, Central and South America by:
Wolters Kluwer Legal & Regulatory U.S.
7201 McKinney Circle
Frederick, MD 21704
United States of America
Email: customer.service@wolterskluwer.com

Sold and distributed in all other countries by:
Air Business Subscriptions
Rockwood House
Haywards Heath
West Sussex
RH16 3DH
United Kingdom
Email: international-customerservice@wolterskluwer.com

Printed on acid-free paper.

ISBN 978-94-035-2220-3

e-Book: ISBN 978-94-035-2224-1
web-PDF: ISBN 978-94-035-2232-6

Printed in the United Kingdom.

About the Author

Maria Wasastjerna is a Partner at Hannes Snellman Attorneys and Co-Head of the firm's competition practice in Finland. She has extensive experience in competition law, regulatory and compliance matters. Before joining Hannes Snellman, Maria gained several years of experience as an in-house lawyer in global corporations, most recently as Lead Competition Counsel at Nokia Corporation. Her professional experience includes working in Cleary Gottlieb Steen & Hamilton's Brussels office, the European Commission's Directorate General for Competition and the Office of International Affairs at the US Federal Trade Commission in Washington DC. Maria is a qualified attorney in Finland and in New York State (USA).

Maria earned her LLD with distinction from the University of Helsinki in 2019. During her doctoral studies, she was a visiting academic at the Institute of European and Comparative Law at the University of Oxford. She also holds LLM degrees from Georgetown University Law Center (2011), where she was a Fulbright-Schuman scholar, and the College of Europe in Bruges (2008). Maria regularly publishes articles, presents at conferences and lectures on competition, compliance and technology-related topics.

Table of Contents

Foreword
by Richard Whish

I was delighted to be asked to write a foreword to Maria Wasastjerna's admirable book *Competition, Data and Privacy in the Digital Economy*. The book, which has been developed from Ms Wasastjerna's PhD on the topic, could hardly be more timely, and it provides a superb account of the critical question of the extent to which data privacy is or should be relevant in the determination of competition law cases. This issue has been hotly debated in recent years, and divergent views have emerged. For some, data privacy is something to be addressed through bespoke legislation, such as the EU's General Data Protection Regulation: competition law has no part to play; for others, privacy is an important 'parameter' of competition, and the competition authorities have been neglectful of this fact. Seen from this perspective, the non-intervention in mergers such as *Facebook/WhatsApp* and *Facebook/Instagram* was a missed opportunity, contributing to the vast market power now held by Facebook. The furore that erupted after the Cambridge Analytica scandal may have been a watershed moment, when many citizens became aware, for the first time, of the dangers that can arise when vast hordes of data may be used in ways that individuals had never contemplated. As I write this foreword we await a judgment from the German Supreme Court in the appeal brought by the Bundeskartellamt against the suspension of the measures which it had ordered against Facebook to prevent it from amalgamating and commercializing data derived from Facebook, WhatsApp and Instagram – a form of 'internal' divestiture of Facebook. The case is of great legal interest, as it finds that Facebook was guilty of an exploitative (as opposed to an exclusionary) abuse of dominance by imposing unfair terms on its users: interestingly the case was brought under German competition law, not Article 102 TFEU. Had the BKA proceeded on the basis of EU competition law the draft decision would have had to be notified to the European Commission under Article 102 TFEU, and it is not impossible that the Commission might have used Article 11(6) of Regulation 1/2003, which would have stayed the German investigation and transferred jurisdiction to itself.

In Ms Wasastjerna's Acknowledgements at the start of the book, she says that 'Competition law is an inspiring discipline, as it continuously offers novel issues to research and write about.' Indeed! If we take 1890 as the start of modern competition law with the passing of the Sherman Act of that year (and acknowledge in passing that the Canadians got there one year earlier!), we can see that competition policy is always in a state of flux. It is inevitable that competition authorities and courts will be influenced by the economic and political considerations of the time. At the end of the 19th and the start of the 20th centuries, the 'trusts' – for example, in railroads, oil, coal – were of huge concern, and the 1912 election that brought Woodrow Wilson to power was fought around the 'antitrust' agenda. An adviser to Wilson in that election was Louis Brandeis, who argued that the trusts should be broken up. He went on to an illustrious career in the Supreme Court, and helped to form the US regime which, until the rise of the 'Chicago school', was deeply suspicious of monopoly, and inclined to assist entry into markets: exclusionary practices were frowned upon. The Chicago school was deeply critical of much of the law that accumulated: a key moment was the publication of Robert Bork's *The Antitrust Paradox*, which has exerted a powerful influence ever since and which has resulted in much laxer enforcement of the Sherman Act, in particular in relation to monopolization under section 2.

In the late 1990s and ever since, many competition authorities have tended to argue that the competition rules are there to promote 'consumer welfare', a phrase that I have always found helpful provided that no one tries to define what is meant by it. There seems little doubt that in the USA there has been a tendency, in particular on the part of adherents to the Chicago school, to interpret consumer welfare to mean that no conduct or merger should be called into question unless it can be shown that the outcome would mean higher prices. If this approach is applied strictly, it can lead to almost no competition law enforcement at all, except in relation to hardcore cartels. This version of the consumer welfare standard will certainly eliminate false positives – wrongly condemning pro-competitive behaviour as anticompetitive; however, there are likely to be many false negatives, where harmful behaviour is permitted to continue.

This is the background to the current debate, prompted by the very rapid emergence of the platform economy, where returns to scale, network effects, the multisidedness of markets and the accumulation of data have given rise to lively debate. Are we back in the 1890s and 1900s, except that the platforms are the modern avatar of the oil trusts and the railroad monopolies? Should the GAFA platforms be broken up as the early trusts were? Can the rules of 1890 and 1914 (in the USA) and of 1957 (the Treaty of Rome) be adapted to deal with the problems of the 2020s? These issues become yet more urgent at a time when the pandemic will almost certainly increase the market power of some platforms yet further. A specific concern in this debate is the rise of 'data-opolies'. What is the role of big data, and what is the relationship between big data and privacy: terms that we often use, and yet which are not free from terminological difficulties, as Ms Wasastjerna's book demonstrates? Of course, if the consumer welfare standard means that the only concern of competition authorities and courts should be with price, competition law will have little role to play, particularly in a system such as that of the USA where belief in the market mechanism to correct market failure is more deeply embedded (not least because of the influence of the Chicago school) than it is in the EU (and elsewhere). In recent years there has been a backlash in the USA against lax enforcement of the competition rules, and the 'New Brandeis' movement has succeeded in introducing new thinking (or reviving old thinking) into the debate. 'Hipster antitrust' was mocked not so many years ago, but quite quickly it came to be seen that it was not necessarily preposterous to argue that the competition policy agenda needed to be reset as the platforms, in particular, accumulated ever-greater market power. This chimed with broader concerns about the increasing concentration of markets, in the USA and further afield. Combined with a manifest rise in inequality, the deterioration of working conditions, insecurity of employment rights, in particular in the gig economy, these issues are now the subject of serious and intense debate; publications such as *The Economist* and the *Financial Times* - hardly the representatives of ivory tower academia (or of hipsters) - have regularly carried features, and indeed editorialized, about the need for more effective competition law enforcement.

This book provides an invaluable insight into these issues, with particular attention being given to whether privacy is a value which should be promoted in competition policy and whether this can be accommodated within a system in which consumer welfare is the standard to be applied. The author asks whether competitive analysis in the digital age should expand its scope to include a broader definition of consumer welfare, the main objective of competition. This book asserts that competition policy is currently undergoing a welcome intellectual shift and that a transformation is taking place as a result of digitalization and the rise of the data-driven economy. I share this view and agree with Tim Wu of Columbia Law School who has said that '[d]ecades of practice have shown that the promised scientific certainty of the Chicago method has not materialized, for economics does not yield answers, but arguments'.

Everyone involved in competition law and policy today will benefit hugely from this splendid book. We will see some major changes, not only in competition law enforcement but also, I suspect, in the competition law tools themselves in the years ahead. For example, the European Commission has just announced its intention to explore the possibility of introducing a new legal instrument modelled on the UK system of 'market investigation references' contained in the Enterprise Act 2002. I believe that the standards of privacy that firms can provide to customers and consumers are indeed one of the 'parameters' of competition and that this will come to be (more widely) accepted. I congratulate Maria Wasastjerna on this excellent contribution to an important debate.

Richard Whish
Emeritus Professor Law, King's College London
8 June 2020

Foreword
by Damien Geradin

The last decade has been marked by rapid development in technology and innovation, with much revolving around sharing personal information. Personal data represents an essential input to a growing number of digital products and services, including search engines, social networks, digital advertising, online dating services and many more. The ability to collect and process large troves of data has not only thus become a source of competitive advantage but also raises competition law issues when firms seek to leverage their data advantage across markets. At the same time, growing concerns over the handling of personal data in the wake of various scandals have led to the adoption of data protection legislation, such as the General Data Protection Regulation (GDPR) and the California Consumer Privacy Act (CCPA), hence creating entirely new bodies of law that could not be foreseen a decade ago.

Maria Wasastjerna's book *Competition, Data and Privacy in the Digital Economy* is therefore extremely timely. A central question in this book, which will be of interest to all competition law researchers and practitioners, is whether competition policy needs to be updated to meet the demands of the digitalized world we live in today and to protect the welfare of consumers. In particular, the author explores whether the price-centric approach in competition assessment, and the reduction of consumer welfare to price considerations in some jurisdictions, is still optimal for data-driven businesses and strategies where the product or service is free and the 'cost' is consumer data privacy.

Many will agree with the author that the answer to that question is probably negative and that privacy considerations can no longer be ignored by competition authorities. Change can already be noticed with the *Facebook* decision adopted by the Bundeskartellamt in 2019 finding a competition breach due to Facebook's practices conflicting with data protection rules, although this decision has been looked at suspiciously by many competition lawyers. The book also makes a strong case that EU competition law is uniquely placed to accommodate privacy as part of its policy goals and assessment. By contrast, for a variety of reasons explained by the author, the US antitrust regime seems less apt to incorporate privacy among its policy goals and to make it part of its antitrust assessment.

The author does not fail to observe that incorporating privacy as part of the competitive assessment of an agreement, a unilateral practice or a transaction is fraught with difficulties. From a general standpoint, privacy is a component of quality, which is in turn a central element or parameter of competition. However, measuring privacy may not be so easy as there may be a subjective element. The author correctly observes, however, that a variety of tools and methodologies can be used to assign a monetary value to personal data and privacy. Developing such tools and methodologies will be a vast area of research for lawyers and economists in the years to come.

The growing interface between competition law and privacy protection also raises important institutional challenges. So far, the authorities in charge of enforcing these regimes have largely worked separately, and Commissioner Vestager has made it clear that data protection authorities (DPAs) do not have a role to play in the competition assessment of mergers raising privacy concerns. But this does not say all. When competition authorities ignore privacy considerations in competition assessments and data protection authorities ignore the competitive dimensions of data privacy, they may take too narrow an approach. The *Google/Fitbit* merger, which is currently examined by the European Commission, represents an important test case as, while this merger could potentially increase competition in the market for so-called wearables, it also raises important privacy questions, such as whether it is reasonable to allow Google to acquire another company that is able to collect large troves of personal data from its users. It is not clear whether Google can be trusted on such matters.

I can certainly foresee some important areas of collaboration between competition authorities and DPAs. For instance, in my practice, I see digital gatekeepers increasingly using privacy-related considerations as a justification for practices that can be harmful to smaller rivals, for instance by depriving them of the data they need to develop and deliver their products and services or by reducing interoperability on privacy grounds. Separating legitimate from illegitimate uses of privacy as a convenient defence to practices harming competition is an area where competition authorities will need the support of data protection authorities. Conversely, competition authorities have an important advocacy role to play in ensuring that data protection rules do not harm competition, by, for instance, increasing concentration as large organizations are generally better equipped to implement these rules and bear compliance costs.

Maria Wasastjerna's book is well structured and contains a wealth of information. Before discussing the interlinkages between competition law and privacy, the author describes the fundamental components of both regimes. This arms the reader with the knowledge required to fully appreciate the central thesis of this book, which is the need for competition law and policy to adapt to the demands of business models powered by the use of data and the provision of free products and services. The book does not only look at the past but also makes a number of proposals for the rethinking of competition policy for the data economy and the introduction of a privacy dimension to competition law's policy goals.

The book's use of the comparative method with an analysis of both EU and US laws and enforcement institutions is also extremely helpful, as is often the case when looking at antitrust matters. In particular, the author's discussion of the price-centric approach to competition analysis developed by the Chicago school is illuminating. It shows why competition authorities have always had difficulties in paying attention to non-price elements, such as privacy considerations, in their competition assessments, in particular in the USA where the Chicago school remains prevalent. While US antitrust agencies and federal courts have historically been a source of inspiration for many competition law regimes across the world, EU competition law has proved to be more adaptable to the assessment of conduct in digital markets, although some progress remains to be made.

This book will be found helpful by a wide audience, including competition specialists (academics, practitioners, enforcers), as well as privacy experts. While it is based on strong theoretical foundations, it is also accessible and practical in nature, and its use is facilitated by the fact it is clearly organized and extremely well-written. This is clearly a must-read for all those interested in competition in digital markets.

Damien Geradin
Professor Competition Law and Economics, Tilburg University
Brussels, 7 June 2020

Preface and Acknowledgements

This book is based on my doctoral dissertation *Competition, Data and Privacy in the Digital Economy: Testing Conventional Boundaries and Expanding Horizons – Towards a Privacy Dimension in Competition Policy?* I presented my dissertation for public defence at the University of Helsinki on 19 October 2019. I would like to express my gratitude to Kluwer Law International and Simon Bellamy for encouraging me to turn my dissertation into this book and enabling the publication of my research of the past four years.

Looking back, my initial decision to pursue a doctorate came from curiosity and a desire to combine the practice of law with a more academic dimension. The topic of my doctoral research and what was to become the final dissertation began to take shape in my mind when working as an in-house counsel at Nokia Corporation, a multinational technology company, and following the developments and the discourse concerning digitalization and big data. Competition law is an inspiring discipline, as it continuously offers novel issues to research and write about. Especially in the digital age with rapid technological developments and increasing access to information, competition law and policy evolve with society and are in a constant state of transformation. In my view, navigating these complexities and understanding the interdependency between the theoretical side of competition law and its application in the business world benefits from one having practical experience in the field.

My research and this book examines the role of privacy in competition law in the digital economy. It explores the growing significance of data protection and looks at the interlinkage between privacy and competition policy, thereby testing conventional boundaries and expanding horizons. With the transition to the data-driven economy, our society has grown to rely on products and services that are free of charge to consumers, but because they have no monetary price, there is hesitation whether, and how, action should follow. The book questions whether competition policy is too fixated on the idea that the only real harm consists of rising prices. Consumers pay for online services with time and data. When many products and services seem free in today's online markets, with user data as the invisible cost, looking only at price effects in competition is, however, misleading. My book asserts that an overly price-centred approach to competition policy risks overlooking significant welfare harms that relate to non-price dimensions, such as privacy and consumer choice.

Since the beginning of my research four years ago, the topic has evolved substantially and been increasingly visible in public discourse. For example, in 2019, a German competition case took traditionally minded lawyers by surprise when establishing a competition breach due to Facebook's practices conflicting with data protection rules, thereby breaking ground in the intersection between competition and privacy. At the time of finalizing the book, the German Federal Supreme Court has just ruled against Facebook and in favour of the national competition authority, and this pioneering case is still under appeal. Moreover, the European Commission has recently proposed new controversial tools for intervention in digital markets, sparking debate among academics, practitioners and policymakers alike. The timeliness of the topic of the book has made the process of writing exceptionally interesting, dynamic and challenging. At a time when protection of personal information and privacy is of growing public concern and the market behaviour of data-driven businesses is scrutinized by the authorities, through this book I hope to provide readers with an overview of the contemporary interplay between competition, data and privacy in the digital economy.

While conducting my research, I have had the privilege of being surrounded by a great network of academics and practitioners, who I want to thank for their support throughout the project. I wish to thank Professor Orla Lynskey, whose work has inspired my research, and who acted as my opponent in the public defence of my dissertation. I would also like to thank my pre-examiners, Professors Ulf Bernitz and Peter Whelan, and my Supervising Professor Johan Bärlund at the University of Helsinki, for excellent guidance along the way. Moreover, I wish to thank all my colleagues, former and current, with whom I have had the pleasure to discuss my research, and in particular my colleagues at Hannes Snellman Attorneys, for their support during the writing of this book. I am also grateful to all my former colleagues at Nokia Corporation, especially Jenni Lukander for being an inspiration, and Ilkka Rahnasto, who encouraged me from the very beginning to pursue a doctorate.

I further wish to thank Victoriastiftelsen and Ella and Georg Ehrnrooths Foundation for financial support for my doctoral studies, including my stay at the University of Oxford as an academic visitor in summer 2018. I also thank the University of Helsinki for supporting my participation in international conferences and seminars to present my research and engage in the academic community.

Finally, and most importantly, my doctorate and this book would not have been possible without the encouragement and support from my friends and family, especially my parents Markus and Hannele Troberg. Still, the biggest thank you of all goes to my wonderful husband Paul, who is also my biggest supporter with an admirable patience and someone who encourages me in all my endeavours and aspirations in life. Thank you for everything.

Maria Wasastjerna
Helsinki, 8 July 2020

List of Abbreviations

ACCC	Australian Competition and Consumer Commission
AG	Advocate General
AGCM	*Autorità Garante della Concorrenza e del Mercato*
CJEU	Court of Justice of the European Union
CMLRev	Common Market Law Review
CUP	Cambridge University Press
DG	Directorate-General
DOJ	Department of Justice (US)
DPA	Data Protection Authority
ECHR	European Convention on Human Rights
ECtHR	European Court of Human Rights
ECN	European Competition Network
EDPS	European Data Protection Supervisor
EL Rev	European Law Review
EU	European Union
FTC	Federal Trade Commission
GDP	Gross Domestic Product
GDPR	General Data Protection Regulation
IECL	Institute of European and Comparative Law
OECD	Organisation for Economic Co-operation and Development
OJ	Official Journal of the European Union
OJLS	Oxford Journal of Legal Studies
OUP	Oxford University Press
SSNDQ	Small but Significant and Non-transitory Decline in Quality
SSNIP	Small but Significant and Non-transitory Increase in Price
TEU	Treaty on the European Union

TFEU	Treaty on the Functioning of the European Union
UK	United Kingdom
USA/US	United States

CHAPTER 1
Introduction

The last decade has been marked by rapid development in technology and innovation, with much revolving around sharing personal information, enabling the development of valuable products and services. Data is the price consumers pay for access to various online offerings and to digital platforms such as Facebook and Google. But how that personal information is treated by businesses has only in recent years become a competition issue. This introductory chapter lays ground for this book, exploring the role of personal information and data protection in competition law in the increasingly digital business environment and data-driven markets. The chapter sets the scene for the reader and presents the scope and objective of the book, making certain limitations and providing the theoretical basis and underpinnings for later discussion. Lastly, the chapter concludes by explaining relevant terminology and giving the reader an understanding of the broad societal relevance, timeliness and interdisciplinary character of the topic of this book.

§1.01 BACKGROUND

Digital transformation continues to bring unprecedented changes to the economy and society, bringing both new opportunities and new risks. When entering the third decade of the 21st century, a sophisticated understanding of the competition law environment is more important than ever, in which companies need to be antitrust compliant in all jurisdictions, considering the economic, political and legal focus on data in particular. One key theme for businesses in the coming years will be the ever-increasing importance of competition law in the digital economy, and in this context, the growing role of data and sharing of personal information. The new decade promises to be testing, with technology and data-driven practices in enforcement authorities' sights, sustainability concerns and climate change front and centre, and a strong focus on consumer welfare, understood broadly. These developments will not be without impact on business, not least as competition law and privacy continue to be also on the political agenda around the world.

The transition from price-driven to data-driven markets has raised questions ranging from whether existing competition laws and enforcement tools are still fit for purpose to how antitrust should interact with data protection law. Competition authorities express concern that market power is too concentrated with a call for increased enforcement, and how authorities and politicians will act to protect competition and markets – as well as privacy and choice – will be decisive for the future. There has been broad debate across the globe as to whether the competition laws are efficient enough in targeting the business models of digital platforms and especially their use of data – practices that have made many of the American technology companies so successful. In this context, the 2020 US presidential candidates and members of Congress from both parties are also vowing to reinvigorate antitrust enforcement in the digital arena.

In Europe, the new European Commission, led by President Ursula von der Leyen, has identified creating a 'Europe fit for the digital age' as a major priority over the next five years and beyond to ensure that Europe makes the most of the enormous potential of the digital age,[1] and unveiled a series of proposals laying out the EU's approach to data and platform regulation, among other. The European Commission envisions Europe to lead the transition to a new digital world, perhaps as part of the Brussels Effect,[2] and heading this development is the EU Competition Commissioner Margrethe Vestager, appointed to an unprecedented second term to stay in charge of Europe's competition rules, with an additional portfolio of overseeing also EU digital policy. The expanded brief covers not only competition enforcement but also the regulation of the digital economy,[3] which to some degree demonstrates how the EU is acknowledging that boundaries between competition, data and privacy are becoming increasingly blurred. What is clear is that the EU will be very active in addressing digital policy issues in the coming years. In her political guidelines, then President-elect von der Leyen called for Europe to grasp 'the opportunities from the digital age within safe and ethical boundaries ... we have to find our European way, balancing the flow and wide use of data while preserving high privacy, security, safety, and ethical standards'.

Another development that will deeply affect the markets and impact the role and meaning of privacy is the outbreak of the coronavirus epidemic (COVID-19) around the world in 2020 and related measures by various governments to face the crisis. These developments and related actions will leave no area in economy, society or law, including competition and data protection, untouched. The developments around this major crisis of humankind and this generation will have an effect on the understanding of what constitutes privacy, reflecting concerns and urgent changes in society and

1. European Commission Communication 'Shaping Europe's digital future' COM(2020)67 (19 February 2020).
2. Anu Bradford, *The Brussels Effect: How the European Union Rules the World* (OUP 2020).
3. Mario Todino and Emilie Ry Schou, 'What Agenda for the Second Term of Commissioner Vestager?' (October 2019) Competition Policy International. Laura Kayali, Melissa Heikkilä and Janosch Delcker, 'Europe's Digital Vision, Explained' Politico (19 February 2020) https://www.politico.eu/article/europes-digital-vision-explained/, accessed 19 April 2020.

current values. The decisions people and governments take in efforts to stop the epidemic will shape the world for years to come,[4] including the notion of people's privacy and individual data protection.

As a result of the digital transformation of the world we live in, what is clear is that data has become a crucial feedstock of the world economy and is commonly referred to as the 'oil of the internet',[5] 'fuel of the future' or the 'currency of the digital economy'. While these industrial metaphors, whether oil or fuel, reflect the economic value of personal data in the digital economy, they fail to recognize that personal data is also essentially linked to the dignity, autonomy and privacy of individuals.

The analogies reflect the commoditization of data and its economic value in the digital economy, where personal information rather than cash has become the currency of payment. However, these same analogies fail to pay heed to the fact that, in addition to having monetary value, personal data is also closely connected to privacy and expression of consumer choice. In this context, there is increasing unease with the privacy of data and the collection and use of personal information raises privacy issues. This is acknowledged, not only by consumer and data protection authorities (DPAs) but also increasingly by competition authorities. In this context, an emerging question is the role of competition law in protecting consumers from privacy risks.

Data is the price consumers pay for access to various online offerings and to platforms such as Facebook and Google. But how that personal information is treated by businesses has only in recent years become a competition issue. While competition law – according to conventional thinking – is interested in data due to its economic value, data protection rules, for their part, deal with personal rights, but not necessarily the market value of data. Nevertheless, the value that individuals assign to protection of their personal data is of great importance to businesses, the legal community, and policymakers.[6]

That value is important to businesses because estimating how highly customers value protection of their personal data enables businesses to predict which privacy-enhancing initiatives may become sources of competitive advantage. The same value is important to legal scholars and practitioners because privacy is an issue that has become increasingly prominent in the law in recent years, largely because of digitalization and the emergence of new technologies. Finally, individual valuations of privacy are important to policymakers, who are often required to choose between policies that trade off privacy for other desirable goals.

The EU legal framework concerning data privacy – the General Data Protection Regulation (GDPR) – brought data protection regulation to the forefront of public discussion, and consumers' views on the value of personal data have been shifting

4. Yuval Noah Harari, 'The World after Coronavirus' Financial Times (20 March 2020) https://www.ft.com/content/19d90308-6858-11ea-a3c9-1fe6fedcca75, accessed 19 April 2020.
5. The Economist, 'Fuel of the Future: Data Is Giving Rise to a New Economy' (6 May 2017): 'Data are to this century what oil was to the last one: a driver of growth and change. Flows of data have created new infrastructure, new businesses, new monopolies, new politics and – crucially – new economics'.
6. Alessandro Acquisti, Leslie K John and George Loewenstein, 'What Is Privacy Worth?' (2013) 42 Journal of Legal Studies 249.

since the wake of the Facebook-Cambridge Analytica scandal, prompting citizens to wake up to their data rights and acknowledging the value of data protection.[7] Concern is growing over consumer welfare and privacy protection in the context of the digital economy and the ever-increasing presence of big data and big analytics, while increasing collection and exploitation of personal information for commercial use raises privacy issues. This is no longer only a question of consumer and data protection but also one of competition policy, with competition regulators increasingly focusing on the complex relationship between data, market power, and competition with the aim of better understanding the possible effects for consumers and digital markets.

Competition issues associated with data now regularly feature on the agenda of competition authorities around the world. The EU Competition Commissioner has highlighted "competition in a big data world' as a new frontier for competition law,[8] and it is commonly acknowledged today that data can be a source of market power.[9] Although amassing and analysing of data by companies is not limited to consumer data, many aspects of big data are targeted specifically at consumers. As noted by the European Data Protection Supervisor (EDPS), '[n]ot all big data is personal, but for many online offerings which are presented or perceived as being "free", personal information operates as a sort of indispensable currency used to pay for those services'.[10] As the amount of information about users and their preferences collected by businesses is rapidly growing, the impact of data as a factor in competition analysis is attracting mounting attention.[11]

The emerging number of businesses that achieve extremely significant turnover based on a business model involving collection and commercial use of personal data has also spurred discussions about the role of data in economic relationships, as well as in the application of competition law to those relationships, in particular as regards the assessment of data as a factor in establishing market power.[12] Instead of talking about monopolies in the traditional sense, the concept of data-opolies is emerging in public discourse to describe the so-called tech giants with significant market power based on data.[13]

7. The scandal, during which data from 87 million Facebook users was illegally accessed from the platform, has also led to wider concerns about Facebook's entire applications ecosystem and data processing practices. *See e.g.* Dina Srinivasan, 'Why Privacy Is an Antitrust Issue' The New York Times (28 May 2019) https://www.nytimes.com/2019/05/28/opinion/privacy-antitrust-facebook.html, accessed 19 April 2020; MLex Comment: 'Regulatory scrutiny of Facebook data-sharing won't be limited to Cambridge Analytica privacy breach' (22 March 2018).
8. Speech by Margrethe Vestager, 'Competition in a Big Data World', DLD 16 (Munich, 17 January 2016) https://ec.europa.eu/commission/commissioners/2014-2019/vestager/announcements/competition-big-data-world_en, accessed 19 April 2020.
9. Joint report by the French and German competition authorities, Autorité de la concurrence and Bundeskartellamt, Competition Law and Data (10 May 2016) 11 (French-German joint report).
10. European Data Protection Supervisor (EDPS), Preliminary Opinion, Privacy and competitiveness in the age of big data: The interplay between data protection, competition law and consumer protection in the digital economy (March 2014) 6 (EDPS Opinion).
11. French-German joint report (n 9) 11.
12. French-German joint report (n 9) 3.
13. Maurice E Stucke, 'Should We Be Concerned About Data-Opolies?' (2018) 2 Georgetown Law Technology Review 275.

In the current economic climate, politicians worry about increasing corporate concentration when a handful of the world's largest companies dominate the technology sectors. Policymakers debate the introduction of platform regulation or breaking up Internet gatekeepers benefiting from network effects. Against this background, the aim of this book – as will be described further in §1.02 – is to take a critical look at competition policy to evaluate whether the system in its current form and with the existing approach is capable of tackling these novel challenges raised by the digital age, especially the role of personal data.

Some of these novel questions appear at the intersection of competition and data protection rules. By and large, privacy is of great importance in a functioning society. Therefore, research on issues related to this area is important. This book is aimed not only at competition scholars and privacy experts because the topic can be of general interest. After all, should not research ultimately be about all of us becoming wiser?

§1.02 SCOPE AND OBJECTIVES

Rapid technological development, the introduction of artificial intelligence, the Internet of Things (IoT), big data and big analytics all have contributed to the economy – and the world around us – going digital. Over the past century, the raw materials, means of production and currency have undeniably changed. Yesterday's oil, steel and railroads are to a large extent today's personal data. This data is collected in masses from our every online interaction and fuels the Internet economy. In the 21st century digital world, data has undoubtedly become a core economic resource.[14] This can also be illustrated in numbers: the value of the EU's data economy is estimated to exceed EUR 7 billion in 2020.[15]

All of these developments are not without effect on competition law. They are giving rise to many new questions, most importantly whether the current approach to competition policy is optimal for the digital age and online markets. This broad question can be translated into a narrower one, namely whether the existing consumer welfare standard that currently guides competition policy and enforcement is capable of addressing anticompetitive conduct in digital markets. One of the biggest challenges for competition authorities in the digital age is how to deal with data and privacy issues in their competitive analysis.

Increasingly, we conduct our lives online. To do this, we grant access to our personal information. During the past decade, companies such as Facebook, Amazon, Alibaba and Google (Alphabet) have sprung up and become powerful by collecting and selling user data. Facebook is described as 'the company responsible for the largest and

14. Commissioner Reding observed already in 2012 that '[p]ersonal data is the currency of today's digital market'. Speech by Viviane Reding, 'The EU Data Protection Reform 2012: Making Europe the Standard Setter for Modern Data Protection Rules in the Digital Age' Innovation Conference Digital, Life, Design (Munich, 22 January 2012) SPEECH/12/26.
15. The estimate is from the study by the Finnish Competition and Consumer Authority (FCCA), Questions related to competition and consumer protection in data economy (February 2019) 11.

most brazen data-collection project in human history'.[16] These data-driven businesses occupy an increasingly important role in the modern economy and digitalization certainly offers tremendous potential for improving people's quality of life, for doing business more efficiently, and for creating revolutionary business models.

Data is commonly acknowledged as having the potential to create significant competitive advantage for companies.[17] Over the last years, competition authorities have increasingly recognized the importance of data in the digital economy, with some of the leading agencies addressing the issue through published reports, investigations, and sector enquiries. One of the most notable examples is the abuse of dominance case by the German competition authority (Bundeskartellamt) against Facebook, opened in 2016 and decided by the authority three years later in 2019.[18]

The case, currently under appeal in German court, concerns the interlinkage between data and market power and looks into Facebook's abuse of market power based on an infringement of data protection rules.[19] According to the Bundeskartellamt's preliminary finding in December 2017 and confirmed by its final ruling in 2019, the social network's breach of data protection amounts to abuse of a dominant position in violation of competition law.[20] In this regard, the German competition authority's antitrust case against Facebook represents a groundbreaking case at the intersection of data protection law and competition law: indeed, the very field of study of this book. The probe is also one of the first cases in which complex issues involving big data, privacy and competition law are colliding.

With the 'big data' trend and the transition from an offline to an online economy, concern is growing about the commercialization and exploitation of personal data and violation of digital privacy. Competition issues associated with personal data and the role of competition law in protecting consumers from potential privacy risks in the modern economy are novel questions – indeed, questions that previously have not received sufficient attention. This is perhaps because the offline economy involved little need to explore these issues. But with the transition to the online economy, where personal data is the new currency, the situation has changed.

The subject of this book, which builds on a doctoral dissertation, began to take shape for the first time in the author's mind when working as a practising lawyer in a multinational technology company, dealing with issues of global competition law and

16. Jake Bittle, 'A Mark Zuckerberg Presidency Isn't Ridiculous – It's Terrifying' The Nation (18 August 2017) https://www.thenation.com/article/a-mark-zuckerberg-presidency-isnt-ridiculous-its-terrifying/, accessed 19 April 2020.
17. Organisation for Economic Co-operation and Development (OECD), 'Supporting Investment in Knowledge Capital, Growth and Innovation' (2013) 319.
18. Bundeskartellamt press releases, 'Bundeskartellamt initiates proceeding against Facebook on suspicion of having abused its market power by infringing data protection rules' (2 March 2016) and 'Bundeskartellamt prohibits Facebook from combining user data from different sources' (7 February 2019); Bundeskartellamt, Case summary: Facebook, Exploitative business terms pursuant to Section 19(1) GWB for inadequate data processing (15 February 2019) (Bundeskartellamt case summary).
19. Bundeskartellamt case summary (n 18) 10–12.
20. Bundeskartellamt press release, 'Preliminary assessment in Facebook proceeding: Facebook's collection and use of data from third-party sources is abusive' (19 December 2017); Bundeskartellamt case summary (n 18).

following developments and the discourse concerning digitalization and big data. Working in a global technology company affords unique insights and enables a 'front-row seat' for the latest developments in law and policy. This in turn enabled the author to reflect on the debate around data and the role of privacy in competition law.

In recent times, the role of data in competition law has been a recurrent theme in Brussels and elsewhere, not least with the EU Competition Commissioner giving several speeches on the subject. This caused the author to think hard about what role personal data, privacy and data protection should play in competition law, and what academia has to say about that. The author was stimulated to address a broad question that was increasingly on her mind, namely the impact on competition law of the digital economy and the increasing importance of data.

In order to tackle this very broad question and undertake meaningful research, some sub-questions need to be formulated and answered. Indeed, this broad question translates into several narrower sub-questions that will be addressed throughout the book. Specifically, three important issues will be considered in more detail: what is the role (if any) of personal data and privacy in competition law? Should competition policy protect privacy among its objectives? Does competition policy to some extent already consider privacy in its goals?

It is worth noting here that one can distinguish between specific goals or objectives and more general aims. Whereas aims can generally be characterized as more idealistic or abstract, goals or objectives are perhaps more concrete as to their nature. However, in this book, this sort of distinction is not followed strictly, and the terminology is used interchangeably.

The whole debate about the role of privacy in competition law has quite a philosophical air to it. This hopefully appeals to the curiosity of the reader, irrespective of legal practitioner or academic, and interest in fields that go beyond law, especially philosophy and the relationship between law and various other disciplines. This book, although focusing on competition law, opens a door to a fascinating world including different legal areas and other disciplines, where notions such as 'privacy', 'fairness' and 'welfare' challenge the reader's mind not only from a strictly legal but also from a theoretical and philosophical point of view.

So, this book sets out to explore the rather complex relationship between data, market power, and competition to seek a better understanding of the possible effects for consumers and digital markets. Leading scholars and policymakers, spearheaded by key stakeholders such as the EDPS, the EU's independent DPA, have started proposing arguments for the inclusion of privacy objectives in competition law to enhance privacy protection and fill regulatory gaps.[21] In examining the role of data privacy in competition policy, this book asks whether privacy goals should be considered in competition policy in the digital age, and if so – how?

It follows that a guiding broader theme of this book concerns the issue of whether current competition policy needs new approaches because of the digitalization of the

21. EDPS Opinion (n 10).

economy. Traditionally, collecting, processing and exploiting personal data for commercial use is seen by many as a question for consumer or data protection rather than one of competition law. However, recent high-profile abuse of dominance cases, as well as certain mergers and acquisitions in digital or Internet markets, have raised the question of the possible competition impact of gaining and exercising control over large data sets, and a desire to better understand the possible consequences for consumers and markets.[22] Indeed, in July 2017, the *Harvard Business Review* published a piece urging competition law to be updated for the digital age, arguing that tomorrow's monopolies would not be judged only in terms of how much they sell but also how much they know about us and how much better they can predict our behaviour than their competitors.[23]

The purpose of competition policy is to secure fair economic competition and to safeguard consumer welfare. Without well-functioning competition and efficient implementation of competition rules, market players can use competitive methods which abuse and exploit personal data by putting consumer privacy at risk and disrespecting the fundamental right to privacy protection. This book questions whether the competition rules written for an offline world which did not know of the Internet are optimal, and whether competition policy needs to be updated to meet the demands of the digitalized world we live in today and to protect the welfare of consumers, offline as well as online.

In digital markets, the concern is that while competition exists in principle, it is chilled by strong network effects and high switching costs.[24] For example, as a consumer, try breaking away from a Facebook profile with hundreds of friends, a Twitter account with thousands of followers or the Microsoft Office suite with its familiar keyboard shortcuts. Not to mention trying to use the Internet without the Google search engine.[25] What this means is that a market failure seems to have occurred as evidenced by lack of consumer choice. The question that arises is whether competition law should correct this kind of market failure?

Generally, competition rules are enforced against companies with significant market power when consumers suffer some demonstrable harm, usually through rising prices. However, in the Internet economy, online services are generally free. This means that the notion of market power is more elusive when consumer harm does not

22. OECD, 'Big Data: Bringing Competition Policy to the Digital Era' (29–30 November 2016) 18 (OECD Big Data).
23. Bala Iyer, Mohan Subramaniam, and Uruppattur Srinivasa Rangan, 'The Next Battle in Antitrust Will Be about Whether One Company Knows Everything About You' Harvard Business Review (6 July 2017) https://hbr.org/2017/07/the-next-battle-in-antitrust-will-be-about-whether-one-company-knows-everything-about-you, accessed 19 April 2020.
24. *See e.g.* European Parliament, 'Challenges for Competition Policy in a Digitalized Economy' (Study for the ECON Committee, Directorate-General for Internal Policies, Economic and Monetary Affairs, 2015) 34: 'Access to digital platform often seems to be free of charge, but by providing the platform operators with personal data consumers do at least pay a price in terms of switching costs.'
25. As a result of the increasing popularity of Google's search engine, usage of the transitive verb 'to google' has become widespread. The neologism commonly refers to searching for information on the Internet, regardless of which search engine is used. It was added to the *Oxford English Dictionary* and to the eleventh edition of the *Merriam-Webster Collegiate Dictionary* in 2006.

necessarily translate into high prices. Many of today's digital businesses capitalize on personal information in various ways. The consumer harm that may follow is without a conventional price tag, but instead the harm may lie in loss of consumer control over personal information: 'consumers are also data subjects, whose welfare may be at risk where freedom of choice and control over one's own personal information is restricted by a dominant undertaking'.[26] In digital markets – when companies provide 'free' services to consumers in exchange for their data – market power is difficult to assess. Market power may be best measured by shares of control over data rather than shares of sales or other traditional measures.[27]

The research conducted for this book examines the market dynamics of the digital economy and the effects on competition and welfare. The key question of the book is whether privacy is a value, which should be promoted in competition policy. The research questions whether competitive analysis in the digital age should expand its scope to include a broader definition of consumer welfare, the main objective of competition. This is done by looking at the two leading competition law jurisdictions, the EU and the United States (USA/US). In particular, the policy goals of EU competition law and US antitrust law are examined to identify whether privacy as a non-price parameter can be considered when enforcing the rules.

In this context, the book explores the interplay between competition law and data protection law. The German Facebook probe is used as a case study, as it is the first competition authority case based on an alleged violation of data privacy. The book engages with the notion that more collaboration should take place between the competition and DPAs to protect consumers from privacy risks. In addition, a theoretical study of the meaning of consumer welfare questions whether welfare should be more widely defined in competition policy to ensure real consumer choice and privacy. With reference to the above, this book aims to contribute to the field of competition law and policy in several ways.

In order to summarize the research objectives of this book and for ease of reading, the main sub-questions that are addressed throughout this book and that the research aims to answer are repeated below. These are the most important issues that will be looked into in detail: what is the role (if any) of personal data and privacy in competition law? Should competition policy protect privacy among its objectives, and if so, how? And finally, does competition policy to some extent already consider privacy in its goals?

Structure. The book is structured into six main chapters. Chapter 1 includes the introduction and presentation of the objective and research questions, as well as the methodologies, theoretical approach and framework of the book. In Chapter 2, the privacy protection regimes in the EU and the USA are explored and discussed. This is followed by Chapter 3, which examines the competition regimes in the respective jurisdictions and the conventional goals of both EU competition policy and US antitrust policy. Chapter 4 analyses the interconnection or interplay between the two legal and policy regimes: privacy protection and competition law. Chapter 5 ties together the

26. EDPS Opinion (n 10) 31.
27. OECD Big Data (n 22) 17.

previous chapters and presents the research findings by proposing a rethinking of competition policy for the data economy and the introduction of a privacy dimension to competition law's policy goals. Chapter 6 reflects on the way forward, offers policy considerations and proposes how this book contributes to research and business practice and ends by offering suggestions for future research.

§1.03 METHODOLOGY AND PERSPECTIVES

A central issue of writing a book is the methodology, as it describes the broad theoretical and philosophical underpinning to the chosen research methods. This chapter outlines the methodologies of the book and its key theoretical elements. It describes where the research fits within existing disciplines and explains the underlying ideology and influences for the book.

Starting from the overarching concept of legal science(s) or jurisprudence, the author understands this notion broadly, encompassing several closely related, yet distinct, fields of study, including the doctrinal study of law or legal dogmatics, legal sociology, legal history and comparative legal study.[28] Although related, these fields of study are commonly regarded as distinct and may differ in their aims, study objects and methods. Thus, the study of law, or jurisprudence, can be divided into many fields depending on the object of study.[29] These various fields are all legal science(s) in the wide sense of the term. With this as a starting point, the reader may recognize in this book elements of many of these closely related fields or disciplines.

Legal dogmatics. Methodologically, the starting point of this book is largely based on traditional legal scholarship in the sense that it relies on legal dogmatics as the guiding research method. Legal dogmatics focuses on interpreting and systemizing the law.[30] It is concerned with current law, referring to law that exists in the present and is both valid and binding.[31] This approach can be defined as scientific knowledge about norms.[32] According to Aulis Aarnio, legal dogmatics is analysis of the action producing norm propositions.[33] As maintained by Aarnio, clarifying the content of the legal order has traditionally been defined as the object of juridical study, but it is legal dogmatics that takes the level of discussion a step further.[34]

However, it is clear that despite legal dogmatics acting as a guiding approach to this book, such an approach cannot be viewed as the principal research method adopted here. Indeed, the methodology of the book goes beyond legal dogmatics. This

28. *See e.g.* Aulis Aarnio, *Luentoja lainopillisen tutkimuksen teoriasta* (Unigrafia Oy, University of Helsinki 2011) 1, 13.
29. *Ibid.*; Aulis Aarnio, *Essays on the Doctrinal Study of Law* (University of Tampere 2011) 19.
30. Aarnio (n 28).
31. *Lex lata/de lege lata.* Ari Hirvonen, *Mitkä metodit? Opas oikeustieteen metodologiaan* (Yleisen Oikeustieteen Julkaisuja 2011) 22.
32. *Ibid.*
33. *Ibid.* For further discussion by Aarnio on legal research, Finnish legal theory and thinking, *see Legal Point of View: Six Essays on Legal Philosophy* (University of Helsinki, Helsinki 1978); Aulis Aarnio, *Oikeussäännösten tulkinnasta. Tutkimus lainopillisen perustelun rationaalisuudesta ja hyväksyttävyydestä* (Juridica 1982).
34. *Ibid.*

is because the book does not limit itself to interpreting and systematizing the law. Rather, the book, especially in Chapter 6, suggests and envisions what the future for the law and legal policy should be: *lex ferenda/de lege ferenda*. This reflects legal policy more than legal dogmatics.

Elements of legal dogmatics, however, are reflected especially in Chapters 3 and 4, studying and describing what the law is, combined with other elements of legal science, such as legal history and comparative legal study. The legal historical perspective and the comparative approach are evident in Chapters 2 and 3.

Further to analysis from the purely legal perspective of legal dogmatics, this book approaches the subject through some elements of contextual analysis of legislation and judicial decisions. Ideologically, one may think that this book resonates with the approach of Scandinavian realism,[35] which, as opposed to law in books, holds that law does not exist based only on legal norms or statutes. They become actual law when applied by the courts, when interpreted or created by judges – not only relying on the words of the legislator.

This kind of contextual analysis necessitates some elements of legal historical and cultural analysis[36] as well as consideration of the philosophical background to the relevant competition policies and privacy regimes. The study of law can be understood as divided into many levels or layers, according to Kaarlo Tuori.[37] The deepest level expresses legal culture. Consequently, comparative legal study in its core amounts to a comparison between legal cultures, comparing the (sedimental) foundations of law.[38]

To clarify, this book does not attempt to carry out a full methodological cultural analysis and empirical study but refers to certain comparative cultural aspects as may be relevant when taking a comparative look at EU competition law and US antitrust law, as well as the notion of privacy in these two jurisdictions respectively. In addition to a cultural dimension, the comparative approach of the book also includes a discussion on values. According to Geert Hofstede, 'In studying "values" we compare individuals; in studying "culture" we compare societies.' However, values are held by

35. For reading on Scandinavian realism, *see* especially Alf Ross, who is commonly considered the founding father of this version of legal realism. Beyond Scandinavian realism, American realism is another famous school of thought, with leading scholars such as Roscoe Pound and Oliver Wendell Holmes. In essence, what they called for was a more pragmatic and public-interested interpretation of law and a focus on how the legal process actually occurred, as opposed to legal formalism. Like, e.g., Pound, realists believe that law does and should serve social ends. Accordingly, judges unavoidably look at considerations of fairness and public policy, and they are right to do so. *See e.g.* Alf Ross, *On Law and Justice* (University of California Press 1959); Oliver Wendell Holmes Jr., 'The Path of the Law' (1897) 10 Harvard Law Review 457; Roscoe Pound, 'The Scope and Purpose of Sociological Jurisprudence' (1911) 24 Harvard Law Review 591 (1911).
36. *See* Geert H Hofstede, *Culture's Consequences: Comparing Values, Behaviors, Institutions, and Organizations Across Nations* (2nd edn, Sage Publications, 2001).
37. Tuori presents law as a multilayered phenomenon based on certain distinctions: between law as a symbolic-normative phenomenon (a legal order) and law as legal practices, and a further distinction within the legal order between its surface level and its subsurface, legal cultural layers. Kaarlo Tuori, *Critical Legal Positivism* (Ashgate 2002).
38. *See e.g.* Aarnio (n 28) 21–23.

individuals as well as by collectivities, and culture presupposes a collectivity. Accordingly, a value can be defined as 'a broad tendency to prefer certain states of affairs over others'.[39]

Economic considerations. In addition to legal dogmatics and legal policy, the research methodology for this book is influenced by economic considerations, especially in terms of examining market power and market effects. This is justified, as competition law exists in close interface with economics. In this context, it is more common to speak about *competition theory* than *economics*.[40] Therefore, the legal dogmatics relied upon in this book involves influences and elements of competition theory. Competition theory and its key concepts and definitions are discussed further in Chapter 3, §3.02.

The influence from competition theory is especially noticeable in some of the chapters of this book, such as Chapter 3 that deals with competition policy goals, examines consumer welfare as the current competition standard and the 'more economic approach' in EU competition law. Chapter 3 also explores the relevant schools of thought for US antitrust policy. These are largely price-centred, especially the Chicago school. Although the book explores some legal and economic findings, the research does not fall under the separate scientific discipline of *law and economics*, which combines legal and economic approaches in one social science.[41]

European legal methodology. In addition to – or perhaps even more than – legal dogmatics as one guiding research method, this book, in exploring EU competition law and policy, rests strongly on European legal methodology as relied on to address European legal sources, such as judicial decisions of the European Commission and the European courts.

Strictly speaking, the term 'EC law' or 'EU law' refers to the law of the European Communities and can be regarded as distinct from the term 'European law'. This is because European legal traditions may be traced back to Roman law and the term 'European law' can therefore be understood as a very broad concept.[42] In this book, however, when discussing EU law, the term European law may also be used interchangeably for ease of reading and convenience. Here, it is noteworthy that EU law is clearly separate and independent as a field of law from, for instance, international law and from national law (even though it is applied by national courts and authorities). As explained by the European Court of Justice (ECJ) in *Van Gend en Loos* and *Costa v*

39. Hofstede (n 36) 5, 15.
40. For a basic overview of competition theory, *see e.g.* Vesa Kanniainen and Kalle Määttä (eds), *Taloustieteellinen näkökulma kilpailuoikeuteen* (Lakimiesliiton Kustannus 2001); Petri Kuoppamäki, *Uusi kilpailuoikeus* (Sanoma Pro Oy 2006) 6.
41. Boudewijn Bouckaert and Gerrit De Geest (eds), *Encyclopaedia of Law and Economics I* (Edward Elgar 2000) 383, 1041.
42. There is hardly such thing as a European common law, as there are many particularities in the law of each of the European countries, making them different from each other. The same applies to the idea of 'Nordic law', which is often referred to as something different from other legal systems due to a common belief that the Nordic countries share the same legal tradition and are very similar in their approach to the law. As noted by Pia Letto-Vanamo, the idea of 'Nordic' law conceals national features. The same could be said about European law. Pia Letto-Vanamo, Ditlev Tamm and Bent OG Mortensen, *Nordic Law in European Context* (Springer 2018).

ENEL, the [European] Community constitutes a new legal order of international law for the benefit of which the states have limited their sovereign rights, albeit within limited fields, and the subjects of which comprise not only Member States but also their nationals.[43]

The book largely focuses on analysing European law at the EU level, as EU competition law and policy is the object of study. However, national case law from EU Member States serves as useful examples of how certain relevant issues have been addressed at the national level. Thus, insights and case examples from other jurisdictions, especially EU Member States, are presented in this book when helpful for involving further perspectives, so that illustrative national case examples may be presented. This is justified because, in the EU, the Modernization Regulation 1/2003 means that the European Commission is not the only body capable of public enforcement of European Community competition law. This means that national competition authorities enforce EU competition policy and contribute to forming EU competition policy through their national enforcement activities. Sometimes, it is not the EU regulator but the national competition authorities that stand at the forefront of developing EU competition law and doing things that are new in terms of competition policy.[44]

In the transition to the digital economy and the related impact on competition law and policy, national competition authorities have taken an active role in analysing new issues and articulating potential risks in studies and reports. The most active national authorities to date have been - especially - the German and French authorities. For example, their joint report on competition law and the role of data is central to this book. Moreover, the German antitrust investigation of Facebook that interlinks competition and privacy concerns is of key importance, as it explores the new territory in which competition and data protection interlink and is the first case examining the interplay between competition and data protection rules.[45]

International and comparative perspectives. The research questions in this book are approached from an international and comparative perspective. A comparative perspective is used to explore differences between European and US competition policy and privacy regimes. The aim is to understand and compare characteristics in EU and US competition policies and their objectives, and what role privacy can play in the respective systems.

43. *See* 26/62 *Van Gend en Loos* (1963) ECR 1, esp 12 and 6/64 *Costa v ENEL* (1964) ECR 585, esp 593.
44. *See e.g.* Foo Yun Chee, 'German Regulator Well Suited to Investigate Facebook: EU's Vestager' Reuters Technology News (7 March 2016) https://www.reuters.com/article/us-eu-facebook-antitrust/german-regulator-well-suited-to-investigate-facebook-eus-vestager-idUSKCN0W91OB, accessed 19 April 2020.
45. Inge Graef and Brendan Van Alsenoy, 'Data Protection Through the Lens of Competition Law: Will Germany Lead the Way?' (LSE Media Policy Project blog, 23 March 2016) https://blogs.lse.ac.uk/medialse/2016/03/23/data-protection-through-the-lens-of-competition-law-will-germany-lead-the-way/, accessed 19 April 2020; Robert McLeod, 'Novel but a Long Time Coming: The Bundeskartellamt Takes on Facebook' (2016) 7 Journal of European Competition Law & Practice 367.

The study of EU competition law benefits substantially from comparison with other competition systems, particularly the wealth of cases found in – and the academic and professional commentary on – US antitrust law. In this book, American antitrust law is used as a point of comparison. This is justified as US antitrust law offers the longest experience in enforcing competition rules.

A comparative perspective is also taken when examining the understanding of privacy and the different privacy regimes between the EU and the USA. This kind of comparative legal methodology of the book includes elements of comparative legal history and analysis of legal cultures. This approach is reflected especially in Chapters 2 and 3.

When exploring privacy and protection of data, the approach used employs a comparative perspective to consider the different approaches to protecting informational privacy and data protection between the EU and the USA. This is done in Chapter 2. This comparative perspective is justified since an understanding of existing views and the legal framework concerning data privacy is of key importance when exploring the interlinkage between privacy and competition policy in Chapter 4, and, further, for evaluating and envisioning the role of privacy in competition policy in Chapters 5 and 6.

In addressing the research questions, it is interesting to look at the different approaches of EU and US regulators concerning competition policy in the data economy. Although seemingly similar, EU competition law and US antitrust law implement different policies and pursue distinct objectives. To date, the most illustrative example of a divide in approaches is *Google Search (Shopping)*.[46] In the future, it might be that the way in which competition law interplays with data privacy will be a question where the transatlantic difference is at its biggest.[47] That is why a comparative approach is needed and justified in this book.

Beyond law, the wider context. This book examines competition law not only in a strictly legal context. Rather, the book explores competition policy in a wider context, which includes societal, political, economic, historical and cultural elements. This approach is evident especially in Chapter 6 when rethinking competition policy for the digital age and envisioning a privacy dimension beyond the conventional limits. One may describe the analysis in this wider context as using elements that can be categorized as sociolegal,[48] or law in context,[49] as it goes beyond an examination in a strictly legal context. This sort of law-in-context approach is also reflected in the proposal to expand the conventional boundaries between competition and data protection law, presented in Chapters 5 and 6.

46. Commission decision 27 June 2017 relating to proceedings under Article 102 TFEU and Article 54 Agreement on the European Economic Area AT.39740 – *Google Search (Shopping)*. For analysis on methodological issues in European and comparative law, *see e.g.* Hannu Tapani Klami, *Methodological Problems in European and Comparative Law* (2nd edn, Yleisen oikeustieteen laitoksen julkaisuja 1997).
47. *See* Chapter 4, §4.04[C] exploring a potential growing transatlantic divergence.
48. Panu Minkkinen, 'Oikeus- ja yhteiskuntatieteellinen tutkimus – suuntaus, tarkastelutapa, menetelmä?' (2017) 7–8 Lakimies 908–923.
49. *See e.g.* William Twining, *Law in Context. Enlarging a Discipline* (OUP 1997) and Reza Banakar (ed.), *Rights in Context. Law and Justice in Late Modern Society* (Ashgate 2010).

Here, it is acknowledged - but questioned - that some critics consider that law is not science because it is not objective.[50] Calling this critique into question can be justified by merely looking, for example, at Ilkka Niiniluoto's definition of science through a list of certain characteristics and noting that law meets such listed criteria.[51] One may also ask: what constitutes science? The theory of Jürgen Habermas concerning *knowledge* and *human interests* is relevant in this regard.[52]

Habermas explores the philosophy of science and analyses the relationship and connection between knowledge and human interests. According to his theory, human interests can be viewed as a threefold division between different forms of knowledge.[53] These are empirical-analytic science with its technical interest; historical-hermeneutic science with its practical interest; and critical knowledge with its emancipatory interest. These distinct forms of knowledge can be transferred to and identified within legal science, noting that the different forms constitute qualitatively different levels in legal research.[54]

Most legal dogmatics carried out in Finland goes at least beyond mere technical interest, as it is often asserted in Finnish legal theory that legal science is hermeneutic by its character. However, legal research can be carried out with an emancipatory form of knowledge interest, as, for example, the scholarly work of Thomas Wilhelmsson demonstrates.[55] This goes beyond achieving an understanding of meaning and description of the legal phenomenon, suggesting by which legal solution *de lege ferenda* or *de lege lata*, and in which direction the law can develop.

In this book, the threefold division between different forms of knowledge is shown so that while strong technical and practical interests drive the work, the aim is also to enter into the deepest qualitative level of critical and emancipatory interest, suggesting a way forward *de lege ferenda*. This approach is reflected in the final Chapters 5 and 6 of the book that explore how to bring competition policy to the digital age by integrating privacy concerns with competition policy goals and suggesting ways of advancing this approach.

The question of knowledge was much explored by Ludwig Wittgenstein, who focused on the problem of *knowledge* and *certainty*, and the difference between these concepts.[56] In order to know something, one must be well informed and be able to provide an argument for what it is that one claims to know. Knowledge requires the possibility of doubt, which, in return, requires argumentation. The knowledge game

50. This issue related to questions of ontology and empirics is discussed by, e.g., Aarnio (n 29) 11, 109–111.
51. These characteristics of science include, e.g., being consistent, systematic, impartial, autonomous, progressive and reflecting a scientific approach. Ilkka Niiniluoto, *Johdatus tieteenfilosofiaan. Käsitteen- ja teorianmuodostus* (Otava 1984).
52. *See e.g.* Jürgen Habermas, *Knowledge and Human Interests* (first published 1968, Heinemann 1981).
53. *Ibid.*, 308–311.
54. Thomas Wilhelmsson, *Critical Studies in Private Law: A Treatise on Need-Rational Principles in Modern Law* (Springer 1992).
55. *Ibid. See also* Aulis Aarnio, *The Rational as Reasonable: A Treatise on Legal Justification* (Reidel Publishing Company 1987) 221.
56. *See e.g.* Ludwig Wittgenstein, *On Certainty* (Basil Blackwell 1969).

includes, as a natural part, doubting, which leads to the challenge of *justification*.[57] If someone doubts an argument presented at a certain point, the argument supporting the knowledge-claim must be strengthened. However, the game of doubt in itself requires certainty, meaning that arguments and proof of these must have a final point. At some point, it must be possible to say, as Wittgenstein considers, we must be able to *trust in something*. So, it all boils down to the notion of trust. This is of central importance to this book and closely connected to the value-based propositions of the book that will be discussed in the following §1.04.

§1.04 THEORETICAL CONSIDERATIONS

This chapter describes the theoretical basis and theoretical considerations for this book and explains its underlying value-based starting point.

The theoretical underpinnings of this book may to some extent suggest reliance on Kaarlo Tuori's perspectivist theoretical understanding of the law. That understanding is based on the assumption that 'law' as such does not exist, but only law as identified by actors (which consequently play a law-creating role).[58] This approach may be especially evident in Chapter 5 of this book, where throughout the underlying understanding of competition law as a political construct is explicitly spelled out and given some elaboration. This understanding of competition law – and law generally – as a political creation reflects the author's view that law is always perspectivist, acknowledging that certain forces influence the 'law' and affect legal discourse. As described by Tuori, theorists (or legal researchers, as in this case) may attain reflexive distance from the object they are analysing but will always remain subjugated to cultural constraints and '*Vorverständnisse*' (or so-called pre-understandings) emanating from the object of study.[59] Of course, this 'perspectivism' applies beyond the theorist or legal researcher to effectively all actors participating in discussion and discourse.

It goes without saying that the author of this book aims to be objective at all times, but what is meant by noting that this book relies on a perspectivist understanding of the law is that there is an inherent acceptance that the research questions addressed in this book may have more than one way of being answered. The answers proposed by the author will inevitably reflect the author's own cultural constraints and *Vorverständnisse*.

The idea of perspectivism is relevant for the multitude of theoretical and disciplinary approaches towards the plurality of legal orders (national, international, European) and the EU as a phenomenon. According to Tuori's theoretical foundations, we may say that the intuitive approach used in this book comes close to a European stand[60] and this book largely reflects a European perspective on (competition) law, if categorized under conventional legal areas.

57. Aarnio (n 28) 39–40.
58. Kaarlo Tuori, *European Constitutionalism* (CUP 2015) 78.
59. *Ibid.*, 5, 9.
60. Tuori (n 58) 342.

The point about having a perspectivist understanding and acknowledging the possibility of alternative answers is related to the more theoretically oriented question and discussion concerning the separation between one right answer and the final answer.[61] Ronald Dworkin presented the famous theory on the one single correct answer.[62] Dworkin bases his theory on pre-existing rights, which takes a different starting point than the one of legal realism mentioned above. Moreover, a key point in his theory is that while the system of rules has gaps, every legal problem can be solved by relying on legal principles. Dworkin's controversial book states that the law as properly interpreted will give an answer. In this, he uses the metaphor of Judge Hercules, an ideal judge, immensely wise and with full knowledge of legal sources. Hercules, argues Dworkin, would always come to the one right answer.[63]

Acting on the premise that the law is a seamless web, Hercules is required to construct the theory that best fits and justifies the law as a whole in order to decide any particular case. Notably, Hercules would also have plenty of time to decide. This is different from the situation in the real world, where, at least in principle, the application of the law and especially law enforcement should be effective and rapid. However, this is not always the situation, especially in the field of competition law. Think only of the *Google Search (Shopping)*, which took more than seven years for the European Commission to decide.[64] Not to mention the famous *Microsoft* that took more than ten years for the EU to resolve.[65]

What is the solution in a given case is something that is often disputed. Lawyers often disagree on how a case should be solved: indeed, Dworkin does not deny that. However, he claims that they are disagreeing about *the* right answer to the case, the answer Hercules would give. Dworkinian critics argue that the law and its legal sources are full of gaps and inconsistencies and that other legal standards, such as principles, are insufficient to solve a hard case. Some of these are incommensurable. In these situations, even Hercules would be in a dilemma and none of the possible answers would be *the* right one.[66]

Dworkin's metaphor of Judge Hercules bears some resemblance to Rawls' veil of ignorance and Habermas' ideal speech situation, in that they propose idealized methods of arriving at valid normative propositions. However, Judge Hercules is difficult to translate from the purely ideal to the practical, as one may contend that it is such a purely idealized construct that if such a figure existed he would arrive at the 'right' answer in every moral dilemma.

Dworkin's one-right-answer theory can also be challenged by noting that deep value-based conflicts ultimately depend on different interests. Can there be one single

61. *See e.g.* Aarnio (n 28) 91–94.
62. 'No Right Answer?' in Peter M S Hacker and Joseph Raz (eds), *Law, Morality and Society. Essays in Honour of H.L.A. Hart* (Clarendon Press 1977) 58; Ronald Dworkin, *Taking Rights Seriously* (Harvard University Press 1978) 357. For further reading, *see e.g.* Michel Rosenfeld, 'Dworkin and the One Law Principle: A Pluralist Critique' (2004) Revue Internationale de Philosophie.
63. Dworkin (n 62) 58.
64. Commission decision *Google Search (Shopping)* (n 46).
65. Case T-201/04 *Microsoft v Commission* [2007] ECR II-3601.
66. Aarnio (n 29) 165.

right answer to every situation in law and the doctrinal study of law? Moreover, is the Dworkinian one-right-answer theory necessary in a well-functioning democratic constitutional state, where it is most relevant to create maximal protection under the law for citizens? This can perhaps be done better, or at least equally well, by making decisions that are justified as well as can be.

As argued by Aulis Aarnio, it is realistic to require that the application and enforcement of laws should aim to create the best possible decisions and outcomes.[67] From a broader perspective, and reflecting something close to a utilitarian approach, law should be assigned the task of attempting to bring the greatest good to the greatest number.[68] Generally, such utilitarianism and positivism can be derived from the philosophy of Jeremy Bentham.[69] Of course, this approach can also be criticized, for example by going against the rights of a minority, and indeed Dworkin challenges the whole theory of utilitarianism that law and its institutions should serve the general welfare and nothing else.[70] This book assumes that competition law is a political construct and inherently susceptible to a range of different values and societal variants. Politics is closely connected to collective aims that can be linked to utilitarianism and positivism.

The theoretical basis for this book can perhaps best be described as a belief in objectives, values and legal principles, and – instead of a Dworkinian one-right-answer approach – the book accepts that the research question concerning the role of privacy in competition law may not have one right answer, as the answer depends on the way one understands, interprets and gives meaning to different factors. What becomes a decisive principle or factor will depend on the *Vorverständnisse*. The book is approached through principles and values as decisive factors of a sort. They are also closely connected to morals. Legal principles transfer the law's interlinkage and connections with values, morals and politics. What the book aims to do is to find perspectives to address the question and identify ways in which privacy can be accommodated in competition law as a policy objective.

Law and justice is no doubt closely connected to fairness. John Rawls' categorization of the principles and conception of justice is presented in the famous *A Theory of Justice*.[71] The resultant theory is known as 'Justice as Fairness', from which Rawls derives his two main principles of justice, reconciling liberty and equality as the basic structure of a well-ordered society.[72] Rawls' conception of justice comprises two main principles of liberty and equality. The principles are, however, intended as a single, comprehensive conception of justice: *justice as fairness*.

67. Aarnio (n 28) 94.
68. Aarnio (n 55) 161.
69. Jeremy Bentham, *An Introduction to the Principles of Morals and Legislation* (first published 1789, 3rd edn Hafner Publishing Co. 1963) 1–7.
70. Ronald Dworkin, (n 62) 357.
71. John Rawls (Belknap 1971).
72. John Rawls, 'Justice as Fairness: Political Not Metaphysical' (1985) 14 Philosophy and Public Affairs 223–251.

In doctoral dissertations in law sometimes, though not often, the author reveals their value-based beliefs and starting point for analysis.[73] In this book, the author's own value-based starting point can be described as a belief in the core concepts, principles and values of trust, choice and fairness. These values will be reflected throughout this book.

Trust, choice and fairness. Why trust? Trust is essential for a functioning marketplace as well as for society as a whole. One may think that, essentially, competition law exists to build trust in markets and society.[74] When competition works the way it should, markets work fairly. Thus, the value of fairness is closely connected to the concept of trust, and central to competition. It should be pointed out, though, that the market is clearly not society. Our societies are much more than the market, but lack of trust in the market can rub off on society as such, and as a consequence, trust in our society is lost. So, one may even argue that the most important currency that societies have - beyond privacy and personal data as this book asserts - is actually trust.

Trust is a central value to the data economy and the digital future. Without it, everything consumers and companies do in the market becomes harder. Consumers cannot live their lives today without trusting in strangers: in the banks that keep their money, in the doctors who treat them when they are ill, in the builders who build their home, and in other drivers on the road. As markets and societies grow, trust becomes even more important, but also harder to achieve, especially when digitalization, big data and new technologies change the way in which consumers and companies in the marketplace interact.

Technological advancement brought about by digitalization can help consumers and actors in the marketplace to trust each other, with features such as ratings and other systems that have made the sharing economy work, for example. However, technology also creates completely novel challenges when it requires trust not only in other people but also in computers and algorithms.

No doubt, computers and algorithms have enormous potential to do a lot of good. They could save time in consumers' everyday lives and make much better use of resources. Algorithms that rely on crunching big data could help doctors prescribe individually designed treatments, and autonomous cars could enable people with disabilities to achieve independence.[75] And there is much more that digitalization and technological advancement can do. But in all of this, trust is a key issue. No one will agree to hand over their medical data, or step into a car driven by an algorithm, unless they trust the companies they are dealing with, unless they rely on technology companies to treat them fairly.

73. For example, Johan Bärlund in his dissertation takes as an analytical starting point the central role of trust for a functioning market economy and consumer protection law. *See* Johan Bärlund, *Reklamation i konsumentavtal – En kontraktsrättslig studie av konsumenten reklamation som en förutsättning för att konsumenten skall kunna åberopa näringsidkarens avtalsbrott* (Kauppakaari Juristförbundets Förlag 2002) 6–7.

74. *See also* Margrethe Vestager, 'How Competition Can Build Trust in Our Societies' TED Talk (New York, 20 September 2017).

75. *Ibid.*

However, studies show that less than a quarter of Europeans trust online businesses to protect their personal information. Indeed, a large section of EU's population is deeply concerned about the use of their personal data, as attested in the 2016 Eurobarometer on ePrivacy.[76] Functioning and fair competition can play a vital role in building the trust needed to make the best of markets and societies. Competition law and policy can help in building the belief in trust and fair treatment that is needed for consumers and companies alike to operate in the markets. Closely connected to trust is also the concept of choice. These values - trust, choice and fairness - are also important for consumer welfare, or well-being, which is a wider understanding of welfare.[77] Trust is important for the area of both competition law and data protection.

Trust can be linked to expectations concerning legal certainty. The notion of legal certainty is closely connected to the essential element of law's ideal dimension, which, as Robert Alexy puts it, is the claim to correctness.[78] Alexy emphasizes the dual nature of law; the law belongs to the realm of facts as well as that of ideals. The core of law's real nature is coercion, or force. Courts and authorities have both the power and the obligation to decide cases. However, the power machinery must follow the principle of legal certainty because it is a central element in people's well-justified expectation of legal certainty.[79]

The claim to correctness reveals another essential feature of law, which is the connection between *law and morals*.[80] This connection is visible also in Gustaf Radbruch's famous formula whereby extreme justice is not law.[81] According to this theory, when encountering a conflict between a statute and a perception of what is just, one has to decide against applying the statute if the legal concept behind the relevant statute seems unbearably unjust or in disregard of human equality before the law. This extreme injustice book means that immoral law, by its foundations, cannot be law at all.[82] Law and morals are, however, connected to each other not only in extreme cases but also *in all cases*.

Moral considerations. Principles are characterized by their close connection to morals.[83] Indeed, law itself is closely connected to morals and values. This is how it should always be. The history of humankind includes many tragic examples that go to show what the consequences can be when law loses its connection with basic humane values and sustainable moral principles: think only of Adolf Hitler and Josef Stalin to name two extremes.

Morals and ethics are the subject of a wide and deep philosophical discussion. The author will not attempt to address that discussion here as it goes beyond the focus and research questions of this book. For that reason, this book will address only a

76. European Commission Directorate General for Communications Networks, Content & Technology, 'Flash Eurobarometer 443 – ePrivacy' (2017).
77. For a discussion on the difference between consumer welfare and well-being, *see* Chapter 5, §5.02.
78. Robert Alexy 'On the Concept and Nature of Law' (2008) 21 Ratio Juris 281, 288.
79. *Ibid.*, 291.
80. Aarnio (n 28) 27.
81. *Ibid.*
82. Aarnio (n 28) 55.
83. Robert Alexy, 'On the Structure of Legal Principles' (2000) 13 Ratio Juris 294–304, 5.

limited number of aspects of the relationship between law and morality, or law and values. However, it may be noted that two dimensions stand out as essential in this relationship.

Moral principles are ingrained in the foundation of law and morals, while values are bound to legal argumentation, being a part of the procedure of justification. In this regard, philosophers, such as Aleksander Peczenik and Herbert Hart, have emphasized the notion of *deep justification* of law[84] and that law has to be in harmony with certain minimum moral requirements.[85] The Hartian criterion for law includes some prima facie principles, or reasons, which are necessary preconditions as regards law and morals (the so-called minimum content of natural law). Relying on the Hartian criterion, Aulis Aarnio lists the most important as being human vulnerability, approximate equality, limited altruism, limited resources, and limited human understanding and strength of will.[86]

When dealing with morals, and especially values, the need for justifications and stating sufficient reasons when taking a position on values is extremely important. After all, values and morals are creations of mankind; they are born and modified in society, tied to time and place. According to Aarnio, when arguing for value-based positions and justifying our position as effectively as possible, we have done what can be expected from us as human beings and what we are capable of.[87] Similarly, as this book aims to explore, competition policy and its goals are also ultimately about values that need to be justified.

Ideological basis. A few words on the researcher's ideology. This is what defines whether the research conducted is largely a question of *expository* or *normative* nature.[88] In this book, there are elements of both the expository and normative nature, meaning that the book examines both what the law is, and also goes a level deeper and asserts what the law ought to be. This normative part is evident especially in Chapters 5 and 6. In addition, the book has elements of an *explanatory* nature in that it explains why the law is the way it is, for example in Chapters 2 and 3. This categorization of research ideology into expository, explanatory and normative has been done in relation to EU law by, for example, Tamara Hervey.[89]

Another way of looking at the notion of a researcher's ideology is as done by Raimo Siltala, who separates a researcher's ideology into two different points of view; studying what the law is, as a societal fact or studying what the law ought to be: law as a societal ideal.[90] The former viewpoint relates to the analytical-descriptive form of study, whereas the latter expresses an ideology which is normative-critical.[91] This separation between law as a fact and law as an ideal goes back to scholars of legal

84. Aleksander Peczenik, *On Law and Reason* (Reidel 1989).
85. Herbert Hart, *The Concept of Law* (Clarendon Press 1961).
86. Aarnio (n 29) 55.
87. Aarnio (n 28) 89.
88. *See* Raimo Siltala, *Oikeustieteen tieteenteoria* (Suomalainen Lakimiesyhditys 2003) 59.
89. Tamara Hervey, Robert Cryer, Bal Sokhi-Bulley and Ali Bohm, *Research Methodologies in EU and International Law* (Hart Publishing 2011). The author had the pleasure of meeting Tamara Hervey in the fall 2017 to discuss and exchange views on research methodologies.
90. Siltala (n 88) 60.
91. *Ibid.*

positivism such as John Austin, Hans Kelsen and Herbert Hart.[92] This categorization of the researcher's ideology also relates closely to the axiological positions of the scholar.[93]

Regulatory theory. This book is concerned with how competition policy addresses data-driven anticompetitive conduct in digital markets and the interlinkage between privacy and competition in these instances. It should be pointed out, however, that competition law is not the only available legal regime for dealing with these issues in the digital world. Circumstances and situations where antitrust intervention is required should be distinguished from those where alternative regimes of intervention exist, such as regulation of digital platforms. Although this book does not go into any detailed considerations on regulatory theory, it does acknowledge recent developments and initiatives in the EU concerning regulatory proposals for tackling online platforms.

While the book does not implement regulatory theory to any significant degree, it should be noted that Chapter 4 evaluates and aims to conceptually and normatively categorize competition and data protection regulation from a regulatory perspective. In addition, the concluding policy considerations in Chapter 6 reflect certain regulatory considerations when assessing the potential of a conjoined approach between competition and DPAs. That approach is explored as it would be able to address the expansion of conventional boundaries between competition and data protection law. Also noted are the plans by some EU Member States to enact stricter regulation on digital platforms through digital agencies that would have extensive antitrust powers.

§1.05 CERTAIN LIMITATIONS

This book analyses the potential privacy dimension in competition policy. In doing so, it questions whether competition law's conventional policy goals are optimal in today's digital economy, with its transformation from price-driven to data-driven markets, and where personal information is acquiring a new value and meaning. A critical evaluation is carried out whether current competition policy properly addresses the challenges brought about by data-driven business models, strategies and markets, where non-price elements, such as privacy, can be of utmost importance, and current shortcomings are identified. Essentially, this book calls into question the current framework – or rather approach – of competition law, specifically its price-centric perspective to the commonly accepted main goal of competition, namely 'consumer welfare', presenting the price-focused system as ill-equipped to capture competitive harm in the digital economy. The book presents potential solutions to the research problem: rethinking traditional competition policy to consider privacy concerns and exploring a conjoined approach between competition and privacy regulators.

92. *See e.g.* John Austin, 'The Province of Jurisprudence Determined' in Wilfrid E Rumble (ed.), *Cambridge Texts* (CUP 1995); Hans Kelsen, *General Theory of Law and State* (Russell and Russell 1945); Hart, (n 85).
93. Siltala (n 88) 59.

The instruments of competition policy can broadly be categorized into state aid, antitrust and merger control rules.[94] The focus of this book when exploring the objectives of competition policy and considering bringing a privacy aspect to competition is mainly on the antitrust side and policy instruments concerning antitrust. More specifically, the book examines policy considerations in terms of unilateral behaviour by companies with market power (dominant companies). The scope of the book does not encompass other competition policy instruments, such as cartels (regulated under Article 101 of the Treaty on the Functioning of the European Union (TFEU) in EU competition law) or state aid. Even though the focus is limited to antitrust-related competition policy instruments, case law from the merger control area is used as examples and points of reference as there are insightful decisions on the EU level dealing with data-focused merger cases.

While the data economy clearly brings new opportunities and benefits for consumers and businesses, at the same time the large amount of data that may be controlled by a limited number of data-driven companies or online platforms generates some competition law concerns. Specific issues or market failures may arise in the data economy in the context of use and processing of personal data. One example is in the context of the so-called privacy paradox, where markets fail to cater to users' privacy preferences.[95] The privacy paradox refers to situations where many users are concerned about privacy, though few actually act on those concerns or situations of dysfunctional equilibrium occurring when users become cynical and fail to read privacy policies.[96] The challenge that arises is whether and to what extent traditional competition law tools and principles can be transferred from the real to the data economy to remedy these kinds of issues or market failures.[97]

In this regard, while competition authorities have so far mainly focused their attention on *exclusionary* practices carried out by online platforms to the detriment of their competitors, such as the recent European Commission decision in *Google search (Shopping)*,[98] in this book the main focus is on *exploitative* abuses in the data economy. Issues regarding relevant market definition and market power are not dealt with here; these are subjects that have already been discussed at length in the literature.[99]

---

94. *See e.g.* European Commission, Xth Report on Competition Policy (2010) 2.
95. Marco Botta and Klaus Wiedemann, 'EU Competition Law Enforcement Vis-à-Vis Exploitative Conducts in the Data Economy – Exploring the Terra Incognita' (2018) Max Planck Institute for Innovation and Competition Research Paper 4.
96. Joseph Farrell, 'Can Privacy Be Just Another Good?' (2012) 10 Journal on Telecommunications and High Technology Law 251; Francisco Costa-Cabral and Orla Lynskey, 'Family Ties: The Intersection Between Data Protection and Competition in EU Law' (2017) 54 CML Rev 21 (2017) 28.
97. Botta and Wiedemann (n 95).
98. Commission decision *Google Search (Shopping)* (n 46).
99. In particular, many scholars have focused their attention on application of the concept of multisided markets, initially developed by Tirole, to online platforms. Further, a number of articles discuss whether and to what extent the accumulation of big data by online platforms may represent an entry barrier in markets. *See e.g.* Daniel L Rubinfeld and Michal Gal, 'Access Barriers to Big Data' (2017) 59 Arizona Law Review 339; Inge Graef, 'Market Definition and Market Power in Data: The Case of Online Platforms' (2015) 38 World Competition 473.

Exclusionary conduct is unilateral behaviour that shuts out rivals from the marketplace. Rather than excluding competitors, *exploitative* conduct is unilateral behaviour that distorts competition by directly harming final consumers or customers. The unilateral imposition of unfair contractual clauses and the imposition of excessive and discriminatory prices are examples of exploitative forms of behaviour that could harm consumers. In EU competition law, unilateral behaviour by companies with market power is regulated under Article 102 TFEU. The corresponding provision in US antitrust law governing behaviour by powerful companies is Section 2 of the Sherman Act. However, unlike in Europe, where EU competition law is the primary tool used to address exploitative abuses, and Article 102 TFEU lists a number of exploitative practices as examples of abuses of dominant position,[100] in the USA, such practices are generally not addressed in the antitrust law framework. This difference in dealing with market conduct of an exploitative nature is discussed further in Chapter 3.

There are certain necessary limitations in the scope of the book. It is worth noting that digitalization of the economy impacts several legal areas and raises previously unexplored issues, indeed many of which go beyond the field of competition law. Examples of impacted and adjacent legal areas include unfair competition and marketing law. These are closely connected to competition law in the sense that they also aim to promote efficient competitive circumstances in the marketplace.[101] This book, however, focuses on the specific legal instruments of competition law and thus does not look further into other legal areas concerning the governance of markets. Nevertheless, access to data is a key issue and a success factor in marketing - especially online advertising - and thus some references are made to this area when relevant and when it serves useful examples.

Additionally, it should be emphasized that this book does not deal with consumer protection law. That said, although consumer protection law falls outside the scope of this book, a few words are none the less worth mentioning concerning its relation to competition law. Concern within competition law over consumer choice is closely connected with the field of consumer protection law. In the context of Nordic competition policy, already in the 1970s, Ulf Bernitz noted that the goals for stronger protection of consumers, both in the Nordics and internationally, would likely come to affect the development of future competition policy.[102] Specifically, Bernitz envisioned

100. Consolidated version of the Treaty on the Functioning of the European Union [2012] OJ C 326/47 (TFEU).

101. For further reading on unfair commercial practices and marketing law from a Nordic perspective, *see e.g.* Ulf Bernitz, *Marknadsrätt. En komparativ studie av marknadslagstiftningens utveckling och huvudlinjer* (Jurist- och samhällsvetareförbundets Förlag AB 1969) ch 1. More generally on market law, *see* Ulf Bernitz, Virpi Tiili and Hannu Pokela, Kansainvälinen *Markkinaoikeus* (Lakimiesliiton Kustannus 1998); Kirsti Rissanen, Virpi Tiili and Pentti Mäkinen, *Markkinaoikeuden perusteet: elinkeino, kilpailu- ja kuluttujalainsäädäntö* (Lakimiesliiton kustannus 1990). For a Finnish perspective, *see* Martti Castrén, *EU-Suomen markkinaoikeus* (Kauppakaari Oy 1997).

102. Ulf Bernitz, *Konkurrens och priser i Norden. En komparativ studie av konkurrens- och prislagstiftningens syften och medel i de nordiska länderna* (Jurist- och samhällsvetareförbundets Förlag AB 1971) 261–262.

that competition law would shape into having a more explicit consumer-oriented profile.[103]

At the EU level, the EDPS has looked into the interconnection between competition law, data protection and consumer protection law and argued for increasing collaboration between regulators in these fields.[104] In Finland, Kalle Määttä has analysed the intersection between competition and consumer protection law.[105] It is clear that a close connection exists between competition policy and consumer policy. It would be a natural extension of the research to look at consumer protection law in addition to, and together with, competition and data protection law. However, the scope of this book does not allow for such an extension of the research objectives and questions. For this reason, integration of consumer protection issues is left for future research activities.

As to perspectives and some limitations in that regard, the book takes an international and comparative perspective when discussing and exploring the characters and inherent differences in European and US competition policies and privacy regimes. The justification for the focus on comparing only the EU and the US legal frameworks is that at present, global competition is largely bipolar. That is, a global business strategy that is successfully challenged by either the European or American competition authorities may have global repercussions and may derail such a strategy in ways that would not necessarily be true if competition agencies in other jurisdictions were to object.

Undoubtedly, however, the phenomenon of digitalization and the growth of the data economy is global. Moreover, it is undeniable that the evolution of competition regimes around the world, for example in Asia and especially the growth of Chinese economic power, is impacting the current and future competition landscape, leading to a multipolar world of competition law and policy.[106] However, for the purposes of this book, while global developments are acknowledged, the analysis focuses on the major established competition regimes in the world, which, according to the author, can be limited to the EU and the USA. Importantly, this delimitation is also justified because of the undeveloped privacy regime in Asia, where to date little emphasis is placed on consumer privacy.

Further to the EU-US comparative perspective, a number of examples from national EU jurisdictions and national competition authorities are used to exemplify certain developments in the data economy and provide additional approaches and interesting insights. In particular, the German antitrust case regarding Facebook's data practices as an abuse of market power is a prime example.

---

103. *Ibid.*
104. EDPS Opinion (n 10).
105. Kalle Määttä, 'Kilpailupolitiikan ja kuluttajapolitiikan yhtymäkohdat: onko niitä? Kilpailu- ja Kuluttajaviraston selvityksiä 4/2013' (Kopioniini Oy 2013).
106. *See e.g.* D Daniel Sokol and William Blumenthal, 'Merger Control: Key International Norms and Differences' in Ariel Ezrachi (ed.), *Research Handbook on International Competition Law* (Edward Elgar 2012) 319.

§1.06 RESEARCH MATERIAL AND SOURCES

The topic of this book being current and dynamic has an impact on the legal sources of the book. The old traditional European view on what constitutes legal sources was that only legal acts or statutes and government proposals (*travaux préparatoires*) for acts amounted to legal sources. However, this approach dates back to the 19th century of Napoleonic France. Since then, the approach has become much more liberal and flexible throughout Europe and Scandinavia.[107] Indeed, the research material for this book extends far beyond mere statutes and government proposals. This is also due to the special character of EU competition law, as will be discussed below.

Legal principles. This book looks at certain legal principles in its analysis of the research questions, especially the principle of fair competition or, more commonly, fairness. EU law is traditionally characterized by giving strong weight to principles in the interpretation of law and allowing for principles-based argumentation.[108] The existing EU principles can be categorized in various different ways; Juha Raitio proposes one approach to EU legal principles as sources of EU law.[109]

With regard to competition law's guiding principles, it should be noted here that competition law is a casuistic field with significant meaning given to praxis. This distinguishes it, for example, from the traditional understanding of sources-of-law doctrine, where government proposals for statutes, or *travaux préparatoires*, hold a central role. In contrast, in EU law the *travaux préparatoires* do not hold a similar important position as legal sources, but rather the interpretation in EU law is more driven by values and the objectives of law.[110] That is, the law is largely interpreted and applied with regard to its *objectives*.[111] Competition law operates with some concepts and definitions that can be viewed as 'open' in the sense that their concrete meaning opens up only when they are applied in practice.[112] This is discussed further in Chapter 3, §3.02.

It should be noted that legal principles are different from legal rules, following the Dworkinian division into rules, principles and policies.[113] While legal rules are

107. Aarnio (n 28) 65.
108. Juha Raitio, *Euroopan integraatio ja Euroopan unionin rakenteet* (Unigrafia Oy 2011) 13.
109. Juha Raitio, *Eurooppaoikeuden tavoitteet ja johtavat periaatteet* (Tampereen yliopisto 1997) 17, 42; Raitio (n 108) 135–238. Raitio bases his treatment of EU legal principles on the scholarly work of Joutsamo, *see e.g.* Kari Joutsamo, Pekka Aalto and Heidi Kaila, *Eurooppaoikeus* (Alma Talent 1996) 22. *See also* Wouter PJ Wils, *Principles of European Antitrust Enforcement* (Hart Publishing 2005).
110. Petri Kuoppamäki, *Markkinavoiman sääntely EY:n ja Suomen kilpailuoikeudessa* (Academic dissertation, University of Helsinki 2003) 24.
111. *Ibid.*
112. *Ibid.*, 23.
113. The discourse on rules and principles was intense following Ronald Dworkin's introduction of the theory of principles in his essay 'The Model of Rules' (1967) 35 University of Chicago Law Review 14. Until Dworkin's essay appeared, the concept of a legal norm was commonly held to be equal to a legal rule, at least within the analytical and positivist tradition of law. *See* Raimo Siltala, *A Theory of Precedent, From Analytical Positivism to a Post-Analytical Philosophy of Law* (Hart Publishing 1998) 38.

applicable in an all-or-nothing fashion,[114] principles possess the extra dimension of weight and sort of elasticity, and their application is characterized by balancing different values.[115] In his dissertation on EU law, Raitio offers an insightful overview of the theories concerning norms, rules and principles in the context of EU law.[116] Alexy understands principles as optimization commands,[117] which captures the structure of weighing or balancing in principles. In addition to legal principles – besides rules, of course – being central to EU law, policies also play an important role in the EU legal system.[118] A more elaborate discussion on the division between principles and policies goes beyond the scope of this book.[119]

Here, it may be noted that theoretical discussion in recent decades concerning legal principles and their role has been active due to the increased attention given to human rights in this context.[120] General principles of law are recognized as legal sources by the Court of Justice of the European Union (CJEU) and the Court of First Instance.[121] According to settled case law, fundamental rights form an integral part of the general principles of law whose observance the CJEU ensures.[122] The Court has broadened the scope of application of human rights, while protection of fundamental rights in the Community legal order has been almost entirely the product of case law.

The research in the book also builds on *case law*, as competition rules are stipulated in a very small number of key provisions and interpretation of these rules is based on judicial decisions. Put differently, competition law is largely a judicial construction as opposed to a legislative one; the scarce and ample wording of both the European Treaties and the US Sherman Act accord courts and regulators a role that these do not enjoy in other legal areas (particularly in non-common law jurisdictions).[123] The case law is mainly from the EU and the USA, as well as from individual

114. On the difference between legal rules and principles, and their interrelationship, *see* Dworkin (n 62) and Robert Alexy, 'Rechtsregeln und Rechtsprinzipien' (1875) Archiv für Rechts- un Sozialphilosophie, Beiheft 25 13–29. For Nordic perspectives on the topic, *see e.g.* Nils Kristian Sundby, *Om normer* (Universitetsforlaget 1974); Torstein Eckhoff, 'Guiding Standards in Legal Reasoning' (1976) 26 Current Legal Problems 205–219 and 'Retningslinjer og "tumregler"' (1980) Tidskrift for retsvidenskab 146–163; Nils Jareborg, 'Regler og riktlinjer' (1979) *Tidskrift for retsvidenskab* 386–410. For the Finnish discourse regarding legal rules and principles, *see e.g.* Juha Pöyhönen, *Juridisista teorioista. Reports from the Project for the Study of Legal Research No 3* (Suomen akatemia 1981) 70–71 and Juha Pöyhönen, *Sopimusoikeuden järjestelmä ja sopimusten sovittelu* (Suomalaisen Lakimiesyhdistyksen julkaisuja 1988) 12; Aulis Aarnio, 'Ottakaamme oikeussäännöt vakavasti' (1989) Oikeus 112–122.

115. Kaarlo Tuori, *Oikeus, valta ja demokratia* (Lakimiesliiton Kustannus 1990) 3–7. Aarnio holds that this dichotomy into rules and principles could be replaced by a division into strict and elastic norms, rules naturally falling into the former category. Aarnio (n 28) 83.

116. Juha Raitio, *The Principle of Legal Certainty in EC Law* (Academic dissertation, Faculty of Law, University of Helsinki 2001) ch 7.

117. Alexy (n 78) 294–304.

118. Juha Raitio, (n 108) 136–137.

119. In the Finnish literature, Pöyhönen has criticized Dworkin's separation of principles and policies, *see* Pöyhönen, *Juridisista teorioista* (n 114).

120. Aarnio (n 28) 83.

121. Takis Tridimas, *The General Principles of EU Law* (2nd edn, OUP 2006) 299.

122. Case 5/88 *Wachauf* [1989] ECR 2609, para. 17; Case C-274/99 *P Connolly v Commission* [2001] ECR I-1611, para. 17; Case C-94/00 *Roquette Frères* [2002] ECR I-9011, para. 23.

123. Alfonso Lamadrid de Pablo, 'Antitrust and The Political Center' (2013) CPI Antitrust Chronicle 3.

EU (national) Member States. As mentioned, the German case against Facebook is important as a pioneer for pursuing a breach of data protection law through competition enforcement.

Legal doctrine, literature. Beyond legal principles and case law, the principal research material consists of legal doctrine and literature in the broader sense. The key literature is mainly European and American legal commentary, with a significant part of the literature originating from the Anglo-American legal tradition. Central sources include research by Ariel Ezrachi and Maurice Stucke and their publications in the competition law field with regard to virtual competition and big data. Much of the research material concerning privacy and data protection consists of European legal literature, and in this regard publications by Orla Lynskey in the fields of data protection and competition law are of great importance.

Institutional documents are significant sources of information, such as the opinions of the EDPS, studies and reports by the Organisation for Economic Co-operation and Development (OECD) and national competition authorities. In particular, the joint report by the French and German competition authorities concerning big data is of key importance, as it provides an overview of relevant competition issues raised by the use of data in digital markets. While the study does not call for increased enforcement action, it explains how the two authorities view the impact and possible risks of data on competition law and identify potential theories of harm.

In addition to traditional legal sources of information, the research for the book benefits from *relevant journals* and *other online resources*, such as blogs and newspapers, which provide up-to-date case commentaries, among others. Their relative importance as legal sources is acknowledged; nevertheless, they are useful for a book topic as current and as rapidly developing as the one dealt with here.

Research visit. The research has benefited from an academic visit at the University of Oxford in England. In the summer of 2018, the author stayed at the Institute of European and Comparative Law (IECL) at the Oxford Law Faculty as an academic visitor. Conducting research and accessing the Bodleian Library's valuable resources on common law significantly furthered the comparative legal study angle of the book. The academic stay also enriched the author's perspectives on the topic of the book and sparked new dimensions of interest.[124]

Practical (dual) perspective. Competition law is a legal field which has inspired and most likely will continue to inspire academic scholars. It is a discipline which is continually changing and thereby offers novel issues to research, learn and write about. Competition law and policy evolve with society and are in a constant state of transformation, not least in today's digital age with increasing access to information in a shifting technological landscape. Navigating these complexities and understanding the interdependency between the academic, theoretical side of competition law and its application in practice in the business world benefits from practical experience in the field: at least the author of this book has benefited greatly from having considerable

124. The author expresses her gratitude to the academic staff at IECL, including John Cartwright, Birke Häcker and Ariel Ezrachi at the University of Oxford Centre for Competition Law and Policy, with whom the author had the pleasure of discussing her research topic.

practical experience of working with competition law. These experiences enable the author to look at competition law both with a practitioner's hat and with that of an academic researcher, and consequently one of the basic premises of this doctoral book is that theory ought to be balanced with what works in practice.[125]

§1.07 INTERDISCIPLINARITY, TIMELINESS AND SOCIETAL RELEVANCE

This book has an interdisciplinary character as it examines the role of privacy in competition policy, which includes an analysis of the competition and privacy regimes in relation to one another. Considerable knowledge can be gained from the intersection between the disciplines of competition law and data protection, especially when considering their similarities and common objectives. This kind of interdisciplinary character of the book makes it both innovative and fresh.

By providing a comprehensive insight into – and critical evaluation of – competition policy in the digital age, and especially the role of privacy and personal data in this context, the book is highly relevant to the understanding of privacy and competition law, and how these two interplay and interconnect with one another. This subject is increasingly under the scrutiny of competition authorities, policymakers and academics alike and will likely continue to be so for the next decade.

The interconnection between privacy and competition presents many emerging questions and issues deserving of further research and exploration.[126] Scholarship on the interaction between competition policy and the protection of personal data is on the increase. With the rise of big data and the digital economy, today increasing attention is focused on this fascinating area, with attempts in the doctrine to understand and analyse the relationship between the two fields of competition and privacy, or data protection, especially in the context of the data-driven economy.

While competition law is a well-established area of EU law and policy, Europe first developed a data protection framework only as recently as 1995.[127] This

125. Not only has the book benefited from this parallel application of a practitioner's and an academic researcher's point of view, but the same dual approach has also made the research project so much more enjoyable and rewarding. The author's varied professional experience from working with competition law in law firms in Helsinki and Brussels, in the European Commission's Directorate-General for Competition and the US Federal Trade Commission's Office of International Affairs in Washington DC, and as in-house legal counsel in a multinational technology company has all been extremely useful and valuable in terms of the research project.

126. This applies especially to issues in the interlinkage between privacy, or data protection, and competition, whereas the intersection between competition law and *consumer protection* has been discussed and previously explored in detail in, e.g., Albertina Albors-Llorens, 'Competition and Consumer Law in the European Union: Evolution and Convergence' (2014) 33 Yearbook of European Law 163; Giorgio Monti, 'The Revision of the Consumer Acquis from a Competition Law Perspective' (2007) 3 European Review of Contract Law 295; Katalin J Cseres, *Competition Law and Consumer Protection* (Kluwer International 2005).

127. Directive (EC) 95/46 of the European Parliament and of the Council of 24 October 1995 on the protection of individuals with regard to the processing of personal data and on the free movement of such data [1995] OJ L 281.

framework has not been much enforced, which may help explain why relatively little attention had previously been given to the relationship between the two fields in Europe.[128] The situation was similarly deficient in the USA, but for different reasons. One of the weaknesses in American privacy law was that there is not really a meaningful body of judicial decisions, as the existing cases have nearly all resulted in settlement agreements. Besides, the primary regulation of privacy in the USA has been studied scarcely in a scholarly way.[129] Nevertheless, the growing importance of personal data for economic activity has been recognized by competition law scholars and, as mentioned, today a growing number of commentaries and articles on the topic are to be found, particularly in the USA. Some are of limited relevance in the EU context given the distinct legal framework and institutional arrangements in the EU.

Timeliness. The topic of the book is timely and important as it sheds light on quickly evolving areas of law and challenges the fairly commonplace assumption that privacy has little or no role and relevance in competition law. At a time when individuals' data privacy is of growing public concern and the market behaviour of data-driven businesses comes increasingly under scrutiny by competition regulators, this book offers academics, policymakers and practitioners something to think about, perhaps even a vision, for the future of a sound competition policy in the digital age.

This book has the ambitious goal of furthering earlier research on competition policy and the role of privacy protection in competition law. The evolution of the data economy, the explosion of personal data collection and novel data-driven business models and strategies all raise new challenges and questions, such as the role of privacy as a competition concern. This in and of itself makes the subject of the book thoroughly current. The research questions are also highly topical due to recent reform of the EU data protection regime, and the entry into force of the GDPR in the EU Member States in May 2018.

The timeliness of the topic makes researching and writing the book not only exceptionally interesting but also challenging at the same time. Important developments are taking place in a short period of time. My research acknowledges the key and most recent developments only until the formal examination of the book and any more detailed, thorough and critical analysis of later developments and their commentary are left for future research endeavours and a potential separate publication.

The joint study by the French and German competition authorities provides an illustrative example of the fast-paced field of study. When published in May 2016, the joint study expressed fresh and up-to-date thinking about the role of data in competition law by the two leading competition regulators in Europe. However, some of the findings quickly became outdated, some in even less than a year. For instance, the study noted that the argument by some scholars[130] that privacy is tantamount to a reduction of product quality has 'remained [...] a theoretical scenario since privacy has

128. Francisco Costa-Cabral and Orla Lynskey, 'The Internal and External Constraints of Data Protection on Competition Law in the EU' (2015) LSE Law, Society and Economy Working Papers 2.
129. *Ibid*.
130. Allen P Grunes and Maurice E Stucke, 'No Mistake about It: The Important Role of Antitrust in the Era of Big Data' (2015) University of Tennessee Legal Studies Research Paper No 269.

so far not emerged as a significant parameter of competition in competition authorities' practice'.[131] This theoretical scenario was turned into practice in December 2016, when the European Commission issued its decisions in *Microsoft/LinkedIn*, in which it explicitly held that data protection is an important parameter of competition.[132] Moreover, in early 2019 the aforementioned *Facebook* case in Germany took more traditionally minded competition lawyers by surprise by establishing an antitrust infringement due to practices conflicting with data protection principles, thereby breaking more ground in the competition/privacy intersection.

Indeed, over recent years the subject has become more visible in EU debates as well as on the international level; the EDPS has repeatedly called for more stringent enforcement of competition rules for the protection of privacy and the OECD has studied the value of user data in competition. Moreover, national competition cases and sector enquiries concerning data and privacy have been on the increase. The timeliness of the book is also reflected in that it looks at recent praxis, such as the European Commission decisions in the *Facebook/WhatsApp* merger,[133] *Microsoft/LinkedIn* and, in particular, the Bundeskartellamt's pioneering *Facebook* opinion.[134]

Societal relevance. The topic of the book has significant societal relevance. A functioning market has enormous importance for society because it leads to more efficient use of resources, increased economic advantage for consumers, high-quality products and services, more affordable prices and, above all, general welfare and well-being for consumers and citizens. A sound competition process also creates strong incentives for technical innovation and improvements in product variety and quality. In consequence, the book is important and of considerable interest from the societal perspective.

The findings of this book can be used for defining a closer-to-optimal competition policy for today's data-driven economy. Significant potential exists for societal impact by identifying market failures, potential privacy harms and flaws in existing competition policy that makes it inadequate for the digital age. The book posits that competition policy goals need to be rethought and it sets out to explore a potential conjoined approach between competition and privacy regulators. Such approach could help in better addressing gaps in the digital markets, dealing with the increasing commercialization of personal user data and the need to protect privacy and preserve consumer integrity. The research results of this book can be used to articulate closer-to-optimal competition policy objectives and envision new approaches to policy cooperation across conventional legal areas.

Fundamental rights. Both the right to privacy and the right to data protection enjoy the status of fundamental rights in the EU. In this context, the book includes an

131. French-German joint report (n 9) 24–25.
132. Commission press release, 'Mergers: Commission approves acquisition of LinkedIn by Microsoft, subject to conditions' (Brussels, 6 December 2016).
133. Case COMP/M.7217 *Facebook/WhatsApp*, C(2014) 7239 (*Facebook/WhatsApp*).
134. Bundeskartellamt case summary (n 18). Facebook successfully appealed the decision to the Düsseldorf Higher Regional Court. Beschluss Facebook gegen Bundeskartellamt VI-Kart 1/19 (V) (26 August 2019).

analysis of fundamental rights, as it examines competition policy in relation to (informational) privacy and data protection. However, the aim of the book is not to discuss fundamental rights beyond the interlinkage between competition and privacy. Thus, decisions of the Court of Human Rights are not explored in any detail but may be used as a point of reference to illustrate relevant developments and helpful perspectives.

§1.08 TERMINOLOGY

A few words on terminology. The terms 'antitrust' and 'competition law' are used interchangeably in this book. This is mostly for convenience and ease of reading. The term 'antitrust' comes from US law, which was originally formulated to combat 'business trusts', now more commonly known as cartels. In the EU and other countries, the term 'competition law' is used more commonly. As noted by Fejø, the reason why the EU provisions have been formed as 'competition rules', '*Wettbewerbsregeln*', or '*regles de concurrence*' and not 'antitrust laws' like the American provisions, has to do with the difference in time of their origin and the motivation for their creation.[135]

However, it is noteworthy that the term 'antitrust' when used in EU competition law may also refer to Articles 101 and 102 TFEU (as opposed to the rules concerning state aid and merger control).[136] In its analysis of the interface between competition and privacy, this book is limited to dealing mainly with abuse of dominance situations, which fall under Article 102 TFEU in EU competition law. Nevertheless, in this book, the term 'antitrust' is used when discussing US antitrust law, whereas 'competition' is used in the context of EU competition law. However, for ease of reading, the terms are also used interchangeably when suitable and convenient.

Another terminological point worth noting is that the concepts of 'privacy' and 'data protection' are often used interchangeably in this book. The laws and regulations that cover 'the management of personal information' are typically grouped under 'privacy' in the USA and under 'protection' in the EU and elsewhere. The EU's regime is of course based on EU terminology. In this book, largely due to its comparative perspective that takes into consideration both jurisdictions, the terms 'privacy' (or 'data privacy') and 'data protection' are in many instances used interchangeably for ease of reading. This choice of terminology is also justified as the concepts of 'privacy' and 'data protection' are commonly considered as overlapping. This reflects the view most prominent in the public perception and in the academic literature.[137]

However, it is important to recognize that even though the two concepts are overlapping, and using the terms interchangeably is generally accepted, strictly speaking, 'privacy' and 'data protection' are also regarded as distinct from each other. While data protection law covers informational privacy, it does not incorporate all

135. *See* Jens Fejø, *Monopoly Law and Market. Studies of EC Competition Law with US American Antitrust Law as a Frame of Reference and Supported by Basic Market Economics* (Kluwer Law and Taxation Publishers 1990) 36.
136. As is done in §1.05 when describing the focus of the book.
137. Orla Lynskey, *The Foundations of EU Data Protection Law* (OUP 2015) 101.

aspects of privacy, such as intrusions on physical seclusion, for example. Further, certain aspects of data protection law are not captured by 'privacy' - for example, unconditional application to personal data in the public domain, or the rights it grants, such as rights of access to data, data security standards and the right to data portability.[138] The relationship between the notions of data protection and privacy is explored in Chapter 2.

§1.09 ETHICS

This brief chapter considers in short ethics (or morals) as an essential element of good research practice, as the topic of ethics in academic discourse and the possibility of academic bias has been the subject of many recent articles and reports in the area of competition law.[139] The recent debate has focused on corporate funding linked to ethical issues, especially where the funding or financial ties are not disclosed.

Good research ethics can have a significant impact on the research community and influence society at large. This book has been written according to good research and ethical norms, and with accountability and respect towards the accuracy and value of the research outcomes. That approach is in line with, for example, David Resnik's view on ethics and key ethical principles.[140]

Finally, ethics makes research meaningful to the researcher and for wider society. This is also in accordance with the key responsibilities for researchers identified in the Finnish Guidelines on Responsible Conduct of Research. Ethical issues foster trust in research, which is closely linked to societal values and compliance with laws. Trust and ethical issues concern everyone involved in research - individuals, institutions, funding bodies, societies and nations - as everyone shares research responsibility. Therefore, the recent debate over funding, impartiality and ethics in competition law research is to be welcomed and perceived as healthy for fostering trust in research.

138. *Ibid.*, 89–130.
139. *See e.g.* Jan Broulík, 'Economics in Antitrust Enforcement and the Private Benefit of Scholarly Commentators' (13 January 2017) TILEC Discussion Paper No 2017-001; Campaign for Accountability, 'Google Academics Inc Report' (11 July 2017) Google Transparency Project (examining Google's considerable financial support for academia).
140. David B Resnik, *The Ethics of Science: An Introduction* (Routledge 1998). In 2017, the author participated in a course on research ethics at the University of Helsinki, during which a wide range of topics were studied, including ethical theories and approaches, key research ethical questions and guiding principles.

CHAPTER 2
The Importance of Privacy in an Increasingly Data-Driven World

In this chapter, the distinct approaches to privacy in the EU and the USA are explored. By looking into the different historical and cultural backgrounds and legal traditions, it is possible to understand why the privacy law framework and the view it reflects on data protection is distinct in these two jurisdictions. Whereas the EU is a jurisdiction wary of private entities amassing personal data, not least after the GDPR, the Americans have traditionally mainly focused on abuses by the government. The transatlantic difference in privacy perceptions is significant for understanding the inter-linking between privacy and competition and for examining the role that data protection can be assigned in competition policy. Lastly, the chapter also considers privacy from a more global perspective by discussing how data protection has evolved in certain jurisdictions around the world.

§2.01 INTRODUCTION

Technology has changed. But even more importantly, our society's attitudes have moved on. We've learned once more that you can't just assume that technology will serve society, and not the other way around. We've come to see that sucking up large amounts of data can help create exciting new services – but also take away our privacy.[141]

141. Margrethe Vestager speech, 'Competition and a Fair Deal for Consumers Online' Netherlands Authority for Consumers and Markets Fifth Anniversary Conference (The Hague, 26 April 2018).

The digital revolution. The digital revolution has been called the Fourth Industrial Revolution.[142] Where previous industrial revolutions liberated humankind from animal power, enabled mass production and brought digital capabilities to billions of people, the digital revolution is fundamentally different. It is characterized by a range of new technologies that are fusing the physical, digital and biological worlds, and having an impact on all disciplines, all industries and the economy.[143] Digitalization has been spurred by the exponential growth of computing power and expansion of Internet access globally. Consequently, global society is undergoing a transformation from an industrial era to an information era, as the economy becomes more information-intensive and data-rich. This has enabled the rise of business models based on the collection and processing of 'big data', a buzzword commonly referred to in the context of the digital economy. The data-driven economy has generated a substantial number of innovations both in terms of new products and services that benefit consumers, and new organization and marketing strategies that increase companies' productivity.[144]

Concept of 'big data'. The concept of 'big data' – originally used by computer scientists and today popularized among academics, regulators and politicians – is widespread across multiple disciplines and industries. However, the term has no single definition and is often used in different ways.[145]

The concept basically tries to capture recent developments in digital technologies and markets. Big data is often described as an accumulation of a significant volume of different types of data, produced at high speed from multiple sources, the handling and analysis of which requires new and more powerful processors and algorithms. The data is stored in massive data servers (called clouds). Big data is also characterized by 'the four Vs', referring to the *volume* of data, the *velocity* or speed at which data is collected, used and disseminated, the *variety* of information aggregated and the *value* of the data. Thus, 'big data' differs from traditional datasets due to these four 'Vs'.[146] According to certain big data researchers, who compiled a survey of all existing big data definitions with a view to generating a more solid term encompassing most of the relevant research areas, '[b]ig data is the information asset characterized by such a

142. The World Economic Forum named the digital revolution the Fourth Industrial Revolution, *see* Klaus Schwab, *The Fourth Industrial Revolution* (Penguin 2016).
143. *Ibid.*
144. OECD, 'Data-Driven Innovation for Growth and Well-Being: Interim Synbook Report' (October 2014) 26.
145. *See e.g.* Jonathan Stuart Ward and Adam Barker, 'The Big Data Conundrum: How to Define It?' MIT Technology Review (3 October 2013) https://www.technologyreview.com/s/519851/the-big-data-conundrum-how-to-define-it/, accessed 19 April 2020; Gil Press, '12 Big Data Definitions: What's Yours?' Forbes (3 September 2014) https://www.forbes.com/sites/gilpress/2014/09/03/12-big-data-definitions-whats-yours/#61a4e10513ae, accessed 19 April 2020.
146. *See e.g.* Ariel Ezrachi and Maurice E Stucke, *Virtual Competition – The Promise and Perils of the Algorithm-Driven Economy* (Harvard University Press 2016) 15; Maurice E Stucke and Allen P Grunes, *Big Data and Competition Policy* (OUP 2016) 16. According to studies by the OECD, each of these 'Vs' has significantly increased over the past decade, *see* n 144.

high volume, velocity and variety to require specific technology and analytical methods for its transformation into value'.[147]

The value of big data increases with the rise of 'big analytics', including algorithms that can access and analyse vast amounts of information and the introduction of machine learning.[148] Nowadays, data analytics is becoming an ever more automated task. This development is accompanied by the increasing use of software that relies on self-learning algorithms and systems using artificial intelligence. In the coming years, data will not be collected only on the Internet but also by an increasing number of sensors installed in electronic devices that interact with each other (the Internet of Things, IoT). This means that the advent of IoT will grow the number of industrial manufacturers and service providers that collect, process and transfer a large amount of data via their devices.

For this book, when referring to the concept of data, it is important to note that data is varied. 'Data' is actually another concept lacking a common definition. In a narrower sense, the term is often used for the results of scientific experiments or measurements. But in a wider sense, the concept is used to refer to (any) information, or the representation of that information, often in combination with it being stored on a computer.[149] Although lacking a universal definition, it is key to acknowledge (and this will be explored in more detail in the following §2.02) that data can be divided, roughly speaking, into personal and non-personal data. In this regard, the EU GDPR[150] provides a broad definition of personal data as 'any information relating to an identified or identifiable individual ("data subject")'.[151] In this book, when discussing data, the focus will be mainly on personal data rather than non-personal data.

In the digital or data economy, data now represents a core economic asset. It has the potential to create significant competitive advantage for companies.[152] Data has even been assigned its own new asset class by the World Economic Forum.[153] The volume of collected data has increased significantly over recent decades and data-driven businesses, strategies and acquisitions will continue to grow as use of data has become a key basis for competition.[154] In 2016, the global flow of data and information

147. Andrea De Mauro, Marco Greco and Michele Grimaldi, 'A Formal Definition of Big Data Based on Its Essential Features' (2016) 65 Library Review 122–135.
148. Ezrachi and Stucke (n 146) 15.
149. *See e.g.* definitions according to *Merriam-Webster* (https://www.merriam-webster.com/dictionary/data) and *Oxford* dictionaries (https://www.oxforddictionaries.com/definition/learner/data).
150. Regulation (EC) 2016/679 on the protection of natural persons with regard to the processing of personal data and on the free movement of such data [2016] OJ L 119 (GDPR).
151. GDPR 4(1).
152. OECD Big Data (n 22) 319.
153. The World Economic Forum, 'Personal Data: The Emergence of a New Asset Class' (January 2011). *See also* World Economic Forum, 'Big Data, Big Impact: New Possibilities for International Development' (2012).
154. McKinsey Global Institute, Big Data: The Next Frontier for Innovation, Competition, and Productivity (June 2011) 2 (noting in 2011 that its 'research suggests that we are on the cusp of a tremendous wave of innovation, productivity, and growth, as well as new modes of competition and value capture – all driven by big data as consumers, companies, and economic sectors exploit its potential'). *See also* n 144, 11 (noting that 'the ICT sector has begun to

generated more value than the global goods trade.[155] This is quite remarkable, as digital data flows were practically non-existent just fifteen years ago, whereas now they exert a larger impact on gross domestic product (GDP) growth than the centuries-old trade in goods.[156]

Some years ago already, *The Economist* noted that data, particularly consumer data, had become 'the new raw material of business: an economic input almost on a par with capital and labour'.[157] As mentioned in the introduction to this book, today data is commonly referred to as the 'oil of the internet' or the 'currency of the digital economy'.[158] While these various analogies reflect the economic value of personal data in the digital economy, what they fail to consider is that personal data is also essentially linked to the dignity, autonomy and privacy of individuals. Business models based on the monetization of personal data abound, yet from a legal perspective this raises questions. More specifically, the large amount of data controlled by a handful of online companies or platforms has generated a number of competition law concerns. As articulated by Botta and Wiedemann, 'a pending question is whether and to what extent the traditional competition law principles can be transferred from the "real" to the data economy'.[159]

It is suggested that the role that competition law played in the wake of the industrial revolution is now being captured by privacy in the digital age, where privacy has become the limiting principle and boundary for balancing between the benefits and risks of an array of technological innovations.[160] A certain point of culmination is the treatment of data and the competition concerns it raises at the intersection between competition law and data protection law, as is done in this book. As phrased by Lynskey, it is because competition law is the only instrument in the legal armour that constrains the exercise of power by private companies that its intersection with data protection laws becomes an inevitable focal point.[161]

The interlinkage between the two policy areas of competition law and data protection also invites discussion on the extent to which the approaches to treatment of

recognise "big data" as a new business opportunity and is making significant investments to catch-up and jump on the "big data" bandwagon').

155. McKinsey & Company, 'Digital globalization: The new era of global flows', McKinsey Global Institute Report (March 2016) 7.
156. *Ibid.*
157. Kenneth Cukier, 'Data, Data Everywhere' The Economist (London, 25 February 2010) http://www.economist.com/node/15557443, accessed 19 April 2020.
158. *See* Chapter 1.
159. Botta and Wiedemann (n 95).
160. Nitasha Tiku, 'Digital Privacy Is Making Antitrust Exciting Again' Wired (6 April 2017) https://www.wired.com/2017/06/ntitrust-watchdogs-eye-big-techs-monopoly-data/, accessed 19 April 2020.
161. Orla Lynskey, 'At the Crossroads of Data Protection and Competition Law: Time to Take Stock' (2018) 8 International Data Privacy Law 179–180. This interconnection between privacy and competition in the data economy has until recent years been relatively underexplored, and has in the past received less attention than, e.g., the general relationship between competition law and consumer protection law. For a discussion on the intersection between competition law and consumer protection law, *see e.g.* Albors-Llorens (n 126) 163; Monti (n 126) 295; Cseres (n 126). In Finland, Kalle Määttä conducted an analysis of the intersection between competition and consumer protection law, *see* Määttä (n 105).

personal data in these fields are, as is often claimed, distinct.[162] The separation between the two policy areas is dealt with in Chapter 4 below, which also looks at overlaps between competition law and data protection (such as both being concerned with imbalances between consumers and dominant companies), and their respective scope of application. A related issue, which goes beyond the scope of this book, concerns data ownership and who owns the data gathered via applications and services. This is a relevant issue; as consumer information has become an asset, consumers may want to sell their own personal data directly to companies.[163] The question concerning the consumers' right to control their own data in the digital market environment is addressed in this book only in connection with consumers' data protection rights.

As reliance on consumer data will continue to grow and more companies will adopt data-driven business models and strategies to achieve a competitive advantage over their rivals, this can raise a range of novel problems, such as modern concerns about diversity of opinions and fake news.[164] For example, one much-discussed Internet business model is that of 'surveillance capitalism', so named in 2015 by the Harvard academic Shoshana Zuboff, which is increasingly seen as a problem following the Facebook-Cambridge Analytica data scandal.[165] While these various novel issues related to data may be relevant generally from a competition law perspective,[166] and may deserve further research to gain a full understanding of their practical implications, they are not within the scope of this book.

§2.02 DEFINITIONS

In the following, before exploring the concept of privacy, certain key definitions relevant to privacy are discussed with the aim of laying the ground for later discussion on the understanding of privacy and data protection from a comparative viewpoint.

162. Botta and Wiedemann (n 95). *See also Facebook/WhatsApp* (n 133) para. 164.
163. For example, Handshake.uk.com offers an application that allows consumers to negotiate a price for their own personal data directly with companies that are interested in buying these data. The basic idea is to create a marketplace for personal data. According to the founders, 'Handshake.uk.com will turn what has previously been stolen into a currency which can be traded.' Natasha Lomas, 'Handshake Is a Personal Data Marketplace Where Users Get Paid to Sell Their Own Data' Techcrunch (2 September 2013) https://techcrunch.com/2013/09/02/handshake/, accessed 19 April 2020.
164. On the relationship between fake news and antitrust, *see e.g.* Sally Hubbard, 'Why Fake News Is an Antitrust Problem' Forbes (10 January 2017) https://www.forbes.com/sites/washingtonbytes/2017/01/10/why-fake-news-is-an-antitrust-problem/2/#4752b2263f0d, accessed 19 April 2020.
165. Jennifer Cobbe, 'Reining in Big Data's Robber Barons' NYR Daily (12 April 2018) http://www.nybooks.com/daily/2018/04/12/reining-in-big-datas-robber-barons/, accessed 19 April 2020.
166. The European Commission has been urged to launch a sector enquiry into online advertisers and platforms to unearth problems with fake news at the request of the European consumer organization BEUC, whose concern is that dominant platforms might be foreclosing information sources by giving preference to their own services. Allegedly, some business models are based on keeping consumers 'hooked' to content that helps increase advertising revenues. *See* BEUC letter to Competition Commissioner Margrethe Vestager, 'A sector inquiry into online advertising practices' (13 March 2018) http://www.mlex.com/ITCMedia/DetailView.aspx?ppo=7&cid=971272&siteid=145&rdir=1, accessed 19 April 2020.

The concept of personal data. Although amassing and analysing large data sets by companies is not limited to consumer data, many aspects of big data are targeted specifically at consumers. As mentioned, data is varied and can be classified into personal and non-personal data. This book focuses on personal data, which, according to the OECD, is generally defined as 'any information relating to an identified or identifiable individual (data subject)'.[167] The value of data lies especially in the fact that it allows some understanding of human behaviour: it reveals patterns of information that enable companies to follow user behaviour and preferences, target their products and services accordingly and thereby monetize those services and products. In its study on the commercial use of consumer data, the UK competition authority found that consumer data can in some business sectors 'be a key competitive asset in targeting offers' because the collection and analysis of consumer data is critical to gain an accurate understanding of how to attract and retain customers.[168] As noted by the EDPS, '[n]ot all big data is personal, but for many online offerings which are presented or perceived as being "free", personal information operates as a sort of indispensable currency used to pay for those services'.[169]

Personal data as currency. Since the European Commission's well-known decision in 2017 in *Google Search (Shopping)* where Google was found guilty of abusing its dominance as a search engine, and slapped with a record fine of EUR 2.42 billion, it is no longer unrealistic to say that individuals pay for supposedly free online services by giving away their personal data.[170] According to the OECD, the expression online 'free' service is generally considered misleading for consumers. The online services delivered, in fact, '... involve non-pecuniary costs (for consumers) in the form of providing personal data, paying attention to ads, or the opportunity costs of reading privacy policies'.[171]

With the transition to the data economy, consumer data has become a new tradeable good.[172] Companies are adopting business models with personal data as a key resource or input and implementing strategies to acquire data-advantage over rivals. Put differently, Tim Wu maintains that human attention is the resource, as an

167. OECD, 'Exploring the Economics of Personal Data: A Survey of Methodologies for Measuring Monetary Value' (2013) OECD Digital Economy Paper No 220, 7. Similarly, the GDPR defines data as 'any information relating to an identified or identifiable individual ("data subject")', *see* GDPR 4(1).
168. The UK Competition and Markets Authority, 'The Commercial Use of Consumer Data: Report on the CMA's Call for Information' (June 2015) CMA 38, 2.88.
169. EDPS Opinion (n 10) 6.
170. European Commission press release, 'Commission fines Google €2.42 billion for abusing dominance as search engine by giving illegal advantage to own comparison shopping service' (27 June 2017): 'Google's flagship product is the Google search engine, which provides search results to consumers, who pay for the service with their data.' *See also* Alec Burnside, 'No Such Thing as a Free Search: Antitrust and the Pursuit of Privacy Goals' (May 2015) CPI Antitrust Chronicle 4.
171. OECD Big Data (n 22) 25.
172. For an analysis of the concept of 'goods' in EU law, *see e.g.* Juha Raitio, *Euroopan unionin oikeuden periaatteet ja perusvapaudet* (Unigrafia Oy 2017) 105. In the context of the EU internal market, goods can generally be defined as products that have monetary value and which can be the object of commercial trade. Raitio notes, however, that digitalization has created interpretational challenges and somewhat blurred the line between what constitutes goods and what amounts to services.

increasingly large sector of the economy, including technology companies such as Google and Facebook, along with parts of the traditional media, actually depend on so-called attentional markets for their revenue.[173]

In whatever way data is defined, the increasing collection and exploitation of personal information for commercial use raises privacy protection issues. Traditionally, this could be seen as a concern only for consumer protection and data protection rather than one of competition policy.[174] However, when personal data has become a valuable commodity that companies compete over, their rivalry falls within the realm of competition law. Recent high-profile cases in digital markets have fuelled the question of the possible competition implications of exercising control over large data sets, as well as a desire to better understand the possible effects for consumers and markets.[175] Besides being a commodity, personal data is also closely linked to the dignity, autonomy, and privacy of individuals, which is protected through data protection law. At the intersection of these two legal fields, competition and data protection law, stands valuable knowledge to be gained. This interconnection is explored when looking in more detail at the relationship between the two regimes governing the use of data.

The definition of privacy. Although privacy is one of the most important concepts of our time, it is also one of the most elusive and vaguest terms. Privacy has no single definition across different jurisdictions and societies.[176] In the data economy, where rapidly changing technologies make information increasingly available, scholars, policymakers and regulators alike are struggling to explain and define privacy. Some concede that the task is impossible.[177] Daniel Solove argues that no single definition of privacy can be workable, but rather that there are multiple forms of privacy, related to one another by family resemblances.[178] According to Neil Richards:

> one of the most difficult (and frustrating) things about privacy is that it has a bewildering variety of meanings. Sometimes it seems as if privacy can mean almost anything – from information collection by Facebook, to lawsuits against the press for publishing celebrity sex gossip, to misuses of personal information leading to identity theft, to 'big data' analysis, to the use of wiretaps by the police to investigate crime, to the ability to enjoy dinnertime at home without a telemarketer calling. In our everyday uses of the English language, and in the technical language of law, the word 'privacy' has been used to mean each of these

173. Tim Wu, 'Blind Spot: The Attention Economy and the Law' (2018) 82 Antitrust Law Journal (holding that antitrust agencies lack tools for assessing market power of companies in these attention markets).
174. OECD Big Data (n 22) 5.
175. *Ibid.*
176. Lee Bygrave, *Data Protection Law. Approaching Its Rationale, Logic and Limits* (Kluwer Law International 2002) 125–127.
177. *See* Daniel J Solove, *Understanding Privacy* (Harvard University Press 2008).
178. *Ibid.* Judith Jarvis Thomson is sceptical about defining the concept of privacy, writing that 'nobody seems to have any very clear idea what [it] is', in 'The Right to Privacy' in Ferdinand David Schoeman (ed.), *Philosophical Dimensions of Privacy: An Anthology* (CUP 1984) 272, 286.

> examples and more besides. We employ it to mean a wide variety of different things, so our use of it often lacks precision.[179]

As scholars of privacy have struggled to define the term, trying definitions that were too narrow or too broad, in recent years many have settled on an understanding of privacy as an umbrella term that encompasses a variety of related meanings. Sociologists Gary Marx and Glenn Muschert, for example, hold that instead of trying to define privacy, one should understand it as 'a family of concepts encompassing personal information'.[180] Philosopher Helen Nissenbaum has argued that we should understand privacy as 'contextual integrity'. Under this view, information is always flowing, but certain flows and restrictions are taken for granted. Only when the norms governing the appropriate flows of information are violated, argues Nissenbaum, does one experience a violation of privacy in context.[181]

Multiple privacy dimensions. What is clear, though, is that the concept of privacy assumes multiple dimensions in a society. These include, among others, physical privacy (protection against physical intrusion and the right to seclusion at home and bodily integrity), informational privacy (limiting access to personal data and rights against unwanted publication of intimate facts), decisional privacy (freedom from government interference with personal life, such as the right to marry and abortion rights), proprietary privacy (rights of celebrities and others to control the attributes of their personal identities), associational privacy (rights to membership, inclusion or access to an otherwise closed group), and intellectual privacy (mental repose, ability to think forbidden thoughts).[182] This categorization is not exhaustive, and no doubt the notion of privacy evolves as society develops and circumstances change.[183]

For the purpose of this book, the most relevant and significant dimension of privacy is informational privacy and the limiting of access to personal data. This form of privacy is increasingly important, as simply operating in a modern economy and in society today requires some degree of disclosure of personal data and foregoing of privacy for various societal and commercial purposes.[184]

Privacy cultures. The delimitation of what constitutes privacy rights changes from society to society and reflects current cultural values.[185] Ideas of privacy have shifted

179. Neil Richards, *Intellectual Privacy: Rethinking Civil Liberties in the Digital Age* (OUP 2015) 8.
180. Gary T Marx and Glenn W Muschert, 'Personal Information, Borders, and the New Surveillance Studies' (2007) 3 Annual Review of Law and Social Science.
181. Helen Nissenbaum, 'Privacy as Contextual Integrity' (2004) Washington Law Review.
182. Anita L Allen and Marc Rotenberg, *Privacy Law and Society* (2nd edn, American Casebook Series, 2011).
183. For an introduction to the various potential dimensions to privacy (Swe. *integritet*) from a Nordic legal perspective, *see e.g.* Johan Bärlund, Frey Nybergh and Katarina Petrell, *Finlands civil- och handelsrätt – En introduktion* (Talentum 2013) 97–100. For further reading on invasions of various personality interests in Europe, *see* Gert Brüggemeier, Aurelia Colombi Ciacchi and Patrick O'Callaghan, *Personality Rights in European Tort Law* (CUP 2010). In their analysis, Brüggemeier et al. study the treatment in different European jurisdictions of personal interests or 'personality rights' with regard to the legal protection of honour and reputation, privacy, self-determination and image.
184. Riku Neuvonen, *Yksityisyyden suoja Suomessa* (Lakimiesliiton Kustannus 2014) 60.
185. James Q Whitman, 'The Two Western Cultures of Privacy: Dignity Versus Liberty' (2004) 113 Yale Law Journal 1151–1221.

remarkably and mutated over time, which can be shown by just looking at varying descriptions and understandings of the privacy concept in literature.[186] Western societies reflect two different cultures of privacy protection: whereas Europeans view privacy as a dignity, Americans view privacy more as a form of liberty.[187] In Europe, personal privacy and control over one's data qualifies as a fundamental, almost inalienable right. The rights to privacy and data protection are enshrined in the EU by the Charter of Fundamental Rights.[188] In the USA, conversely, privacy and data are treated mostly as an asset that can be freely traded.[189] This, some argue, creates an EU/US divide - or, even more strongly put, a collision - in privacy protection.[190] Others talk about privacy conflicts or a 'transatlantic clash'.[191]

When describing values in the cultural context and how Europe and the USA reflect different privacy cultures, as mentioned above, it is also necessary to say something about what is meant by value. The term *value* can be understood as a broad tendency to prefer certain states of affairs over others.[192] The concept of value is used in all social sciences (anthropology, economics, political science, psychology and sociology) with different although not completely unrelated meanings. According to Geert Hofstede, value is an interdisciplinary term, and nearly all our other mental programmes, such as attitudes and beliefs, carry a value component.[193] *Norms* of value refer to collectivity.[194] Importantly, it is values that form the core of culture. When speaking of cultural values, what is meant is the collective phenomenon of culture, which consists of the unwritten rules of a social game.[195]

Here, it is not argued that a transatlantic clash of distinct privacy cultures is taking place. It is not necessary to look at the differences between the two jurisdictions of the EU and the USA in the form of conflicting interests. Rather, the different forms of privacy protection can be understood as a reflection of their own cultural and legal histories, which are distinct for both the European and American jurisdictions and their

186. *See e.g.* André Bertrand, *Droit a la vie privée et droit a l'image* (LexisNexis/LITEC 1999) 2 (discussing public defecation by early modern kings of France); Bernard Beignier, *La vie privée*, in Rémy Cabrillac et al. (eds), *Libertés et droits fondamentaux* (5th edn, Dalloz 1999) 139, 139–141 (discussing nude bathing in the Seine and other early modern examples).
187. Whitman (n 185) 1151–1221. *See also* Filippo Maria Lancieri, 'Digital Protectionism? Antitrust, Data Protection, and the EU/US Transatlantic Rift' (2019) 7 Journal of Antitrust Enforcement 1–27.
188. Charter of Fundamental Rights of the European Union [2000] OJ C364/01 and [2010] OJ C83/389 (EU Charter of Fundamental Rights).
189. *See generally*, Whitman (n 185) 1151–1221.
190. Paul M Schwartz, 'The EU-US Privacy Collision: A Turn to Institutions and Procedures' (2013) 126 Harvard Law Review 1966.
191. Whitman (n 185) 1153.
192. *See* Hofstede (n 36) 5–6.
193. *Ibid.*, 6.
194. Norms of value refer to values actually held by the majority (statistical norm or the desired, i.e. what people actually desire) or pertaining to what is ethically right (absolute or deontological norm or the desirable, i.e. what people think they ought to desire). On values, culture and the distinction between the desired and the desirable, *see* Hofstede (n 36) 6–7.
195. Culture is defined as the collective programming of the mind that distinguishes the members of one group or category of people from others. Geert H Hofstede, Geert Jan Hofstede and Michael Minkov, *Cultures and Organizations: Software of the Mind. Intercultural Cooperation and Its Importance for Survival* (3rd edn, HarperCollins 1994) 6–9.

respective societies. These differences in culture and history have led to two different privacy regimes developing in Europe and the USA. This is of great importance when considering the question of what role privacy plays, and should play, in competition law and policy.

Although a transatlantic clash of privacy cultures is not necessarily taking place, none the less it cannot be denied that distinct attitudes have provoked some tense and costly transatlantic legal and trade battles over time. For example, it can be mentioned in this context that the EU and the USA experienced a trade conflict over protection of consumer data in the 1990s, only problematically resolved by a 2000 'safe harbour' agreement, which was later struck down.[196]

In more recent times, the spread of the coronavirus epidemic (COVID-19) around the world in early 2020 and related actions by various governments to face the crisis will probably also have an effect on the understanding of what constitutes privacy, reflecting concerns and urgent changes in society and current values. The decisions people and governments take in efforts to stop the epidemic will shape the world for years to come.[197] This includes the understanding of privacy and data protection.

The decisions that governments take may concern new surveillance tools enabling so-called under the skin surveillance, referring biometric surveillance systems. For example, Israel authorized its national security agency to deploy surveillance technology normally reserved for battling terrorists to track coronavirus patients and Chinese authorities deployed surveillance tools to closely monitor people's smartphones, track their movements and identify anyone they came into contact with.[198] According to Yuval Noah Harari, in this time of crisis, humankind faces a particularly important choice between totalitarian surveillance and citizen empowerment:

> A big battle has been raging in recent years over our privacy. The coronavirus crisis could be the battle's tipping point. [...] If we fail to make the right choice, we might find ourselves signing away our most precious freedoms, thinking that this is the only way to safeguard our health. It remains to be seen, and this may take many years to come, how the understanding of privacy and data protection will possibly change and evolve as a result the coronavirus – one of (if not the) biggest global crisis of humankind and our generation.

In the following §2.03, some context from mainly legal, but also historical and cultural, dimensions will be provided to explain the diverse backgrounds to the privacy regimes in Europe and the USA and their different approaches to informational privacy and control over data. Understanding this background and acknowledging the divergent privacy views is important when later (in Chapter 3) looking at the distinctions between competition law objectives in Europe and the USA, and when analysing the

196. This involved the EU Data Privacy Directive (Council Directive 95/46 of 24 October 1995 on the protection of individuals with regard to the processing of personal data and on the free movement of such data, 1995 OJ (L 281) 31). For documents on the Safe Harbour Agreement, *see* Daniel J Solove and Marc Rotenberg, *Information Privacy Law* (2003) 743–754. The safe harbour framework was later struck down by the CJEU in *Schrems*, *see* n 223.
197. Harari (n 4).
198. *Ibid.*

interlinkage between competition and privacy laws and their scope of application in the data economy (in Chapter 4).

§2.03 THE EU'S APPROACH TO DATA PRIVACY

[A] Privacy as a Dignity and Fundamental Right

An important starting point is acknowledging that privacy and data protection, though connected and overlapping, are commonly regarded as two separate rights in the EU. These rights enjoy legal protection that originates in constitutional documents, most notably in the EU Charter of Fundamental Rights. Article 8 of the EU Charter sets out a right to protection of personal data, which sits alongside, and in addition to, the right to privacy set out in Article 7 of the Charter. Further, Article 8 of the European Convention on Human Rights (ECHR) grants legal protection to the 'right to respect for private and family life'. The European Court of Human Rights (ECtHR) has acknowledged in its case law that the right to privacy as granted by Article 8 of the ECHR must be interpreted to include a right to data protection.[199]

While the inclusion of a right to data protection in the EU Charter reflects the recognition of such an independent right in several EU Member States, no 'common constitutional tradition' exists in terms of data protection across the EU.[200] Several Member States, including Finland, treat the right to data protection as a subset of the right to privacy. For example, Section 10 of the Finnish Constitution, entitled 'the right to privacy', states that:

> Everyone's private life, honor and the sanctity of the home are guaranteed. More detailed provisions on the protection of personal data are laid down by an Act.[201]

In a similar fashion, the CJEU in its decisional practice conflates the rights to data protection and privacy, often treating data protection as a subset of the right to privacy. This arguably reflects a narrower view of data protection, a view which is prominent in the public perception and academic literature.[202] Lynskey considers different ways of conceptualizing the relationship between data protection and privacy, arguing that the link between the two rights is best reflected by understanding data protection as an independent right serving many functions including, but not limited to, the protection of privacy.[203] Data protection offers individuals enhanced control over their personal data by giving them more rights over more types of information than the right to privacy when applied in the context of data processing. Others see data protection as a

199. *See e.g. Leander v Sweden*, judgment of 26 March 1987 (Appl no 9248/81) and *Rotaru v Romania*, judgment of 4 May 2000 (Appl no 28341/95).
200. Lynskey (n 137) 89.
201. 731/1999, Fi. *Suomen perustuslaki*.
202. *See e.g.* Alan Westin, *Privacy and Freedom* (Athenaeum 1967) 158; Daniel Solove, *The Digital Person: Technology and Privacy in the Information Age* (NYU Press 2004); Andrew Charlesworth, 'Clash of the Data Titans? US and EU Data Privacy Regulation' (2000) 6 European Public Law 253.
203. Lynskey (n 137) 90.

facet of the right to privacy: as the most recent phase in the evolution of the right to privacy to encompass elements of information control.[204]

The distinction between privacy and data protection is conceptually noteworthy but not the primary concern of this book. It suffices to acknowledge that data protection and privacy are two separate rights and that data protection considerably overlaps with the right to privacy, as they both ensure informational or data privacy, which, in terms of this book, is the most relevant and important dimension of privacy.

Privacy as dignity. In the EU, human dignity is recognized as an absolute fundamental right. The dual nature of personal data, which encompasses both an economic and a dignitary value, is acknowledged through a strong level of protection. Lynskey describes this dual dignitary-economic role for personal data as personal data leading 'a double life in digital society'; on the one hand, personal data is a digital reflection of our physical and spiritual selves, and, on the other hand, personal data has an economic life as a result of the informative insights that can be gleaned from such data.[205]

The distinct rights to data protection and privacy mentioned above form part of Europe's common constitutional regime and reflect the deeper underlying values of respect and personal dignity.[206] In the words of the European Commission:

> [b]eing European means the right to have your personal data protected by strong, European laws. [...] Because in Europe, privacy matters. This is a question of human dignity.[207]

In the notion of dignity, privacy or the right to a private life, to be autonomous, in control of information about oneself, to be let alone, plays a crucial role. Privacy is not only an individual right but also a social value. Historically, in other parts of the world, such as the USA, privacy has often been regarded as an element of liberty, the right to be free from intrusions by the state. To some extent, however, this distinction between Europe and other parts of the world can be held as relative since it is also an element of privacy in the EU. European privacy culture, as far as one can describe it as one homogeneous culture[208] that builds on values of respect and personal dignity, reflects the privacy doctrines that were shaped especially by the German and French

204. For example, in the American context, Solove argues that 'the constitutional right to information privacy has emerged in the courts as a spin-off of the regular constitutional right to privacy'. Solove (n 177) 8.
205. Orla Lynskey, 'Non-price Effects of Mergers' (2018) Background note for 129th OECD Competition committee meeting 6–8 June 2018, 1.
206. Without our privacy, we lose 'our very integrity as persons', declared Charles Fried some fifty years ago. Charles Fried, 'Privacy' (1968) 77 Yale Law Journal 474, 477. Many others have since agreed that privacy is somehow crucial to our 'personhood'. *See e.g.* Jeffrey H Reiman, 'Privacy, Intimacy, and Personhood' in Schoeman (n 164) 300, 310; Jonathan Kahn, 'Privacy as a Legal Principle of Identity Maintenance' (2003) 33 Seton Hall Law Review 371.
207. Former president Jean-Claude Juncker, European Commission, Exchanging and Protecting Personal Data in a Globalized World, COM(2017)7 2.
208. It is acknowledged that cultural variations and distinctions exist within Europe and its various Member States regarding the understanding of privacy. However, analysing variations of privacy cultures within Europe goes beyond the scope for the purpose of this book, which takes a predominantly legal comparative approach that focuses on looking at the EU and the USA.

privacy heritage. For example, German data protection law is deeply anchored to the concept of human dignity, whereas French data protection is rooted in the notion of individual liberty.[209] The Belgian data protection law has privacy foundations. These privacy cultures centred around citizens' rights to preserve a respectable public image before third parties, and the right to control one's image, name, and reputation, as well as the right to informational self-determination.[210] Under this approach, a primary enemy of one's privacy was the media or private third parties who are capable of publishing incorrect information about someone.[211] It has been argued that, in a sense, Europe's privacy culture was advocated in the USA by Samuel Warren and Louis Brandeis in 1890,[212] but it never much prospered in the USA due to its direct collision with other constitutionally protected values such as freedom of speech.[213]

Fundamental rights dimension. The role of individual rights at the heart of the EU data protection system is reflected by privacy and data protection constituting rights enshrined in the EU Treaties and in the EU Charter of Fundamental Rights. The right to data protection is set out in Article 8 of the EU Charter of Fundamental Rights, and the right to privacy is set out in its Article 7.[214] As mentioned, the fundamental right to data protection is distinct from the right to privacy, which concerns information that invades personal privacy.

The right to data protection is a broad right to limit processing of all information relating to oneself. In addition, Article 16 of the TFEU obliges the EU to lay down data protection rules for the processing of personal data. The EU is unique in imposing such an obligation in its constitution. It is common for Europeans to maintain that they respect a 'fundamental right to privacy' that is either weak or wholly absent in the 'cultural context' of the USA.[215] Europeans may refer with pride to the ECHR, which protects 'the right to respect for private and family life', and to the EU Charter of Fundamental Rights, which protects both 'respect for private and family life' and 'protection of personal data'. By the standards of these documents, some scholars argue that American privacy law may seem, from the European point of view, to have 'failed'.[216]

Concept of data protection. As mentioned, the notion of data protection originates from the right to privacy. However, privacy is explicitly recognized as a human right

---

209. *See* Lynskey (n 137) 104.
210. For a discussion on the German right to informational self-determination, *see* Edward J Eberle, Dignity and Liberty: Constitutional Visions in Germany and the United States (2002) 7 Law Faculty Scholarship 87–92.
211. Whitman (n 185) 1160–1162.
212. Samuel D Warren and Louis D Brandeis, *The Right to Privacy* (Harvard Law Review 1890) 193–220.
213. Richards (n 179) 27.
214. EU Charter of Fundamental Rights (n 188). The entry into force of the Lisbon Treaty in 2009 gave the Charter of Fundamental Rights the same legal value as the constitutional treaties of the EU. Thus, the EU institutions and bodies and the Member States are bound by it.
215. Ken Gormley, 'Long Live the Constitution (Subject to Change)' (2002) Pittsburgh Post-Gazette, at F1 (a description of the European sense that the Charter of Fundamental Rights sets Europe apart from the USA).
216. David A Anderson, 'The Failure of American Privacy Law' in Basil S Markesinis (ed.), *Protecting Privacy* (OUP 1999) 139.

while data protection is not – at least not yet.[217] The protection of personal data has been central to EU law already for decades, from the original Data Protection Directive in 1995[218] to adoption of the GDPR, replacing the former legislative instrument.[219] EU law has gradually developed towards granting strong protection for personal data and also emphasizing its importance from a legal policy perspective in Europe.[220] Recent case law of the EU courts has supported this development of ever-increasing protection of personal data with noteworthy decisions such as *Digital Rights Ireland*,[221] *Google Spain*,[222] *Schrems*,[223] and *Tele2 and Watson*.[224]

EU data protection law can be characterized as pursuing several goals. One of these goals is economic – to facilitate the establishment of the internal market[225] – while another is rights-based – to protect fundamental rights in personal data processing. EU data protection law entitles individuals to exercise specific data protection rights and obliges (public or private sector) parties that process their data to respect those rights. The multiple objectives of EU data protection legislation, market harmonization and fundamental rights have led some to classify data protection as a hybrid regulation, or a 'cluster concept'.[226]

In recent years, the right to data protection has been a much-discussed topic and present in public and academic debate alike due to the entry into force of a new EU regulatory framework, the GDPR, in May 2018, after long preparation.[227] The GDPR aroused considerable discussion and debate among policymakers and technology companies expressing concerns about tougher rules, increased complexity and stricter enforcement,[228] not to mention the increased costs for companies in ensuring compliance with the new rules. The estimate by consultancy company Ernst & Young

217. Note, however, the case law of the ECtHR, which acknowledges that the right to privacy as given in Article 8 of the ECHR is interpreted to include a right to data protection.
218. Directive 95/46/EC of the European Parliament and of the Council of 24 October 1995 on the protection of individuals with regard to the processing of personal data and on the free movement of such data, OJ L 281 of 23.11.1995.
219. The GDPR entered into force on 24 May 2016 and applies from 25 May 2018.
220. Susanna Lindroos-Hovinheimo, 'Henkilötietojen suoja EU-oikeudessa – yksityisyyttä yhteisön kustannuksella?' (2018) 1 Lakimies 52.
221. Combined cases C-293/12 and C-594/12 *Digital Rights Ireland* and *Seitlinger and Other*.
222. Case C-131/12 *Google Spain SL and Google Inc. v Agencia Española de Protección de Datos (AEPD) and Mario Costeja González* [2014] ECR 317.
223. Case C-362/14 *Maximillian Schrems v Data Protection Commissioner* [2015] ECR.
224. Combined cases C-203/15, *Tele2 Sverige AB v Post- och telestyrelsen* and C-698/15 *Secretary of State for the Home Department v Tom Watson, Peter Brice and Geoffrey Lewis*.
225. As will be explored in Chapter 5, EU data protection law was originally enacted also as an instrument of market integration.
226. This refers to the fact that data protection regulation reflects both economic and social regulations, which will be examined in greater detail in Chapter 4. For further discussion on the objectives of data protection law and the categorization of data protection from a regulatory perspective, *see* Lynskey (n 137) 46–88.
227. Tobias Bräutigam and Samuli Miettinen, *Data Protection, Privacy and European Regulation in the Digital Age* (University of Helsinki 2017).
228. *See e.g.* Ludwig Siegele, 'New EU Data Rules Will Get Tough on Privacy' The Economist (The World in 2018 Special Issue, December 2017) http://www.theworldin.com/article/14563/edition2018new-eu-data-rules-will-get-tough-privacy, accessed 19 April 2020.

provides an illustrative example, according to which 'the world's 500 biggest corporations spend a total of USD 7.8 billion to comply with GDPR'.[229] The new GDPR established one single pan-European set of rules for governing personal data instead of twenty-eight national (EU Member State) laws. According to the EDPS, 'the GDPR is the most comprehensive and progressive piece of data protection legislation in the world, updated to deal with the implications of the digital age'.[230]

[B] The EU Data Protection Regime

This chapter gives an introduction to the key characteristics of the EU data protection framework. EU data protection law seeks to ensure the free flow of personal information while respecting the fundamental rights to privacy and data protection.[231] Data protection and privacy are instrumental in both preserving and promoting fundamental values and rights and to exercise other rights and freedoms – such as freedom of speech or the right to assembly. Data protection is about protecting any information relating to an identified or identifiable natural (living) person, including names, dates of birth, photographs, video footage, email addresses and telephone numbers. Other information such as IP addresses and communications content – related to or provided by end users of communications services – are also considered personal data. Data protection aims to ensure fair processing, which includes collection, use and storage, of personal data by both the public and private sectors.

The first legal instrument that is relevant to data protection originates from 1948, the United Nations Universal Declaration of Human Rights, which talks about the right to privacy (family, home and correspondence). This was followed by the ECHR in 1950, which gave legal effect to some rights under the United Nations Universal Declaration of Human Rights and made those rights binding on the signatory states. Article 8 of the ECHR established the right to privacy and family life, mentioning specifically the prohibition of interference by public authorities. All EU Member States are parties to the ECHR, so that any breach can be taken to the ECtHR. The Lisbon Treaty provides that the EU should also access the ECHR, which would allow individuals to challenge acts by the EU before the court. This, however, has not happened, at least yet, and whether EU accession is going to happen is not clear.

The 1995 Data Protection Directive set out a detailed framework for the data protection right, including specific legal grounds for personal data processing. It also established regulatory bodies for enforcement by national and subnational DPAs as primary enforcers. In an effort to keep up with the fast pace at which technology-based services are developing and evolving, in recent years, the European Commission has modernized its data protection framework. This process culminated in the adoption of

229. Jeremy Kahn, Stephanie Bodoni and Stefan Nicola, 'It'll Cost Billions for Companies to Comply with Europe's New Data Law' Bloomberg Businessweek (22 March 2018) https://www.bloomberg.com/news/articles/2018-03-22/it-ll-cost-billions-for-companies-to-comply-with-europe-s-new-data-law, accessed 19 April 2020.

230. *See* the website of the EDPS, https://edps.europa.eu/data-protection_en.

231. Lynskey (n 137) 46–75.

the GDPR in May 2016. The EU's ePrivacy legislation was also adapted to align with the new rules.[232] EU data protection law comprises a mix of primary and secondary law. The GDPR, as secondary law, must be interpreted in the light of the Charter rights to privacy and data protection.[233]

The GDPR seeks to clarify existing rights and obligations while introducing changes to improve compliance and enforcement. The GDPR has been described as 'one of the most important pieces of legislation brought into force in 2018'.[234] The reform broadens rights for consumers over their data, creates a stronger level of protection and gives the individuals more control over their personal data. This aims also to increase general consumer trust in the digital economy.[235] The issue of trust is something that is central to the data economy and will be examined in more detail in later chapters. It suffices to say here that recent scandals revolving around data privacy are not only testing consumer trust in online platforms and more broadly in liberal democracy but also at the same time stressing the need to improve trust.

The GDPR creates new rights for individuals in the digital environment and several new and detailed obligations for cooperation. Despite the novelty of the GDPR, the principal structure of the EU legal framework applicable to personal data processing has stayed largely unchanged, with certain distinct key features, as also identified by Lynskey. These features are explored in the following:

(i) *Broad scope of application.* The first key feature of EU data protection law is its broad scope of application. This is a result of the expansive definition of terms such as 'personal data' and 'processing'. Personal data is defined as any information relating to an 'identified or identifiable individual',[236] while processing means 'any operation or set of operations which is performed upon personal data, whether or not by automatic means'.[237] It applies to personal data processing conducted by natural and legal persons and public and private bodies, with limited exceptions.[238] For example, in *Google Spain,*[239] the CJEU supported the broad scope of application of the data protection regime by adopting an expansive interpretation of 'processing' to ensure the law would not be deprived of its effect.[240]

---

232. The ePrivacy Regulation is a regulation on privacy and electronic communications that will repeal Directive 2002/58/EC.
233. Case C-73/07 *Satamedia* [2008] ECR I-9831; *Schrems* (n 223).
234. Siegele (n 222).
235. European Commission, Exchanging and Protecting Personal Data in a Globalized World, COM(2017) 3. *See also* Vestager (n 70) (on building consumer trust for the digital future with the help of competition law).
236. Directive 95/46, Article 2(a); GDPR, Article 4(1). *See also* Lynskey (n 137) 177 concerning the broad scope of application.
237. Directive 95/46, Article 2(b); GDPR, Article 4(2).
238. For example Directive 95/46, Article 2.
239. Case C-131/12 *Google Spain*. Many commentators interpreted the CJEU's opinion as a call for a new 'right to be forgotten'. For a case commentary, *see e.g.* Susanna Lindroos-Hovinheimo, 'Legal Subjectivity and the "Right to Be Forgotten": A Rancièrean Analysis of Google' (2016) 27 Law & Critique 289–301.
240. *Ibid.*, para. 29.

(ii) *Legal basis for processing.* A second key feature of the EU data protection regime is that personal data processing is not automatically prohibited when it falls within the scope of the legal framework. Rather, the data protection regime could be said to legitimize personal data processing, in that it makes processing permissible provided a legal basis exists in conjunction with compliance with the safeguards set out in secondary legislation.[241]

The legal basis most frequently relied upon for processing is the consent of the individual 'data subject'.[242] The role of consent has not changed significantly with the enactment of the GDPR, apart from the extension of its definition that consent now also has to be 'unambiguous'.[243] The GDPR states that consent 'means any freely given, specific, informed and unambiguous indication of the data subject's wishes by which he or she, by a statement or by a clear affirmative action, signifies agreement to the processing of personal data relating to him or her'.[244] There are further specifications on the conditions for valid consent.[245] For instance, the burden of proof that consent was given in the first place lies with the data controller,[246] and the data subject is free to withdraw consent at any time.[247]

The term 'explicit consent' – as opposed to 'consent' – has not been defined in the GDPR, even though it is used several times within the Regulation.[248] 'Explicit consent' is relevant for the processing of special categories of personal data, such as those revealing the racial or ethnic origin of the data subject or those concerning their health.[249] In these cases, an express statement of consent is necessary, thereby raising the threshold in terms of how consent is given by the data subject.[250]

An interesting and highly relevant recent case regarding 'consent' that falls between the areas of data protection and competition law concerns the WhatsApp messaging service in Italy. In May 2017, the Italian competition authority *Autorità Garante della Concorrenza e del Mercato* (AGCM) imposed a EUR 3 million fine on WhatsApp over data sharing with its parent company, Facebook. This happened at roughly the same time as the European Commission decision on the aftermath of *Facebook/WhatsApp* and

241. Directive 95/46, Articles 6 and 7; GDPR, Articles 5 and 6. The GDPR relies on the traditional principle under EU data protection law that processing personal data is prohibited unless a legal basis for the processing can be invoked by the data controller.
242. GDPR, Article 6(1)(a).
243. GDPR, Article 4(11).
244. GDPR, Article 4 (11).
245. GDPR, Article 7.
246. GDPR, Article 7(1).
247. GDPR, Article 7(3). In the Recitals of the GDPR, further and more detailed explanations are given. *See* in particular Recitals 32, 33, 42 and 43 GDPR.
248. GDPR, Article 22(2)(c), 49(1)(a).
249. GDPR, Article 9.
250. Express consent does not necessarily have to be in writing, but the express character of its grant must be ensured. *See* Article 29 Data Protection Working Party (2017), 'Guidelines on Consent under Regulation 2016/679: 17/EN WP259' 18–19, available at http://ec.europa.eu/newsroom/article29/document.cfm?doc_id=50053 (22.5.2018).

privacy policy changes, though based not on competition concerns but on an infringement of Italian consumer protection law.[251]

The main issue was that WhatsApp asked users to consent to sharing of their data with Facebook in a way that users were given the impression that they could not use the app unless they gave consent – de facto forcing users to accept the new terms of use in full. In addition, the authority questioned WhatsApp's use of one 'accept' button and the fact that it was difficult for them to find and use the options not to share data. In fact, all twenty-eight EU DPAs asked WhatsApp in 2016 to stop sharing users' data with Facebook due to doubts over the validity of users' consent.[252] This is an issue that is relevant also in the German dominance probe into Facebook, which will be analysed in Chapter 4 in connection with exploring the interplay between data protection and competition laws. Here, however, the authority chose to pursue a breach of law under competition rules instead of consumer protection law, as in the Italian case.

The idea that consent serves as a legal basis for the processing of personal data mirrors the notion of 'informational self-determination', which is one of the leading principles of European data protection law.[253] Data subjects, or individuals, should be allowed to decide autonomously whether and to what extent personal data relating to them can be processed.[254]

To be lawful, personal data processing can also rely on legal bases other than consent, such as necessary compliance with a legal obligation or performance of a contract.[255] Generally, data processing conducted online relies not on consent but on a catch-all legal basis, whereby processing is permissible provided it is necessary for the purpose of the legitimate interests of the data controller or by a third party to whom the data is disclosed. Of the compliance safeguards, the so-called purpose limitation principle should be highlighted. According to this principle, personal data must be 'adequate, relevant and not excessive in relation to the purposes for which they are collected and/or further processed'.[256]

---

251. *Autorità Garante della Concorrenza e del Mercato* of 11 May 2017 in the WhatsApp Inc case, para. 36. The original text of the decision in Italian is available at: www.agcm.it (20 August 2018). *See also Autorità Garante della Concorrenza e del Mercato press release*, 'WhatsApp fined for 3 million euro for having forced its users to share their personal data with Facebook' (Rome, 12 May 2017).
252. *Ibid.*
253. The term 'informational self-determination' was created by the German Federal Constitutional Court in its judgment on a national census in 1983 (*Volkszählungsurteil*) and was expressly acknowledged by the Court as a fundamental right (*Recht auf informationelle Selbstbestimmung*), Bundesverfassungsgericht, judgment of 15 December 1983, NJW 1984, 419.
254. Botta and Wiedemann (n 95) 25.
255. *See* Directive 95/46, Article 7; GDPR, Article 6. GDPR, Article 6(1) provides an exhaustive list of legal bases, e.g. contractual necessity (GDPR, Article 6(1)(b)) and legitimate interests pursued by the data controller (GDPR, Article 6(1)(f)).
256. Directive 95/46, Article 6(1)(c); GDPR, Article 5(1)(c): adequate, relevant and limited to what is necessary in relation to the purposes for which they are processed ('data minimization').

(iii) *Subjective rights*. The third key feature of the data protection regime is that it is a rights-based framework. This basically means that it grants individuals subjective rights over their personal data, such as the right to access personal data,[257] the right to delete personal data in certain circumstances,[258] and the right to information regarding the processing of their personal data.[259]

Through this framework described above, data protection in the EU can be described as a comprehensive system of checks and balances determining the limits between permissible and impermissible data processing. In doing so, the system aims to reconcile individual rights and other social interests. This also means that the right to protection of personal data is not an absolute right but 'must be considered in relation to its function in society'.[260] Where the right to data protection conflicts with other fundamental rights, such as freedom of expression, then the rights at issue must be balanced. For example, in the above-mentioned 'right to be forgotten' Google case, there was a balancing between the fundamental privacy interest in being forgotten and other societal interests, initially left to Google, such as the legitimate interests of Internet users and the media in accessing information.[261]

Another feature of the GDPR that has been expected to improve the effectiveness of data protection is the right for supervisory authorities to impose fines on companies in breach of the rules. Consequently, companies will need to take their data protection responsibilities even more seriously and potentially introduce reforms to meet their obligations under the EU rules, with possible fines of up to 4% of global turnover for serious violations.[262]

One of the aspects of the GDPR that has been particularly anticipated as a potential enhancer of competition policy is the right to data portability. Data portability refers to the user's right provided for in the GDPR to move data from one company to another.[263] This right to data portability can have pro-competitive effects because if users are able to take their data with them, they will not necessarily be trapped any longer within a certain company's ecosystem, which may currently often be the case.[264] In other words, data portability could help lower switching costs for consumers.

The right to data portability could help in solving some of the 'lock-in' effects that users of online services are experiencing, for example in digital markets for social networking. In this regard, Facebook is the most obvious example, where users experience being locked in and they cannot take their data and move it to another

257. Directive 95/46, Article 12(a); GDPR, Article 15.
258. Directive 95/46, Article 12(b); GDPR, Article 17.
259. Directive 95/46, Articles 10 and 11; GDPR, Articles 13 and 14.
260. EDPS Opinion (n 10) 13.
261. *Google Spain* (n 216).
262. The GDPR fining system is inspired by the EU competition regime, as it uses the same methodology in large part, in particular the determination of fines in terms of a percentage of the overall turnover of the concerned company.
263. GDPR, Article 20.
264. Daniel Zimmer, Editorial: 'Digital Markets: New Rule for Competition Law' (2015) 6 Journal of European Competition Law & Practice.

platform. This will be explored later in connection with the German Facebook case in Chapter 4, §4.04[B].

However, there are many dimensions to these so-called lock-in situations and this multidimensionality most likely makes the right to data portability inadequate in completely solving the problems around the 'lock-in' effect. Chapter 4 of this book will discuss the problems around the 'lock-in' effect in the context of looking at other limits of data protection law in ensuring sufficient privacy protection in the data economy.

As to the effect of the GDPR on competition policy as a possible enhancer, the EU Competition Commission has reportedly noted that the new EU data rules will have a positive impact in that they assist in unlocking the potential of big data and help empower consumers.[265] Indeed, the GDPR gives citizens the 'right to be forgotten', transfer their data to different service providers and limit the extent of companies' data gathering. This may also lead to building trust in digital markets and making citizens more comfortable with how their data is handled by service providers. In this sense, the new European privacy rules can be viewed as promoting competition by giving consumers more choice and more control – something that competition is also about.

These competition-enhancing effects of the GDPR can also be viewed as raising the question of the need for EU competition law to concern itself with data protection. As the GDPR aims to strengthen and unify privacy enforcement tools in Europe, by the same token it can be asked whether EU competition law has a role to play in preventing exploitative abuses that affect the personal data of final consumers. In other words, does the GDPR protect privacy sufficiently so that no gap remains that competition law needs to fill?

These issues are addressed to some extent in the context of exploring the privacy dimension in competition policy in Chapter 5. Suffice to say here that, despite the implications of the GDPR resonating well with a competition-based rationale, the rights under the GDPR can also be differentiated from competition law. While the right to data portability under the GDPR is well aligned with competition law and bears many of the trappings of a competition law remedy, such as the potential to reduce barriers to entry, stimulate innovation and lower switching costs for individuals, the GDPR right to data portability can also be decoupled from the logic of competition law. However, a more detailed elaboration on this aspect goes beyond the scope of this book.[266] Nevertheless, it is worth recalling that, by and large, competition law is the only instrument in the legal armour that constrains the exercise of (market) power by private companies, and therefore competition law's intersection with data protection law has become an inevitable focal point in the digital age.

265. Lewis Crofts, 'New EU Data Rules to Help Competition, Unlock Big Data Potential, Vestager Says' MLex ITC & Media (13 April 2018).
266. For further analysis on this topic, *see* Orla Lynskey, 'Aligning Data Protection Rights with Competition Law Remedies? The GDPR Right to Data Portability' (2017) 42 European Law Journal.

§2.04 THE AMERICAN UNDERSTANDING OF PRIVACY

[A] Privacy as a Liberty

Whereas the dignitary value of personal data is recognized in the EU, as explored in the previous chapter, the American notion of privacy is based on its underlying values of liberty, self-government and self-determination.[267] Under this view, the threat to someone's privacy and liberty is not the market, but rather abusive power by governmental authorities.[268] Suspicion of the state stands at the foundation of American privacy-related thinking, starting from the late 18th century and the Bill of Rights, with its circumscription of state power, while American scholarly writing and court doctrine take it for granted that the state is the prime enemy of privacy.[269]

In the USA, 'privacy' begins with the Fourth Amendment to the American Constitution, whereby the right to privacy is the right against unlawful searches and seizures, protection from state invasion in the sanctity of their own homes, or wherever else individuals have 'reasonable expectations of privacy'.[270] Supreme Court Justice Louis Brandeis famously described the right to privacy as 'the right to be let alone – the most comprehensive of rights and the right most valued by civilized men'.[271] Over time, the American privacy concept has evolved and matured into a more far-reaching right against state intrusion into individuals' lives. The right to be left alone from government intervention has been expanded to encompass other areas of American policymaking such as abortion rights, in the famous Supreme Court *Roe v Wade* decision of 1973.[272]

It is worth underlining here that the American understanding of privacy rests on the right against state intrusion (as opposed to intrusion by individuals or companies) and it is this approach to privacy protection that goes to explain, at least in part, the suspicion against government intervention and protection. This also has wider implications for the American understanding of the notion of privacy and the importance played by the protection of privacy.

[B] Fragmented and Sectoral Codification

The belief that privacy concerns are mostly a public-private relationship has implications for how protection of personal privacy is codified in the USA. The right to privacy is protected under the Privacy Act of 1974, but this Act applies solely to governmental agencies. Relationships between private parties are left on their own to follow freedom

267. Whitman (n 185) 1211–1216.
268. According to Whitman (n 185) 'state action will raise American hackles much more often than European ones'. 1211–1216.
269. *Ibid.*
270. *Katz v United States*, 389 US 347 (1967) 389. For the common view that this is the origin of the American right to privacy, *see e.g.* Jeffrey Rosen, *The Unwanted Gaze: The Destruction of Privacy in America* (Random House 2000) 5.
271. *Olmstead v United States* 277 US 438 (1928), 478. *See also* Richards (n 179).
272. *Roe v Wade* 410 US 113 (1973).

to contract provisions and limits. Only certain specific sectors and activities, such as healthcare and credit reporting, face more stringent federal regulation or specific state statutes.[273] Thus, unlike the EU privacy regime and the privacy laws of many other industrialized nations, which protect all personal data in an omnibus fashion, privacy law in the USA is sectoral, with different laws regulating different industries and economic sectors. This sectoral approach in the USA leaves significant areas uncovered. Technological development and changes in business practices have resulted in growing gaps in the US privacy legal regime.[274] Notably, the fragmented statutory laws do not directly address data collection in the digital age carried out by private parties.[275] Nor is there a federal law that directly protects the privacy of data collected and used by merchants such as Macy's or Amazon, or the many forms of data collection commonly in use by companies such as Facebook and Google. State laws and privacy tort law are ineffective at dealing with this kind of data collection.[276] There are those who contend that its consumer protection laws are the primary method American society uses to protect privacy.[277]

In the absence of a national privacy standard, the federal states appear to be left to develop their own standards of privacy by consent decree, and perhaps the default US privacy statute may become the California Consumer Privacy Act signed into law in 2019.[278] The law, which some have referred to as groundbreaking, perhaps by US standards, mandates certain disclosure obligations, opt-out rights for California residents, statutory damages for victims of data theft and data security breaches.

Nevertheless, EU law's regulatory comprehensiveness and the GDPR stands in contrast to the lack of an overriding federal policy and US law's fragmented standards, which provide few limits on the collection, use and disclosure of personal data.[279] As

273. For example, the Health Insurance Portability and Accountability Act (1996, Pub I, No 104–191, 110 Stat 1936 (codified as amended in scattered titles of USC), 'HIPAA') protects the privacy of health data, but a different regime governs the privacy of financial data. In fact, several laws regulate financial data depending upon the industry. Health data is not even uniformly protected: not all health data is covered by the HIPAA and various constitutional and state laws can protect health data more strictly than the HIPAA. *See e.g.* Joy I Pritts, 'Altered States: State Health Privacy Laws and the Impact of the Federal Health Privacy Rule' (2002) 2 Yale Journal of Health Policy, Law & Ethics 327, 330–48 (comparing state and federal statutes governing health privacy).

274. For example, new technologies and business models, such as mobile health apps and wearable fitness bands, mean that health data can be in the possession of entities not covered by any applicable health data regulation, such as the HIPAA. As mentioned in the introductory part of this chapter on p 31, data is increasingly collected not only on the Internet but also by sensors installed in electronic devices that interact with each other through IoT, which also implies that the number of industrial manufacturers and service providers that collect, process and transfer a large amount of data via their devices will only increase.

275. Daniel J Solove and Woodrow Hartzog, 'The FTC and the New Common Law of Privacy' (2014) 114 Columbia Law Review 583–587.

276. *Ibid.*

277. *See e.g.* Robert H Lande, 'The Microsoft-Yahoo Merger: Yes, Privacy Is an Antitrust Concern' (2008) 714 FTC: Watch 2.

278. AB-375 (2017–2018 Session).

279. *See e.g.* James P Nehf, 'Recognizing the Societal Value in Information Privacy' (2003) 78 Washington Law Review 1, 58 (discussing 'holes in this patchwork of sector specific privacy laws'); Joel R Reidenberg, 'Privacy Wrongs in Search of Remedies' (2003) 54 Hastings Law

a result of the sectoral approach lacking an effective 'catch-all' provision, the American cultural norm is that personal data is treated as an 'asset', freely tradeable in private transactions, subject only to limitations typically applicable to other private contracting. This view was reflected in the litigation between the US Department of Justice (DOJ) and Microsoft, where the DOJ required Microsoft to hand over personal emails stored in a server located in Ireland by claiming that the data constituted mere business records of Microsoft.[280]

The contrast between privacy protection in the EU and the USA is also visible when looking at the powers granted to privacy regulators in the two jurisdictions. In the EU, agencies enjoy investigative powers, and with the new GDPR further strengthening the level of protection, the EU-wide regulator may impose fines on companies for privacy violations up to 4% of their annual global turnover.[281] In the USA, the Federal Trade Commission (FTC) is the leading federal agency responsible for overseeing privacy violations in private transactions under its mandate to regulate 'unfair or deceptive acts or practices in or affecting commerce'.[282] Because so many companies fall outside sector-specific privacy laws, the FTC, which has many mandates, and which is initially responsible for enforcing consumer protection and competition laws, is in many cases the primary source of privacy regulation and the most important component of the US privacy regulatory system.[283] But in contrast to the EU regulator, however, 'the Federal Trade Commission has a limiting mandate, lacks fining authority absent consent decree and contains a bipartisan split of commissioners that may dampen its aggressiveness'.[284]

Despite their differing privacy frameworks, the US and EU privacy regimes do share the common general objectives of promoting transparency and consumer control. The FTC regulates private information markets under a so-called system of informed consent, where the role of the agency is to ensure that consumers enjoy full access to the conditions of transactions to make informed decisions, including some form of opt-out possibility from the system.[285] Whereas the FTC does not regulate what may be done with data, the agency enforces privacy policies. Many companies today, and almost every large company, have privacy policies. The FTC can bring an action against a company for breaching its privacy policy. The main federal safeguards are

---

Journal 877, 887–88 (asserting US informational privacy 'is protected only through an amalgam of narrowly targeted rules ... [that] leave many significant gaps and fewer clear remedies').

280. *Microsoft Corporation v US* (15 F Supp 3d466 (SDNY 2014). The ruling was reversed by the Second US Circuit Court of Appeals (*Microsoft v US*, No 14-2985).
281. GDPR, Article 83.
282. Federal Trade Commission Act, 15 USC, Section 5.
283. Solove and Hartzog (n 269) 588.
284. Lior Strahilevitz, 'Towards a Positive Theory of Privacy Law' (2013) 113 Harvard Law Review 2036. *See also* Ryan Moshell, '... and Then There Was One: The Outlook for a Self-Regulatory United States Amidst a Global Trend Toward Comprehensive Data Protection' (2005) 37 Texas Technology Law Review 357, 383 (discussing the 'FTC's inadequacy and toothlessness in ensuring privacy protection').
285. FTC, 'Privacy Online: Fair Information Practices in the Electronic Marketplace – A Report to Congress' (May 2000) https://www.ftc.gov/reports/privacy-online-fair-information-practices-electronic-marketplace-federal-trade-commission, accessed 19 April 2020.

found in general prohibitions on 'deceptive' or 'unfair' commercial acts and practices.[286] Indeed, since the spread of the Internet in the 1990s, the FTC has applied this authority to both online and offline commercial data practices. Much of the FTC's enforcement activity has focused on data security where cases have been brought against companies charged with failing to take reasonable steps to safeguard consumer data.[287]

Outside the data security context, the FTC has relied on the prohibition of deception to allege that companies have violated express or implied representations as to what consumer data they would collect or how data would be used or shared. For example, in the case of Snapchat, the FTC alleged that the mobile app deceptively promised users that their videos and photo messages would permanently disappear after a brief time set by the user when, in fact, recipients had readily available means to keep photos and videos.[288]

The FTC has also challenged retroactive changes to data practices made without affirmative express consent, such as Facebook's revamp of its platform in 2009, which unfairly overrode users' privacy settings that had restricted access to certain information, including profile picture and friends list, without its users' informed consent.[289] The agency has become a more active privacy regulator after a series of high-profile settlements for consumer rights violations concerning data collection.[290] In terms of imposing fines or other forms of non-voluntary sanctions, the FTC has traditionally had little power, although at the time of finalizing this book, interesting developments are taking place, as the FTC has created headlines by awarding one of its largest fines ever (in the form of a settlement decision) to Facebook for privacy breaches, following investigations arising from the Cambridge Analytica scandal and other allegations regarding the social network's handling of user data.[291] However, as noted in Chapter 1, §1.07, this book considers the key and recent developments only until the formal examination of the book, and any more detailed and thorough analysis of later developments are left for future research endeavours, including the mentioned FTC record fine against Facebook.

It has been said that one of the weaknesses in American privacy law is that there is not really a significant body of judicial decisions, as the cases have nearly all resulted

286. 15 USC Section 45(a). *See also* 45 (n) '[An unfair] act or practice causes or is likely to cause substantial injury to consumers which is not reasonably avoidable by consumers themselves and not outweighed by countervailing benefits to consumers or to competition.'

287. For example, following what was at the time the largest violation of payment card data, in 2008 the FTC accused the TJX Companies of having engaged in unreasonable (and therefore unfair) practices by storing and sharing personal data in its network in unencrypted text, not requiring network administrators to use strong passwords and failing to use firewalls to limit access among its users. *See* Complaint 2-3, The TJX Cos., FTC Docket No. C-4227 (1 August 2008).

288. Complaint, 2-4, *Snapchat Inc.*, FTC File No 132 3078 (8 May 2014).

289. Complaint, 7-9, *Facebook Inc.*, FTC Docket No C-4635 (27 July 2012).

290. Solove and Hartzog (n 269) 585.

291. *Ibid.*; FTC press release, 'FTC Imposes $5 Billion Penalty and Sweeping New Privacy Restrictions on Facebook' (24 July 2019). According to the FTC's press release, the settlement with Facebook imposes a historic penalty, new privacy restrictions and significant requirements to boost accountability and transparency.

in settlement agreements.[292] As mentioned, the primary regulation of privacy in the USA has not been studied very much in a scholarly way,[293] especially compared to the situation in the EU.

The differences between the EU and the US privacy protection regimes are also illustrated in the famous decision by the CJEU striking down the safe harbour framework that had enabled the sending of EU related data to servers in the USA (*Schrems*).[294] In its judgment, the court declared the old EU-US safe harbour framework based on the Commission's 2000 decision invalid, essentially calling for a higher level of data protection as required by EU law: stronger obligations for companies handling the personal data of Europeans and more robust monitoring and enforcement by US authorities.[295]

In the wake of the Facebook-Cambridge Analytica debacle, increased attention has focused on the value of data protection. Citizens are waking up to their data rights, and voices are heard maintaining that the time has come for the USA to adopt its own laws similar to those of the GDPR in Europe.[296] The privacy scandals have changed the calculus about the benefits of self-regulation, and it has been proposed that the USA should borrow from Europe's data protection laws:[297]

> The failings of America's self-regulatory approach are becoming clearer by the week. Large parts of the online economy are fuelled by data that consumers spray around without thought. Companies' arcane privacy policies obfuscate what they do with their users' information, which often amounts to pretty much anything they please. Facebook is embroiled in crisis after news that data on 87m users had been passed to a political-campaign firm. Identity-theft is widespread; the annual cost to American consumers exceeds USD 16bn, according to some estimates. On March 29th Under Armour, a clothing brand, said that hackers had gained access to information about 150m users of its MyFitnessPal app. These scandals are changing the calculus about the benefits of self-regulation.

American companies must implement the requirements stemming from the GDPR to cover their operations in Europe, because the law also applies to organizations or companies not established in the EU that offer goods and services to individuals in the EU or monitor their behaviour, something that is very common with digital service providers whose offerings are accessed globally by users (Facebook being an obvious

292. Solove and Hartzog (n 269) 585.
293. *See* Costa-Cabral and Lynskey (n 128).
294. *Schrems* (n 223).
295. Since the *Schrems* decision, an agreement on a new framework, called the Privacy Shield, for transatlantic exchanges of personal data for commercial purposes has been negotiated between the EU and the USA. The new arrangement is said to live up to the requirements of the CJEU concerning ensuring in practice a sufficient level of data protection as required by EU law. *See* European Commission press release, 'EU Commission and United States agree on new framework for transatlantic data flows: EU-US Privacy Shield' (Strasbourg, 2 February 2016) IP/16/216.
296. *See e.g.* arguments by consumer advocate Jessica Rich, 'Beyond Facebook: It's High Time for Stronger Privacy Laws' Wired (8 April 2018) https://www.wired.com/story/beyond-facebook-its-high-time-for-stronger-privacy-laws, accessed 19 April 2020.
297. The Economist, 'America Should Borrow from Europe's Data-Privacy Law' (5 April 2018) https://www.economist.com/news/leaders/21739961-gdprs-premise-consumers-should-be-charge-their-own-personal-data-right, accessed 19 April 2020.

example of this). For this reason, one could imagine that they could – in theory – apply the same rules and protections to users based in North America and elsewhere around the world. No doubt with nearly 100 articles, the GDPR is complex and far from perfect, but it is suggested that the USA could draft a '2.0' version, choosing the best parts of the EU Regulation.[298] Some parts of the GDPR are likely out of step with America's constitutional guarantee of free speech: a 'right to be forgotten' of the kind that the GDPR enshrines would probably not fly. However, the benefit of the USA adopting GDPR-type laws would be to have a similar regime on both sides of the Atlantic that would help keep the data flowing across borders and help restore consumer trust in online service providers.[299]

In whatever direction the situation may evolve in the future, the current situation is that EU law's comprehensiveness stands in contrast to US law's fragmented standards, which is a reflection of two different privacy cultures. For the purpose of this book, the central takeaway from this chapter is that the American cultural norm is that personal data is treated as an 'asset' freely tradeable in private transactions, as opposed to the European approach to privacy as a dignity. This distinction plays an important role when this book moves on to explore competition policy objectives and to examine whether and how the element of privacy can be considered as part of competition law goals.

§2.05 SUMMARY

In this chapter, the different approaches to privacy in the EU and the USA have been explored. As the discussion clearly shows, the different historical and cultural backgrounds and legal traditions explain why the privacy law framework and the view it reflects on privacy protection is distinct in these two jurisdictions. As can be seen from the transatlantic comparison of privacy regimes, EU law's comprehensiveness stands in contrast to US law's fragmentation and relatively hollow standards, which provide few limits on the collection, use and disclosure of personal data. The EU has codified a fundamental right to privacy and data protection that is overseen by an increasingly powerful body of dedicated regulators. In this sense, the EU system has no parallel in the USA, where the FTC oversees data markets as part of its obligations to protect consumers in general. Whereas the EU has developed into a jurisdiction wary of private (and public) entities amassing personal data, the American jurisdiction is still mainly focused on abuses by the government.

With the GDPR, the European approach to data privacy as a core right of individuals is further strengthened. In this sense, a stark contrast exists between the European view of privacy and data protection as an inalienable right, and the Americans treating it more as a freely tradeable asset. Moreover, this contrast is likely to increase unless the American view towards privacy protection undergoes some changes. Although some voices argue that the USA should look to the evolution of

298. *Ibid.*
299. *Ibid.*

thought and practice in Europe regarding protection of privacy, this would not happen overnight. As mentioned, some elements in the GDPR are likely out of step with America's constitutional guarantee of free speech. However, the benefit of the USA adopting stronger data protection laws would, among other things, be the strengthening of consumer trust in online service providers and the data economy more broadly, something that is fundamentally important for a functioning market economy and liberal democracy.

The transatlantic difference in privacy perceptions explored in this chapter is significant for understanding and analysing the interlinking between privacy and competition that will be undertaken in Chapter 5, and for examining the role and meaning that privacy protection can be assigned in competition policy (Chapter 6). In the following, the distinct competition policy goals between EU competition law and US antitrust law will be explored as a next step in addressing the central question of the proper place of privacy in competition law and policy in the digital economy.

CHAPTER 3

Competition Policy in the Digital Economy

While the EU and US competition regimes look similar at first glance and share the same basic principles, their policy objectives have evolved in very different directions until the present day. Europe's approach and underlying philosophy to competition diverges in many ways from that in the USA. Most notably, non-price dimensions are deeper embedded in EU competition law, which is multidimensional and provides a range of policy goals, including the ordoliberal understanding of freedom of choice and fairness. Conversely, US antitrust policy is more price-driven and less interventionist, which, as this chapter explores, is largely a consequence of the influential Chicago school. This chapter explores the distinct policy goals in EU competition law and US antitrust law as part of addressing the larger question of the proper place of privacy in modern-day digital competition policy.

§3.01 INTRODUCTION

This chapter explores the main features that competition laws and policies have exhibited in the past in Europe and the USA until the present day. This introductory §3.01 addresses the fundamental question: why have competition laws and policies at all? Understanding this issue lays the basis for understanding and critically analysing competition policy objectives. Section §3.02 introduces certain key concepts and economic theories to provide a further basis for clarifying what competition policy is about. Section §3.03 takes a somewhat historical approach by aiming to show through a historical review that, in the practice of competition law, a number of public policy considerations and objectives have been, and currently are, used. These objectives are discussed and the distinction – and possible conflict – between economic and non-economic objectives is introduced. Armed with this discussion, the key question of this book, namely, the role of privacy, if any, in competition policy, can then be explored.

Why have competition rules? Competition effectively means a struggle or contention for superiority. In the commercial world, this means striving for customers' business in the market place.[300] But why do we have competition rules at all? Why not just leave it to businesses to compete? One may ask, is it not it in their interests to compete as freely as possible – and moreover in the interest as consumers since more competition leads to better products and services, lower prices and more innovation and choice? For the most part, it probably is. The problem is that, sometimes, businesses may be tempted to avoid competition.[301] Competition rules are essentially there to make sure that companies do not misuse their power to undermine competition. The crucial paradox is to limit some sorts of economic freedom for the sake of freedom itself. This might sound obvious, but it has not been a feature of the economic policies pursued in many places around the globe.[302]

Historically, an ideological struggle between capitalism and communism has been ongoing, especially in the 20th century, with many countries expressing suspicion of competitive markets and preferring state planning and management of the economy. However, in the wake of the millennium, significant changes occurred, leading to widespread demonopolization, liberalization and privatization. Coupled with the growth of international trade and rapid technological development, these phenomena have given rise to powerful economic forces impacting upon individuals and societies in many different ways. Underlying these developments is a growing consensus that on the whole markets deliver better outcomes than state planning.[303] Moreover, central to the idea of markets is the competitive process.

Adam Smith and the 'invisible hand'. An inherent part of the competitive process is individual economic freedom, meaning the freedom to act and interact with others, and hence to compete. Adam Smith referred to the overall system of this action and interaction as a 'system of natural liberty' that allowed and required individuals to act freely concerning exchange transactions in the market.[304] According to Smith, competitive markets would lead self-interested individuals by an 'invisible hand' to promote the general welfare, although it was no part of their intention. In other words, competitive markets result in enhanced welfare for consumers:

> Although an individual undertaking striving to maximize profits intends only his own gain ... he is in this, as in many other cases, led by an invisible hand to promote an end which was no part of his intention ... By pursuing his own interest he frequently promotes that of society more effectually than when he really intends to promote it.[305]

300. *See e.g.* Richard Whish and David Bailey, *Competition Law* (8th edn, OUP 2015) 4.
301. In the words of the EU Competition Commissioner: '... the temptation to avoid competition is powerful. It's rooted in motives that are as old as Adam and Eve. In greed for yet more money. In fear of losing your position in the market, and all the benefits that position brings. And when greed and fear are linked to power, they create a dangerous mix. [...] Competition rules can ... [make] sure that greed and fear don't overcome fairness. Because those rules mean that companies can't misuse their power to undermine competition'. *See also* Vestager (n 63).
302. Lamadrid de Pablo (n 123) 3, 5.
303. Adam Smith, *The Wealth of Nations* (Cannan, University of Chicago, 1977) 477.
304. *Ibid.*
305. *Ibid.*

Today, with changes related to the data economy and evolving data-driven businesses, the arising concern is that the invisible hand of competition, which should safeguard consumer welfare, is being replaced by the *digital hand*.[306] The new economic reality with big data and big analytics is changing the dynamics of competition. The characteristics of competitive markets are displayed but competition is driven by different forces (the digital hand). Ezrachi and Stucke argue that consumers have no idea about how, and the extent to which, they are possibly being exploited.[307] Ezrachi and Stucke draw an analogy to the 1998 American movie *The Truman Show* – a controlled environment which is nothing more than a façade.[308] Such an environment has the potential to deliver relative well-being to its subjects, but the main beneficiary, of course, is the one controlling the ecosystem. But before looking 'behind the façade' (in the words of Ezrachi and Stucke) of competition in digital markets and exploring the shortcomings of competition policy in the data economy, this chapter will examine the origins of competition law to lay the ground for later analysis.

Competition law as a legal field has existed almost as long as trade has been subject to regulation.[309] The origins of current competition law are found in the USA, where the Sherman Act, drafted in 1890, prohibited the monopolization of markets and cartels between businesses. The law was complemented in 1914 with rules concerning mergers in the Clayton Act. These antitrust laws were enacted to address the problems created by capitalism, industrial mass production and to limit the powers of the 'business trusts' that led to market concentration and small companies going bankrupt in the USA.[310] Around the same time, cartels became common in the industrialized European countries, where competition laws were enacted to create common rules and institutional safeguards to preserve competitive markets. The first European modern competition law was passed in Germany in 1923.[311]

In the comparative context, at first glance, the competition regimes and policies in Europe and the USA might look very much the same. Indeed, these jurisdictions share a consensus about the basic theory of competition that markets deliver better outcomes than state planning, and central to the idea of a market is the process of competition.[312] Promoting competition is broadly accepted as the best available tool for promoting consumer welfare. In practice, however, the policy objectives in EU competition law and US antitrust law are quite different and competition cases under

306. Ezrachi and Stucke (n 146) 27.
307. *Ibid*.
308. *Ibid*.
309. Olli Wikberg, *Johdatus kilpailuoikeuteen* (Talentum 2011) 17. For a historical overview of competition law development, *see e.g.* Kuoppamäki (n 40) 18–21.
310. The phrase 'antitrust' is said to derive from the technical device adopted in the late 19th century for vesting shareholdings (held by a number of businesses) in individual trustees, who then issued trust certificates to those businesses for whose benefit the pooling of interest had taken place, normally to facilitate the operation of cartels and other restrictive agreements. Joanna Goyder and Albertina Albors-Llorens, *Goyder's EC Competition Law* (5th edn, OUP 2009) 3 (fn 1).
311. Wikberg (n 309) 18.
312. Whish and Bailey (n 300) 4.

review in both jurisdictions can have contrasting outcomes across the two jurisdictions. This is true especially in the digital economy and is because of different prevailing sets of considerations and underlying competition policy goals. Europe's approach to competition diverges in many ways from that dominating in the USA. For example, as will be explored in the following chapters, non-price dimensions are more significantly embedded in EU competition law. In contrast, US antitrust policy is much more focused on the role of price. As will be shown, the different approaches of the two regimes lead to distinctive assumptions as to how online markets work and how they should be monitored by governments.

This chapter analyses the distinct goals of EU and US competition law. It explores the shifts in objectives over time and the development of the two competition policies. Understanding the underlying policy motives is of fundamental importance, as the goals shape how law and policy are implemented and enforced. As will be explored, despite the EU and US competition systems sharing the same basic principles, their policy goals have evolved in different directions until the present day. That point is significant for this book, which considers the interlinking between competition and privacy protection, and whether privacy considerations can and should be included in the objectives of competition policy in the data economy. That analysis cannot be carried out without first taking a critical look at the situation today.

§3.02 COMPETITION THEORY, KEY CONCEPTS AND DEFINITIONS

This chapter will outline the central elements of competition theory and the basic concepts relevant for this book. A detailed discussion on the economic theories that have been advanced in support of competition and the role of legal rules in maintaining an effective competitive structure lies outside the scope of this book. As noted above, the methodology in this book is influenced by competition theory, which is viewed as a subcategory of economics.[313] Therefore, this chapter will look at the basic considerations of competition theory and explain some key economic concepts central to this book. A theoretical introduction of this kind is necessary as the concepts constitute the foundations for the understanding and application of competition law and policy.

Competition theory. Starting from the concept of competition theory itself, the term 'competition theory' refers to the field of social science that studies economic competition in the market economy.[314] Beyond looking at markets, competition theory also considers the interplay between existing financial systems, society and the legal system. Thus, in effect, competition theory is not only about economics in the narrow sense. That is, competition can also be studied through the means of other disciplines, such as legal discipline (clearly), sociology, political sociology and historical studies.[315]

313. Kanniainen and Määttä (eds) (n 40).
314. For a detailed explanation of the economics of competition, *see* Luc Peeperkorn and Vincent Verouden, 'The Economics of Competition' in Jonathan Faull and Ali Nikpay (eds), *The EC Law of Competition* (first published 1999, 3rd edn, OUP 2014) ch. 1.
315. Wikberg (n 309) 23–26; Kuoppamäki (n 110).

The discipline of economics and economists as its high priesthood study competition as an economic form of competition.[316] Neoclassical *price theory* or parameter theory[317] focuses on the interrelationship between prices and quantity, whereas the economic theory of *industrial organization* looks at competition through market structures. In simplified terms, the different approaches can be explained according to whether conclusions are drawn based on the conduct or performance of companies or according to structural factors of the markets (Structure-Conduct-Performance (SCP)).[318] In addition to these approaches, competition and competitive behaviour is studied with the help of *game theory*, which examines situations of strategic interaction using mathematical models.[319] Game theory has been applied extensively to study the strategic behaviour of companies, especially in oligopolistic markets.[320]

Beyond the discipline of economics, on a higher level, competition can be studied as an institution. This approach sets competition tasks that go beyond economic efficiency and adequacy, placing the process of competition at the heart of the market economy and connecting it to a wider societal context, where sound competition forms a part of the legal infrastructure of a market economy.[321] This book follows the aforementioned approach of looking at competition as an institution, which goes beyond studying competition only as an economic (in the strict sense) form of competition. This approach is taken to address the central research question of the role of privacy in competition policy and to examine whether existing competition policy goals are optimal for the data economy, where personal data and privacy increasingly shape markets.

Competition policy. The next concept that must be considered is that of competition policy itself. To give 'competition policy' – or antitrust policy, as it is called in the USA – an exact or precise definition is not an easy task.[322]

Massimo Motta has suggested the following definition: 'the set of policies and laws which ensure that competition in the marketplace is not restricted in a way that is detrimental to society'.[323] This definition is empty unless one specifies what 'detrimental to society' means. This, in turn, calls for a specification of the objectives of competition policy. Motta, as an economist, like many other scholars with an economic background, argues that *economic welfare* is the objective that competition

316. Kalle Määttä, *Oikeustaloustieteen aakkoset* (Helsingin Yliopisto 1999).
317. On the development from price theory towards parameter theory, *see e.g.* Arne Rasmussen, *Pristeori eller parameterteori. Studier omkring virksomhedens afsætning* (2nd edn, Erhvervsøkonomisk Forlag, Nyt Nordisk Forlag 1977) 17.
318. The SCP model is closely connected with the Harvard school of thought, *see* below §3.04[C].
319. As a formal theoretical analysis, game theory started with the book by the mathematician John von Neumann and the economist Oskar Morgenstern, *Theory of Games and Economic Behaviour* (Princeton University Press 1944).
320. An oligopoly is a market structure in which there are few suppliers, but at least two, and the main characteristic is that the companies in such a market realize or believe that their individual behaviour concerning price, output, etc. has a perceptible influence on the market outcome and therefore may provoke reactions from competitors. *See* Faull and Nikpay (n 314) 25–35.
321. Olli Wikberg (n 309) 24.
322. Massimo Motta, *Competition Policy: Theory and Practice* (CUP 2004) 30.
323. *Ibid.*

authorities and courts should pursue.[324] This brings him to define competition policy as 'the set of policies and laws which ensure that competition in the marketplace is not restricted in such a way as to reduce economic welfare'.[325]

This definition is arguably incomplete in the sense that it limits the ultimate goal of competition to within purely economic parameters and ignores the 'non-economic' side of competition. Thus, adopting this perspective would not be possible without certain restrictions concerning the notion of economic welfare, the concept of which will be discussed below.[326] In this regard, the definition of competition policy as presented by Kuoppamäki is more in line with the understanding of the essence of competition policy as perceived in this book. To define competition policy precisely is challenging because of its complex and nuanced character.[327] Therefore, it makes more sense to understand and describe competition policy as the product or outcome of many layers or areas.

According to Kuoppamäki, competition policy can be viewed as consisting of three areas: (i) setting objectives for competition policy (*hypostasis*), (ii) detecting problems regarding functioning competition (*diagnosis*), and (iii) selecting means to remedy identified competition issues (*therapy*).[328]

Moreover, competition policy objectives can be viewed and examined from different perspectives. First, objectives can be approached from a *legal* perspective, looking at the objectives written out in competition statutes and provisions, and how these objectives are manifested by the court and authorities in their practice. Second, competition policy objectives can be viewed from a *politico-economical* perspective, which examines the effects of competition on economic welfare and efficiency.[329] Third, competition policy objectives can be examined from a broader social policy perspective, which considers the social and economic implications of the competition process and policy.

The different competition policy perspectives and different research directions are reflected in a number of schools of thought. These schools of thought display distinct (social) policy perspectives and different (politico-economical) research directions and are discussed in later chapters of this book (Chapter 4, §4.3 and §4.4). Let it suffice to say here that the common factor among the different schools of thought and their policy recommendations is explained by differences in the understanding or belief in how well the markets can self-correct their own failures. Another distinction relates to the ability of the authorities and the courts to tell the difference between harmful and restrictive competitive practices on the one hand and efficient and pro-competitive activity on the other.[330]

324. *Ibid.*
325. *Ibid.*
326. *See* §3.02.
327. *See* Kalle Määttä, *Uusi kilpailurajoituslaki* (Edita Publishing Oy 2004) 39, who notes that in some cases the distinction between competition law and competition policy can be likened to a line drawn in water.
328. Kuoppamäki (n 110) 98–99. Similarly, *see* Wikberg (n 309) 25.
329. On the concept of efficiency in EU competition law, *see e.g.* Giorgio Monti, *EC Competition Law* (CUP 2007) 44; Määttä (n 316) 43.
330. Wikberg (n 309) 25.

If attempting to conceptually differentiate between competition theory and competition policy, in the sense of what each of these is, the core of competition theory is found in economics and its study of causalities and determinants, whereas competition policy focuses more on examining questions around policy objectives, such as for what reason and by what means. It is difficult to draw an exact distinction between competition theory and competition policy, as these two areas are closely intertwined in many respects.[331] However, in this book the focus lies more on competition policy rather than on theory, although elements of both are present, especially as policy goals cannot be examined without relying on basic theoretical foundations. Nevertheless, rather than staying within the boundaries of competition theory, the book addresses questions around competition policy objectives, as it examines whether privacy has a place in the goals of competition policy. Therefore, the questions that are looked at are exactly those mentioned, namely *for what reason* should privacy be considered as an element and value worth protecting by competition law and *by what means* should this be done; that is, how in practice should privacy be included in competition policy objectives.

Generally, the wider objectives of competition policy can be categorized in various ways, for instance, by looking at broader goals or values. For example, Kuoppamäki approaches the general objectives of competition policy through the broader aims or values of efficiency, freedom and justice (or fairness).[332] Timonen argues on the basis of Jacquemin that the broader aims of competition laws in different jurisdictions can be summarized into three goals: (i) decentralizing economic power and related protection of individual freedom, (ii) protecting the economic freedom (latitude) of market actors, and (iii) promoting consumer welfare through emphasis on allocative and dynamic efficiencies.[333]

This kind of categorization is naturally very high-level and does not take into account differences in various national competition policy goals with variants in their enforcement philosophy[334] or the distinctions between EU and US competition law. However, this summary or categorization of the broader goals of competition law in different jurisdictions goes to illustrate the availability, or existence, of a range of competition law open-ended objectives, and that depending on the interests to be promoted or supported, different values are put forward as a driver for the enforcement of competition laws. As Ezrachi notes, competition law can be considered as a form of

331. Kuoppamäki (n 110) 98–99.

332. *Ibid.*, 28–55. For further reading on the aims or values of justice and fairness in EU competition law, *see e.g.* Wouter PJ Wils, *Efficiency and Justice in European Antitrust Enforcement* (Hart Publishing 2008).

333. Pekka Timonen, *Määräysvalta, hinta ja markkinavoima. Julkisesti noteeratun yrityksen määräysvallan siirtymisen oikeudellinen sääntely* (Lakimiesliiton Kustannus 1999) 219; Alexis Jacquemin and PH Admiraal, *Merger & Competition Policy in the European Community* (Basil Blackwell 1990) 3–4.

334. *See e.g.* Ariel Ezrachi, 'Sponge' (2017) 5 Journal of Antitrust Enforcement 2. Ezrachi discusses, among other things, competition law's susceptibility to national peculiarities and the variety of goals depending on national interests.

domestic or regional social policy with regard to its inherently dynamic nature and its wide-ranging goals and scope.[335]

Indeed, over time many different values have been advocated in the name of competition law, as will be examined in later chapters. What this multitude of values also shows is that competition law is political. Kuoppamäki views the discourse on competition policy as consisting of two layers, the political level and the operative level.[336] One may think that this is all the more true today when observing the public discussion and politics around competition objectives in digital markets.[337] According to Ezrachi, competition law is intrinsically predisposed to a wide range of values and considerations. Moreover, 'its true scope and nature are not "pure" nor a "given" of a consistent objective reality, but rather a complex and, at times, inconsistent expression of many values'.[338]

Broadly speaking, looking at the above categorization of goals, the research question of the book concerns the first mentioned goal of decentralizing economic power and the related protection of individual freedom, as it examines protection of privacy in competition policy. This, according to Kuoppamäki, 'non-economic side' of competition law was evident when enacting the US Sherman Act in 1890 and in the German competition act after World War II.[339] In recent years, this side of competition law has again been lifting its head with the rise of the data protection, privacy and fundamental rights discourse. However, the research question of the book also goes beyond the first mentioned goal of decentralizing economic power and the related protection of the individual, as the book also presents a rather consumer-centric view when attempting to (re)consider the concept of consumer welfare and what this notion in fact means in the data economy. Therefore, when addressing the research question, the book inevitably also goes deeply into the area of the third goal, namely that of promoting consumer welfare, the definition of which will be examined below.[340]

As noted by Kuoppamäki with regard to competition law's principle of interpretation, competition law operates with definitions that can be viewed as 'open' in the sense that their concrete meaning opens up only when they are applied in practice.[341] Competition law is a casuistic field with significant meaning given to praxis.[342] In this regard, Määttä describes how in competition law a realistic form of interpretation is often preferred due to the law's flexible character.[343] The law is largely interpreted and applied with regard to its *objectives*. This differentiates it from, for example, the traditional understanding of the doctrinal study of legal sources where *travaux préparatoires* hold a central role. In contrast, in competition law they do not hold a

335. *Ibid.*
336. Kuoppamäki (n 110) 28–29. The author has had the pleasure of discussing and exchanging views about her research and writing with Petri Kuoppamäki on several occasions.
337. Ariel Ezrachi and Maurice E Stucke, 'Emerging Antitrust Threats and Enforcement Actions in the Online World' (2017) 13 Competition Law International.
338. Ezrachi (n 334) 2.
339. Kuoppamäki (n 110) 30–31.
340. *See* §3.02.
341. Kuoppamäki (n 110) 23 (Fi. *tulkintaperiaate*).
342. *Ibid.*, 24.
343. Määttä (n 316) 37 (Fi. *realistinen tulkintatapa*).

similar important position as legal sources, but rather interpretation is more driven by the values behind the law and the objectives of the law.[344]

Timonen contends that significant purposive consideration attaches to competition statutes since the law operates with general definitions, not all of which can be understood only by relying on conventional doctrinal methods, but rather require, for example, considering 'economic realities' and the use of legal economics.[345] This approach has been criticized by Määttä for detaching legal reasoning from economic argumentation.[346]

It may be argued that it is impossible to give an exact answer to the question where the law ends and where economics begins in competition law. Theoretically, both law and economics can be traced back to the discipline of philosophy. As noted by John Stuart Mill, philosophy forms the origins and roots of social sciences.[347]

However, for what is relevant here, it is noted that the objectives of competition law are a significant feature in interpreting competition provisions and principles. This makes the research question of this book all the more important. Further, as reflected by Kuoppamäki, competition law is characterized by open definitions, which grants the decision-maker considerable leeway or discretion in their decision-making. This discretion and the decisional outcome must be in accordance with the objectives of the law.[348] From an outsider's perspective, the application and interpretation of competition law may seem unpredictable and even lacking in legal certainty, but, looking from the inside, the decision-maker's discretion is restricted by existing praxis and precedents that constitute the framework within which one operates.[349]

Definition of consumer. Competition law is concerned about individuals as aggregate consumers. The fundamental assumption of competition law is that the competitive process and rivalry between companies increases the welfare of consumers. Consumers want better products and services, and companies succeed in the marketplace by providing them.[350] Whereas competition law is concerned about individuals as aggregate consumers, EU data protection law, for example, involves protection of data subjects who are natural persons and thus may include consumers.[351]

According to the definition by the European Commission, under EU competition law 'the concept of "consumers" encompasses all direct or indirect users of the products covered by the agreement, including producers that use the products as an

344. *Ibid.*
345. Timonen (n 333) 355–356 (Fi. *tarkoituksenmukaisuusharkinta*).
346. Kalle Määttä, 'Taloustieteen hyödyntäminen kilpailunrajoitusten sallittavuutta arvioitaessa' in Kanniainen and Määttä (eds) (n 40) 86.
347. *See* John Stuart Mill, *Utilitarianism* (first published 1861, OUP 1998).
348. Kuoppamäki (n 110) 26–27.
349. On the importance of court precedents and case law in EU (competition) law, *see* Paul Craig and Gráinne De Búrca, *EU Law: Text, Cases and Materials* (6th edn, OUP 2015) 72.
350. For example, the EU courts have recognized that competition law protects both the interests of the consumer and competition 'as such' and that there is a link between the two. *See* Joined Cases C-501, 513, 515 and 519/06P, *GlaxoSmithKline* [2009] ECR I-9291; Case C-209/10 *Post Danmark I* [2012] ECR I-0000, para. 20.
351. This is further discussed in Chapter 4, §4.02 when analysing the common goals of competition and data protection law, which include the protection of consumer welfare.

input, wholesalers, retailers and final consumers, that is, natural persons who are acting for purposes which can be regarded as outside their trade or profession'.[352]

Consumerism versus producerism. With respect to the definition of 'consumer' in competition law, Whitman's distinction between *consumerism* and *producerism* is worth a note.[353] According to James Whitman, the concept of consumer interest includes varieties of "consumerism"; additionally, it is essential to distinguish between consumer *economic* interest, such as an interest in low prices, shopping convenience, and the like, and consumer *protection* interest, an interest in legal guarantees of the safety and quality of products and services.[354]

Whitman thus draws a distinction between *consumerism* and *producerism* – that is, separating a producerist legal order on the one hand from a consumerist legal order on the other – and argues that this contrast between producerism and consumerism is of considerable value for understanding the comparative law of the economy.[355] While producerism revolves around rights and interests on the supply side of the market, consumerism, by contrast, focuses more on rights and interests on the demand side of the market: on the consumer's economic interest. This is understood primarily as an interest in competitive prices. In contrast, a producerist legal order focuses on the interest of some class of producers or distributors, such as workers, small shopkeepers, or the competitors in a given industry. Whitman argues that producerist legal orders can take forms quite different from consumerist ones in terms of economic regulation under the law of antitrust and in terms of fundamental conceptions of the nature of rights.[356]

The differences between consumerism and producerism mirror the differences in the politics of the law and the differences in the values embraced by different legal cultures.[357] Yet of course consumers and producers are not two different classes of persons. All productive members of society in a modern economy can feature both of these identities, while individuals are all both 'consumers' and 'producers'. A worker when working is a producer; but when shopping, the same worker is or becomes a consumer. Correspondingly, as Whitman rightly argues, the choice between emphasizing consumer rights and emphasizing producer rights is not a choice between favouring 'the' economic class of consumers or favouring 'the' economic class of producers. Rather, it is a choice about which of these two identities is regarded as deserving protection by law.[358]

352. European Commission Guidelines on the Application of Article 81(3) of the Treaty [2004] OJ C101/97, para. 84.
353. James Q Whitman, 'Consumerism Versus Producerism: A Study in Comparative Law' (2007) 117 Yale Law Journal 340, 361.
354. *Ibid.*
355. *Ibid.*, 346. According to Whitman, '[t]he best way to analyze many of the dominant legal conflicts in today's world is indeed through the lens of conflict between law oriented toward producer interests and law oriented toward consumer interests, between law oriented toward rights on the supply side and law oriented toward rights on the demand side'.
356. *Ibid.*, 371.
357. *Ibid.*
358. *Ibid.*

Consequently, whether the citizen's interests in the guise of 'consumer' are more fundamental than their interests in the guise of 'producer', or vice versa, is a value choice. In this book, value choice leans inevitably more towards protecting the citizen's interests in the guise of 'consumer', as the role of protecting individuals' personal data and privacy is issues that closely link to the individual in the role of consumer, rather than producer. This is in line with the approach taken in EU competition law generally according to Simon Bishop and Mike Walker, who state that the welfare of consumers is valued higher than that of producers.[359]

Consumer welfare. In recent years, many competition authorities have stressed the central importance of consumer welfare when interpreting and applying competition law.[360] But what does consumer welfare mean as the (main) aim of competition policy? Consumer welfare is concerned with gains explicitly for consumers rather than for society at large.[361] This does not mean that competition law is applicable only where a specific increase in prices to end-consumers can be shown.[362] In EU competition law, for example, it is recognized in case law that consumers can be indirectly harmed by action that harms the competitive structure of the market.[363] According to Whish and Bailey, there is no inconsistency in this statement or the proposition that EU competition law is oriented around promoting consumer welfare.[364]

Consumer welfare expresses the benefits of competition. Competition law is based on the assumption that competition can reduce prices and increase all types of efficiency, including *allocative, productive* and *dynamic* efficiency.[365] At its simplest, the benefits of competition are lower prices, better products and services, wider choice and greater efficiency than would occur under conditions of monopoly. According to neoclassical economic theory, social welfare is maximized in conditions of perfect competition.[366] In this context, 'social welfare' refers to achieving allocative and productive efficiencies, the combined effect of which is that society's wealth overall is maximized. Consumer welfare, which is concerned with gains explicitly for consumers rather than for society at large, is also maximized under perfect competition.[367]

As will be shown, this book calls into question the understanding of consumer welfare advocated by economists that *economic welfare* is the sole objective that

359. Simon Bishop and Mike Walker, *The Economics of EC Competition Law* (2nd edn Sweet & Maxwell 2002) 29.
360. Whish and Bailey (n 300) 19. For further discussion, *see* Joseph Farrell and Michael L Katz, 'The Economics of Welfare Standards in Antitrust' (2006) 2 Competition Policy International.
361. Whish and Bailey (n 300) 5; Bishop and Walker (n 359) paras 2.17–2.19.
362. Whish and Bailey (n 300) 19.
363. Bishop and Walker (n 359) paras 2.22–2.26.
364. Whish and Bailey (n 300) 20–21. For critical discussion, *see* Oles Andriychuk, 'Rediscovering the Spirit of Competition: On the Normative Value of the Competition Process' (2010) 6 European Competition Journal 575.
365. Michal S Gal, 'The Social Contract at the Basis of Competition Law' in L Lianos and D Gerard (eds), *Competition Policy: Between Equity and Efficiency* (CUP 2017).
366. *See* Richard Whish, *Competition Law* (5th edn, LexisNexis 2003) 2–3. On industrial economics and competition generally, *see* Jean Tirole, *The Theory of Industrial Organization* (MIT Press 1988); Peeperkorn and Mehta (n 314); Bishop and Walker (n 359).
367. Bishop and Walker (n 359) paras 2.22–2.26.

competition policy should pursue.[368] Such a narrow price-centred understanding of the aim of competition policy disregards objectives or policy considerations other than economic efficiency, such as protection of privacy. Inadequate protection of consumer data and individuals' privacy can no doubt be detrimental to society. Therefore, the statement that *economic welfare* is the sole objective that competition policy should seek to protect is questioned as failing to consider the meaning of consumer welfare, or well-being, and what aspects this entails – a thought that will be developed further in Chapter 5.

Allocative efficiency. In an attempt to transform the consumer welfare standard into workable benchmarks, competition authorities have often approximated them through use of the consumer surplus benchmark.[369] Allocative efficiency (or Pareto efficiency) refers to the scenario under perfect competition where economic resources are allocated between products and services in such a way that it is not possible to make anyone better off without making someone else worse off. In this scenario, consumer surplus (the net gain to a consumer when buying a product) is at its largest.

In this regard, it should be borne in mind that competition economics can be classified into schools. Which school of thought is most appropriate with respect to competition law is closely linked to the question which theory of harm should be considered. This in turn is effectively about which welfare or surplus standard should be applied: the consumer surplus standard or the total welfare standard.[370]

Indeed, economic efficiency as a competition objective is based on a welfare standard of either total welfare or consumer welfare. Whether total welfare, consumer welfare, or an entirely different standard is the right formulation of economic efficiency has long been debated. Whereas some within the academy argue for the strengths of the consumer surplus standard,[371] others assert that the consumer welfare standard is the predominant objective.[372] Others again support a 'trade-off' model[373] or maintain that competition should be the primary goal of antitrust.[374] By and large, however, two goals have dominated the debate and indeed more widely modern academic and policy

368. *See e.g.* Motta (n 322).
369. Ariel Ezrachi 'EU Competition Law Goals and the Digital Economy' (Working paper, 6 June 2018) 8. The working paper was published in August 2018 as a discussion paper by BEUC, the European Consumer Organisation, in connection with its project on the role of competition law enforcement and policy in shaping fairer and consumer-oriented digital markets in Europe. Ezrachi, in the role of academic advisor to BEUC, prepared a discussion paper which considers the EU competition goals emerging from the EU treaties and case law and suggests how these goals should guide competition authorities and courts when applying EU competition law in digital markets. *See also* Barak Y Orbach, 'The Antitrust Consumer Welfare Paradox' (2010) 7 Journal of Competition Law & Economics 133 (arguing that surplus is the only realistically applicable benchmark for competition purposes).
370. Doris Hildebrand, *The Role of Economic Analysis in EU Competition Law: The European School* (Kluwer Law International 2009) 95.
371. *See e.g.* Farrell and Katz (n 360) 3.
372. John B Kirkwood, 'The Essence of Antitrust: Protecting Consumers and Small Suppliers from Anticompetitive Conduct' (2013) 81 Fordham Law Review 2425.
373. Alan J Meese, 'Reframing the (False?) Choice Between Purchaser Welfare and Total Welfare' (2013) 81 Fordham Law Review 2197.
374. Barak Y Orbach, 'How Antitrust Lost Its Goal' (2013) 81 Fordham Law Review 2253.

discourse: *total welfare* (the overall surplus from producers and consumers) and *consumer welfare* (the surplus only from consumers).[375]

Productive efficiency. Apart from allocative efficiency, economists consider that under conditions of perfect competition, products and services are produced at the lowest cost possible, meaning that as little of society's wealth as necessary is used up in the production process.[376] One way that companies in a competitive market try to undercut the prices of their rivals is by reducing their cost of production.[377] Therefore, competition is said to be conducive to productive efficiency.[378] Productive efficiency is achieved because a company (producer) is unable to sell above cost (customers would desert it if it did so) and it will obviously not sell below cost (because that would leave it without profit). Above all, if a company were to charge above cost, other competitors would move into the market in the hope of profitable activity.[379]

Dynamic efficiency. A further benefit of perfect competition is that it can produce the dynamic effect of stimulating innovation as competitors seek to produce new and better products and services for consumers in the battle of striving for consumers' business.[380] This kind of dynamic efficiency is a particularly significant feature in data-driven and technology-rich markets as it stimulates important technological research and development. The notion of dynamic efficiency is particularly relevant for this book. This is because dynamic efficiency encompasses important non-price parameters of competition, including choice and quality. These parameters will be examined in this book as increasingly important aspects of competition policy in the digital age, bearing in mind that this book focuses on digital markets, which are characterized by rapid technological development.

Some economists have questioned the assumption of dynamic efficiency, arguing that only monopolists enjoy the wealth to innovate and undertake expensive research.[381] Joseph Schumpeter was a proponent of the idea that the motivation to innovate was the prospect of monopoly profits and that, even if existing monopolists earned such profits in the short term, outsiders would in due course enter the market and take their place.[382] A 'perennial gale of creative destruction' would be enough to protect the public interest, and therefore one should not be concerned about short-term monopoly power. Empirical research shows that neither monopolists nor fierce competitors are superior in this respect. However, it seems clear that the assertion that

375. The difference between welfare and surplus is noted, but the term 'welfare' is used here because the debate has been framed as between consumer welfare and total welfare. For a discussion on the difference between welfare and surplus, *see e.g.* Orbach (n 369) 133.
376. Whish and Bailey (n 300) 5.
377. *Ibid.*
378. For discussion, *see* John Vickers, 'Concepts of Competition' (1995) 47 Oxford Economic Papers 1.
379. Whish and Bailey (n 300) 5.
380. Whish and Bailey (n 300) 6.
381. *See e.g.* John Kenneth Galbraith, *American Capitalism: The Concept of Countervailing Power* (Houghton Mifflin 1952).
382. Joseph A Schumpeter, *Capitalism, Socialism, and Democracy* (first published 1942, 3rd edn, Harper & Brothers 1950).

only monopolists can innovate is incorrect.[383] The Schumpeterian approach to short-term monopoly is something that in recent times has been called into question in tandem with rising concern over increasing concentration in digital markets,[384] a trend that is also touched upon in this book.

Market power. A crucial concept in competition law, and especially in the economics of competition law, is market power. Traditionally, market power is defined as the power to raise price beyond a competitive level in a profitable way.[385] Since the lowest possible price a company can profitably charge is the price which equals the marginal cost of production,[386] market power is commonly referred to as 'the difference between the prices charged by a company and its marginal costs of production'.[387] Importantly, market power is also defined as the power to exclude competitors from the market, or the possibility to act independently of consumers and thus to weaken competitive parameters.[388]

Market power is also the common denominator of the different normative areas of competition. Indeed, in the prohibition of cartels, abuse of a dominant position and merger control alike, the fundamental issue is regulation of market power.[389] Market power is also the connecting link between these instruments, or areas, of competition policy.

Market dominance relates to the concept of market power and means wielding a significant amount of such power.[390] What constitutes a significant amount of market power for a company depends on the market in question and other factors, such as competitive pressures imposed on the company. It also depends under which national competition law market power is assessed, and in particular whether market power is assessed under EU competition rules or US antitrust law, as these look at market power with different approaches. It can be held that EU competition policy reflects the idea that monopolies are 'bad'; this is even said to be 'the basis of competition policy'.[391] When compared to the USA, one may say that Europe maintains the view that market

383. *See* Frederic M Scherer, *Industrial Market Structure and Economic Performance* (first published 1970, 2nd edn, Houghton Mifflin 1994).
384. The Economist, Schumpeter 'The University of Chicago Worries about a Lack of Competition' (12 April 2017) https://www.economist.com/news/business/21720657-its-economists-used-champion-big-firms-mood-has-shifted-university-chicago, accessed 19 April 2020.
385. Motta (n 322) 40.
386. In a model where companies sell perfectly identical products, have zero fixed costs and choose prices, price is equal to marginal cost at the equilibrium. This is the so-called Bertrand model. For a description of the model, *see e.g.* Motta (n 322) ch. 8.
387. An alternative definition is to define market power not by how far the prices are with respect to marginal cost, but by how close they are to monopoly prices. Motta notes that these definitions are conceptually very similar, and, operationally, one is not easier to define than the other: the former requires an estimation of marginal costs, the latter of the industry's monopoly prices. *See* Motta (n 322) 40–41.
388. Bishop and Walker (n 359).
389. Kuoppamäki (n 110) 5.
390. *See e.g.* Wallace Peterson (ed.), *Market Power and the Economy. Industrial, Corporate, Governmental and Political Aspects* (Kluwer Academic Publishers 1988). For general discussion on market power and abuse thereof, *see e.g.* Arttu Mentula, Hannu Pokela and Tuomas Saraste, *Määräävän markkina-aseman väärinkäyttö kilpailuoikeudessa* (Kauppakaari Oy, Lakimiesliiton Kustannus 1998).
391. Motta (n 322) 39.

power is probably harmful, or a so-called big is bad ideology,[392] so the greater the number of businesses in any given market the better.[393]

The issue of how to measure market power in practice is addressed by competition laws establishing certain minimum market power thresholds below which some rules do not apply, under the presumption that companies with little market power can do little harm. Different thresholds are often adopted for different types of market practices, which have different potential for harming competition. Consequently, in many circumstances, competition policy will be concerned only with those companies having 'large enough' market power. 'Large enough' will to some extent be arbitrary, and might differ according to the particular competition problems being scrutinized.[394]

For example, while under US antitrust law the qualification of dominance normally requires that a company maintains market shares around 70%–75% for five years, under EU competition law the rebuttable presumption of dominant market power is that a company is dominant if it controls above 50% of the market.[395] The presumption of dominance in EU competition law has its origins in well-known and often cited cases such as *Hoffmann-La Roche*, *AKZO* and *Hilti*.[396] In addition to the relatively low threshold for the characterization of dominance, EU competition law has developed a view that companies with significant market power have a 'special responsibility' not to distort competition in the market.[397] The scope of the responsibility is considered in relation to the degree of dominance held by the company.[398]

Monopoly power. In the USA lawfully acquired monopolies are generally free to charge supra-competitive prices.[399] In Europe, the situation is different, as EU competition law prohibits exploitative practices – such as imposing abusive contracting terms and charging 'excessive prices' – that lead to direct loss of consumer welfare.[400] An excessive price is one that bears no relationship to the economic value of the product, amounting to unfair pricing or rent extraction.[401]

However, enforcing exploitative abuse cases involves some challenges. These include how to determine costs, and how consumers value products, for example. Consequently, there has not been an abundance of cases in Europe pursuing this theory of harm. At the same time, European competition authorities have shown a willingness

392. *See e.g.* Motta (n 322).
393. Already in an earlier European Community known as the (Eastern) Roman Empire, the Constitution of Emperor Zeno of 483 AD prohibited, in addition to price-fixing, monopolization in relation to clothes, fish, sea-urchins and other goods, the sanction for breach being perpetual exile.
394. Motta (n 322) 41 fn 3.
395. Phillip E Areeda and Herbert J Hovenkamp, *Fundamentals of Antitrust Law* (4th edn, Aspen Law & Business 2011) 319.
396. Cases 85/76 *Hoffmann-La Roche* [1979] ECR 461; C-62/86 *AKZO v Commission* [1991] ECR I-3359 and T-30/89 *Hilti AG v Commission* [1991] ECR II-1439.
397. Case 322/81 *Michelin v Commission* [1983] ECR 3461, para. 57.
398. Robert O'Donoghue and Atilano Jorge Padilla, *The Law and Economics of Article 82 EC* (Hart 2006) 166.
399. *See e.g.* the judgments in *United States v Alcoa*, 148 F.2d 416 (2nd Cir 1945) and *United States v Grinnell*, 384 US 563 (1966) and more recently *US Supreme Court, Verizon Communications Inc v Trinko*, 40 U.S. 398 (2004).
400. O'Donoghue and Padilla (n 398) 603–604.
401. *Ibid.*

to bring more exploitative cases and clarify the methodology behind exploitative abuses,[402] especially on a national level. In this context, the German competition authority's investigation into Facebook's unfair terms and conditions is the most vivid example.[403] As will be explored later, no comparative doctrine on exploitative abuses exists in the USA. Consequently, at times there has been US criticism that Europeans are overly paternalistic in their law enforcement. This phenomenon is explored in Chapter 3 when looking at US antitrust law objectives and in Chapter 4 when analysing the German Facebook case interlinking competition and privacy issues.

Or monopoly-like power? To better reflect the power of monopolies in the digital economy, some argue that it would be more correct to describe large and powerful data-driven companies as having 'monopoly-like' powers rather than having monopoly power.[404] According to Scott Galloway, this description of power as 'monopoly-like' aims to reflect that most big technology companies have not used their power to do the one thing that most economists would describe as the whole point of assembling a monopoly, which is to raise prices for consumers.[405]

While this concept of monopoly-like power is appealing, one may say that the argument fails in that it relies on the underlying assumption that consumers always pay in traditional monetary currency. It does not recognize the fact, which is central to this book, that it is commonplace today for consumers to pay with their personal information instead of conventional currency for accessing online offerings in the data economy.[406]

Data-opolies. Similar to Galloway's concept of monopoly-like (market) power, Stucke describes the emergence of 'data-opolies' in the data economy.[407] These data-opolies are generally companies that control a key online platform through which a significant volume and variety of personal data flows. Speed or velocity in acquiring

402. *See e.g.* speech by Margrethe Vestager, 'Protecting Consumers from Exploitation' Chilling Competition Conference (Brussels, 21 November 2016) https://ec.europa.eu/commission/commissioners/2014-2019/vestager/announcements/protecting-consumers-exploitation_en, accessed 19 April 2020. According to Vestager, examples of some exploitative abuse cases are the European Commission's investigation into Gazprom, the pharmaceutical sector and standard-essential patents, where competition has not been enough to provide a real choice and dominant businesses are said to exploit customers by charging excessive prices or imposing unfair terms.
403. *See* Chapter 4, §4.04[B]. For developments in other EU Member States, *see e.g.* Luis Ortiz Blanco and Pablo Ibáñez Colomo, 'Evolving Priorities and Rising Standards: Spanish Law on Abuses of Market Power in the Light of the 2008 Guidance Paper on Article 82 EC' in Lorenzo Federico Pace (ed.), *European Competition Law: The Impact of the Commission's Guidance on Article 102* (Edward Elgar 2011) ch. 4.
404. Scott Galloway, 'Opinion: The Case for Breaking up Amazon, Apple, Facebook and Google' (8 February 2018) http://www.stern.nyu.edu/experience-stern/faculty-research/case-breaking-amazon-apple-facebook-and-google, accessed 19 April 2020 (full article as published in Esquire https://www.esquire.com/news-politics/a15895746/bust-big-tech-silicon-valley/?src=nl&mag=esq&list=nl_enl_news&date=020818, accessed 19 April 2020.
405. *Ibid.*
406. *See* Chapter 2, §2.01.
407. Stucke (n 13). *See also* Maurice E Stucke, 'Here Are All the Reasons It's a Bad Idea to Let a Few Tech Companies Monopolize Our Data' Harvard Business Review (27 March 2018) https://hbr.org/2018/03/here-are-all-the-reasons-its-a-bad-idea-to-let-a-few-tech-companies-monopolize-our-data, accessed 19 April 2020.

and exploiting personal data can help these companies obtain significant market power. Whereas Stucke calls them data-opolies, Lynskey approaches platform power by arguing that such notion should be replaced by the broader concept of a 'digital gatekeeper' to adequately reflect the power over information flows and individual behaviour that such gatekeeper companies can exercise.[408]

Stucke and Lynskey essentially raise the same point as Galloway: data-opolies or digital gatekeepers are different from the conventional monopolies of the offline world, because in contrast to the earlier monopolies, data-opolies are unlikely to exercise their power (only) by charging higher prices to consumers. But they also go one step further and warn that this does not mean they are harmless; data-opolies can raise other significant concerns, including less privacy, degraded quality, a transfer of wealth from consumers to data-opolies, less innovation and dynamic disruption in markets in which they dominate, as well as political and social concerns.[409] Current commonly referred to data-opolies are Google, Apple, Facebook, and Amazon, and it has become commonplace to talk about these companies by referring to them as GAFA for short.[410] The concern about data-opolies and how this may translate into less privacy and degraded quality for consumers will be further discussed in Chapter 4 of the book in connection with analysing the interlinkage between competition law and data privacy.

With the transition to the digital or data economy, the question whether data can lead to market power in products and services has been under much debate among competition experts.[411] A joint report by the German and French competition authorities proclaims that 'the issue of data possibly contributing to market power is most likely to arise and is, in many respects, the most interesting one from a competition standpoint'.[412] Debated issues are whether personal information can constitute a barrier to entry or otherwise lead to market power. In this regard, network effects also play a significant role.

Network effects. Certain markets are characterized by 'network effects'. Network effects occur when the value of a product or service for a customer increases when the

408. Stucke (n 407); Orla Lynskey, 'Regulating "Platform Power"' (2017) LSE Law, Society and Economy Working Papers 1.
409. Stucke (n 407). Lynskey elaborates on a theory of 'gatekeeper harm' in 'Regulating "Platform Power"' (n 408) 12.
410. The Economist created its own nuanced acronym, BAADD, 'too big, anticompetitive, addictive and destructive to democracy'. The Economist, 'The Techlash Against Amazon, Facebook and Google – And What They Can Do' (20 January 2018) https://www.economist.com/news/briefing/21735026-which-antitrust-remedies-welcome-which-fight-techlash-against-amazon-facebook-and, accessed 19 April 2020.
411. *See e.g.* David S Evans, 'Multi-sided Platforms, Dynamic Competition, and the Assessment of Market Power for Internet-Based Firms' (2016) University of Chicago Coase-Sandor Institute for Law & Economics Research Paper No 753; Michal S Gal and Daniel L Rubinfeld, 'The Hidden Costs of Free Goods: Implications for Antitrust Enforcement' (2016) 80 Antitrust Law Journal 36; Graef (n 99) 501; D Daniel Sokol and Jingyuan Ma, 'Understanding Online Markets and Antitrust Analysis' (2017) 15 Northwestern Journal of Technology and Intellectual Property 43.
412. French-German joint report (n 9) 25. *See also* speech by Vestager (n 8).

number of other customers also using it increases.[413] In this sense network effects can have positive effects on competition since consumers benefit as a product becomes more popular. The telecommunications sector is a classic example of a traditional industry characterized by network effects; the more customers that are connected to a particular telephone network, the more valuable the network is to each customer. The increased utility is of value both to the operator and to subscribers. Similar benefits accumulate to consumers where the amount of users of a payment system, such as Visa, increases, or where a particular technology, such as the Windows operating system for computers, becomes widespread. Comparably, the value of an airline to its consumers increases in tandem with the increase in the number of airports that it serves and routes that it operates. These examples reflect how network effects can positively affect competition since consumers are better off as the popularity of a product or service increases.

On the other side of the coin, network effects also give rise to the possibility of one or only a few companies dominating a market, especially in view of the likelihood of 'tipping effects', where all customers in a particular market decide to opt for the product of one company or for one particular technology. Facebook's social network illustrates these network effects.[414] This issue will be further explored in Chapter 3 in connection with the German competition authority's abuse of dominance case against the social network based on breach of data protection rules. Several other examples of network effects also exist in the technology industry, such as Google's Search engine, or Amazon's e-commerce service, just to name a couple.

Indirect network effects and two-sided markets. In digital markets, the vast majority of online service providers use a two-sided, or multisided, business model, whereby to attract users, the product or service (such as search services, and provision of content, such as newspaper articles, weather information, videos, hotel and restaurant reviews) is offered at zero price, while the producers generate the revenues necessary to fund the free service and make a profit through online advertising.[415] Two-sided markets are characterized by indirect network effects: the more users on one side, the more users on the other. It has been suggested that companies do not profit directly from the market on the user side, but from the market on the advertising side.[416] Services that are free at the point of user access are subsidized in order to draw users as a result of the positive feedback loop between the number of users and the

413. Whish and Bailey (n 300) 12. Noteworthy cases in this respect are Case COMP/M.8124 *Microsoft/LinkedIn* C(2016) 8404 at 341; *United States v Microsoft* 253 F.3d 34, 49 (D.C. Cir. 2001); *United States v Bazaarvoice* No 3:2013cv00133 (ND Cal 2014).

414. *See e.g.* Stucke and Grunes (n 146) 200–205.

415. There is a flourishing doctrine on two-sided or multisided markets. *See e.g.* Jean-Charles Rochet and Jean Tirole, 'Platform Competition in Two-Sided Markets' (2003) 1 Journal of the European Economic Association 990; Evans (n 411); David S Evans, 'The Online Advertising Industry: Economics, Evolution and Privacy' (April 2009) Journal of Economic Perspectives 37; Jean-Charles Rochet and Jean Tirole, 'Two-Sided Markets: A Progress Report' (2006) 37 RAND Journal of Economics 645; David S Evans and Richard Schmalensee, 'The Industrial Organization of Markets with Two-Sided Platforms' (2007) 3 Competition Policy International 151.

416. Maurice E Stucke and Ariel Ezrachi, 'When Competition Fails to Optimize Quality: A Look at Search Engines' (2016) 18 Yale Journal of Law & Technology 70.

advertising sold. According to Evans, in these markets, also referred to as 'markets for attention',[417] dynamic competition can easily upset market power by consumers turning their attention elsewhere.[418]

In two-sided markets in the data economy, where products are offered to users for free and monetized through targeted advertising, personal data is often described as the currency that is paid by users in return for receiving the 'free' product.[419] In other words, the price effectively paid by consumers for free goods is the loss of their privacy.[420] As explained by Newman, consumers trade their attention and personal information to access zero-price products, and it is this dynamic exchange that brings zero-price markets within the scope of antitrust law.[421]

With the fast pace of development in digital markets, this loss of privacy now extends beyond advertising breaks or banner ads, as personal information and search entries are analysed by data mining software, possibly involving a much higher degree of intrusiveness. With the rise of big data and big analytics, companies are able to move beyond 'data mining' to 'reality mining'.[422] This may come to penetrate everyday experience, communication and even human thinking.[423] For example, companies may use disclosed customer data for purposes that are not in consumers' best interests. Health apps from health insurance companies or online payment apps by credit card companies may be used to gather data about consumers' lifestyle, the information of which can then be used to set discriminatory prices or even deny a service.[424]

Another way of describing the incredible speed at which companies can access and process large datasets in real time is that the term 'forecast' is being replaced with 'now-cast', referring to accurately forecasting events occurring in the present, near-present or very recent past, such as traffic conditions, virus outbreaks, home/auto sales and restaurant crowds.[425] In this regard, the auto industry is following the lead of the technology sector by collecting used data via sensors and services in cars (connected cars).[426]

The speed of data processing and predictive ability can enable companies to deliver more timely and relevant information to consumers and avoid staleness and lag. However, the ability to generate and process large datasets can also be associated

417. *See also* Tim Wu's description of 'attention markets' (n 173).
418. Evans (n 404) 28.
419. Stucke and Grunes (n 146); Ezrachi and Stucke (n 146).
420. OECD Big Data (n 22) 18.
421. John M Newman, 'Antitrust in Zero-Priced Markets' (2015) 164 University of Pennsylvania Law Review 149.
422. EDPS, 'Towards a New Digital Ethics: Data, Dignity and Technology' (11 September 2015) Opinion 4/2015 6.
423. *Ibid.*
424. European Parliament, Challenges for Competition Policy in a Digitalised Economy (Study for the ECON Committee, Directorate-General for Internal Policies, Economic and Monetary Affairs, 2015) 34–35.
425. OECD Big Data (n 22) 2.
426. Christina Rogers, 'What Your Car Knows about You' The Wall Street Journal (18 August 2018) https://www.wsj.com/articles/what-your-car-knows-about-you-1534564861, accessed 19 April 2020.

with market power.[427] This is a result of economies of scale, economies of scope and network effects, as well as real-time data feedback loops.[428] Even if these effects do not necessarily lead to market dominance or market tipping, they should be considered as part of a competitive analysis in data-driven markets.

Beyond competition theory. Having in this chapter described the conventional understanding of competition theory, it is important to recognize that a theoretical analysis of perfect competition does not sufficiently explain business conduct in the 'real' world. This is particularly true in today's increasingly complex, technology-based digital world. Theory is based on certain misleading presumptions, such as consumers having perfect information about market conditions. Indeed, consumers seldom have access to perfect information about market conditions. As is commonly held in the data-driven economy, in practice a strong asymmetry of information often prevails between individuals and businesses. This issue is further explored in Chapter 5.

Another misleading assumption that stems from economic theory is that all businesses always act rationally. This, we know from real-life experience is unlikely to occur in practice. Individuals, consumers and businesspeople alike are human beings, driven by emotions and previous experiences.[429] They are not rational calculating machines, even though this is sometimes maintained by classical economic theories. One may jokingly question whether classical economists have not left their lecture halls enough to venture into the real world.[430]

Furthermore, an inherent paradox subsists in the theoretical concept of competition and the competitive process, which is worth recognizing when analysing competition policy goals: namely, competitions are there to be won. This means that sometimes some competitors simply win. By producing products and services in the most efficient way possible, by being the most innovative and the most responsive to customers' wishes, one company may succeed in seeing off its competitors. One may question whether it is not rather odd if that company could then be condemned for being a winner (a monopolist)? In the words of Judge Learned Hand in *US v Aluminium Co of America*:

> [A] single producer may be the survivor out of a group of active companies, merely by virtue of his superior skill, foresight and industry ... The successful competitor, having been urged to compete, must not be turned upon when he wins.[431]

Judge Learned Hand's remarks about the successful competitor who should not be turned upon when winning are echoed by those who defend powerful technology companies in the data economy, that are accused of monopolistic behaviour and exploitation of user data in digital markets, such as Facebook and Google. Indeed, one of the issues with monopolists in data-driven markets is that they reflect the chicken or the egg causality dilemma; it can be argued that monopolists are not successful because

427. *Ibid.*
428. *Ibid.*
429. Gal and Rubinfeld (n 411) 401.
430. In this regard, behavioural economics may provide some more useful guidance, as discussed in Chapter 5, §5.03[B].
431. 148 F 2d 416 (2nd Cir 1945).

they have a lot of data, but they have a lot of data because they are successful, which is really the source of their intellectual capital and analytical ability to create added value. Using competition policy to discourage them from doing so would be tantamount to discouraging success. How should this dilemma be best resolved? The solution lies in finding the right balance between economic freedom and interventionist enforcement: in short, creating and enforcing sound competition policy. This will be pondered when responding to the research question of the book and will be addressed in more detail in Chapter 5 when envisioning optimal competition policy goals for the digital age.

§3.03 MULTIDIMENSIONAL EU COMPETITION POLICY

[A] Multiple Objectives

§3.03 deals with European competition law and policy. Here, the purpose is not to provide a complete description of the history of competition law in Europe, but rather to help understand the key circumstances in which EU competition law was created and enforced, and with what underlying policy objectives.

To start with, it should be noted that in Europe there are two different levels of competition jurisdiction: national and supranational. The focus in this chapter – as in this book generally – is on competition law at the EU level, and not on the national competition laws of the various EU Member States. However, a cursory look is taken at Germany because its history and recent case law are interesting in many respects. Noteworthy in this regard, too, is that the influence of the German legal tradition is widespread both in Europe as a whole and in the Nordic countries.[432] The regional history has affected the evolution of EU competition law. For instance, its philosophical foundations were influenced to a large extent by the German ordoliberal school, which reflects humanist values protecting individual freedom from governmental and private power.[433]

Generally, the competition laws in most European countries to a large extent reproduce the same features as the laws introduced by the Treaty of Rome and its successive modifications.[434] Although a high degree of convergence prevails between EU and domestic competition law, which were modelled upon the key provisions of EU competition law, nevertheless the possibility remains that different outcomes can occur depending on which system is applied.[435] After all, competition law is intrinsically open to a wide range of values and considerations that can be of a national or domestic character.[436]

432. Interestingly, nearly all basic legal concepts used in Nordic (or Scandinavian) law are derived primarily via German law. Ulf Bernitz, 'What Is Scandinavian Law? Concept, Characteristics, Future' (2007) 50 Scandinavian Studies in Law 13, 28.
433. The ordoliberal school of thought is discussed in §3.03[B].
434. Motta (n 322) 9.
435. Much has been written about the issue of possible conflicts between EU and domestic competition law over the years. However, the starting point is that EU law takes precedence

Another important observation when discussing EU competition law is that it is truly multidimensional. This – something already touched upon in the previous chapter – means that many different objectives can be pursued under EU competition law. Depending on which scholarly work one goes to, different policy goals are mentioned by academics and scholars as being the primary objectives of EU competition law. This reflects the numerous overarching EU competition law goals that have existed, and indeed still do. Although in recent times the central importance of the consumer welfare standard is stressed when interpreting and applying competition law,[437] many different policy goals have been pursued in the name of competition law. Some of these were not rooted in conceptions of consumer welfare in the technical sense at all, and some were unfavourable to the pursuit of allocative and productive efficiency.[438] The outcome has sometimes even been contradiction and inconsistency.[439]

Ezrachi describes the key goals and values of EU competition law as its 'unique DNA', which together can be understood as representing the ethos of competition law in Europe.[440] However, this diversity of objectives is not without challenge or controversy. Moreover, the various goals have not always been clearly outlined.

Among the range of goals that have been pursued under EU competition law – beyond consumer welfare – are European integration in the form of the single market imperative, protection of the market structure, economic freedom and freedom of choice, as well as the notion of fair competition.[441] As will be discussed, the European Commission has attempted an economic effects-based approach to EU competition law,[442] while the Courts have not endorsed any single objective, but left themselves discretion in this regard. The CJEU has defined the concerns of competition law to be multiple, including, for example, consumer welfare, the interests of competitors and the structure of the market.[443]

Absent any prescribed single unifying objective for competition law in the EU Treaties, there has been much debate over time concerning potential competition

over national law. *See* Case 6/64 *Costa v ENEL* (n 39). For further discussion, *see e.g.* Christopher Stephen Kerse and Nicholas Khan, *EC Antitrust Procedure* (5th edn, Sweet & Maxwell 2005) para. 5.56.

436. In some cases, national competition authorities might weigh in regional policy matters, such as unemployment and other local policy issues. For example, South African law specifically provides that in certain circumstances the position of historically disadvantaged people (the victims of apartheid) should be considered. South African Competition Act 1998 (Act No. 89 of 1998) (SA) 16), Section 2(f).

437. *See e.g.* Whish and Bailey (n 300) 19–20.

438. *Ibid.*

439. *See* Okeoghene Odudu, 'The Wider Concerns of Competition Law' (2010) 30 OJLS 599–613.

440. Ezrachi (n 369) 6.

441. A vast literature exists on the goals of competition law. For analysis of the different goals adopted by competition law, *see e.g.* Daniel Zimmer (ed.), *The Goals of Competition Law* (Edgar Elgar 2012); Dina L Waked, 'Antitrust Goals in Developing Countries: Policy Alternatives and Normative Choices' (2014) 38 Seattle University Law Review 945.

442. This more economic approach to EU competition law and policy is discussed in greater detail in §3.02[C].

443. Joined Cases CJEU C-501/06P, C-515/06P and C-519/06P, *GlaxoSmithKline Services Unlimited, formerly Glaxo Wellcome plc v Commission* [2009] ECR I92916.

policy aims including efficiency, market integration and consumer welfare. The multidimensional character of EU competition law makes the precise role of the system contestable. This position was well summarized in the late 1990s by Richard Whish, writing that although 'the debate about what is meant by a restriction of competition under [EU competition law] has been with us for 30 years' we are no 'closer to an acceptable solution to this central conundrum of competition law'.[444]

To illustrate these various competition goals and values that coexist with one another and how they can be viewed as somehow centring around the concept of consumer welfare, Figure 3.1 is helpful.[445]

Figure 3.1 Competition Goals

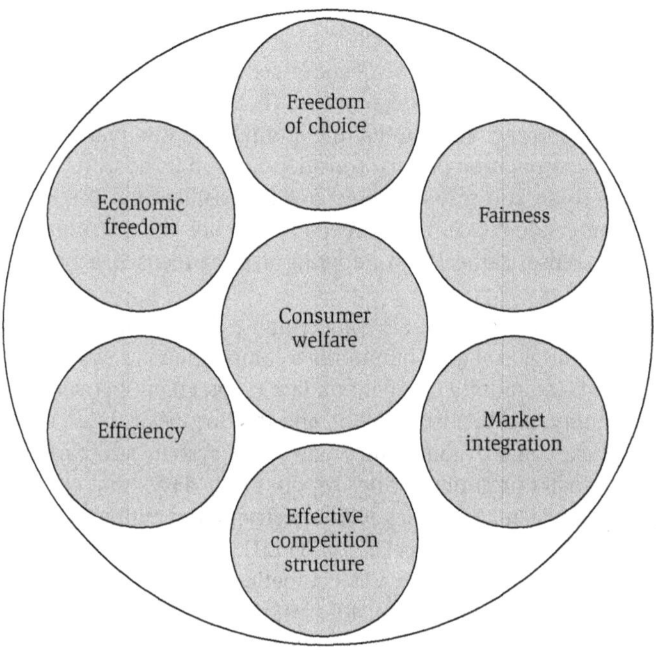

Source: created by the author.

The figure does not imply a hierarchy among goals but reflects their multitude. For the research question of this book, it is key to find out where privacy fits among the goals and values. Whereas critics may argue that privacy has no place at all within the multitude of competition goals, one may also consider that privacy fits rather well in many different places, such as close to the value of fairness or next to, or as part of, consumer choice. Some may even argue that privacy should constitute a value of its own. Going forward in this book, the best place where privacy fits among the goals and values of competition law will be considered throughout.

444. Cited in Odudu (n 439) 601.
445. Similarly, *see* Ezrachi (n 369).

So, much like the concept of privacy, the precise definition of which is still debated by privacy scholars,[446] the goals of competition law is also a topic that continues to be questioned and disputed by antitrust scholars across different jurisdictions and societies. This also has the consequence that if the meaning of privacy is unresolved, some reluctance may be shown to adding the notion of privacy to competition law's policy goals that are already under debate. However, just because of ongoing academic discourse and discussion around the central concepts in competition law as well as in data protection law, respectively – which in any event should be viewed as a positive phenomenon fostering free exchange of opinions – this should not preclude consideration of privacy protection as a value also deserving attention in competition policy.

In the following, the differing competition objectives, including the various evolutionary phases in EU competition law, will be further explored. Emphasis is placed on two key concepts in EU competition policy: consumer welfare and freedom of choice, or consumer choice, which are addressed each in their own chapters. These policy goals are examined in more detail and in their historical context, partly relying on a law-in-context perspective,[447] to lay the ground for later analysis of competition policy potentially incorporating privacy considerations in its goals (Chapter 5). Such a merging of competition and privacy objectives is possible only if competition law's policy goals are understood to centre on freedom of choice and consumer welfare in the non-price centred sense, rather than adopting a price-focused economic efficiency approach.

When discussing the goals of EU competition policy, it makes sense to first step back and look at the origins of the Community's competition law system. This includes the development of Community competition law enforcement between the European Economic Community, established in 1958, and the European Union of today.[448] It is commonplace to explain EU competition law as a system structured around four pillars. The first two are prohibition rules set out in the TFEU that cover the antitrust field; agreements between companies which restrict competition (Article 101 TFEU) and abuse of a dominant position (Article 102 TFEU). The third pillar is merger control. The fourth pillar is state aid. The EU competition rules derive from two basic competition provisions applicable to businesses, namely Articles 81 and 82 (now 101 and 102) of the Treaty establishing the European Community (the EC Treaty or the Rome Treaty), substantially amended several times since its entry into force.[449]

The EC Treaty's overarching goal was to create a common market based on an economic union between EU Member States. This objective received a major boost from the creation of the single market in 1993. The Treaty on the European Union (TEU) marked a further substantial stage in the integration of the Member States by

446. *See* discussion in Chapter 2, §2.02.
447. On the perspectives used in this book, *see* Chapter 1.
448. Generally on the development of European integration, *see* Craig and De Búrca (n 349).
449. For general works on the EC Treaty, *see e.g.* David Vaughan and Aidan Robertson (eds), *The Law of the European Union* (OUP, 2003 and supp); Trevor Hartley, *The Foundations of European Community Law* (5th edn, OUP 2003); Craig and De Búrca (n 349).

establishing a European Union that embraces a wide range of additional areas of cooperation.[450]

According to the TEU, the 'Union is founded on the values of respect for human dignity, freedom, democracy, equality, the rule of law and respect for human rights, including the rights of persons belonging to minorities. These values are common to the Member States in a society in which pluralism, non-discrimination, tolerance, justice, solidarity and equality between women and men prevail.'[451] Among others, the aims of the European Union are to promote 'the well-being of its peoples',[452] to 'establish an internal market',[453] promote 'the sustainable development of Europe based on balanced economic growth and price stability, a highly competitive social market economy, aiming at full employment and social progress'[454] and ensure 'an open market economy with free competition'.[455]

Competition policy is one of several instruments used to advance these goals. Protocol No 27, annexed to the EU Treaties, states that 'the internal market as set out in Article 3 of the Treaty on the European Union includes a system ensuring that competition is not distorted'. Over the years, the EU competition rules have been applied, interpreted and clarified through case law and official publications.[456]

The development of the Community has been quite remarkable, considering that what started as cooperation between six Member States has become an economic and political union of twenty-eight Member States. This holds true today despite the Brexit crisis and the rise of various protectionist and anti-European movements.[457] Nevertheless, with all its imperfections, the internal single market is a reality, and with the European Commission's plan for an integrated digital market,[458] a digital single market is under way that intends 'individuals and businesses seamlessly to access and exercise online activities under conditions of fair competition, and high level of consumer and personal data protection'.[459]

---

450. For further discussion, Peter Roth and Vivien Rose (eds), *Bellamy & Child, European Community Law of Competition* (6th edn, OUP 2008) 2–3.
451. Consolidated Version of the Treaty on European Union [2012] OJ C 326/13 ('TEU'), Article 2.
452. Article 3(1) TEU.
453. Article 3(3) TEU.
454. *Ibid.*
455. Articles 119, 120, 127, 170, 173 TFEU.
456. Ezrachi (n 369) 1.
457. As a response to the EU crisis, in January 2017, the European Commission issued an insightful White Paper on the future of Europe containing ideas and reflections for relaunching the European project, available at https://ec.europa.eu/commission/white-paper-future-europe/white-paper-future-europe-drivers-europes-future_en.
458. On the European Commission's digital single market strategy, *see* European Commission, 'Shaping the Digital Single Market' https://ec.europa.eu/digital-single-market/en/policies/shaping-digital-single-market, accessed 19 April 2020.
459. *Ibid.* Forecasts indicate the potential dimensions of the digital transformation in Europe, where a digital single market could contribute EUR 415 billion yearly to the economic performance of the EU and create hundreds of thousands of new jobs. For example, the market volume of the IoT is estimated to be some EUR 1.9 billion in 2020. *See* German Federal Ministry for Economic Affairs and Energy, White Paper on Digital Platforms of the Economic Affairs Ministry (20 March 2017).

When looking at the development of EU competition policy and trying to understand its evolutionary process, three phases can be identified according to Rein Weisseling.[460] The first phase reflects that initially the competition provisions were inserted into the Treaty of Rome with a view to their role in the process of market integration. In this phase, the European Commission enforced the competition rules by constant reference to ensuring free flow of products and services, thus promoting market integration.[461]

Subsequently, in the second phase, competition policy was employed to establish a broader Community industrial policy. Exemptions to competition rules were granted to forms of transnational cooperation between businesses, to promote broader Community policy aims (e.g., employment in crisis sectors).[462]

The third phase expanded the scope of competition policy even further and altered the character of competition law enforcement; control of corporate mergers and liberalization of public economy sectors commenced by the end of the 1980s. Noteworthy in this respect is that both of these were highly political exercises. This underscores the political character of competition law, something that is central to this book and that will also be developed further later on.

Thus, the European Community's competition policy developed gradually and incrementally for the first two decades largely as a reactive policy, though since the 1980s as a much more active one.[463] Similarly, the scope of EU competition policy has widened gradually: from the focus in the 1960s on restrictive practices to tackling monopolies in the 1970s until in the 1980s and 1990s it expanded into merger control and monitoring of state subsidies.[464]

Looking at the historical development of national competition laws in Europe, the principle of economic freedom stands out. In these countries, and especially in Germany, the development of competition law was inspired by the principle of economic freedom. Another governing principle of competition law was freedom of contracting. This implied that in Germany, as in many other countries, price agreements actually used to be permitted.[465]

As a result, cartel activity was active around the turn of the 18th century.[466] Under the effect of the Great Depression and the bankruptcy of many firms, in 1930, participation in cartels was made compulsory for companies operating in sensitive

460. Rein Wesseling, *The Modernisation of EC Antitrust Law* (Hart 2000) 48.
461. *Ibid.*, 48–49.
462. *Ibid.*
463. Michelle Cini and Lee McGovan, *Competition Policy in the European Union* (MacMillan Press Ltd 1998) 30.
464. *Ibid.*, 36. For further reading on the evolution of EU competition law and policy, *see e.g.* Paul Craig and Gráinne De Búrca, *The Evolution of EU Law* (OUP 1999).
465. Historically, in many Central European countries, such as Germany, Austria, the Czech Republic, Switzerland, Hungary and Holland, cartel activity was accorded favourable treatment. One explanation for this is that in the past, there was an idea that cartels were a useful instrument for controlling the instability created by cut-throat competition and price warfare. For further discussion, *see* Motta (n 322) 9, 11 fn 33.
466. For further reading on the evolution of German competition law, *see e.g.* Scherer (n 383); Kai-Uwe Kühn, 'Germany' in Edward M Graham and J David Richardson (eds), *Global Competition Policy* (Institute for International Economics 1997).

sectors. This compulsory cartel participation was made more extensive under the Nazi regime with the aim of controlling the national industry and strengthening the sectors relevant for warfare.[467] This idea of having companies cooperate closely or merging their operations to strengthen them and create 'national champions' of a sort, capable of outperforming foreign rivals, is widespread. For example, after World War II, the Allies (the USA and the British) wanted to impose antitrust laws upon Germany and Japan not only to promote economic progress but also to break up excessive concentrations of economic power, which they saw as a potential future threat. Accordingly, cartels and trusts were prohibited by the occupation authorities.[468] In 1957, Germany passed a competition law. One central principle behind German competition policy is still protection of economic freedom.[469] This philosophy is reflected in that mergers are scrutinized because they could lead to the formation of dominant entities that might endanger the economic freedom of competitors. Cases against abuse of a dominant position are seen in the same perspective, and it is argued that German competition law tends to protect smaller competitors.[470]

Integration motivation. Competition law has always been of central importance for the European Community, with one important dimension of EU competition policy being integrational motivation. After all, the initial focus of the European competition regime and the EU overall was to integrate the economies of the Member States.[471] This integrational motivation of EU competition policy is unique and constitutes a fundamental difference between EU competition law and competition systems in other jurisdictions, particularly in the USA, which has no similar objective.

The integrational objective fulfils a different function, which has often been characterized as being both negative and positive, in the sense that EU competition law has a role of preventing measures attempting to maintain the isolation of one domestic market from another (negative role),[472] as well as a role of encouraging trade between Member States 'by levelling the playing fields of Europe' and facilitating cross-border transactions (positive role). The concept of competition policy lies at the very heart of efforts to establish a common market and therefore can even be viewed as the

---

467. Motta (n 322) 10.
468. For example, the breaking up of the German chemical company IG Farben into BASF, Bayer and Hoechst dates from this period.
469. *See* Kühn (n 466).
470. Motta (n 322) 11 fn 33. *See also* Giuliano Amato, *Antitrust and the Bounds of Power: The Dilemma of Liberal Democracy in the History of the Market* (Hart 1997).
471. Generally on the integration of Europe, *see* Raitio (n 108). Article 2 of the EC Treaty makes it clear that market integration is seen as an important objective of EU competition law: 'The Community shall have as its task, by establishing a common market and progressively approximating the economic policies of Member States, to promote throughout the Community a harmonious development of economic activities, a continuous and balanced expansion, an increase in stability, an accelerated raising of the standard of living and closer relations between the States belonging to it.' *See also* Claus-Dieter Ehlermann, 'The Contribution of EC Competition Policy to the Single Market' (1992) 29 CML Rev 257.
472. In other words, internal barriers to trade within the EU, such as export bans, national cartels and market-sharing, should be dismantled.

foundation stone of the entire European Union.[473] The CJEU has stated that maintaining effective competition is so essential 'that without it numerous provisions of the Treaty would be pointless'.[474]

Effective competition. Many attempts have been made over time to categorize and classify in different ways the objectives of EU competition law. One model was that presented above by Ariel Ezrachi. Another way of thinking about it is in line with Bishop and Walker, who divide EU competition law's goals into the 'integration goal' and the 'economic goal'. Whereas the 'integration goal' refers to promotion of integration between EU Member States, as touched on above, the 'economic goal' refers to promotion of effective and undistorted competition.[475]

The goal of maintaining 'effective competition' can be found in the wording of the main competition rules. For example, Article 102 TFEU prohibits '[a]ny abuse by one or more undertakings of a dominant position ... in so far as it may affect trade between Member States'. The EU Merger Regulation states that '[a] concentration which creates or strengthens a dominant position as a result of which effective competition would be significantly impeded in the common market or in a substantial part of it shall be declared incompatible with the common market'. But what is meant by effective competition? If one looks back to the theoretical considerations presented in the previous chapter, efficiency as competition law's policy goal aims to prevent practices that decrease allocative, dynamic or productive efficiency. According to standard competition economic theory, unless companies possess and exercise market power, they are unable to affect competition adversely.[476] Effective competition can therefore be defined as *absence of market power.*

As discussed above, the definition of market power – the core concept in competition law – is understood as the possibility to act independently in the market, which traditionally translates into power to weaken competitive parameters by raising prices. Indeed, standard economic theory defines market power as the ability to raise prices above the competitive price level.[477] This is where it becomes a bit tricky when bringing traditional competition law and policy goals into the digital age and data-driven markets. This is because, in the digital economy, online services are generally offered for 'free' (zero price, although the currency is personal data).[478] This turns the traditional notion of market power in competition law into a slippery concept, as conventional consumer harm does not necessarily translate into higher prices. Rather, the harm may lie in consumers giving away and losing control over their personal data. As suggested by the OECD, an online service delivered involves non-pecuniary costs

473. Lee McGowan and Stephen Wilks, 'The First Supranational Policy in the European Union: Competition Policy' (1995) 28 European Journal of Political Research 141.

474. Case 6/72 *Europemballage and Continental Can v Commission* [1973] ECR 215 [1973] CMLR 199, para. 24.

475. Bishop and Walker (n 359) 3.

476. *Ibid.*

477. *Ibid.*

478. As noted above, in reality, despite commonly referring to 'free' online offerings, individuals pay for supposedly free online services by giving away their personal data. Therefore, the expression online 'free' service can be generally considered misleading for consumers. *See* Burnside (n 170).

for consumers through providing personal data, paying attention to ads, or the opportunity costs of reading privacy policies.[479]

The implications from this are multifold, and competition may be negatively affected as businesses active in online markets become extremely powerful by collecting and exploiting consumer data. For example, this may result in competitors being excluded from the market. Moreover, and most importantly, consumers can be negatively affected. But the problem is that the conventional competition concept of market power based on prices, as well as the notions of market dominance and consumer welfare,[480] may not be optimal for identifying this sort of consumer harm and grappling with the realities of the data economy, where price equals personal information. This problem will be further explored in Chapter 4 on the interlinkage between privacy and competition, and further in Chapter 5 when envisioning the optimal competition policy for the data-driven digital world.

Fairness. A discussion on the goals and values of EU competition law must address the concept of fairness. In competition parlance, the notion of 'fair' competition is common. The concept of fairness echoes a moral norm embodied in EU competition rules.[481] Recently in Europe, increased focus has been placed on fairness, especially in speeches by the EU Competition Commissioner Margrethe Vestage when addressing the goals of competition enforcement and defining her task as competition commissioner as a promoter of 'fair competition'.[482] She has also approached the subject of fairness in moral terms, drawing parallels between competition policy and religious norms.[483] In the context of the digital economy and personal data as currency for online transactions, the Commissioner has stated that consuming free services against the disclosure of one's data 'doesn't have to be a problem, as long as people are happy that the data they share is a *fair* price to pay for the services they get in return' (emphasis added).[484]

Article 102 TFEU stipulates that abuses of market dominance may be born from, among other things, the direct or indirect imposition of *unfair* purchase or selling prices, as well as by other *unfair* trading conditions. In this regard, a concern for fairness has triggered competition intervention in some cases involving exploitative prices imposed on consumers.[485]

479. OECD Big Data (n 22) 25.
480. The key concepts in competition law have been discussed in Chapter 3.
481. Ezrachi (n 369) 15.
482. *See also* Vestager (n 74); Vestager 'Competition for a Fairer Society' Speech at 10th Annual Global Antitrust Enforcement Symposium (Georgetown, 20 September 2016); 'Working Together to Support Fairer Competition Worldwide' Speech at UCL Jevons Institute Conference (London, 3 June 2016); 'The Values of Competition Policy' Speech at CEPS Corporate Breakfast (Brussels, 13 October 2015).
483. Speech by Margrethe Vestager, 'Luther and the Modern World' Speech at 9th Luther Conference and the award ceremony of the Luther Rose 2016 (Copenhagen, 14 November 2016) ('In my work on competition, I sometimes say that what is at stake is as old as Adam and Eve. For all the economic theories and the business models, it all comes down to greed').
484. Speech by Margrethe Vestager, 'Making Data Work for Us', Data Ethics event on Data as Power (Copenhagen, 9 September 2016).
485. Case 26/75 *General Motors Continental v Commission* [1975] ECR 1367; Case 27/76 *United*

Looking at the value of fairness in the context of the digital economy, Ezrachi argues that fairness 'may be viewed as ensuring equal opportunities for as efficient competitors and the protection of consumers. It is used to guaranty the legitimate expectations of economic operators and consumers'.[486] Fairness also serves as an abstract normative value which is promoted by the competitive process,[487] as well as ensuring a fair result of market outcome. Importantly, fair competition cultivates trust in markets.[488]

In the context of fairness, concerns regarding possible data- and privacy-related activities, which have exploitative effects, are relevant. Privacy can be woven into discussion of fairness as a value since the role played by data and privacy has become important in shaping digital markets. In its more abstract form, fairness can be seen as a guide, rather than an independent enforcement benchmark.[489] Exploitative conduct is unilateral behaviour that distorts competition by directly harming final consumers, rather than excluding competitors. The imposition of excessive and discriminatory prices and the imposition of unfair contractual clauses are examples of exploitative conduct that could harm consumers. This will also be discussed further in later chapters.

Fairness as a policy goal can be criticized as a vague and subjective concept, and fairness has been condemned as 'a vagrant claim applied to any value that one happens to favor'.[490] Sceptics hold that the notion can easily be misapplied by less efficient competitors to promote their own goals at the expense of consumers.[491] However, in terms of the concept of fairness, economics has always played a major part. Adam

---

Brands v Commission [1978] ECR 207; Case C-177/16 *Autortiesību un komunicēšanās konsultāciju aģentūra (AKKA)/ Latvijas Autoru apvienība (LAA)* (judgment of the court of 14 September 2017) not yet published; *Deutsche Post AG* (Case COMP/C-1/36.915) Commission Decision 2001/892/EC [2001] OJ L331/40.

486. Ezrachi (n 369) 15, citing Daniel Zimmer, 'On Fairness and Welfare: The Objectives of Competition Policy – Comment on David J Gerber, Christian Ahlborn and A Jorge Padilla' in Claus-Dieter Ehlermann and Mel Marquis (eds), *European Competition Law Annual 2007 – A Reformed Approach to Article 82 EC* (Hart Publishing 2008).
487. 'Healthy and vigorous competition is of fundamental importance to a fair EU economy and society', *see* European Commission, Staff working document accompanying the Report on Competition Policy 2016, SWD (2017) 175 final, 59.
488. In the 2016 'State of the Union' speech by Jean-Claude Juncker, former President of the European Commission, it was stated that 'a fair playing field also means that in Europe, consumers are protected against cartels and abuses by powerful companies. (...) The Commission watches over this fairness. This is the social side of competition law. And this is what Europe stands for'. *See* speech as quoted in European Commission, 'Report on Competition Policy' (2016) 2.
489. Ezrachi (n 369) 16.
490. Phillip E Areeda and Herbert Hovenkamp, *Antitrust Law: An Analysis of Antitrust Principles and Their Application* (4th edn, Wolters Kluwer 2015) 111d. *See also* Louis Kaplow and Steven Shavell, 'Fairness Versus Welfare' (2001) 114 Harvard Law Review 961, 969–970.
491. For further discussion on the concept of fairness in EU competition law, *see* Maurits Dolmans and Wanjie Lin, 'Fairness and Competition Law: A Fairness Paradox' (November 2017) 4 Concurrences Review 1–20 (suggesting there is a fairness paradox: while competition law should reflect the values of fairness, if fairness were actually employed in substantive decision-making as a goal, that would lead to unequal and inefficient results). For a conceptual analysis of fairness at the intersection of EU competition and data protection law, *see* Harri Kalimo and Klaudia Majcher, 'The Concept of Fairness: Linking EU Competition and Data Protection Law in the Digital Marketplace' (2017) 42 EL Rev 210.

Smith wrote his treatise on ethics (the lesser-known, but equally important, *Theory of Moral Sentiments*)[492] almost twenty years before he finished *The Wealth of Nations*[493] and recognized that the desire to trade is a fundamental part of the human social instinct; in particular, he identified fairness as playing a critical role in human interaction.[494]

Besides the above-mentioned integrational goal, effective competition and the concept of fairness, other objectives and values can impact on EU competition law and enforcement. Some of these are dictated by economic and political reasons related to historical and cultural aspects. For instance, EU competition law may be applied and developed in the light of policy concerns such as public health, social protection, consumer protection, environmental concerns, investment, transportation and regional development.[495] The ordoliberal approach to EU competition law is another example. In the following, this school of thought and the closely related concept of freedom of choice, also central to EU competition policy, will be explored.

[B] Ordoliberalism and Freedom of Choice

In addition to the goals of market integration and effective competition, competition policy in Europe traditionally assigns importance to the concept of 'freedom of choice' as a theory of harm.[496] The concept is the result of the evolution of the ordoliberal school of thought. Here, the term 'ordoliberalism' refers to the perspective that emphasized the important role of private law and competition rules for the proper functioning of competitive markets.[497]

In this context, competition law is seen as a tool that can deprive businesses of economic and associated political power, thereby helping safeguard individual freedom.[498] This role for competition fits within the broader competition law goal (as summarized by Timonen) of decentralization of economic power and protection of individual freedom.[499] The ordoliberal school contributed to assigning competition law a political and social dimension. This, some argue, goes back to the scars of the totalitarian state in Germany and its Nazi history, which was closely associated with support from influential interest groups and highly cartelized industrial complexes.

492. First published 1759, CUP 2002.
493. Adam Smith, *The Wealth of Nations* (W. Strahan and T. Cadell 1776).
494. *Ibid.*
495. Ezrachi (n 334) 5.
496. Paul Nihoul, 'Freedom of Choice: The Emergence of a Powerful Concept in European Competition Law' in Paul Nihoul et al. (eds), *Choice – A New Standard for Competition Law Analysis* (Concurrences Review 2016) 9.
497. Peter Behrens, 'The "Consumer Choice" Paradigm in German Ordoliberalism and Its Impact on EU Competition Law' in Nihoul (n 496) 11.
498. *Ibid.*
499. *See* discussion in §3.02. The other two goals in the summary or categorization of the broader goals of competition laws include protecting the economic freedom (latitude) of market actors and promoting consumer welfare. For a transatlantic comparative discussion, *see* René Joliet, *Monopolization and Abuse of Dominant Position: A Comparative Study of American and European Approaches to the Control of Economic Power* (Université de Liège Faculté de Droit 1970).

Moreover, the origins of the understanding of a social market economy (*soziale Marktwirtschaft* in German) promoting social policies to create a welfare state, as implemented in West Germany in 1949, were strongly inspired by ordoliberalism.

Moreover, the forming of EU competition policy, especially in its early days, was significantly influenced by German ordoliberalism,[500] even though the school is not widely known outside Germany and is generally not as famous as the Chicago and Harvard schools.[501] According to ordoliberal views, competition policy has broader objectives than mere economic efficiency, and as competition is necessary for a liberal constitutional state, control over power and preserving the protection of democracy necessitates competition policy.[502] Competition policy can prevent concentrated markets that could allow businesses excessive economic power that, in turn, may lessen economic efficiency and pervert political decision-making. Companies with economic and market power might acquire special rights, which might result in weakened competition. In this context, the economy and politics, the state and society are analysed through chains of interactions. Ordoliberalism aims to protect economic freedom as a value in itself, which is achieved by limiting excessive economic power.[503]

Ordoliberal thinking captures the dynamic concept of competition as an information-producing process of interaction between market participants, contrary to the static approach to competition.[504] Accordingly, competition is seen as a dynamic process of discovery between consumers and businesses.[505] The concept of competition as a dynamic process of discovery was developed by Friedrich Hayek.[506] As more nuanced views of the ordoliberal school evolved into forming different strands of

500. On the development and influence of German ordoliberalism, *see* Heinz Rieter and Matthias Schmolz, 'The Ideas of German Ordoliberalism (1938–1945): Pointing the Way to a New Economic Order' (1993) 1 The European Journal of the History of Economic Thought 87–114; David J Gerber, 'Constitutionalizing the Economy: German Neo-Liberalism, Competition Law and the "New" Europe' (1994) 42 American Journal of Comparative Law 25; AJ Nicholls, *Freedom with Responsibility: The Social Market Economy in Germany 1918–1963* (Clarendon Press 1994).
501. This is largely due to much of the scholarly work existing only in German. The ordoliberal school or Freiburg school as it is commonly referred to was born in the 1930s in Germany and became the leading school of thought after World War II until 1960. Leading thinkers were economist Walter Eucken and lawyer Franz Böhm. Petri Kuoppamäki provides further reading on ordoliberalism and the school's influence on EU competition policy, *see* Kuoppamäki (n 110) 189–204.
502. Kuoppamäki (n 110) 191.
503. Wernhard Möschel, 'The Proper Scope of Government Viewed from Ordoliberal Perspective: The Example of Competition Policy' (2001) 157 Journal of Institutional and Theoretical Economics (JITE) 3, 4. *See also* Christian Ahlborn and Carsten Grave, 'Walter Eucken and Ordoliberalism: An Introduction from a Consumer Welfare Perspective' (2006) CPI Antitrust Chronicle.
504. Behrens (n 497) 20.
505. *Ibid.*
506. *See* Friedrich A Hayek, *Individualism and Economic Order* (The University of Chicago Press 1963) 94–96 ('[Consumers'] knowledge of the alternatives before them is the result of what happens on the market, of such activities as advertising, etc.; and the whole organization of the market serves mainly the need of spreading the information on which the buyer is to act).

contemporary ordoliberalism, Hayek's concept was complemented by the Schumpeterian notion of rivalry as a process of 'creative destruction'.[507]

The common denominator for these variants of contemporary ordoliberal approaches to competition is that they all build on the core belief, dating back even to Adam Smith, that competition should be understood as a 'system of interaction between choice making individuals who by making their choices reveal their preferences and produce the kind of information that other individuals need to make their choices'.[508]

As will be shown, it is rather challenging trying to bring that ordoliberal core belief and choice-centred approach to competition into today's data economy. The basic problem boils down to the simple fact that, in concentrated markets, consumers are deprived of choice between different suppliers or service providers, and thus are denied the important individual freedom associated with competition. The higher the degree of concentration, the lower the number of alternatives available to consumers and the more limited becomes consumers' freedom of choice. Under this view, an important task for competition enforcers would be to protect consumer welfare by looking at consumer choice as a guiding aim, and ensuring that consumer choice is not unduly restricted by abusive or anticompetitive behaviour by dominant companies. Indeed, there is a 'freedom of choice' approach to EU competition law, and European enforcers have affirmed restriction of consumer choice as a theory of harm behind violations of, for example, Article 102 TFEU.[509]

As will be shown, the 'freedom of choice' approach to EU competition law is completely different from American views of dominance abuses.[510] This focus in EU competition law on consumers' freedom of choice is sometimes said to protect competitors instead of competition.[511] Some argue that preserving choice has translated into enforcement that disfavours efficient competitors.[512] However, what it essentially boils down to is a difference in the politics of competition law and differences in legal cultural and historical values. This is similar to the different views concerning consumerism and producerism as presented by Whitman.[513]

After all, EU competition law has numerous objectives, and the historical origin of consumer choice is grounded in German ordoliberalism, which, arguably, is closely connected to Germany's Nazi history. An abundant theoretical and empirical literature examines the influence of ordoliberalism on EU competition policy.[514] Certain features

507. Schumpeter (n 382) ch. 7. The notion refers to a process of constant emergence and erosion of market power, where one or some innovative businesses strive to outcompete rivals who are then challenged in turn to overtake the lead by better innovation and so on.
508. Behrens (n 497) 22.
509. Nihoul (n 496) 9.
510. Andrew I Gavil, William E Kovacic and Jonathan B Baker, *Antitrust Law in Perspective: Cases, Concepts, and Problems in Competition Policy* (Thomson/West 2008) 639–640.
511. Whish and Bailey (n 300) 22.
512. *See* William E Kovacic, 'Transatlantic Turbulence: The Boeing-McDonnell Douglas Merger and International Competition Policy' (2001) 68 Antitrust Law Journal 805.
513. *See* discussion in §3.02.
514. Petri Kuoppamäki explores the importance of ordoliberalism for the development of competition law in Kuoppamäki (n 110) 189–204.

reflecting ordoliberal thinking are deeply rooted in European competition enforcement, such as the prohibition on exploitative abuses and the importance placed on freedom of choice as a theory of harm.[515] It has been argued that Article 102 TFEU is in fact a product of ordoliberalism.[516] However, over time, efforts have been made to replace ordoliberal principles with neoliberalism and an efficiency-enhancing rationale in competition enforcement, not least with DG Competition's 'more economic approach', as will be discussed below.[517]

Today, ordoliberalism is reflected in a systematic holistic approach to competition in a societal context, where competitive markets are viewed as a tool for promoting and protecting more important societal purposes.[518] This approach puts an emphasis on competition performing a social function, which arguably can be held as the most significant function of all, and that the market economy should serve its citizens, not the other way around.[519] This practical perspective on competition is highly current because with the evolution of the data economy and business models based on the collection and commercialization of users' personal data, this kind of social function of competition and protecting the rights of individual citizens, such as data protection and privacy, are increasingly important. Conceptually, ordoliberalism can be understood as not only a school of thought but also more of an entire political and economic philosophy and it can be widely applied to competition policy.[520]

The ordoliberal understanding of competition policy does not confine itself to mere economic-technical efficiency measurements but looks at the market economy more widely, including goals involving freedom, efficiency and fairness. This understanding of an ordoliberal take on competition policy is of key importance for this book, as many aspects of ordoliberalism resonate with today's rising criticism about insufficient competition in digital markets and calls for a rethink of competition policy to better serve consumers. One can identify significant parallels between the conventional ordoliberal view on competition policy and calls for a revised, more interventionist approach to competition law today to deal with concerns regarding possible data and privacy-related activities which have exploitative effects, as well as digital markets being concentrated in the hands of a few big data-driven companies.

Some fascinating similarities can be found in the thinking of modern competition scholars such as Ezrachi and Stucke about competition policy (as articulated in their books *Virtual Competition* and *Big Data and Competition*, for example) and the

515. Nihoul (n 496) 9.
516. *See e.g.* David J Gerber, *Law and Economics and Competition in Twentieth Century Europe Protecting Prometheus* (OUP 1998) 264. This view has been contested by Pinar Akman, *The Concept of Abuse in EU Competition Law. Law and Economic Approaches* (Hart Publishing 2012) 49-105.
517. For a discussion on the influence of ordoliberalism, neoliberalism and the Chicago school on EU competition policy, *see e.g.* Dzmitry Bartalevich, 'The Influence of the Chicago School on the Commission's Guidelines, Notices and Block Exemption Regulations in EU Competition Policy' (2016) 54 Journal of Common Market Studies 267.
518. *Ibid.*, 201-202.
519. *Ibid.*, 202.
520. Alison Jones and Brenda Sufrin, *EU Competition Law: Texts, Cases and Materials* (5th edn, OUP 2014) 33.

traditional ordoliberal understanding of competition policy as a necessary tool not only for preserving price competition but also for exercising control over power and preserving protection of democracy. This goes to the broader question whether, and to what extent, societal goals should be included in competition analysis, a topic that has recently been gaining increasing attention.[521] What is interesting is that this current debate shares many similarities and elements of traditional ordoliberal thinking about competition policy. Consequently, it seems that ordoliberalism may be making a comeback to the approach that should guide competition policy in the digital age.

Indeed, freedom of choice is becoming a real concern today in data-driven markets, which are increasingly concentrated. This concern is expressed in public by many policymakers and regulators. For example, the EU Competition Commissioner observes that:

> Digital technology is transforming every part of our lives [...]. And we're seeing signs that competition might not be working the way it should. There's evidence that some markets might be getting more concentrated, with more of the market in the hands of just a few companies.[522]

This market concentration indicates some sort of market failure in that competition is not working the way it should. For example, with regard to Facebook, one of the so-called super-platforms of the digital economy and heavily criticized in the light of the Cambridge Analytica scandal concerning misuse of personal data, it is noted that '[i]f there was competition, we'd not be stuck with Facebook. In a competitive market, bad behaviour is not left unpunished. Users flee in droves to the next best alternative'.[523] Indeed, as noted by Robert Lande already in 2008 in the context of defending privacy issues as an antitrust concern in the context of the *Microsoft/Yahoo* merger, '[w]hen a market is competitive, any information-heavy firm that does not respect consumers' privacy rights will pay a penalty'.[524] In practice, this does not seem to be happening today because consumers are without effective choice, and therefore cannot exercise their freedom of choice. Despite the data privacy scandal with Cambridge Analytica, there seems to have been little, if any impact on Facebook with Zuckerberg commenting at the Congressional hearing: 'I don't think there's been any meaningful impact that we've observed.'[525]

---

521. Anne Witt, 'Public Policy Goals under EU Competition Law – Now Is the Time to Set the House in Order' (2012) 8 European Competition Journal 443; Beata Mäihäniemi, *Imposing Access to Information in Digital Markets Based on Competition Law – In Search of the Possible Theory of Harm in the EU Google Search Investigations* (Academic dissertation, Faculty of Law, University of Helsinki 2017) 11.
522. Speech by Margrethe Vestager, 'The Importance of Being Open – And Fair' European Conference (Harvard University, 2 March 2018).
523. Nicolas Petit, 'A Quick and Dirty Note on FB, Competition and Individualism' Symphony of disruption (Symphony of Disruption blog, 29 March 2018) https://symphonyofdisruption.org/author/ieje/, accessed 19 April 2020. *See also* Dina Srinivasan, 'The Antitrust Case Against Facebook' (10 September 2018) 16 Berkeley Business Law Journal.
524. Lande (n 277) 2; COMP/M.5727 *Microsoft/Yahoo! Search Business* C[2010] 1077.
525. Petit (n 523).

An ordoliberal understanding of competition as a dynamic process is highly relevant for addressing the current problems of competition policy today. An ordoliberal would address the existing restriction on consumers' freedom to choose and lack of choice in increasingly concentrated digital markets as a competitive harm and market failure that competition policy should seek to protect as its primary objective. Whereas data protection laws can ensure more informed choice, competition enforcement can be used to deconcentrate markets to facilitate more choice. With the digitalization of the economy and growing concerns about insufficient or failing competition in online markets, the need arises for a more ordoliberal approach to competition that distances itself from a focus on price-based static consumer harm (the static approach to competition) and instead defines competition as a dynamic concept.

There are some signs of an emerging comeback of ordoliberal thinking in competition policy. Calls for a more dynamic approach to competition law are being made in the European Commission. The head of the EU's DG Competition, Johannes Laitenberger, proposed a more 'dynamic perspective' in EU competition analysis that would look beyond a traditional focus on prices to longer-term effects, especially in terms of the digital economy and new technologies.[526] A static, short-term, price-centric perspective will fail to deliver the benefits of competition, and given that digital markets frequently involve services provided for free and monetized through advertising, the need is for a 'stronger focus' on other parameters of competition, such as 'quality, *choice* and innovation'.[527]

[C] The 'More Economic Approach' and Consumer Welfare

Despite the multitude of goals when initially enacting EU competition legislation, today, the consumer welfare standard, discussed above in §3.03, is most commonly understood as the principal aim of EU competition policy. This is because, over time, efforts were made in the European Commission's DG Competition to narrow the goals of EU competition law and embrace the concept of consumer welfare as the sole guiding principle. This was done with the aim of implementing a more economics-based approach to EU competition law and policy.

This more economic approach was introduced with the advent of modern economics and because of influences from the US Chicago school.[528] There were some concerns that past competition policy lacked clear objective and rational criteria for consistent enforcement and had had counterproductive effects on efficiency and innovation.[529] Thus the goal of maintaining 'effective competition' was to be understood as the objective to enhance efficiency in the sense of maximizing consumer

526. Speech by Johannes Laitenberger, 'EU Competition Law in Innovation and Digital Markets: Fairness and the Consumer Welfare Perspective' MLex/Hogan Lovells event EU Competition Law Enforcement 2.0 (Brussels 10 October 2017).
527. *Ibid.*
528. *See* §3.02.
529. Robert H Bork, *The Antitrust Paradox: A Policy at War with Itself* (Free Press 1978).

welfare and achieving optimal allocation of resources.[530] This meant that EU competition policy transitioned away from political goals to promoting consumer welfare and more efficient allocation of resources in the economic sense.

The EU's 'more economic approach' was promoted in particular by EU Competition Commissioner Mario Monti, according to whom preserving competition is not an end in itself, as '[t]he ultimate policy goal is the protection of consumer welfare'.[531] According to Monti, the purpose of introducing the more economic approach to EU competition policy was to give the EU's 'cumbersome and complicated competition provisions a radical overhaul in order to bring them into holding with modern economic thinking'.[532] The Commission, under the leadership of Monti, put forward consumer welfare as the primary competition goal but with little explanation or reasoning.

The shift to a 'more economic approach' was formalized in the EU during the modernization process in the 1990s to the early 2000s. As part of the shift, the Commission established the Chief Competition Economist team at DG Competition in 2003. Moreover, it introduced various soft law instruments in the form of (non-binding) interpretative guidelines.[533] These include a discussion paper on the application of Article 102 TFEU to exclusionary abuses (the 2005 Discussion Paper), which in its outline of the traditional analysis injected a more economically inspired approach to assessing abuse,[534] and the 102 Guidance Paper published in late 2008,[535] which expressed the European Commission's modern approach.[536]

These guidance papers recognize 'consumer welfare' as the prime objective of EU competition law. For example, the European Commission's Guidelines on the Application of Article 101(3) state: 'The objective of Article [101] is to protect competition in the market as a means of enhancing consumer welfare and of ensuring an efficient allocation of resources.'[537] Similar statements are found in the Horizontal Merger

530. As discussed in Chapter 3 on competition theory, traditional economic theory indicates that products and services are produced most efficiently where there is perfect competition, or, more realistically, workable competition. *See also* Scherer (n 383); Richard Lipsey and Alec Chrystal, *Economics* (10th edn, OUP, 2003).
531. Mario Monti speech, 'The Future for Competition Policy in the European Union' (London, 9 July 2001). Monti also stated: '[T]he goal of competition policy, in all its aspects, is to protect consumer welfare by maintaining a high degree of competition in the common market.' *See also* his speech given at the formal introduction ceremony of the new President of the Bundeskartellamt, 'Festveranstaltung Präsidentenwechsel Bundeskartellamt' speech/00/6 (13 January 2000) http://europa.eu/rapid/press-release_SPEECH-00-6_en.htm?locale=fi, accessed 19 April 2020.
532. Mario Monti, 'A Competition Policy for Today and Tomorrow' (2000) 23 World Competition 1.
533. Ariel Ezrachi, *EU Competition Law – An Analytical Guide to the Leading Cases* (5th edn, Bloomsbury Publishing 2016) 211.
534. *Ibid.*
535. Guidance on the Commission's enforcement priorities in applying Article 82 [102 TFEU] of the EC treaty to abusive exclusionary conduct by dominant undertakings [2009] OJ C45/02 (Article 82 Guidance Paper).
536. Ezrachi (n 533) 211.
537. European Commission Guidelines (n 352) para. 13.

Guidelines, the Vertical Guidelines, the Technology Transfer Guidelines and the Guidelines on Article 102 Enforcement Priorities.[538]

This introduction of the more economic approach driven by the Commission can be criticized for having little bearing on the case law of the EU courts at the time;[539] it is argued that the approach was a construction of the European Commission and inspired by American ideologies.[540] Nevertheless, this new emphasis on economics came to have significant methodological and substantive implications for EU competition law. The methodological changes brought about the use of abstract economic theory and concepts. A key substantive change was infusing a more economic legal objective into competition law by using the concept of consumer welfare. Despite the more economic approach being a construction of the Commission, with debatable support in the judiciary, and none in the actual Treaty provisions, adherence to the consumer welfare model of competition policy continued under the next EU Competition Commissioner, Neelie Kroes, who in 2005 declared without elaboration that:

> [c]onsumer welfare is now well established as the standard the Commission applies when assessing mergers and infringements of the Treaty rules on cartels and monopolies. Our aim is simple: to protect competition in the market as a means of enhancing consumer welfare and ensuring an efficient allocation of resources.[541]

538. Guidelines on the assessment of horizontal mergers under the Council Regulation on the control of concentrations between undertakings, OJ (2004) C 31/03, para. 61; Guidelines on Vertical Restraints, OJ [2010] C 130/01, para. 7; Guidelines on the application of Article 101 of the Treaty on the Functioning of the European Union to technology transfer agreements, OJ (2014) C 89/03, para. 5; and Article 82 Guidance Paper (n 535) para. 5.
539. One may also argue, however, that the General Court played a role in pushing the Commission to develop its economic reasoning. This was done by the court overturning three consecutive Commission decisions based on insufficient economic reasoning, as the merger decisions were annulled on the grounds of manifest errors of assessment. In addition, in the period between 1990 and 2000, the EU spearheaded by the Commission received criticism by academia and practitioners due to several Commission decisions that were conflicting with FTC decisions in cases of international scope. An example is the merger between General Electric and Honeywell that was only prohibited by the EU but not by the USA, which was heavily criticized. *See e.g.* Jeremy Grant and Damien J Neven, 'The Attempted Merger Between General Electric and Honeywell: A Case Study of Transatlantic Conflict' (2005) 1 Journal of Competition Law and Economics 2.
540. Anne C Witt, 'The European Court of Justice and the More Economic Approach – Is the Tide Turning?' XXXth CLaSF Workshop on Antitrust at the Intersection of Law and Economics, Competition Law Scholars Forum (CLaSF) and the Graz Institute of Corporate and International Commercial Law (Graz 19 April 2018). *See also* Anne C Witt, *The More Economic Approach to EU Antitrust Law* (1st edn, Hart Publishing 2016) 9.
541. Speech by Neelie Kroes, 'European Competition Policy – Delivering Better Markets and Better Choices' European Consumer and Competition Day (London, 15 September 2005). *See also* speech by Joaquín Almunia, 'Competition – What's in It for Consumers?' (Poznan, 24 November 2011) ('Consumer welfare is not just a catchy phrase. It is the cornerstone, the guiding principle of EU competition policy'), and on his nomination as competition commissioner, Almunia spoke in similar terms: 'All of us here today know very well what our ultimate objective is: Competition policy is a tool at the service of consumers. Consumer welfare is at the heart of our policy and its achievement drives our priorities and guides our decisions'; 'Competition and Consumers: The Future of EU Competition Policy' European Competition Day (Madrid, 12 May 2010).

There have been attempts to find support for the Commission's more economic approach by referring to early European Commission reports on competition policy, which can be read so that European competition policy was aimed at the promotion of consumer welfare: '(...) competition policy endeavours to maintain or create effective conditions of competition by means of rules applying to enterprises in both private and public sectors. Such a policy encourages the best possible use of productive resources for the greatest possible benefit of the economy as a whole and for the benefit, in particular of the consumer'.[542]

However, there is also evidence of lack of support, because the European Commission has explicitly acknowledged that 'competition policy cannot be pursued in isolation, as an end in itself, without reference to the legal, economic, political and social context'.[543]

One can debate whether the attempts by DG Competition to implement a more economics-based approach in EU competition law have been rightful and successful. In academic discourse, doubts are expressed whether the Commission has managed to move to an economics-based approach, especially when interpreting Article 102 TFEU.[544] Moreover, despite the Commission's attempts to increase the use of economic analysis, the EU courts have not always followed the more economic approach. For example, in her Opinion in *Post Danmark II*, Advocate General Kokott held that 'the added value of expensive economic analysis is not always apparent and can lead to the disproportionate use of resources'.[545] She also noted that aiming at solving issues (such as price-based exclusionary effects analysed in the case at hand) cannot succeed simply by applying mathematical models, because it does not ensure legal certainty as it is open to various interpretations.[546] Therefore, all the circumstances of the case should be taken into account, which implies that legal requirements and objective justifications should not disregard facts and economic realities.[547]

Compared to price-focused US antitrust law, which will be looked at in the following, revamping EU competition policy to become only about consumer welfare in the economic sense – driven by price – has not been completely resolved or unanimous. In other words, the multidimensionality of EU competition law still exists and various goals can still be advanced as objectives under EU competition policy. In this book, the focus lies on exploring whether a role for privacy exists among this multitude of goals. This is part of the wider research question considering a potential privacy dimension in competition policy.

542. *See* European Commission, First Report on Competition Policy (April 1972) 12.
543. European Commission, XXIInd Report on Competition Policy (1992) 13.
544. For further reading, *see e.g.* Pinar Akman, 'The Reform of the Application of Article 102 TFEU: Mission Accomplished' (2016) 81 Antitrust Law Journal.
545. Case C-23/14 *Post Danmark A/S v Konkurrencerådet* [2015] Opinion AG Kokott.
546. *Ibid.*, para. 67.
547. *Ibid.*

§3.04 PRICE-CENTRIC US ANTITRUST POLICY

[A] Single Economic Goal

After reviewing EU competition law and its key policy goals, in this chapter US antitrust law and policy will be examined. Similarly to the previous chapter, the purpose here is not to provide a comprehensive outline of the history of antitrust law in the USA, but rather to track the origins of modern US competition law and policy to understand the circumstances in which US antitrust law was founded, and with what underlying policy goals.

Over the past forty years, competition policy has transformed across both Europe and the USA. Starting in the 1970s, the USA went through an antitrust revolution as it moved from various public interest goals and political elements to a singular goal based on economic analysis.[548] In Europe, by contrast, the (attempted) shift to greater focus on economic analysis in competition law began in earnest only in the early 2000s with the above-mentioned 'more economic approach'. While this approach did not move EU competition law to an economics-based approach centred only around price effects, in the USA antitrust analysis is driven predominantly by price and economic efficiency, or some variation of it, as the sole policy goal.[549] This stands in stark contrast to EU competition law's multiple and varied policy objectives, some of which are dictated by economic and political reasons related to historical and cultural aspects.

Originally, the legislative tools for enforcing US antitrust law were created in response to the formation of trusts and monopolies and the concentration of American business arising from post-Civil War industrialization. In the early days of American antitrust enforcement, the rules were used to target the victims of market power, such as trade unions and their officers.[550] The Clayton Act (as amended in 1950) gave the antitrust agencies and courts 'the power to brake this force at its outset and before it gathered momentum'.[551] President Woodrow Wilson announced the antitrust initiative to Congress in his 1914 State of the Union Address, declaring, '[w]e are all agreed that private monopoly is indefensible and intolerable'.[552] The speech resulted in the passage of the FTC and Clayton Acts of 1914, which led to the establishment of a new agency dedicated to protecting consumers and competition from deceptive or unfair trade practices: the FTC.[553]

548. *See e.g.* Einer Elhauge, 'Harvard, Not Chicago: Which Antitrust School Drives Recent U.S. Supreme Court Decisions?' (2007) 3 Competition Policy International 59; Bruce H Kobayashi and Timothy J Muris, 'Chicago, Post-Chicago, and Beyond: Time to Let Go of the 20th Century' (2012) 78 Antitrust Law Journal 147.
549. Roger D Blair and D Daniel Sokol, 'Welfare Standards in US and EU Antitrust Enforcement' (2013) 81 Fordham Law Review 2499.
550. Ezrachi (n 334).
551. *Brown Shoe Co. Inc v United States*, 370 US 294 (1962).
552. President Woodrow Wilson, Address to a Joint Session of Congress on Trusts and Monopolies (20 January 1914) http://www.presidency.ucsb.edu/ws/index.php?pid=65374, accessed 19 April 2020.
553. For discussion on the origins of the FTC, *see* Marc Winerman, 'The Origins of the FTC: Concentration, Cooperation, Control, and Competition' (2003) 71 Antitrust Law Journal 1.

The enactment of the Sherman Act in 1890 enabled the DOJ to undertake criminal and civil prosecutions for unreasonable restraints of trade and monopolistic abuses. The US Supreme Court in 1958 noted that:

> The Sherman Act was designed to be a comprehensive charter of economic liberty aimed at preserving free and unfettered competition as the rule of trade. It rests on the premise that the unrestrained interaction of competitive forces will yield the best allocation of our economic resources, the lowest prices, the highest quality and the greatest material progress, while at the same time providing an environment conductive to the preservation of our democratic political and social institutions.[554]

Interpretation of the Sherman Act's antitrust provisions evolved over the years along with dynamic economic conditions and changing enforcement philosophy. The relatively abstract language enabled the courts to develop and adjust the realm of antitrust law; modern application of US antitrust law has been characterized by an attempt to reduce its susceptibility to non-economic considerations.[555]

When discussing the history of US antitrust policy in the following, the development of this policy is divided into three different phases or schools: the Harvard school, the Chicago school, and the Post-Chicago school. These will be discussed in turn below.

The Harvard school. The Harvard school flourished in the 1950s. The school was based on the prevailing industrial organization economics of the time with a focus on the effects on market prices of concentration and entry barriers.[556] There was a view that concentration in a market would facilitate tacit or explicit collusion among companies and that high barriers to entry would increase the margins and profits of dominant companies.[557] The school reflected the so-called Structure-Conduct-Paradigm idea, which can be summarized as a belief that the structure of the market would shape the behaviour of companies. This behaviour would then shape the performance of the market, such as the profitability of companies and general consumer welfare.[558] Effectively, this assumption meant that scholars of the Harvard school were distrustful of highly concentrated markets, often advocating break-ups.[559]

---

554. *Northern Pacific Co. v United States*, 356 US 1 (1958).
555. Richard Hofstadter, 'What Happened to the Antitrust Movement' in Richard Hofstadter (ed.), *The Paranoid Style in American Politics, and Other Essays* (first published 1965, Vintage Books 2008); Gary Minda, 'Antitrust at the Century's End' (1995) 48 SMU Law Review 1749, 1762; Harry First and Spencer Weber Waller, 'Antitrust's Democracy Deficit' (2012) 81 Fordham Law Review 2543, 2544.
556. The Harvard school relied greatly on the scholarly works of Joe Bain. *See e.g.* Joe Bain, 'Economies of Scale, Concentration, and the Condition of Entry in Twenty Manufacturing Industries' (1954) 44 The American Economic Review 15–39; Joe Bain, 'Relation of Profit Rate to Industry Concentration: American Manufacturing, 1936–1940' (1951) 65 The Quarterly Journal of Economics 293–324; Joe Bain, 'A Note on Pricing in Monopoly and Oligopoly' (1949) The American Economic Review 448–464.
557. Leonard W Weiss, 'The Structure-Conduct-Performance Paradigm and Antitrust' (1979) 127 University of Pennsylvania Law Review 1105–1106.
558. Herbert Hovenkamp, *The Antitrust Enterprise: Principle and Execution* (Harvard University Press 2008) 36–38.
559. Richard A Posner, 'The Chicago School of Antitrust Analysis' (1979) 127 University of Pennsylvania Law Review 944–947.

The school's philosophy and US antitrust policy in general at the time focused on whether companies had the *power* to engage in anticompetitive conduct, less on their *incentive* to do so.[560] The *Alcoa* judgment in 1945 somewhat altered this position in establishing that possessing a monopoly was not illegal under Section 2 of the Sherman Act.[561] The Supreme Court later clarified in *Grinnel* that an illegal act arises solely from 'the wilful acquisition or maintenance of that power as distinguished from growth or development as a consequence of a superior product, business acumen, or historic accident'.[562]

This new position basically meant that lawfully acquired monopolies were (and are) free to charge supra-competitive prices, thanks to their market position, as these prices reflect a reward for their superior efforts. As a result of this new approach, the Harvard school, and US antitrust policy in general, shifted its focus.[563]

[B] The Chicago School and Price Theory

No picture of American antitrust law would be complete without paying heed to the Chicago school and its influence on US antitrust law and policy. The Chicago school of economics challenged the views of the Harvard school and brought US antitrust policy to a new phase where the focus of enforcement shifted from *power* to *incentives*, and from *structuralism* to *price theory*.[564]

Chicago's influence in policymaking obtained a hold in the 1970s with the influential scholarly works of Stigler,[565] Posner[566] and Bork.[567] According to the philosophy of the Chicago school, the scope of competition policy should be reduced to fighting cartels and dealing with large horizontal mergers, where a clear theory of harm could be articulated.[568] The Chicago school promotes the idea that markets tend to self-correct. This approach is also acknowledged as a 'laissez-faire' attitude. In 1978, Robert Bork published *The Antitrust Paradox*, which held that the major goal of antitrust policy should be to promote 'business efficiency', which from the 1980s onwards came to be measured in consumer prices. It was a shift that took the USA away from an antitrust policy predicated on the welfare of the 'citizen', and one that clearly served the laissez-faire politics of the Reagan administration.

---

560. Jorge Padilla and David S Evans, 'Designing Antitrust Rules for Assessing Unilateral Practices: A Neo-Chicago Approach' (2005) 72 University of Chicago Law Review 76.
561. *Alcoa* (n 399) 148.
562. *Grinnel* (n 399) 571.
563. Posner (n 559) 927–931; Richard A Posner, *Antitrust Law: An Economic Perspective* (University of Chicago Press 1976).
564. Lina Khan, 'Amazon's Antitrust Paradox' (2017) 126 Yale Law Journal 718–719; Posner (n 559).
565. George J Stigler, *The Organization of Industry* (University of Chicago Press Economic Books 1983).
566. Posner (n 559). *See also* by Richard A Posner, *Economic Analysis of the Law* (Aspen Law and Business 1998); *Antitrust Law* (2nd edn, The University of Chicago Press 2001).
567. Bork (n 529).
568. Posner (n 559) 928.

According to Richard Posner, the essence of the Chicago school approach to antitrust is that 'the proper lens for viewing antitrust problems is price theory'.[569] The Chicago school's view is based on strong confidence in the efficiency of the markets driven by profit-maximizing rational actors. The Chicago school based itself on microeconomic analyses and defended the position that rational companies are not able to obtain or enhance monopoly power by means of unilateral action, as in that case they would trade profits for pure market share. The school's vision of industrial organization builds on a simple theoretical presumption that 'rational economic actors working with the confines of the market seek to maximize profits by combining inputs in the most efficient manner. A failure to act in this fashion will be punished by the competitive forces of the market'.[570]

Chicago's rationale spread to many of the traditional areas of antitrust analysis, emphasizing the possible efficiency- or welfare-enhancing justifications for problematic conduct and abusive practices.[571] The Chicago school's impact on US antitrust policy was strengthened by the appointment of more conservative judges and justices throughout the 1970s and 1980s. In particular, the scholarly works of Bork were influential and presented a normative reasoning that the Sherman Act was intended to enhance consumer welfare, which Bork interpreted as banning only conduct that reduced allocative efficiency.[572] Although Bork used 'consumer welfare' to mean 'allocative efficiency', courts and authorities largely measured it through effects on consumer prices.[573] Thus consumer prices became the dominant metric for assessing competition. Judges affirmed many of Bork's views and, over time, many of the per se approaches to unilateral conduct were reversed by the Supreme Court, paving the way for a rule of reason analysis. All of this gave rise to the 'Chicago era' in US antitrust law.[574]

The Chicago school dissociates itself from the idea that the aim of antitrust laws can be many-sided. Instead, the representatives of the Chicago school advocated making economic efficiency the only goal of American antitrust policy. This also involved the implication that social and other political aims should not be included as policy goals to the detriment of economic efficiency. Thus, the recommendation of the Chicago school is that interpretation and judgment of antitrust laws be made solely on the basis of relevant economic theory. Many of the basic arguments of the school are, however, questionable.[575]

---

569. Posner (n 559) 925, 932.
570. Marc Allen Eisner, *Antitrust and the Triumph of Economics: Institutions, Expertise, and Policy Change* (first published 1987, The University of North Carolina Press 1991) 107.
571. Posner (n 559).
572. William E Kovacic, 'Public Choice and the Origins of Antitrust' in Fred S McChesney and William F Shughart II (eds), *The Causes and Consequences of Antitrust* (University of Chicago Press 1995) 245.
573. *See* Bork (n 529).
574. Padilla and Evans (n 553) 74.
575. For early criticism of the Chicago school, *see e.g.* Jens Fejø, *Monopolret og marked. Studier i EF-konkurrenceretten med US-amerikansk antitrustret som sammenligningsgrundlag og med støtte i markedsøkonomisk grundteori* (Jurist- og økonomforbundets forlag 1985) 97–103 and in English in Fejø (n 135); and more recent criticism is presented in Khan (n 564); Lina Khan, 'The Ideological Roots of America's Market Power Problem' (2018) 127 Yale Law Journal 960.

The Post-Chicago school. Over time, the Post-Chicago school took over and became the prevailing antitrust policy in the USA.[576] It combined microeconomic tools, which were the foundations of the Chicago school, with other methodologies, such as game theory, and identified certain failures of the Chicago rationale.[577] For example, the Post-Chicago approach to antitrust expressed restrictions on Chicago's pro-market views, holding that much of the business conduct analysed could have both consumer welfare-enhancing and -diminishing effects, depending on their characteristics.[578] With the rise of the Post-Chicago school, strong formal economic reasoning and the role of economic experts grew in importance. In general it can be noted that both the Chicago and Post-Chicago schools increased antitrust law's technicality and the use of abstract neoclassical economic theories and concepts.[579]

In sum, one of the crucial developments in US antitrust law and interpretation over the last century has been the shift to consumer prices becoming the dominant metric for assessing competition. The Chicago school revolution in US antitrust law entailed a move away from market structure and competitive process, and price theory came to replace a structure-based view of competition.[580]

This has naturally involved implications for doctrine and enforcement. Whereas until the late 1970s antitrust law used to be seen as key to preserving economic and political freedom, the Chicago and Post-Chicago schools turned antitrust into a technical concern and broadened the gap between antitrust enforcement and public concern.[581] Moreover, this shift discarded 'the historic concern about halting the momentum toward concentration in an industry, in order to arrest the economic, political, and social harms from concentrated economic power in their incipiency'.[582] According to Stucke and Ezrachi, 'antitrust's noneconomic goals were jettisoned'.[583]

Today, US antitrust policy can be characterized as relying on strong economic analysis and on the maximization of consumer surplus in the sense of total consumer surplus.[584] Despite the successful penetration of the Chicago school's thinking, Bork's view of consumer welfare as total welfare was never adopted by the courts, which generally understand consumer welfare as total consumer surplus.[585] This rule of reason approach largely governs US antitrust analysis of unilateral conduct, setting a high burden of proof for plaintiffs, including the American government, when bringing

576. Hovenkamp (n 558) 38–39.
577. There are a number of scholarly works concerning game theory. For further reading on game theory in a legal context, *see e.g.* Douglas G Baird, Robert H Gertner and Randal C Picker, *Game Theory and the Law* (Harvard University Press 1994, 4th edn 2000); Louis Philips, *Competition Policy: A Game-Theoretic Perspective* (CUP 1995).
578. Padilla and Evans (n 553) 74.
579. Maurice E Stucke and Ariel Ezrachi, 'The Rise, Fall, and Rebirth of the U.S. Antitrust Movement' Harvard Business Review (15 December 2017) https://hbr.org/2017/12/the-rise-fall-and-rebirth-of-the-u-s-antitrust-movement, accessed 19 April 2020.
580. Khan (n 564) 717.
581. Stucke and Ezrachi (n 579).
582. *Ibid.*
583. *Ibid.*
584. Einer Elhauge, 'Tying, Bundled Discounts, and the Death of the Single Monopoly Profit Theory' (2009) 123 Harvard Law Review 435–439.
585. *Ibid.*, 437–438.

claims against dominant companies under Section 2 of the Sherman Act. In practice, there has been very little antitrust enforcement and few prosecutions concerning abuse of dominance in the USA.[586]

The scarce enforcement against dominant companies in the USA is also explained by US antitrust law allowing companies with lawfully acquired market power to earn supra-competitive profits (or charge excessive prices) that follow from their market position. This stands in stark contrast to the special obligation prescribed for dominant companies by EU competition law, whereby they have 'a special responsibility not to allow their conduct to impair undistorted competition on the common market'.[587] An outstanding example in this regard is the opinion of Judge Learned Hand cited earlier[588] that reflects the diverging approaches to competition in the EU and the USA and shows that the American judge's opinion does not fit well with EU competition law's 'special' responsibility of dominant companies. As mentioned, when comparing to the US, EU competition policy reflects more of a 'big is bad' ideological perspective, whereas enforcement is less aggressive in the USA and the antitrust authorities tend to be sceptical of complaints by competitors. The general view is that US antitrust policy encourages monopolists.

Illustrative in this respect are the comments in 2018 by the head of the Antitrust Division of the US DOJ addressing the enforcement gap with Europeans: 'European competition law still imposes a "special duty" on dominant market players, while we in the US do not believe any such duty exists.'[589] He acknowledged his agency's 'particular concerns in digital markets' but absent 'demonstrable harm to competition and consumers, we are reluctant to impose special duties on digital platforms, out of our concern that special duties might stifle the very innovation that has created dynamic competition for the benefit of consumers'.[590]

On another occasion, the Assistant Attorney General defended the lack of enforcement action in the USA against major technology players such as Google and Facebook, saying that the absence of antitrust intervention reflects the success of US antitrust law because American business has produced so many significant innovators:[591]

> I define US antitrust law's success as the fact that we have these innovators. We have the Googles and the Facebooks and the Microsofts and the Ubers and the AirBnBs coming out of the United States. How many of those innovative companies are coming out of Europe or Korea or China?

586. Stucke and Ezrachi (n 579).
587. *Michelin v Commission* (n 397) para. 57.
588. *See* above §3.02.
589. Speech by Assistant Attorney General Makan Delrahim, 'Good Times, Bad Times, Trust Will Take Us Far: Competition Enforcement and the Relationship Between Washington and Brussels' Remarks at the College of Europe (Brussels, 21 February 2018).
590. *Ibid.*
591. Leah Nylen, 'US Hands-Off Approach Has Helped Google, Uber, Others Thrive, DOJ's Delrahim Says' Mlex ITC & Media (22 June 2018) citing speech by Makan Delrahim, Assistant Attorney General for Antitrust, The 40th Anniversary of Robert Bork's The Antitrust Paradox (n 529).

Clearly, there have been, and will continue to be, some differences between the US and EU approaches to antitrust enforcement and how dominant companies are treated.[592]

So, in contrast to EU competition law, there is no comparative doctrine on exploitative abuses in US antitrust law. The ruling of the US Supreme Court in *Trinko* suggested that the Sherman Act sanctions only exclusionary conduct that harms competitors, rather than exploitative abuses that harm consumers.[593] In *Trinko*, the US Supreme Court stated that:[594]

> The mere possession of monopoly power, and the concomitant opportunity to charge monopoly prices, is not only not unlawful; it is an important element of the free-market system. The opportunity to charge monopoly prices – at least for a short period – is what attracts business acumen in the first place.

This leads to an interesting issue, namely which law is used to address problematic market conduct of an exploitative nature. Unlike in Europe, where EU competition law is the primary tool used to address exploitative abuses, in the USA such practices are not addressed by antitrust laws, but they are rather prosecuted in the context of the American consumer law framework.[595] The US FTC can investigate discriminatory pricing and unfair contractual clauses under Section 5 of the FTC Act.[596] This stands in contrast to the situation in Europe, where Article 102 of the TFEU specifically lists a variety of exploitative conduct as examples of abuse of a dominant position.[597]

Another diverging point between EU and US antitrust law is the role of fairness as a value and philosophical foundation. In the US, the concept of fairness as an underlying purpose and policy goal of antitrust law has generally been less evident in competition rhetoric than in the EU.

One may note, however, that in recent times, with increasing public concern and criticism against concentration in digital markets, the notion of fairness has been referred to by some antitrust enforcers also in the USA. Interesting in this regard is former US Assistant Attorney General Renata Hesse referring to 'promot[ing] the

592. Similarly, *see* speech by Makan Delrahim, Assistant Attorney General for Antitrust, Antitrust and the Digital Economy: 'New Challenges for International Cooperation?' Bocconi University Milan, reported by MLex Market Insight, US Reluctant to Impose Special Duties on Digital Platforms, Delrahim tells antitrust audience in EU (25 May 2018).

593. Botta and Wiedemann (n 95) 6 fn 7.

594. *US Supreme Court, Verizon Communications Inc v Trinko*, 40 U.S. 398 (2004).

595. For a comparison of the EU and US approach to sanction exploitative conducts under competition law, *see* Michal Gal, 'Monopoly Pricing as an Antitrust Offense in the US and the EC: Two Systems of Belief about Monopoly?' (2004) 49 Antitrust Bulletin 343–384.

596. Section 5(a) provides the FTC the power to prosecute 'unfair methods of competition and unfair or deceptive acts or practices in or affecting commerce'. Federal Trade Commission Act, 15 USC, Sections 41–58, as amended.

597. By studying the *travaux préparatoires* of the Rome Treaty, Pinar Akman has concluded that the initial intention of the EU founding fathers was to address and sanction via Article 102 TFEU primarily exploitative conduct, rather than exclusionary practices. *See* Pinar Akman, 'Searching for the Long-Lost Soul of Article 82 EC' (2009) 29 OJLS 267–303.

interests of the public over the power of the few' and 'the ultimate goal of antitrust, economic fairness'.[598] She continued:

> The language of economic theory does not sound like the language of economic fairness that is the raw material for most popular discussions about competition and antitrust. [...] Animating the beliefs of ordinary Americans who demand vigorous antitrust enforcement are the value of fairness and the belief that properly functioning competitive markets are themselves fair. To say it another way, competition is fair because it gives a chance to the small business owner to succeed in her business venture, because it delivers lower prices to consumers, and because it drives the innovation that improves products, business processes, and more.[599]

Nevertheless, the dominating view in US antitrust law places little emphasis on fairness or other social, political or non-price dimensions.[600] Similarly, in US antitrust law, one does not see much of another underlying core value of EU competition law, namely freedom of choice.

The 'freedom of choice' approach to EU competition law is different from the traditional American views on abuses of dominance.[601] With its concern in competition enforcement about choices for consumers, EU competition law has generally had a more distributive character than its American counterpart.[602]

This focus in Europe on consumers' freedom of choice is sometimes said to protect competitors instead of competition.[603] Some argue that preserving choice has translated into enforcement that disfavours efficient competitors.[604] Compared to the USA, it is true that Europe has more of an interventionist flavour and can be regarded as a more favourable jurisdiction for a finding of a competition infringement.[605] This is perhaps also explained by EU competition rules having numerous objectives embedded in the law. At times, EU's more interventionist competition enforcement (in comparison with the USA) has been called protectionist. One may wonder whether there is any truth in this.

Protectionism. The classic complaint about the protection-of-competition goal is that it can become protectionist by protecting the inefficient against the efficient. This

598. Renata Hesse, 'And Never the Twain Shall Meet? Connecting Popular and Professional Visions for Antitrust Enforcement', Presentation at the Global Antitrust Enforcement Symposium (Washington, DC, 20 September 2016).
599. *Ibid.*
600. For example, former FTC Chair Maureen Ohlhausen, 'Antitrust Enforcement in the Digital Age' Georgetown University (12 September 2017) ('Given the clear consumer benefits of technology-driven innovation, I am concerned about the push to adopt an approach that will disregard consumer benefits in the pursuit of other perhaps even conflicting goals').
601. Gavil et al. (n 510) 639–640.
602. Nihoul (n 496) 9.
603. Whish and Bailey (n 300) 22.
604. *See* Kovacic (n 512) 805.
605. *See* generally Francesco Russo et al., *European Commission Decisions on Competition* (CUP 2010) 113–197, analysing and classifying all competition decisions of the European Commission from 1962 to 2009.

is captured in the often misused slogan that 'competition is meant to protect competition, not competitors'.[606] Perhaps the most famous criticism against the EU's 'big is bad' ideological perspective came from former US President Barack Obama, who called the EU's actions protectionist in an interview in 2015:[607]

> [Americans] have owned the Internet. Our companies have created it, expanded it, perfected it in ways that [European companies] can't compete. And oftentimes what is portrayed as high-minded positions on issues sometimes is just designed to carve out some of their commercial interests.

In response to the European Commission investigations into Google, Facebook and other American companies, Obama is quoted as saying:[608]

> In defence of Google and Facebook, sometimes the European response here is more commercially driven than anything else. As I've said, there are some countries like Germany, given its history with the Stasi, that are very sensitive to these issues. But sometimes their vendors – their service providers who, you know, can't compete with ours – are essentially trying to set up some roadblocks for our companies to operate effectively there.

The European Commission's investigations and decisions in recent years against big technology companies for not only anticompetitive behaviour but also other issues such as tax avoidance and mishandling of private data have come under criticism and been described as aggressive and as unfairly targeting American companies.[609] Current US President Trump has also voiced his concern on European antitrust protectionism, tweeting about 'Europeans using privacy and antitrust to harm American jobs'.[610]

One should be mindful of believing this protectionist chatter and rhetoric. In reality, these concerns seem to rest on a few famous anecdotes. There is little evidence that the EU would systematically use its authority to protectionist ends by deliberately

606. *See e.g.* Tim Wu, 'After Consumer Welfare, Now What? The "Protection of Competition" Standard in Practice' (April 2018) Competition Policy International Antitrust Chronicle 8.
607. Kara Swisher, 'White House. Red Chair. Obama Meets Swisher' Recode (15 February 2015) https://www.recode.net/2015/2/15/11559056/white-house-red-chair-obama-meets-swisher, accessed 19 April 2020.
608. *Ibid.*
609. For example, in 2016, the European Commission ordered Ireland to reclaim EUR 13 billion in back taxes on the basis that the company had illegally received a tax break that was not available to others. In June 2017, the European Commission fined Google a record USD 2.7 billion in *Google Search* for unfairly favouring some of its own services over those of rivals (*see* n 46). In January 2018 another record USD 1.2 billion fine was issued to chip maker Qualcomm for abuse of dominance to squeeze out competitors in the EU. Sarah Lyall, 'Who Strikes Fear into Silicon Valley? Margrethe Vestager, Europe's Antitrust Enforcer' The New York Times (5 May 2018) https://www.nytimes.com/2018/05/05/world/europe/margrethe-vestager-silicon-valley-data-privacy.html, accessed 19 April 2020. For public media criticism against EU enforcement actions, *see e.g.* Chad Bray, 'EU Fines Qualcomm $1.2 Billion Over Apple Deal' New York Times (24 January 2018) https://www.nytimes.com/2018/01/24/business/eu-qualcomm-fine-antitrust.html, accessed 19 April 2020.
610. Tweet by @realdonaldtrump: 'Europeans use privacy and antitrust to harm American jobs. Very sad. WILL REACT!' *See* Tiku (n 160).

targeting American companies (with the alleged aim of facilitating the creation of European national champions).[611]

[C] Self-Correcting Markets or Failing Laissez-Faire

As the discussion on the development of US antitrust law shows, starting in the 1970s, enforcers and courts abandoned political, social and moral goals of antitrust and shifted to a single economic goal, namely maximization of economic welfare. Consumer prices became the dominant metric for assessing competition. This reflected the wide adoption of the Chicago school and Bork's assertion that '[t]he only legitimate goal of antitrust is the maximization of consumer welfare', best pursued through promoting economic efficiency.[612]

However, this quest for a single economic goal in US antitrust law can also be seen as a sort of failure, as Stucke argues.[613] Today US antitrust law is criticized for not having either an antitrust movement or much enforcement.[614] The main reason for this is over-reliance on an incomplete notion of competition coming from the Chicago school's simplified assumptions of self-correcting markets that are made up of rational, self-interested market participants.[615] Especially in today's digital economy, it can be argued that US antitrust law's pegging competition to consumer welfare defined as short-term price effects is ill-equipped to capture the architecture of market power.[616]

Looking back at the historical foundation of the antitrust statutes, current criticism against price-driven US antitrust law contends that the goal of consumer welfare in an economic sense did not actually have a foothold in the antitrust statutes. The US Supreme Court simply followed Bork's policy prescriptions and in 1979 declared, without further elaboration or discussion, that 'Congress designed the Sherman Act as a "consumer welfare prescription".'[617] This philosophy wound its way into US antitrust policy, although the statement by the Supreme Court has widely been regarded as erroneous by antitrust scholars.[618] After all, antitrust laws were originally intended to protect consumers and competitors against concentrations of market

611. For discussion and challenging of European antitrust protectionism in the context of merger control in particular, *see* Anu Bradford, Robert J Jackson Jr and Jonathon Zytnick, 'Protectionism? An Empirical Analysis' (2017) 15 Journal for Empirical Legal Studies 165–191. This analysis of more than 5,000 merger cases reported to the EU competition regulator between 1990 and 2014 reveals no evidence of protectionism. If anything, the results suggest that the EU is less likely to challenge transactions involving non-EU acquirers, according to the analysis.
612. *See* Bork (n 529) 7; 405: 'The only goal that should guide interpretation of the antitrust laws is the welfare of consumers ... In judging consumer welfare, productive efficiency, the single most important factor contributing to that welfare, must be given due weight along with allocative efficiency.'
613. Maurice E Stucke, 'Reconsidering Antitrust's Goals' (2012) 53 Boston College Law Review 551.
614. Stucke and Ezrachi (n 579).
615. Stucke (n 613) 551.
616. Khan (n 564) 742.
617. *Reiter v Somotone Corp*, 442 US (1979) 330, 343 (quoting Bork at 66).
618. *See* Barak Orbach, 'Foreword: Antitrust's Pursuit of Purpose' (2013) 81 Fordham Law Review 2151, 2152.

power. Antitrust policy was a reaction to the excesses of corporate America and 'robber barons'[619] at the beginning of the 20th century.[620]

The orientation of US antitrust law towards material rather than political and social ends has been described as embracing 'concentration over competition'[621] with vocal critics, such as Lina Khan, today maintaining that 'the United States has a monopoly problem'.[622] Economic factors that are easier to measure, such as impacts on price and output, have become disproportionately important in the application of US antitrust law.[623] According to Eleanor Fox, Chicagoans 'assert an ahistorical view of antitrust' by rationalizing the history of antitrust to fit their economic efficiency-based model.[624] In doing so, they ignore historical antitrust goals by declaring that the only significant objective of the Congress that passed the Sherman Act was to enhance consumer welfare, 'a term that they then misdefine'.[625]

Fox is one of many leading critics who question the Chicago view that antitrust is solely about consumer welfare defined as wealth maximization.[626] Looking back at the evolution and legislative history of US antitrust, she argues that in fact there has been a range of policy goals beyond, including non-price aspects, such as concern for consumers, concern for the 'little man', interest in access, diversity, and pluralism, and condemnation of exploitation.[627] Over time, these non-price dimensions were forgotten in the quest for a single price-centric approach to antitrust law.

'The New Brandeis' movement. In the USA, a new group of scholars and antitrust activists is rebelling against Chicago school dictates and expressing concern about the state of US antitrust enforcement and policy.[628] They are calling into question the philosophy of competition policy and antitrust that has prevailed in America for the last

619. 'Robber baron' is a derogatory metaphor of social criticism originally applied to certain late 19th-century American businessmen who used unscrupulous methods to acquire wealth. The metaphor appeared as early as in 1859, when *The New York Times* characterized unethical business practices by Cornelius Vanderbilt. Historian TJ Stiles says the metaphor 'conjures up visions of titanic monopolists who crushed competitors, rigged markets, and corrupted government. In their greed and power, legend has it, they held sway over a helpless democracy'. *See* TJ Stiles, '"Robber Barons or Captains of Industry?" The Gilder Lehrman Institute of American History' (June 2010) 24 History Now.
620. *See* discussion on the origins of US antitrust law in §3.01.
621. Khan (n 564) 742.
622. *Ibid.*, 564. *See also* Lina Khan, 'The New Brandeis Movement: America's Antimonopoly Debate' (2018) 9 Journal of European Competition Law & Practice 131; Khan (n 575) 960.
623. Khan (n 564) 564.
624. Eleanor M Fox, 'The Battle for the Soul of Antitrust' (1987) 75 California Law Review 918.
625. *See* Eleanor M Fox, 'Consumer Beware Chicago' (1986) 84 Michigan Law Review 1714; Eleanor M Fox, 'The Politics of Law and Economics in Judicial Decision Making: Antitrust as a Window' (1986) 61 New York University Law Review 554, 585–588.
626. Fox (n 625) 918; Eleanor M Fox, 'The Modernization of Antitrust: A New Equilibrium' (1981) 66 Cornell Law Review 1140. For further discussion, *see* Robert Pitofsky (ed.), *How the Chicago School Overshot the Mark: The Effect of Conservative Economic Analysis on US Antitrust* (OUP 2008) 56.
627. *Ibid.*, describing how politicians have called for a halt to the dangerous trend towards industrial concentration and argued for preserving 'small, independent, decentralized business', and thus saving the country from a fate like Nazism. *See also* Hans B Thorelli, *The Federal Antitrust Policy: Origination of an American Tradition* (Johns Hopkins Press 1955) (presenting a Swedish scholar's detailed history of American antitrust).
628. The Economist, Schumpeter (n 384).

thirty-five years. This more progressive and antimonopoly school of thought is led by younger scholars such as Lina Khan, author of the debated article 'Amazon's Antitrust Paradox', and this school has been labelled or named the 'New Brandeis movement'.[629]

According to the New Brandeis movement, focusing antitrust exclusively on consumer welfare is a mistake. A range of other interests can be harmed, and these deserve protection. The movement argues that antitrust law's focus on consumer welfare should be replaced with a broader social and political antimonopoly programme:

> Focusing antitrust exclusively on consumer welfare is a mistake. For one, it betrays legislative intent, which makes clear that Congress passed antitrust laws to safeguard against excessive concentrations of economic power. This vision promotes a variety of aims, including the preservation of open markets, the protection of producers and consumers from monopoly abuse, and the dispersion of political and economic control.[630]

As the name suggests, the new movement traces its intellectual roots to Justice Louis Brandeis, who served on the Supreme Court between 1916 and 1939. Brandeis was a strong proponent of America's Madisonian traditions, which aim at a democratic distribution of power and opportunity in the political economy. Brandeis wrote: '[w]e can have democracy in this country, or we can have great wealth concentrated in the hands of a few, but we can't have both'.[631] Before reaching the Supreme Court, Brandeis advised President Woodrow Wilson in the election of 1912, condemning 'the curse of bigness' and favouring break-ups of those trusts that the Sherman Act had yet to dismantle.[632] Brandeis influenced America's antimonopoly regime, along Madisonian lines, for the industrial era, and his philosophy held sway into the 1970s.

With the rise of this more progressive and antimonopoly New Brandeis school, the American antitrust movement could perhaps be undergoing an emerging change. Supporters of the movement describe this potential shift as a 'rebirth'[633] or 'the pendulum is swinging the other way'.[634] Indeed, there are some signs of increasing calls for US antitrust policy to be reinvigorated; for example, the Obama administration's council of economic advisers linked rising market power with inequality and other ills; US Senators have suggested reinvigorating competition policy; and the

629. David Dayen, 'This Budding Movement Wants to Smash Monopolies' The Nation (4 April 2017) https://www.thenation.com/article/this-budding-movement-wants-to-smash-monopolies/, accessed 19 April 2020.
630. Khan (n 564) 710, 743. For an argument critiquing this kind of interpretation of the Sherman Act, *see* Joseph V Coniglio, 'How the "New Brandeis Movement" Already Overshoots the Mark: Sketching an Alternative Theory for Understanding the Sherman Act as a Consumer Welfare Prescription' (2017) October Competition Policy International North America Column.
631. As an interesting side note, there seems to be little evidence of the origins of this well-known quote by Brandeis, *see* Peter Scott Campbell, 'Democracy v. Concentrated Wealth – In Search of a Louis D. Brandeis Quote' (2013) University of Louisville School of Law Legal Studies Research Paper Series No 2014-11.
632. Under President Wilson, Congress closed Sherman Act loopholes with the Clayton Antitrust Act and created the FTC to combat monopoly power.
633. Stucke and Ezrachi (n 579); Khan (n 622) 131–132.
634. Stucke and Ezrachi (n 579).

Democratic Party has identified antitrust enforcement as a key pillar of its economic agenda.[635]

Others are more critical of the New Brandeis movement, arguing that 'courts should not look to adjudicate the merits of abstract social or political theories' and US antitrust policy 'should not involve philosophical exercises in social or political theory in the light of the difficulties associated with formulating objective enforcement standards'.[636]

In many ways, the increased attention towards the policy goals of US antitrust law echoes discussions in Europe, where the competition community is debating whether and to what degree competition law should embody values of fairness.[637] The New Brandeis movement's concern with the effects of market concentration and monopolies on economic freedom appears similar to that of ordoliberals such as Walter Eucken, who saw market power as a threat to the individual's liberty to participate in economic life.[638] Despite the American jurisdiction not sharing the same ordoliberal legal and historical tradition with Europe, calls by the New Brandeis movement for a more dynamic approach to US antitrust policy may indeed suggest the beginning of an intellectual shift that, if further developed and materialized, would bring EU and US antitrust policy closer to each other. The unease in the USA with the current antitrust model and how it seems non-optimal for the digital age would support a more ordoliberal approach that would be more inclusive towards non-price policy goals in antitrust law. Whether this fits well with the current situation in the US lacking doctrine on exploitative abuses is another question.

§3.05 SUMMARY

In this chapter, the different policy goals of EU and US competition law have been explored. Even though the EU and US competition regimes look similar at first glance and share the same basic principles, their policy objectives have evolved in very different directions until the present day. Europe's approach and underlying philosophy to competition diverge in many ways from that in the USA. Most notably, non-price dimensions are more significantly embedded in EU competition law, which is multidimensional and provides a range of policy goals, including the ordoliberal understanding of freedom of choice and the concept of fairness. Conversely, US antitrust policy is much more focused on the role of price, which is a consequence of the influential Chicago school that excluded political and social goals from US antitrust law.

Despite the divergent approaches to competition policy in the EU and the USA, a common trend affects both jurisdictions, which is digitalization and data becoming increasingly important in shaping markets as an enormously valuable asset, and a new kind of currency. With the transition to a data-driven economy and an increasingly

635. Khan (n 622) 131.
636. *Ibid. See also* Coniglio (n 630) and by the same author 'Why the "New Brandeis Movement" Gets Antitrust Wrong' (2018) Law 360.
637. Khan (n 622) 131.
638. *See e.g.* Ahlborn and Grave (n 503).

technological and complex landscape, competition policy in both the EU and the USA will somehow need to consider these changes and adapt to a new market reality. As explored in this chapter, in Europe there are now calls for a more dynamic approach to competition to reflect traditional ordoliberal thinking characterized by rejection of a static approach to competition but rather defining competition as a dynamic concept. The time may be ripe for a comeback of ordoliberalism in EU competition policy.

Similarly, in the USA, the digitalization and increasing concentration of technology markets have brought about an emerging rebellion against Chicago school thinking of competition as dominated by price effects. The New Brandeis movement wants to change the current laissez-faire approach to US antitrust policy and operate a more interventionist enforcement against monopolies. To what degree this intellectual movement will influence the American competition regime in the coming years is an open question. Currently, these voices are mainly of a small group of scholars, meaning that to date US antitrust law remains heavily price-oriented. In other words, one may conclude here that US antitrust law currently leaves little room for a non-price dimension to play a role in American antitrust policy.

Conversely, EU competition law's multidimensional character gives weight to policy goals other than price, enabling – at least in theory – inclusion of data privacy among its non-price competition parameters. This interlinkage between privacy and competition will be discussed in the following chapter.

CHAPTER 4

Interlinkage Between Competition and Data Privacy

According to the traditional view and conventional treatment of competition and privacy, the regimes are completely separate areas with distinct aims. However, increasingly the two fields of competition and data protection law coexist and interact with each other. This chapter explores indications that the historical hard line between competition and privacy is softening, looks at similarities and commonalities between the fields and considers potential for convergence and synergies. The role of privacy is becoming more visible especially in EU competition law with the growing attention from national competition authorities and academia. This development has culminated in the German Facebook dominance case, where the Bundeskartellamt was a pioneer in merging competition and data protection law in a bold precedent. This chapter explores these recent developments and discusses the increasing interplay between competition and privacy. The chapter questions whether in this context there is transatlantic divergence or convergence and whether US antitrust law is lagging behind EU competition law. Lastly, the chapter looks at possible implications more broadly from a global perspective.

§4.01 INTRODUCTION

You cannot talk about privacy in the digital age without talking about market power. It is a fact that today only a few companies determine what most people see on the Internet. This is possible because those companies have accumulated staggering amounts of data.[639]

639. Speech by Giovanni Buttarelli, 'Privacy and Competition: Big Issues for Big Data' IAPP Global Privacy Summit (Washington, DC, 27–28 March 2018).

This book asserts the idea that the conventional boundaries between competition law and privacy are undergoing some sort of convergence and increased interconnection. The traditional strict and distinct separation between the two areas no longer holds true in the new data economy. In this regard, at a global privacy summit in Washington, DC in 2018, it was proclaimed that in the coming years European regulators would increasingly be looking to dissolve the traditional wall between privacy and antitrust.[640] Germany's competition authority is already 'deeply convinced privacy is a competition issue',[641] and the French competition agency sees 'the importance of privacy rules [in] really shaping the way the market is working, and this needs to be taken into account in our competitive analysis'.[642]

In and of itself, the role played by data and privacy in shaping markets in the digital economy increasingly supports considering them as parameters in a competition assessment.[643] This would mean that competition regulators will likely need with increasing frequency to tackle privacy and the accumulation and use of personal data as a dimension in competitive assessment in investigations and merger reviews.[644] One may wonder whether this is desirable, and if so, how it can be done. In other words, provided it is conceptually clear that privacy can play a role in competition, how to overcome the challenges in making this approach fully operational? In the following Chapters 5 and 6, this book aims to address these open questions.[645]

Data protection is undoubtedly of generally growing importance with the ever-increasing presence of data-driven businesses and digital services present in the modern economy and society. The passing of the EU's comprehensive new privacy law, the GDPR, which has more teeth than its predecessor, has made digital privacy a buzzword across industries and sectors. The data privacy scandal concerning Facebook and Cambridge Analytica has surely alerted citizens to the topic. It is suggested that, in the digital age, privacy has become the new antitrust, and the importance that antitrust had in the industrial revolution is being overtaken by privacy in the digital age.[646] Looking at the big picture, the setting looks quite similar, with increasing concentration of corporate control over markets, consumers, and even to some extent the political process. The power of Zuckerberg and Gates is perhaps not much unlike

640. *Ibid.*
641. Andreas Mundt, 'Policy and Enforcement Choices' Online Markets and Offline Welfare Effects, Oxford Center for Competition Law and Policy Conference (22 May 2017).
642. Isabelle de Silva (French Competition Authority) cited by Vesela Gladicheva, 'EU Privacy Rules Key to Competition Analyses, Head of France's Antitrust Watchdog Says' (4 May 2018) GCR Live, 7th Annual Telecoms, Media & Technology.
643. Ezrachi (n 369) 18.
644. Speech by Edith Ramirez, 'Privacy and Competition: Big Issues for Big Data' IAPP Global Privacy Summit (Washington, DC, 27–28 March 2018).
645. This topic is elaborated in two articles by the author that relate to and in substance largely form part of this book, *see* Maria Wasastjerna, 'EU Competition Policy for the Digital Economy' (2019) 24 Columbia Journal of European Law; 'The Role of Data and Digital Privacy in Merger Review' (2019) 14 European Competition Journal 417– 444.
646. Omer Tene, 'Privacy Is the New Antitrust' IAPP Privacy Perspectives (15 January 2015) https://iapp.org/news/a/privacy-is-the-new-antitrust-introducing-the-ftc-casebook/, accessed 19 April 2020.

that of Ford and Rockefeller.[647] Then, as now, the harm of monopolies and privacy infringements is not easy to articulate and quantify. Much like the Chicago school critics who proclaimed antitrust policy as based on insubstantial economics, other critics are now arguing that privacy harms, especially as elements of a competition assessment, are fluid and imprecise. While some of the overarching policy questions remain the same, others are more specific to privacy in digital markets, such as what is a reasonable level of protection in terms of one's personal information.

Faced with these novel issues raised by the data economy, competition authorities are making data and its implications for competition law a key focus.[648] It is now generally accepted that data is the price consumers pay for access to various online offerings and to platforms like Facebook and Google.[649] But how that data is to be treated has only recently become a competition issue. Whereas this question concerning data and how personal information is treated by businesses is obviously of concern to data protection and consumer agencies, it is now also of real interest to competition authorities, who are grappling with the question how data should play a role in competition policy.

The first tentative steps have been taken by some authorities and academics in identifying the challenges and articulating possible concerns raised by the data-driven economy for competition policy. These will be discussed in the following and throughout when examining the interplay between privacy and competition.

In particular, national competition authorities in Europe have actively been contributing to the discourse through reports, investigations and cases. As a result of numerous reports and studies looking into competition in the digital age, 2019 has even been referred to as a 'year of reports'.[650] Clearly, an ongoing trend is under way where, through diverse enquiries and studies, national authorities articulate the possible risks connected to data, especially in the context of companies collecting and commercializing the personal data of online users. This activity by national agencies is interesting and means that they are contributing to the shaping of competition policy in the data economy. Some commentators have hinted that this activity by national authorities in Europe shows that they – not the European Commission – are now the main regulators in the driving seat in the digital age. Wherever the balance lies, it is clear that activities by the various national agencies are helpful in understanding the impact on competition law of the big data phenomenon and how personal data should be considered in competition law and policy. The follow-up question that naturally arises is that if 2019 was the 'year of reports', will 2020 and the coming years be the 'years of action'?

The various key developments, cases and reports so far in the field are compiled and presented in Figure 4.1. The aim is to provide a high-level and non-exhaustive overview and illustration of the rising tide of investigations and efforts related to data and privacy.

647. *Ibid.*
648. Speech by Vestager (n 8).
649. *See* discussion in Chapter 2, §2.02.
650. *See e.g.* Freshfields Bruckhaus Deringer, 'The Digitised Economy' (2019) https://www.freshfields.com/en-gb/our-thinking/campaigns/antitrust-10-key-themes/the-digitised-economy/, accessed 19 April 2020.

Figure 4.1 Increase in Data-Related Competition Cases and Studies

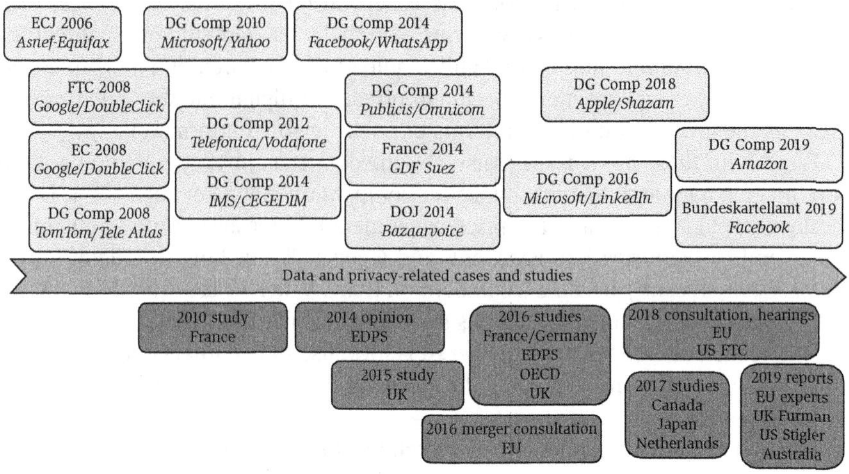

Source: created by the author.

With regard to the figure, a few specific items are worth emphasizing. The UK authority was among the first national agencies to look into the role of data in competition law with the 2015 report by the UK Competition and Markets Authority on the commercial use of consumer data.[651] The authority launched a digital markets strategy and opened a market study on online platforms and digital advertising following publication of a report by the digital competition expert panel led by Professor Jason Furman (former economic adviser to President Obama).[652] The German and French competition authorities have also taken a leading role in focusing on competitive conditions in the digital economy and the role of privacy by publishing a joint study addressing the potential risks associated with the use of algorithms, in addition to their previous 2016 joint study examining the interplay between data and competition law.[653] Following and closely connected to the 2016 report, the German Facebook investigation was opened. In February 2018, the German authority launched a sector enquiry into online advertising, which followed an earlier sector enquiry into online advertising by the French authority in 2016.[654] The Netherlands also carried out a big data-related enquiry, looking into digital platforms and their large-scale data

651. CMA, 'The Commercial Use of Consumer Data: Report on the CMA's Call for Information' (June 2015) (n 168).
652. Jason Furman, Diane Coyle, Amelia Fletcher, Derek McAuley and Philip Marsden, Unlocking digital competition, Report of the Digital Competition Expert Panel (March 2019). The latter Furman report, commissioned by Philip Hammond, advocates for establishing a new independent digital markets unit in the UK, among other far-reaching initiatives.
653. French-German joint report (n 9).
654. Press release, 'Bundeskartellamt launches sector inquiry into market conditions in online advertising sector' (1 February 2018); Autorité de la concurrence, Avis n°18-A-03 portant sur l'exploitation des données dans le secteur de la publicité sur interne (6 March 2018).

collection, and the Dutch Authority for Consumers and Markets released an article entitled 'Big platforms, big problems?' exploring how personal data collected by online platforms can be a source of market power and whether competition law is adequate as an instrument to protect the privacy interests of platform users.[655]

The European Commission has also confirmed its interest in big data, in particular with regard to privacy issues and data as an asset, both in several speeches by the EU Competition Commissioner and, most notably, in the European Commission's 2018 public consultation and commissioned expert report concerning competition policy for the digital era released earlier in 2019.[656] The expert report by three academics considers how EU competition law and policy should evolve to promote pro-consumer innovation in the digital age. The Commission's response to the commissioned report is keenly awaited in the competition community. Further, corporate ownership of data and privacy concerns were key issues in the Commission's competitive assessment of *Microsoft/LinkedIn* and more recently in *Apple/Shazam* and *Google/Fitbit*.[657]

It is not only the authorities in Europe that have been actively following the developments. The OECD issued an insightful paper in 2016 on the implications of big data for competition enforcement and addressed the importance and value of user data and privacy in competition.[658] The intersection between data and competition law is also an emerging field of interest of competition authorities beyond Europe. For example in Japan, a variety of new laws and guidelines have been introduced to regulate digital platforms, including new digital transparency legislation, amended merger guidelines and guidelines on abuse of superior bargaining position concerning use of personal data. The Japanese competition agency has also shown interest in Facebook's data collection practices as a potential competition issue.[659] Canada's competition bureau has factored in big data when modifying its merger guidelines.[660]

655. Dutch Authority for Consumers and Markets, 'Big platforms, big problems?' (September 2016). Available in Dutch: https://www.acm.nl/sites/default/files/old_publication/publicaties/16333_toezicht-online-platforms.pdf, accessed 19 April 2020.
656. *See* speech by Vestager (n 8); European Commission, 'Shaping Competition Policy in the Era of Digitisation' Call for Contributions (12 July 2018); Jacques Crémer, Yves-Alexandre de Montjoye and Heike Schweitzer, Competition Policy for the Digital Era (European Commission 2019).
657. *Microsoft/LinkedIn* (n 413) 8404; Case COMP/M.8788 *Apple/Shazam*, Commission decision of 6/9/2018, not yet reported. The Commission's interest in data is also reflected in the authority weighing possible changes to merger rules to better capture data-focused mergers, *see* European Commission press release, 'Mergers: Commission seeks feedback on certain aspects of EU merger control' (Brussels, 7 October 2016) IP/16/3337 and more recently speech by Margrethe Vestager, 'Keeping the EU Competitive in a Green and Digital World' (Bruges, 2 March 2020). In addition, the question whether the data-driven economy requires introducing changes to the EU merger rules is evaluated in the expert report commissioned by the European Commission concerning competition policy for the digital era, *see* Crémer, de Montjoye and Schweitzer (n 656) 110–124.
658. OECD Big Data (n 22).
659. MLex, 'Japanese Antitrust Chief Says Facebook Data-Collection Competition Issues on JFTC's Radar' (2 April 2018).
660. MLex Market Insight, 'Canada's Competition Enforcers Pondering Big Data, Including in Mergers' (30 March 2017).

In the USA, the FTC has conducted public hearings on competition law in the digital age, created a permanent Technology Enforcement Division and is preparing digital guidelines relating to digital platforms in conjunction with the DOJ.[661] In addition, the so-called Stigler report was published by a group of competition experts and academics at the University of Chicago – of all places, considering its traditionally conservative approach to antitrust – that engaged in the analysis of market concentration, monopoly and digital platforms.[662] Also, the Australian Competition and Consumer Commission (ACCC) published recommendations, which the government followed with a series of proposed regulatory reforms, following an in-depth digital platforms enquiry with the focus more on the effect of digital search engines, social media platforms and other digital content aggregation platforms on competition in the media and advertising services markets.[663] One of the consequences of the increased attention to data in competition law is that powerful digital companies are already facing rising pressure by competition authorities who are looking into alleged abusive practices related to the treatment of data.[664] On this note, the German competition authority's antitrust case against Facebook concerning alleged misuse of user personal data reflects a groundbreaking development in this field.[665] It is a case, the first of its kind, right at the intersection or interface between data protection and competition laws. The final outcome of the case is still pending in an appeals process in German courts.

Before embarking on a closer examination of the relationship between privacy and competition, it is worth recalling the main thrust of the previous chapters. As shown from the transatlantic comparison of privacy regimes in Chapter 2, the view on protecting personal data is notably distinct in these two jurisdictions. EU law's comprehensiveness and fundamental rights protection stands out in contrast to US law's fragmentation and relatively hollow standards, which provide few limits on the treatment of personal data. The EU has generally seen a more favourable approach to state intervention and the German tradition (as well as Germany's Nazi history) has influenced the evolution of a consent-based privacy system expressing the individual's willingness to be protected by the state.

661. US FTC Hearings on Competition and Consumer Protection in the 21st Century, Hearings on Competition & Consumer Protection, Public comment topics and process, available at https://www.ftc.gov/policy/advocacy/public-comment-topics-process#1. Separately, US State Attorneys General have individually and collectively launched investigations into digital platforms.

662. Stigler Center for the Study of the Economy and the State, The University of Chicago Booth School of Business, Report by the Committee for the Study of Digital Platforms, Market Structure and Antitrust Subcommittee (15 May 2019) (Stigler report).

663. Press release Australian Competition and Consumer Commission, 'ACCC commences inquiry into digital platforms' (4 December 2017) https://www.accc.gov.au/media-release/accc-commences-inquiry-into-digital-platforms, accessed 19 April 2020; and final report published in 2019, the Digital Platforms Inquiry Final Report (26 July 2019).

664. Laurence Frost, France to Sue Google, Apple over Developer Contracts' Reuters (14 March 2018) https://www.reuters.com/article/us-apple-google-france/france-to-sue-google-apple-over-developer-contracts-minister-idUSKCN1GQ0SP, accessed 19 April 2020; Bryan Menegus, 'Amazon Japan Raided by Antitrust Agency' Gizmodo (15 March 2018) https://gizmodo.com/amazon-raided-in-japan-by-antitrust-agency-1823794268#, accessed 19 April 2020.

665. Bundeskartellamt press releases and case summary (n 19).

The USA, on the contrary, has always shown mistrust against state power, as is also reflected in that the Sherman Act was originally adopted against Rockefeller and monopolies. As discussed in Chapter 3 when comparing EU and US competition policy goals, EU competition policy - due to its historical and cultural background influenced by ordoliberalism and political aspects - is more flexible to including non-price competition objectives than US antitrust policy, which is predominantly price-driven. Recalling the underlying competition policy motives is of fundamental importance in considering the interlinkage between competition and privacy protection. Moreover, the goals shape how law and policy are implemented and enforced.

As will be shown, the different approaches both to privacy protection and the distinct underlying policy goals of EU and US competition law affect the outcome of the question of the role of privacy in competition policy. These distinct approaches lead to distinctive assumptions on how privacy as a non-price dimension can and should play a role in competition law and policy enforcement in digital markets.

The starting point is that EU competition policy is more apt to incorporate privacy among its non-price competition objectives than US antitrust policy. This statement relies on the understanding that the data economy is characterized by market failures that, in principle, justify the application of competition policy, in spite of overlaps with the policy area of data protection. EU competition law is more apt to incorporate privacy because it generally focuses on *harm to competition*, which allows for other goals beyond economic efficiency, especially considering that market integration was the original competition law mission in the European Community. Conversely, US antitrust law - due to its heavily price-centred focus - is less likely to merge privacy and antitrust goals.

An inevitable consequence of the growing role of data protection law is confluences and potential normative conflicts with other legal fields.[666] This chapter examines the interlinkage between the fields of data protection and competition law. Attempts have been made in the doctrine to analyse and systematize the relationship between competition and privacy in digital markets.[667] However, many distinct and conflicting views are circulating, while scholars and competition enforcers are yet to reach a common understanding on this topic. This book aims to contribute to the current discourse and provide it with some additional perspectives to take the discussion further.

---

666. Eija Warma and Jussi Nieminen, 'Tietosuoja ja kilpailuoikeus - määräävässä markkina-asemassa olevan yrityksen toimitusvelvollisuudesta ja tietosuojalainsäädännöstä' (2016) 4 Defensor Legis 550.

667. *See* especially Costa-Cabral and Lynskey (n 128) 21; Grunes and Stucke (n 126); Allen P Grunes and Maurice E Stucke, 'Debunking the Myths Over Big Data and Antitrust' (2015) University of Tennessee Legal Studies Research Paper No. 276; Damien Geradin and Monika Kuschewsky, 'Competition Law and Personal Data: Preliminary Thoughts on a Complex Issue' (2013) 2 Concurrences; Maureen K Ohlhausen and Alexander P Okuliar, 'Competition, Consumer Protection, and the Right (Approach) to Privacy' (2015) 80 Antitrust Law Journal; Lisa Kimmel and Janis Kestenbaum, 'What's up with WhatsApp? A Transatlantic View on Privacy and Merger Enforcement in Digital Markets' (2014) Antitrust 48; Darren S Tucker, 'The Proper Role of Privacy in Merger Review' (2015) 2 Competition Policy International Antitrust Chronicle.

In the previous chapters, data privacy and competition policy were considered in turn. In this chapter, the two are considered together, so that the focus is on the interlinkage between competition and privacy. This is because, when examining the role of data privacy in competition law, which is the central research question of this book, it comes naturally as a next step to explore the relationship between competition and data protection law. Considerable knowledge is to be gained at the intersection between the disciplines of competition law and data protection. This book challenges the relatively traditional assumption that privacy has little or no role or relevance in competition law.

This book also asserts that despite the conventional separation of the two legal frameworks, the regimes share some important commonalities. Most notably, both show a concern for the welfare of the individual.[668] In Europe, both policies also seek to achieve market integration.[669] In addition, both fields of law are concerned with power asymmetries in which a consumer or individual often occupies a weaker position relative to a company.[670] These commonalities between two legal frameworks facilitate their intersection.

Certainly, the systems involve distinct aims and methods, and their material scope and normative objectives differ in many ways. However, in view of the common objectives of the two legal regimes and other shared similarities, it is possible to identify potential synergies. Synergy potential can be found, for example, through cooperation between the competition and DPAs. The synergy potential based on commonalities is examined in more detail in Chapter 6 when envisioning a conjoined approach to privacy and competition.

In the following chapters, the interlinkage between competition and data privacy is explored. This is done by first looking at how the regimes have traditionally been treated as distinct from each other (§4.02). Second, the commonalities and similarities between the regimes are identified (§4.03). Third, the increasing interplay between competition and privacy is examined by identifying recent important developments, especially the German competition authority's *Facebook* opinion, which falls right at the intersection between competition and data protection law (§4.04).

§4.02 TRADITIONALLY SEPARATE REGIMES

This book challenges the conventional boundaries between competition law and privacy in the data economy; but before doing so, one needs to understand what those conventional boundaries are and how the traditional separation between regimes has played out in practice.

The traditional view has been that, as such, privacy and data protection concerns are typically regarded as matters falling outside the scope of competition law enforcement and protected through their own dedicated laws.[671] In this sense, traditionally,

668. Costa-Cabral and Lynskey (n 128) 21.
669. *Ibid.*
670. *Ibid.*
671. Ezrachi (n 369) 18–19.

the legal fields of competition and data protection have been treated as separate, with distinct aims.[672] This is true for both the EU and the US. Examples of this thinking and application can be found in the case law of competition authorities and courts.

For example, in merger cases, the European Commission has explicitly excluded data protection considerations from the application of competition law, such as in its decisions in *Google/DoubleClick*[673] and *Facebook/WhatsApp*.[674] In the Facebook press release it wrote:

> In the context of this investigation, the Commission analyzed potential data concentration issues only to the extent that it could hamper competition in the online advertising market. Any privacy-related concerns flowing from the increased concentration of data within the control of Facebook as a result of the transaction do not fall within the scope of EU competition law.[675]

The General Court has stated something similar, albeit only in passing. This was in *Asnef* in 2006, which concerned a register containing credit and solvency information about individuals.[676] The Court said:

> any possible issues relating to the sensitivity of personal data are not, as such, a matter for competition law, they may be resolved on the basis of the relevant provisions governing data protection.[677]

Some discussion has taken place on the relationship between competition and privacy in the context of data ever since the 2008 case of *Google/DoubleClick*, a case in which personal data was, for the first time, analysed as an asset, and which received significant public attention.[678]

Today, the existing debate can be viewed as somewhat polarized in that there are those who strongly advocate competition enforcement to prevent consumer harm in the form of privacy of consumers,[679] whereas others see data as just another type of input or strategic asset, thus taking the traditional view that privacy concerns always fall outside the scope of intervention by competition enforcers.[680]

---

672. Warma and Nieminen (n 666) 569.
673. Case COMP/M.4731 *Google/DoubleClick* C(2008) 927.
674. *Facebook/WhatsApp* (n 133) 7239.
675. European Commission press release, 'Mergers: Commission approves acquisition of WhatsApp by Facebook' (Brussels, 3 October 2014).
676. The subject matter of the case was unconnected; it was a reference from a Spanish court on the question whether agreements between financial institutions to share information on customer credit or solvency are liable to restrict competition and the possibility of exemption.
677. Case C-238/05 *Asnef-Equifax*, Judgment of the Court of 23 November 2006, para. 63.
678. *Google/DoubleClick* (n 673). Speech by Joaquín Almunia, 'Competition and Personal Data Protection', Privacy Platform event: Competition and Privacy in Markets of Data (Brussels, 26 November 2012).
679. Grunes and Stucke (n 126); Grunes and Stucke (n 667).
680. *See e.g.* Darren S Tucker and Hill B Wellford, 'Big Mistakes Regarding Big Data' (December 2014) Antitrust Source 3; D Daniel Sokol and Roisin Comerford, 'Does Antitrust Have a Role to Play in Regulating Big Data?' in Blair and Sokol (n 542); Geoffrey A Manne and Ben Sperry, 'The Problems and Perils of Bootstrapping Privacy and Data into an Antitrust Framework' (2015) CPI Antitrust Chronicle. For a comprehensive list of literature reflecting both sides of the debate, *see* Cyril Ritter, 'Bibliography of Materials Relevant to the Interaction of Competition

As will be shown, it is possible on the whole to identify a gradual change in the traditional approach on the separation between competition law and data protection. However, this development has mostly been taking place in Europe, where national competition authorities, the European Commission and academia are driving the debate and thereby contributing to the field's development. This development is, at least to date, not as evident in the USA, although there are signs that this may be shifting, as discussed further in §4.04[D].

The gradual change in approach to the conventional separation between competition law and privacy and a more welcoming attitude to a potential privacy dimension in competition analysis is visible when looking and comparing, for example, the European Commission's assessment in *Google/DoubleClick*, *Facebook/WhatsApp*, and the more recent *Microsoft/LinkedIn* and *Apple/Shazam*.[681] In the two former cases, the Commission strictly dismissed any privacy-related concerns and held that privacy harms flowing from the increased concentration of data resulting from the transaction fell outside the scope of EU competition law.[682] In its more recent review of Microsoft's acquisition of LinkedIn in 2016, the Commission approved the deal only after Microsoft offered certain commitments related to data, including securing competitors' access to certain data. More importantly, in this case, the Commission explicitly held that:

> data privacy was an important parameter of competition.[683]

When commenting on the decision, the EU Competition Commissioner held that:

> by getting commitments from Microsoft that will keep the market open, we've helped to allow companies to compete to protect privacy more effectively.[684]

The development towards a more welcoming attitude to a potential privacy dimension in competition law goes back to *Google/DoubleClick*, which is commonly viewed as the first competition case to treat personal data as an asset in a merger.[685] At the time of the transaction, DoubleClick was the leading provider of an ad-serving technology which targeted ads and monitored their performance, whereas Google, besides being active in online search, provides online advertising space and collects large amounts of personal data.[686] The merger aimed to 'combine not only the two firms' products and services, but also their vast troves of data about consumer

---

Policy, Big Data and Personal Data' (29 September 2016) https://papers.ssrn.com/sol3/papers.cfm?abstract_id=2845590, accessed 19 April 2020.

681. *Microsoft/LinkedIn* (n 413) 8404; *Apple/Shazam* (n 657). On this development generally, *see also* Wasastjerna (n 645).
682. Commission press release (n 675).
683. Commission press release (n 132). *See also* speech by Laitenberger (n 526).
684. Speech by Margrethe Vestager, 'What Competition Can Do – And What It Can't' Chilling Competition Conference (25 October 2017).
685. *Google/DoubleClick* (n 673). Almunia (n 678). However, depending on how one categorizes what constitutes a relevant case from a data and privacy perspective, there are earlier cases where data has played a role, such as in, e.g., *TomTom/Tele Atlas* and other cases mentioned in Figure 4.1. For further reading, *see e.g.* Wasastjerna (n 645).
686. Commission press release, 'Mergers: Commission clears proposed acquisition of DoubleClick by Google' (Brussels, 11 March 2008).

behaviour on the internet'.[687] During the case review, several market operators and civil society groups challenged the merger due to competition concerns and on the basis of privacy.

Opponents of the merger argued that the mere combination of the two companies' assets, especially personal data, would allow the new entity to achieve a market position that could not be replicated by competitors and would thus lead to their progressive marginalization and foreclosure.[688] Publishers and advertisers would have no choice but to have recourse to the merged entity.[689] In the USA, the planned data consolidation also raised concerns among privacy advocates, who filed a complaint with the FTC objecting to the merger on privacy grounds.[690]

During the competitive assessment of the *Google/DoubleClick*, the effect of the increase in the amount of personal information obtained by the combined entity was considered by the competition authorities. However, the investigation found that the combination of information on search behaviour and web-browsing behaviour would not give a competitive advantage in the advertising business that could not be replicated by other players that have access to similar web-usage data.[691] The agencies' market definition has since been criticized as flawed in that the agencies missed the point that other markets were also involved, and especially that they overlooked that the acquisition of DoubleClick may have strengthened Google's position in the multiplatform online advertising market.[692] The merger was cleared unconditionally on both sides of the Atlantic, but in the USA the transaction saw one FTC Commissioner, PJ Harbour, write a strong dissenting opinion claiming that the merger threatened consumer privacy:

> [i]f the Commission closes its investigation at this time, without imposing any conditions on the merger, neither the competition nor the privacy interests of consumers will have been adequately addressed.[693]

---

687. Dissenting Statement of Commissioner Pamela Jones Harbour, *Google/DoubleClick*, FTC File No. 071-0170 (20 December 2007), available at http://www.ftc.gov/sites/default/files/documents/public_statements/statementmatter-google/doubleclick/071220harbour_0.pdf.
688. *Google/DoubleClick* (n 673) 359.
689. Geradin and Kuschewsky (n 667) 12.
690. Complaint and Request for Injunction, Request for Investigation and for Other Relief, *The Electronic Privacy Information Center in the Matter of Google, Inc. and DoubleClick, Inc.* (20 April 2007).
691. Almunia (n 678). Besides, the agencies decided that Google and DoubleClick were not close actual or potential competitors in any markets for online advertising or services. The Commission has relied on similar reasoning, where rivals' access to data post-merger was considered sufficient despite concerns regarding large data pools creating entry barriers, in cases COMP/M.6314 *Telefónica UK/Vodafone UK/Everything Everywhere/JV (Mobile Wallet JV)*, C(2012) 6063; COMP/M.7023 *Publicis/Omnicom*, C(2014) 89, and COMP/M.7337 *IMS/CEGEDIM*, C(2014) 1025.
692. *See* European Parliament, Challenges for Competition Policy in a Digitalized Economy (Study for the ECON Committee, Directorate-General for Internal Policies, Economic and Monetary Affairs, 2015) 54.
693. Harbour Dissenting Statement (n 687).

Since leaving the agency, Harbour has continued to urge enforcers to develop a more sophisticated analytical framework for evaluating the antitrust implications of privacy and big data.[694]

The European Commission, in its approval of *Google/DoubleClick* under EU competition law, made it clear that it assessed the merger only under EU competition law and that the decision was without prejudice to the obligations of the merging parties under privacy legislation. Similarly, in the USA, the FTC concluded that antitrust laws did not provide a basis to impose conditions on a merger (purely) to safeguard privacy. In its closing statement, the FTC held that 'privacy considerations, as such, do not provide a basis to challenge this transaction'.[695] However, it was explicitly recognized that privacy can be a non-price dimension of competition and that the FTC therefore would have the authority to act where a transaction is likely to reduce competition on that basis.[696] This ability to act may, however, also rely on the FTC's powers under the consumer law framework under which it can address unfair contractual clauses (Section 5 FTC Act).

The European Commission largely echoed its *Google/DoubleClick* analysis in the subsequent review of online social networking company Facebook's acquisition of mobile messaging company WhatsApp, and it cleared the merger unconditionally in 2014.[697] The competition analysis focused on the market for advertisements and the potential harm to advertisers resulting from an increase in Facebook's market power through increased data collection capability. The outcome of the Commission assessment was that even if Facebook were to collect and use data from WhatsApp for advertising purposes, valuable user data would remain available to competitors beyond Facebook's exclusive control.[698]

What is important to underline is that the Commission did not examine whether personal data from end users may be collected to a greater extent due to the combination; that is, how consumers' privacy may be affected.[699] Concerns about Facebook holding a significant amount of data were dismissed as strictly a privacy issue, outside the scope of competition law. The case illustrates the challenges of examining the impact of a merger, or performing a competitive assessment more generally, on two-sided or multisided digital markets. In such markets, competition authorities consider the implications of a merger often only on the advertising side but fail to take into account the impact on the 'free' side. This is where the problem lies, as

694. *See* Pamela Jones Harbour, 'The Transatlantic Perspective: Data Protection and Competition Law' in H Hijmans and H Kranenborg (eds), *Data Protection Anno 2014: How To Restore Trust?* (Intersentia 2014) 225; Pamela Jones Harbour & Tara Isa Koslov, 'Section 2 in a Web 2.0 World: An Expanded Vision of Relevant Product Markets' (2010) 76 Antitrust Law Journal 769.

695. Statement of FTC, *Google/DoubleClick*, FTC File No. 071-0170, 3 (20 December 2007) (FTC Google/DoubleClick Statement), available at http://www.ftc.gov/system/files/documents/public_statements/418081/071220googledc-commstmt.pdf.

696. Kimmel and Kestenbaum (n 667) 48.

697. *Facebook/WhatsApp* (n 133).

698. European Commission press release (n 675).

699. *Facebook/WhatsApp* (n 133) para. 164: 'For the purposes of this decision, the Commission has analysed potential data concentration only to the extent that it is likely to strengthen Facebook's position in the online advertising market or in any sub-segments thereof.'

ignoring the effects on the 'free' side of markets may make consumers worse off – through a lowered degree of privacy protection. In *Facebook/WhatsApp*, the Commission considered the data concentration only on the advertising side of the market but did not analyse whether consumers might be harmed if Facebook were to start collecting and using data from WhatsApp users, which was dismissed as a privacy issue going beyond the reach of competition law.[700] The review of *Facebook/WhatsApp* missed the true driver for the deal – capturing more users and monetizing yet more personal data – and ended merger ended with an unconditional clearance because there were no 'conventional' competition concerns – notwithstanding that Facebook actually paid USD 21 billion at the time, or USD 55 per user.[701]

At the time, lively discussion, controversy and objections surrounded the case; in particular, concerns were expressed regarding Facebook's compliance with data protection rules and privacy. The European Commission chose not to deal with the question whether merger clearance should be conditional on strict compliance related to data protection. Conversely, the FTC in its review of the merger in the USA took another approach and sent a letter to the merging parties urging them to continue to honour the promises made to consumers with respect to WhatsApp's privacy policies as well as public statements about privacy made when the transaction was announced.[702] The European Commission rather stated, as it had in *Google/DoubleClick*, that any privacy-related concerns arising from the increased concentration of data as a result of the transaction fall within the scope, not of EU competition rules but of EU data protection rules.[703] While it recognized privacy as one of many parameters of competition between consumer communications apps, and while noting that users increasingly value privacy and security, the Commission concluded that most consumer communications apps on the market do not compete mainly on privacy features.[704]

Since then, things have taken a new turn. During the case assessment, Facebook had pledged that it would not merge the two user bases. However, two years after being granted unconditional clearance for the merger, the company started doing so in 2016.[705] This development led the Commission to question Facebook about its privacy policy changes.[706] Notably, when the acquisition was announced back in 2014, WhatsApp told users that its messaging product and Facebook's existing Messenger app would continue to operate as stand-alone applications and the transaction would not change anything in terms of the treatment of personal data by WhatsApp. As a

700. *Ibid.*
701. Cristina Caffarra and Tommaso Valletti, 'Google/Fitbit Review: Privacy IS a Competition Issue' CEPR Policy Portal (4 March 2020).
702. Failure to honour these promises could constitute deceptive or unfair practices in violation of the FTC Act. *See* Letter from Jessica Rich, Director, Bureau of Consumer Protection, FTC, to Erin Egan, Chief Privacy Officer, Facebook, Inc, and Anne Hoge, General Counsel, WhatsApp Inc (20 April 2014).
703. *Facebook/WhatsApp* (n 133) para. 164.
704. *Ibid.*, 174.
705. Kimmel and Kestenbaum (n 667) 51.
706. Aoife White and Peter Levring, 'Facebook Grilled by EU's Vestager Over WhatsApp Merger U-Turn' Bloomberg Technology (9 September 2016) https://www.bloomberg.com/news/articles/2016-09-09/facebook-grilled-by-eu-s-vestager-over-whatsapp-merger-u-turn, accessed 19 April 2020.

response to privacy concerns raised about the transaction at the time, Facebook's Chief Executive Mark Zuckerberg was reported as proclaiming that Facebook was 'absolutely not going to change plans around WhatsApp and the way it uses user data'.[707]

Finally, in December 2016, the Commission sent Facebook a formal statement of objections for allegedly having provided incorrect or misleading information during the 2014 merger review.[708] According to the charges, the technical possibility of automatically matching Facebook users' IDs with WhatsApp users' IDs already existed in 2014, contrary to Facebook's statements at the time. The outcome of the Commission's investigation was that Facebook received a hefty fine amounting to EUR 110 million – the first time a company had ever been fined for disclosures since the entry into force of the 2004 Merger Regulation. When commenting on this in public, the Commission had stressed that the decision is unrelated to privacy or data protection issues, holding that the fact 'that they didn't merge data wasn't the decisive factor when the merger was approved', noting, however, that this 'was still a part of the decision'.[709] Some have been doubtful of this: 'Now, it [the Commission] claims to have received "incorrect or misleading information" at the time. We dare say that the Commission was probably the only party actually misled [...]' and 'it [the Commission] has merely bent over backwards to emphasise just how unrelated this new investigation is to its 2014 merger clearance decision'.[710]

In this illustrative example of *Facebook/WhatsApp*, the Commission, years after its clearance decision, decided to take action against Facebook – eventually imposing a heavy fine in connection with the combined entity's privacy degradations. The question that arises is whether consumers would not be better off today if the Commission had already in its initial case review also assessed the impact of the merger on the free side of the market, considered the implications for consumers in addition to advertisers, and probed for possible negative effects on non-price parameters, such as privacy protection. Critics also ponder whether Facebook achieved a goal of preventing another competing social network platform from emerging.[711]

Another interesting case from the data and privacy perspective is *Microsoft/LinkedIn*, where data featured as a central issue in the Commission review of Microsoft's acquisition of the LinkedIn professional social network in 2016.[712] Critics of the deal, such as Internet software company Salesforce – whose own bid to buy LinkedIn failed – argued that acquiring LinkedIn would give Microsoft exclusive access to data on how the social network's 450 million users interact. This, so the argument

707. *See* Facebook, WhatsApp blog (19 February 2014) https://blog.whatsapp.com/499/Facebook, accessed 19 April 2020; WhatsApp blog, Why We Don't Sell Ads (18 June 2012) https://blog.whatsapp.com/245/Why-we-dont-sell-ads?, accessed 19 April 2020.

708. European Commission press release, 'Mergers: Commission alleges Facebook provided misleading information about WhatsApp takeover' (Brussels, 20 December 2016) IP/16/4473.

709. European Commission press release, 'Mergers: Commission fines Facebook €110 million for providing misleading information about WhatsApp takeover' (Brussels, 18 May 2017) IP/17/1369.

710. Rating Legis blog, 'Merry Christmas, WhatsApp Users' (23 December 2016) http://ratinglegis.eu/en/eu-commission-looks-at-facebook-whatsapp-deal-again/, accessed 1 August 2019.

711. Caffarra and Valletti (n 701).

712. *Microsoft/LinkedIn* (n 413).

went, would give Microsoft too much control over data and create an unfair advantage over rivals through restricting access to that information, which pre-merger was only available to LinkedIn.[713]

In this case, the Commission went further than before in its analysis by looking at privacy and explicitly noting that data privacy can be an important parameter of competition This time, the merger was not unconditionally cleared, but the outcome of the Commission's review led to commitments being required from Microsoft. This was to protect competition between professional social networks, in three respects. First, for five years, PC manufacturers and distributors can choose whether or not to instal LinkedIn on Windows. Second, competing networks will continue to enjoy certain interoperability with Microsoft products. Third - and importantly - competing networks will be granted access to data stored in Microsoft Cloud.[714]

In its assessment, the Commission stressed the importance of privacy as a parameter of competition. Here, it was explicitly noted that data privacy can be an important parameter of competition and constitutes an important driver of customer choice.[715] The assessment looked at whether existing or potential competitors exist in the market offering a greater degree of privacy protection to users than LinkedIn. The concern was whether the transaction would restrict consumer choice in relation to privacy when choosing which professional social network to use. According to the Commission's investigation:[716]

> the results of the Commission's investigation revealed that, today, in Germany and Austria, Xing seems to offer a greater degree of privacy protection than LinkedIn. For instance, during the registration process, XING asks users to actively accept XING's privacy policy and Terms & Conditions by ticking a box, whereas LinkedIn users accept LinkedIn's privacy policy automatically when they press the button 'join now'. Moreover, when XING introduces new services which have an implication on how it collects and/or uses its members' data, it explicitly seeks active consent from the members. In addition, regardless of whether members give their consent in such specific cases or not, they will be able to continue to use XING as such without losing any of the functions to which they previously had access. In contrast, when LinkedIn makes changes to its collection, storing, processing or usage of personal data, LinkedIn only informs the members of those changes and considers that LinkedIn members agree with those changes, if they continue to use LinkedIn's services after they have been notified of the changes.

713. Nick Wingfield and Kate Benner, 'How LinkedIn Drove a Wedge Between Microsoft and Salesforce' New York Times (5 November 2016) https://www.nytimes.com/2016/11/06/technology/how-linkedin-drove-a-wedge-between-microsoft-and-salesforce.html, accessed 19 April 2020. Also relevant for the case was whether Microsoft's exclusive use of LinkedIn's metadata, in conjunction with artificial intelligence software under development by companies, including Microsoft, could give rise to an unfair competitive advantage. *See* Richard Waters, 'Data Mining: Microsoft-LinkedIn Deal Raises New Competition Concerns' Financial Times (3 November 2016) https://www.ft.com/content/d5ceda60-a1e1-11e6-82c3-4351ce86813f, accessed 19 April 2020.
714. Commission press release (n 132). Competition authorities elsewhere, such as in the USA, Canada, Brazil and South Africa, approved the transaction unconditionally.
715. *Microsoft/LinkedIn* (n 413) para. 350, n 330.
716. *Microsoft/LinkedIn* (n 413) para. 350.

The above shows that privacy can be taken into account in a competition assessment to the extent that consumers see privacy as a significant factor of quality, and the merging parties compete with each other on this factor. In this instance, the Commission concluded that data privacy, as an important dimension of competition between professional social networks on the market, could have been negatively affected by the transaction.[717]

Apple/Shazam constitutes another interesting case and important addition to the series of merger cases involving the use of customers' personal data.[718] In 2018, the Commission accepted referral requests from Austria, France, Iceland, Italy, Norway, Spain and Sweden concerning the proposed acquisition by Apple of Shazam, a developer and distributor of music recognition apps for smartphones, tablets, and personal computers. The Commission opened an in-depth merger investigation and focused in its assessment on potential anticompetitive effects coming from Apple's access to commercially sensitive data about customers and rivals regarding digital music streaming services. The transaction was approved by the Commission after a careful review of the acquisition of commercially sensitive data sets, here Shazam's user and music data.

One takeaway from the case is the challenge of assessing market power in the presence of zero or non-monetary pricing. In its merger analysis, the Commission noted the inconvenience of using market shares as a proxy for market power in fast-growing sectors that are characterized by frequent market entry and short innovation cycles.[719] However, while acknowledging the inadequacy of market shares as a measurement of market power and recognizing the existence of a problem with its estimation of market power, the Commission did not go further to conduct a more holistic enquiry that would lead to more solid conclusions. *Apple/Shazam* does confirm, however, that data is market power and constitutes an important consideration in competition law and the case contributes to the discussion on rethinking competition law in the digital economy. When commenting on the decision, the EU Competition Commission noted that:[720]

> Data is key in the digital economy. We must therefore carefully review transactions, which lead to the acquisition of important sets of data, including potentially commercially sensitive ones, to ensure they do not restrict competition.

Another interesting merger in the series of recent cases where the use of customers' personal information and privacy plays a central role is Google's plan to buy well-known fitness tracker Fitbit Inc. for USD 2.1 billion, a deal that raised concerns and opposition from especially privacy advocates. The European Data Protection Board, the body advising the Commission on the application of EU data

717. *Ibid.*
718. *Apple/Shazam* (n 657). For an insightful discussion on the decision, *see* Nicolo Zingales, 'Apple/Shazam: Data Is Power, But Not a Problem Here' (December 2018) Competition Policy International 5.
719. *Apple/Shazam* (n 657) para. 162. *See also* Zingales (n 718) 5.
720. European Commission press release, 'Mergers: Commission clears Apple's acquisition of Shazam' (Brussels, 6 September 2018) IP/18/5662.

protection law, issued a statement highlighting the privacy implications of the merger, and pointing to concerns that the possible further combination and accumulation of sensitive personal data regarding European users by a major tech company 'could entail a high level of risk to the fundamental rights to privacy and to the protection of personal data'.[721] Interestingly, the statement was not received with much enthusiasm from the EU Competition Commissioner Vestager, who was reported to have indicated that DG Competition's review of *Google/Fitbit* will not involve privacy regulators.[722] *Google/Fitbit* not only shows the difficulties in assessing mergers in the digital sector[723] but also demonstrates the institutional implications that may follow when the interface between competition and privacy issues is becoming very broad. As the role of data and the competition/privacy interface grows even broader, perhaps going even further than viewing privacy as a parameter of competition,[724] it is likely that there will be more of these institutional clashes going forward.

The above review of certain data-focused merger cases illustrates that, traditionally, competition authorities examined transactions mainly through the lens of price competition, meaning also that they have avoided entering into a detailed analysis of harm when such harm is harder to quantify – such as the impact of a merger on privacy protection.

This price-centric approach may still work relatively well when datasets are simply bought and sold. An example of this kind of case is *TomTom/Tele Atlas*.[725] TomTom, a manufacturer of portable navigation devices and navigation software, acquired Tele Atlas, which was one of the main suppliers of navigable digital map databases, a key input for such navigation devices and software. In its review of the deal, the Commission considered the significant competitive advantage of data in digital map markets. While ultimately clearing the merger, the Commission did note that the merged entity would likely have the ability to exercise market power but lacked the economic incentives to do so.[726]

However, relying on a price-centric approach in competition assessment is less optimal for data-driven businesses and strategies where the product or service is free and the 'cost' is consumer data privacy. *Google/DoubleClick* serves as a good example, where critics of the deal argued that the combination of the companies' valuable sets of user information amounted to a significant reduction in the *quality* of the search product for the many millions of individuals with high privacy preferences.[727] This

721. Natasha Lomas, 'Google Gobbling Fitbit Is a Major Privacy Risk, Warns EU Data Protection Advisor' Techcrunch (20 February 2020) https://techcrunch.com/2020/02/20/google-gobbling-fitbit-is-a-major-privacy-risk-warns-eu-data-protection-advisor/, accessed 19 April 2020.
722. Aoife White and Hamza Ali, 'Google-Fitbit Probe Isn't for Data Watchdogs, Vestager Says' Bloomberg (25 February 2020) https://www.bloomberg.com/news/articles/2020-02-25/google-fitbit-probe-is-for-me-not-data-watchdogs-vestager-says, accessed 19 April 2020.
723. Also the US and Australia, among other jurisdictions, are probing Google/Fitbit, *see* ACCC, Request for submissions: Google's proposed acquisition of Fitbit (27 February 2020).
724. Caffarra and Valletti (n 701).
725. COMP/M.4854 *TomTom/Tele Atlas*, C(2008) 1859.
726. *Ibid.*, para. 230.
727. Peter Swire, 'Protecting Consumers: Privacy Matters in Antitrust Analysis' Center for American Progress (19 October 2007).

brings the discussion to the question whether privacy should play a role in competition analysis as an element or subcategory of the concept of quality – and, if so, how? The answer to this question is not straightforward, especially as the introduction of a privacy dimension into competition analysis is not without criticism, with opponents representing a more conventional view that privacy concerns do not fall within the scope of competition authorities' powers.[728] These issues will be discussed further in Chapter 5 of this book where the focus is on looking at the challenges of measuring potential privacy harms in competition assessment.

The above cases in which data and privacy issues have played a role also exemplify how, in the past, the competition and data protection regimes have been treated as quite distinct from each other. This has been done to the extent that competition authorities have refrained from looking at privacy concerns even when they have been apparent, such as in *Facebook/WhatsApp*. The divergences between the two regimes are often referred to when explaining why competition and data protection law have and should be treated as separate from each other. In the following, the central differences between competition and data protection law are examined. This is done largely from an EU perspective, as the EU rules on data protection provide a better comparative metric than the fragmented US data protection framework.

Economic or non-economic activity. First, one may look to the divergences between the fields of competition law and data protection according to his/her respective focus areas. Competition law applies to all economic activity, given that the competition law provisions apply to 'undertakings', meaning any entities engaged in economic activity.[729] Data protection law can be distinguished as it only applies to the activity of personal data processing, and the scope of data protection law applies irrespective of whether personal data processing is an economic or non-economic activity.[730]

Nature of harm. Further, the nature of the types of harm that competition law and data protection address can be differentiated. As discussed in previous chapters, competition law traditionally focuses primarily on economic harm. By doing so, it considers whether there is a negative impact on the different competition parameters, mainly price, which affects consumer welfare. While data protection can also prevent economic harm (for example, by dealing with information and power asymmetries), this is not the principal goal of the data protection rules, which focus on seeking to ensure the free flow of personal information. The data protection rules in Europe also seek to prevent harm to fundamental rights, such as privacy, freedom of association and non-discrimination.[731]

728. Sokol and Comerford (n 680) in Blair and Sokol (n 549) 6.
729. For example, joined cases C-180-184/98 *Pavlov* [2000] ECR I-6451, para. 74. Notably, certain provisions of the GDPR also apply to 'undertakings', such as 'binding corporate rules' (Article 47) and 'general conditions for imposing administrative fines' (Article 83).
730. Case C-101/01 *Lindqvist* [2003] ECR I-12971.
731. *See* Chapter 2, §2.03. New forms of privacy discrimination are arising due to increasing access to data in modern society, think only of China's so-called social credit system for flights and trains to stop people who have committed misdeeds from taking such transport. *See* Kim

Distinct methods. In addition to competition and data protection law being able to address different types of harm, the two systems employ distinct methods. In this regard, data protection law appears more related to consumer protection law. Ohlhausen and Okuliar note that 'antitrust laws are focused on broader macroeconomic harms, mainly the maintenance of efficient price discovery in markets, whereas the consumer protection laws are preoccupied with ensuring the integrity of each specific contractual bargain'.[732] So, whereas competition is seen as catering for the availability of *consumer choice*, data protection provides consumers with the relevant information for the effective *exercise of that choice*.[733] From this perspective, competition and data protection law intervene to address market behaviour at different points on the same spectrum.[734] Competition law applies to correct market failures that are external to the individual, such as companies abusing their market power, while data protection law applies to correct internal failings, such as information and power asymmetries preventing individuals from enjoying control over their personal data.[735]

These divergences described above are sometimes referred to when explaining why competition and data protection law have been treated as separate systems. However, this book maintains that the reason for the past application of competition and data protection as absolutely separate systems is that it was not before digitalization of the economy and the emergence of big data and data-driven businesses that a real need has arisen to consider the two regimes together.

The transition to the data economy, the role played by privacy in shaping markets and the potentially enormous implications that this poses for consumers necessitates looking beyond the divergences of the two systems and exploring a more holistic approach. Such an approach focuses on the concerns that competition law and data protection share in common. In particular, shared concerns about the welfare of individuals and the power asymmetries between consumers and online service providers have come to attention with the transition to the online economy. These shared concerns and common objectives will be analysed below. Moreover, today's online markets in which consumers deal with personal information as a new currency have revealed areas of overlap as well as gaps in regulation. This calls for healthy discussion and debate over whether a more holistic approach which would involve considering both systems is desirable and useful. This book aims to contribute to that discussion and bring some new perspectives.

Coghill, 'China to Bar People with Bad "social credit" from Planes, Trains' Reuters (16 March 2018) https://www.reuters.com/article/us-china-credit/china-to-bar-people-with-bad-social-credit-from-planes-trains-idUSKCN1GS10S, accessed 19 April 2020. There are also plans to enable the Google search engine in China as a state-monitored service, and no doubt these kinds of services endanger not only privacy but also raise wider concerns regarding society and democracy.

732. Ohlhausen and Okuliar (n 667) 121.
733. Neil W Averitt and Robert H Lande, 'Using the "Consumer Choice" Approach to Antitrust Law' (2007) 74 Antitrust Law Journal 176.
734. Costa-Cabral and Lynskey (n 128) 11, 15.
735. *Ibid.*, 18.

§4.03 SIMILARITIES AND COMMON OBJECTIVES

[A] Regulatory Hybrids

Competition and data protection law both influence the exercise of economic activity and seek to enhance the interests and benefits of individuals. As discussed, they just do this at different ends of the same spectrum. Whereas data protection law safeguards the integrity of individual decision-making concerning personal data processing (for example, when consent is used as the legal basis for data processing), competition law protects consumers against unlawful exercise of market power.[736]

Regulatory hybrids. It is possible to identify similarities between competition and data protection law when looking at the regimes from a broadly regulatory perspective. Regulation is traditionally viewed from the perspective of its objectives, with economic and social regulation being the archetypal forms of regulation.[737] In this respect, both competition and data protection laws are hybrids. Data protection is a hybrid or a cluster concept as the data protection regime reflects elements of both economic and social regulation.[738] Competition law is also of a hybrid nature between economic policy and social regulation.[739] These hybrids are looked into in more detail in the following by considering both the economic and social sides of the relevant regulation.

Economic regulation. Economic regulation is associated with the regulatory state; it intervenes directly in market decisions by structuring the market (for example, by reducing barriers to entry) and influencing the behaviour of businesses in the market. Competition law has clear market structuring features associated with economic regulation as it influences the behaviour of businesses in the market by, for example, regulating pricing practices. Competition rules also aim to reduce power asymmetries, which reflect an economic regulation objective in the sense that resources can be fairly allocated in the market provided that transactional parties enjoy equal bargaining power.

Similarly, data protection reflects aspects of economic regulation. Data protection has market structuring features as it harmonizes the protection offered to personal data, thereby removing barriers to the free flow of personal information to national markets for operators complying with data protection requirements. These entities can be active in EU markets and engage in cross-border data transfers, contributing to the creation of a market for personal data. Further, as will be discussed, data protection regulation reduces information asymmetries. Reduction of such asymmetries reflects an economic regulation objective: in order for resources to be efficiently or fairly allocated in a market system, parties to any transaction must have equal bargaining power. Equal bargaining power is put at risk by information asymmetries. By granting

736. Costa-Cabral and Lynskey (n 128) 15.
737. Lynskey (n 137) 76.
738. *Ibid.*, 76–88.
739. Ioannis Lianos, 'The Poverty of Competition Law' (2018) 2 CLES Research Paper Series.

individuals subjective rights over their data, data protection contributes to minimizing information asymmetries.[740]

Social regulation. Social regulation pursues societal aims without having overt economic goals.[741] Yet, even though social regulation does not pursue economic goals, it has economic effects, cost and benefits and is founded on an economic premise, namely the correction of market failures.[742] These kinds of market failures would prevent achieving the societal aim in the absence of regulatory intervention. A clear example of societal regulation is consumer protection.[743] Consumer protection rules seek to protect consumers from false and misleading advertising, thereby correcting the market failure of information asymmetry.[744] Data protection regulation involves elements of social regulation in that it aims to correct market failures in order to pursue societal aims. In this context, market failures might include a skewed market resulting from asymmetric information, or failure by the market to account for externalities.[745]

Competition law also encompasses elements of social regulation. It has the goal of correcting market failures, such as power imbalances in the context of abuse of dominance cases where a market player enjoys significant market power and is able to act independently without having regard to other actors. Further, competition rules reflect social regulation as they aim to correct market failures in order to pursue the welfare of consumers, which can be understood as a societal aim.

This observation arguably challenges the conventional understanding by some that competition law should only reflect economic regulation. In this regard, one must recall the distinctions between EU competition law and US antitrust law. Whether consumer welfare is interpreted in the narrow Chicago school sense tied strictly to price effects,[746] or more broadly so as also to include non-price related competitive parameters, such as privacy, affects whether competition regulation fits the definition of social regulation. The more competition law is interpreted as also pursuing social and non-price related goals, such as privacy, the more it approximates to social regulation. Ezrachi describes this stretching of competition law's application to protect social goals as the inherent 'sponge' properties of the law or the 'instrumentalisation' of competition law, 'advancing goals which may go beyond the competitive process as understood by many'.[747]

With regard to the social regulation side of EU competition law, it should be noted that although EU competition policy through its multidimensional character is able to

740. *Ibid.*, 77.
741. Cento Veljanovksi, 'Economic Approaches to Regulation' in Robert Baldwin, Martin Cave and Martin Lodge (eds), *The Oxford Handbook of Regulation* (OUP 2010) 18.
742. *See e.g.* Joseph E Stiglitz, 'Government Failure vs. Market Failure: Principles of Regulation' in Edward J Balleisen and David A Moss (eds), *Governments and Markets: Towards a New Theory of Regulation* (CUP 2009) 18.
743. Lynskey (n 137) 78.
744. At EU level, consumer protection law aiming to address such power asymmetries is, e.g., the Unfair Commercial Practices Directive 2005/29/EC and the Unfair Contract Terms Directive (Council Directive 93/13/EEC of 5 April 1993 on unfair terms in consumer contracts [1993] OJ L95/29).
745. Veljanovksi (n 741) 20–22.
746. *See* above Chapter 3, §3.02.
747. Ezrachi (n 334).

address and pursue various policy objectives, it can be asserted that, initially, the EU model of competition was conceived as a tool more of economic, rather than social, policy and regulation. As discussed in Chapter 3 when exploring the goals of EU competition policy, the purpose of the competition rules of the European Community, and later the EU, was to assist the formation of a common or single internal market. At that stage, the social policy dimension was left more to the policy discretion of Member States, some of which made the choice of developing their domestic model of competition law.[748] Then, as mentioned, a specific form of neoliberalism developed in Germany when developing German competition law. The influence of this German ordoliberal school of thinking is significant not only on German competition law but also more broadly on EU competition policy.[749] Although some groups in ordoliberal thinking were quite close to neoclassical economics, other groups were inspired by the principle of the 'social market economy'.[750] As this book suggests, elements of ordoliberal thinking, especially concerning the freedom of choice concept, resonate well with today's concerns raised by digitalization and the use of consumers' personal data, as well as the broader issue of threats to democracy and freedom of speech.

While elements of EU competition law still reflect its origins as an economic instrument in Europe, the European competition model has evolved and today can also be likened to social regulation if one understands and interprets competition law as pursuing broader societal objectives.[751]

Interestingly, while current US antitrust law can arguably be more likened to economic regulation due to its narrow economic focus and price-centricity, at least until the early 1970s, antitrust in the USA was conceived of as a form of social regulation.[752] Antitrust scholars (especially representing the New Brandeis movement) underline that the American antitrust model was initially conceived as a tool of social policy.[753] The US antitrust objectives included ensuring that small- and medium-size companies would have access to the market and protecting workers from exploitation through institutions of countervailing power, such as workers' unions.[754] To ensure that markets afford equal opportunities to all, market access and protection of the competitive process were regarded as essential. So, when comparing the starting points and subsequent development of EU and US competition law, it seems that whereas EU competition policy has transitioned from representing economic regulation to also

748. Some Member States developed their domestic competition laws, focusing on some form of social regulation of their specific brand of capitalism, whereas others relied on price regulation through public ownership of significant parts of their economy. The latter would be the example of effectively all other Member States founding the EU. The relatively small role of competition law as a tool of social regulation at the beginning may also be explained by the European social model which relies on the constitution of a powerful social welfare state.
749. *See* Chapter 3, §3.03[B].
750. Viktor J Vanberg, 'The Freiburg School: Walter Eucken and Ordoliberalism' (2004) Freiburg Discussion Papers on Constitutional Economics No. 04/11.
751. *See e.g.* Motta (n 322) 15 ('Social reasons are [also] taken into account in European competition policy').
752. *Ibid.*
753. Khan (n 575) 960.
754. *Ibid.*

including elements of social regulation, US antitrust law started off as social regulation but has developed into more economic regulation.

Today, broader societal objectives are in demand in the modern economy with growing concerns relating to values such as freedom, democracy and the right to privacy. New competition dynamics in the digital economy raise questions as to the normative scope of competition law. This book aims to address the normative issue of how it 'should' be in the shape of analysing whether privacy should play a role in competition policy. On the whole, competition law can be said to represent hybrid regulation encompassing dimensions of both economic and social regulation, similar to data protection law. The hybrid nature of competition law means that it is not only a tool of economic order but also a form of social regulation. The more competition law is interpreted as pursuing other societal objectives, such as privacy, and thereby fulfilling social regulation purposes, the more competition and data protection law share similarities and can more easily interplay, for example, through a conjoined approach. This conjoined approach is examined in more detail in Chapter 6.

[B] Welfare of the Individual and Power Asymmetries

In the following, the common objectives that competition and data protection law share are explored. Most importantly, both systems seek to protect the welfare of the individual and overcome power asymmetries, which will be addressed in this chapter. Further, both regimes are concerned with advancing EU market integration, which is dealt with in §4.03[C].

The shared concerns and commonalities between the regimes have important implications in that they facilitate the intersection of the two systems. This interlinking enables the development of a conjoined approach, which will be explored in Chapter 6 as a policy consideration for the way forward. The intersection of competition and privacy is illustrated in Figure 4.2, where shared concerns are placed within the circles.

Figure 4.2 Intersection of Competition and Privacy

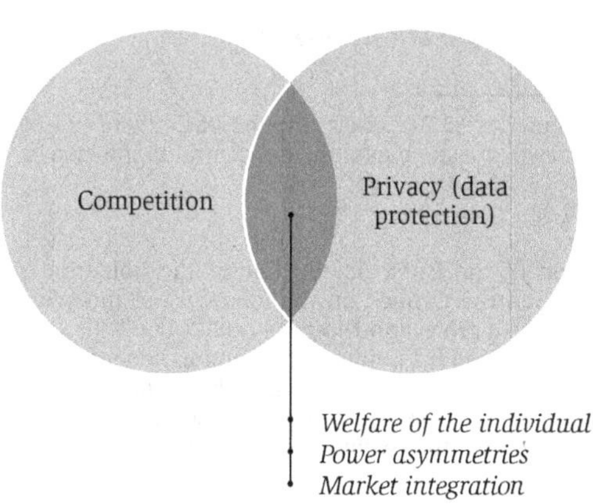

Source: created by the author.

Welfare of the individual. Both competition and data protection law share a concern for the welfare of the individual. Competition law is concerned about individuals as aggregate consumers. The fundamental assumption of competition law is that the competitive process and rivalry between companies increases consumer welfare. Simply put, consumers want better products and services, and companies succeed in the marketplace by providing them.[755]

Data protection law involves the protection of data subjects who are natural persons, thus including consumers. In markets where consumers value privacy in a product or service, and express awareness and sensitivity as to its data protection conditions, the competitive process can enhance data protection and foster privacy as a competitive advantage. In certain markets, consumers may consider a more privacy-friendly service to be of higher quality than a service which has an unclear or ambiguous privacy policy.[756] For example, in the provision of security services, private banking, and legal and medical services, privacy constitutes a competitive parameter according to which companies typically compete.[757] It is thus possible that in such markets a company's failure to respect data protection and address the expectations of privacy-aware consumers could damage their market power.[758] Today, some Internet search services strive to differentiate themselves from their competitors in the marketplace on a privacy basis. The search engine DuckDuckGo, which does not track users or customize results (as opposed to Google search), is one example.[759]

Competition and data protection law's shared concern for individual welfare interacts so that, whereas data protection provides baseline protection for individuals, competition enhances or increases the options available to consumers. A key question that arises in this respect with regard to consumer options is whether enough options are available in today's digital markets and whether consumers truly have freedom of choice when using online services.

Here, the point made by the EDPS is worth stressing: the consumer's single most effective power to influence the market through competition is the ability to change services.[760] The EU Competition Commissioner explains it thus:

> competition gives consumers the power to demand a fair deal. It means companies know that if they don't offer a good price, and a proper service – well, then their customers will simply go somewhere else.[761]

755. *See* discussion in Chapter 3, §3.01 concerning the basic theory of competition that markets deliver better outcomes than state planning, and central to the idea of a market is the process of competition.
756. EDPS Opinion (n 10) 33.
757. *Ibid.*
758. *Ibid. See also* Opinion of the EDPS on the Communication from the Commission to the European Parliament and the Council on the follow-up of the Work Programme for better implementation of the Data Protection Directive [2007] C 255/01.
759. As an interesting side note, the EU Competition Commissioner has stated in an interview that she prefers to search the Internet with DuckDuckGo and Microsoft's Bing. *See* Rowland Manthorpe, 'Europe vs Silicon Valley: Behind Enemy Lines with the Woman Deciding Google's Fate' Wired (27 June 2017) http://www.wired.co.uk/article/who-is-margrethe-vestager, accessed 19 April 2020.
760. EDPS Opinion (n 10) 33.
761. *See also* Vestager (n 74).

This important observation misses one important point, though. In the data economy, with increasingly concentrated technology markets, consumers may sometimes lack real choice. This is due to limited competition or monopolistic markets that prevent them from influencing the market by exercising their power of choice. As noted above with regard to Facebook in the light of the Cambridge Analytica scandal and misuse of personal data, '[i]f there was competition, we'd not be stuck with Facebook'.[762] Indeed, in a competitive market, bad behaviour should not go unpunished and users should move to the next best alternative on the market. This problem concerning market failure and restriction of consumer choice in digital markets is explored further in relation to the German Facebook case below.

Power asymmetries. Another challenge for consumers in the modern economy is the existence of power asymmetries in the market. This is a shared concern for competition and data protection law. Both these fields of law often deal with power asymmetries in which the individual or consumer is usually in a weaker position than other market players, usually big companies. Data protection law seeks to protect individuals throughout the data processing cycle.[763] The legal framework ensures the legality of processing and that the individual can exercise rights vis-à-vis the data controller (often a company) at all times. Competition law also safeguards consumers against the market power of companies. The protections provided by both fields of law are mutually reinforcing in that less individual control over personal data may result in market power (or more market power) for a company. That market power may then allow the company to impose unfair data processing conditions on individuals.[764]

A particular concern with power asymmetry worth mentioning is that it could lead to consent, which is central to data protection law, becoming 'illusory'.[765] This risk is present in situations where consumers have little, if any, room to negotiate terms and conditions of use with a service provider. This may arise, for example, when free online services do not offer users an alternative version of a provider's services and collect personal information for reasons exceeding marketing purposes. Such a 'significant imbalance' between provider and user could call into question the validity of the user's consent to the processing of their personal information, as well as the legality of data processing and the existence of a genuine choice.[766]

The shared concern for power asymmetries by competition and data protection law and the risk of 'illusory' consent is reflected in the German competition case against Facebook[767] analysed in §4.04 below.

762. Petit (n 523).
763. Lynskey (n 137) 14.
764. Costa-Cabral and Lynskey (n 128) 22.
765. According to the EDPS, 'where there is a limited number of operators or when one operator is dominant, the concept of consent becomes more and more illusionary'. EDPS Opinion (n 10) 35.
766. *See* Article 7(a) of the Data Protection Directive.
767. Bundeskartellamt press release (n 19).

[C] Market Integration

In addition to the common objectives of protecting the welfare of the individual (or the consumer) and addressing power asymmetries, competition and data protection law both seek to advance EU market integration. As mentioned, the EU Data Protection Directive was enacted as an instrument of market integration.[768] The GDPR is intended to further this objective by replacing the Directive with a Regulation to ensure more substantive harmonization as well as procedural harmonization by introducing a new EU agency to assure uniform data protection enforcement.[769]

Competition law promotes the EU single market by preventing interstate trade barriers. Initially, the European competition regime focused on integrating the economies of the Member States.[770] Thereafter, competition law has evolved through phases.[771] This evolution began with preventing restrictive practices that interfered directly with the goal of market integration and public obstacles to interstate trade. Competition law later developed a goal of enabling the liberalization of public economy sectors and control of corporate mergers.[772] One may take the view that competition law works mostly through negative integration, while data protection law is an instrument of positive integration.[773]

As the discussion of the common objectives of competition and data protection law shows, the two fields of law are distinct through their divergences but at the same time closely intertwined, thanks to sharing several normative concerns. The shared concerns between competition and data privacy have in recent years led to increased intersection between the regimes. This interplay and its culmination in the German Facebook case are explored in §4.04.

§4.04 INCREASING INTERPLAY AND TESTING OF CONVENTIONAL BOUNDARIES

[A] Increasing Interplay

Despite competition and data protection law sharing similarities and common goals, in practice collaboration between authorities and policymakers in these respective fields has in the past been quite limited. In 2014, there was a sort of breaking point when the EDPS initiated a public debate about the interplay between competition and data protection by publishing a discussion paper on privacy and competitiveness in the age

768. Directive 95/46/EC of the European Parliament and of the Council of 24 October 1995 on the protection of individuals with regard to the processing of personal data and on the free movement of such data, OJ L 281 of 23.11.1995.
769. GDPR, Article 20.
770. Ehlermann (n 471) 257.
771. *See* Chapter 3, §3.03[A] above for a description of evolutionary phases.
772. Wesseling (n 460) 48. *See also* European Commission, White Paper on modernization of the rules implementing Articles 85 and 86 of the EC Treaty (Commission Programme No 99/027, 28 April 1999).
773. Costa-Cabral and Lynskey (n 128) 21–22.

of big data.[774] The EDPS called for more interaction between policies with the aim, among other, to incentivize privacy-enhancing services and minimize potential for consumer harm.[775] In particular, it encouraged cooperation between the relevant EU authorities in responding to the challenges of digital markets and suggested that the policies of competition law and data protection should have more dialogue in the context of the data economy.[776] The idea was that more dialogue between regulators and experts across policy areas could aid enforcement of rules on both competition and privacy protection, as well as stimulate markets for privacy-enhancing services. As part of this call for regulatory collaboration, the EDPS also initiated the development of a so-called conjoined approach. This led, in 2016, to the EDPS founding a Digital Clearinghouse to bring regulators together.[777]

Until the 2014 EDPS discussion paper, it is fair to say that relatively little attention had been directed towards this topic. Apart from the controversy around the *Google/DoubleClick* merger case in 2008, which caught the attention of privacy advocates especially in the US, the relationship between competition and data protection law used to be relatively underexplored. At the time of the discussion paper, interest in the privacy and antitrust circuits was too limited to elaborate further on the topic, with some thinking it was strange or even improper to consider 'merging' competition and privacy.[778] This sceptical approach is to some extent also seen in the competition assessments in *Google/DoubleClick* and *Facebook/WhatsApp*, where privacy concerns were strictly dismissed by the regulators as lying outside the scope of their review. Today, with the growing role of personal data shaping markets and being central to the whole digital economy, more and more attention is being paid to the interlinkage between these two legal fields, and rightfully so.[779] Academia and policymakers alike have shown new and profound interest in this intersection of fields and competition authorities are actively taking part in the debate on competition and privacy by studying the role of data in competition law through various reports and investigations.[780]

Spearheaded by the EDPS, reformers are presenting arguments for integrating privacy into competition law and calling for a broader approach to personal data protection through promotion of closer integration with other, market-shaping, EU law

774. EDPS Opinion (n 10).
775. *Ibid.*, 37-38.
776. *Ibid.* The EDPS includes consumer protection law in its proposal for more collaboration between the different fields. The scope of this book does not go into any detail on the role and interlinkage with consumer protection law in the discussion but acknowledges that this interconnection merits further research in the future, *see* Chapter 6, §6.05.
777. Alec J Burnside, 'Antitrust, Privacy & Big Data - Setting the Scene' (3 February 2015) Lexology; EDPS, 'Opinion 8/2016 on coherent enforcement of fundamental rights in the age of big data' (23 September 2016) 15).
778. Burnside (n 777).
779. Examples of some leading scholarly work include Burnside (n 170 and 777); Costa-Cabral and Lynskey (n 128); Geradin and Kuschewsky (n 667); Ohlhausen and Okuliar (n 667); Grunes and Stucke (n 126); Grunes and Stucke (n 667); Kimmel and Kestenbaum (n 667); Tucker (n 667).
780. *See* §4.01 and Figure 4.1 showing the rising tide of cases and studies in the field.

policies, especially competition law.[781] One of the main drivers for this is the general concern regarding information and power asymmetries in data-driven markets. While the EU data protection framework aims to ensure individuals control over their personal data through mechanisms such as consent, information rights, and rights to access, rectify, and delete data, asymmetries in information and power are currently frustrating individual control.[782] This can play out in such a way that, for example, data processing practices can be ambiguous, with online services offered on a 'take it or leave it' basis, leaving little scope for consumer choice.[783] This issue is relevant in the Facebook dominance case.[784]

However, some have questioned the role, if any, for EU competition law in seeking to protect privacy and personal data after the entry into force of the GDPR. One may wonder whether there is a need for EU competition law to try to prevent abuses that affect the personal data of (final) consumers after the GDPR's introduction of strengthened privacy enforcement tools in Europe, such as the right to data portability.

The reality is that there are limits to data protection law in the context of the data economy. There are more dimensions to a so-called 'lock-in' situation, and this multidimensionality makes the right to data portability inadequate in completely solving the problems around the 'lock-in' effect. The GDPR and the right to data portability are inadequate as there may not be other alternatives in the marketplace for consumers to go to, meaning that there is a market failure and lack of consumer choice. This is when competition law needs to step in to try to fix the market failure - provided it is steered by consumer choice as a policy objective. Further, despite consumers having a right to data portability based on the GDPR, there may be strong network effects that keep them from switching or leaving the online service provider or platform in question, as the *Facebook* case exemplifies. Certain markets may be characterized by these high social switching costs.

Therefore, due to the inadequacy of data protection law in solving all market failures concerning data protection and the existence of a sort of 'gap' in regulation, this book suggests that through the shared policy goal of protecting the welfare of the consumer - understood broadly as including non-price related social goals - competition and data protection law, as two hybrid regulations, can work together to address the timely concerns of information and power asymmetries in the data economy. This is possible through advancing and developing a conjoined approach. This proposal for dealing with these issues aims to contribute and give direction to the current discussion on the normative scope of competition law in the age of digitalization and take that discussion a step further. Moreover, it attempts to offer some conceptual change to the thinking about competition and data protection law together, while not attempting to suggest too far-reaching substantive reform. The practical implications of this approach are discussed further in Chapter 5, §5.03.

781. EDPS Opinion 8/2016 (n 777); EDPS Opinion (n 10).
782. Costa-Cabral and Lynskey (n 128) 12.
783. For discussion on the notion of consent under data protection law, *see* Fred H Cate and Viktor Mayer-Schönberger, 'Notice and Consent in a World of Big Data' (2013) 3 International Data Privacy Law 67.
784. *See* §4.04[B].

One should, however, be mindful that this proposal towards a more holistic conjoined approach that combines the policies of competition and data protection is directed mainly with EU competition law in mind. Why is this? In essence, EU competition law is uniquely placed to accommodate privacy issues as part of its policy goals and thereby capable of developing a joined-up approach between competition and privacy. It is possible to develop a conjoined approach between competition and data protection law with regard to EU competition policy, but less so under US antitrust law. This is not only because it is the European national competition authorities that so far have shown the most interest in the role of data in competition law, which would in any case somehow indicate that the US authorities do not want to combine antitrust and privacy issues. There are voices arguing that the USA should look to the evolution of thought and practice in Europe regarding the intersection of privacy and competition laws.[785]

Rather, the main reason why EU competition law is uniquely placed to foster a conjoined approach and include a privacy-friendly competition policy goes back to what has been discussed in the previous chapters concerning the distinct privacy cultures and the different competition policy goals that exist in the EU and the USA. These differences and special characteristics make Europe better placed to take into account privacy concerns in EU competition policy, in contrast to US antitrust law.

Moreover, EU competition law is arguably better placed than US antitrust law to accommodate privacy concerns because, again in contrast to the American system, EU competition law can address exploitation of consumers and not only foreclosure of competitors. This, in essence, is what the German case against Facebook is about, discussed in the following, where Facebook abused its dominant position by exploiting consumers through imposing unfair contract terms.[786]

[B] Testing Conventional Boundaries: The German Facebook Case

The *Facebook* case started in 2016 when the German competition authority (Bundeskartellamt) opened an investigation into Facebook for a suspected infringement of data protection provisions as an abuse of a dominant position.[787] The investigation targeted allegations that Facebook, the world's biggest social network with 1.6 billion monthly users, had abused its market power by infringing data privacy rules. According to the theory of harm, Facebook's position allows it to impose contractual terms and conditions that its users would not otherwise accept but for its

785. Charles McConnell, 'Stucke: US Should Follow Europe's Lead on Privacy' Global Competition Review (14 August 2017) https://globalcompetitionreview.com/article/usa/1145542/stucke-us-should-follow-europes-lead-on-privacy, accessed 19 April 2020.

786. For further discussion on the historical evolution of EU competition law and its unique position to incorporate privacy concerns, *see* Maria Lancieri (n 187) 1-27.

787. Bundeskartellamt press release, Bundeskartellamt initiates proceeding against Facebook on suspicion of having abused its market power by infringing data protection rules (2 March 2016). This case is discussed by the author in an article that in substance forms part of this book, *see* Maria Wasastjerna, 'Blurred Lines: The German Facebook Case and the Interlink Between Competition Law and Data Protection' (2018) Finnish Competition Law Yearbook 23-34.

market power, meaning that because of the company's size, users have no choice but to consent to the social network's terms and conditions, which are in violation of data protection provisions.[788]

The Bundeskartellamt issued a preliminary finding in December 2017, holding that the social network's data practices amount to abuse of a dominant position.[789] At the same time, the German authority also published a more detailed paper as background information to the proceedings.[790] In February 2019, the national agency's final ruling came out that confirmed that Facebook abused its dominant position as a social network in Germany by imposing exploitative business terms on its users. The decision prohibits Facebook from making the use of its social network conditional on the collection of user and device related data and combining that information with the Facebook accounts without the users' consent.[791]

The condition highlighted as particularly problematic by the Bundeskartellamt is that Facebook conditions access to its social network on the unlimited collection of data generated by users going on third-party websites and Facebook merging that data with the users' Facebook account and using it for numerous data processing activities. These third-party sites include services owned by Facebook, such as WhatsApp and Instagram, and websites and apps of other operators with embedded Facebook Application Programming Interfaces, or APIs.[792] Via APIs, data is transmitted to Facebook and collected and processed by Facebook when a user visits other websites and when, for example, a user does not even press a 'like button' but has called up a site into which such a button is embedded.

The Bundeskartellamt differentiates between user data generated through using Facebook ('on Facebook') and user data obtained from third-party sources ('off Facebook'), which include Facebook-owned services WhatsApp and Instagram, and websites and apps of other operators with embedded Facebook APIs.[793] In this case, the focus is on collection and use of data from third-party sources, whereas collection and use of data on the Facebook network itself is not covered. In other words, the Bundeskartellamt did not examine the permissibility of using data generated from the use of Facebook's social network itself.

While Facebook has not been ordered to pay a fine, the competition authority's opinion imposes on the social network an obligation to change the way it collects data from users in Germany. The Bundeskartellamt's ruling requires an implementation plan from Facebook for an internal divestiture: user data from Instagram and WhatsApp are not allowed to be integrated with the Facebook user profile without explicit

788. *Ibid.*
789. Bundeskartellamt press release, Preliminary assessment in Facebook proceeding: Facebook's collection and use of data from third-party sources is abusive (19 December 2017).
790. Background paper of the case: Bundeskartellamt, Background information on the Facebook proceeding (19 December 2017) (Bundeskartellamt background paper).
791. Bundeskartellamt press release, Bundeskartellamt prohibits Facebook from combining user data from different sources (7 February 2019); Bundeskartellamt case summary (n 18).
792. *See* Bundeskartellamt background paper (n 790) 2; Bundeskartellamt press release, Preliminary assessment in Facebook proceeding: Facebook's collection and use of data from third-party sources is abusive (19 December 2017).
793. Bundeskartellamt background paper (n 790) 3.

and adequate consent.[794] The same goes for information collected on third-party websites.

Exploitative conduct. The Bundeskartellamt's approach is novel in the sense that so far, most discussions of exploitative abuses take price as their starting point, and competition authorities have traditionally understood exploitative conduct mostly as an instrument against excessive pricing.[795] However, in *Continental Can* the CJEU (then the ECJ) made clear that the potentially abusive practices mentioned in the text of Article 102 TFEU (then Article 82 EC) do not form 'an exhaustive enumeration of the sort of abuses of a dominant position prohibited by the Treaty'.[796] Exploitative conduct may thus concern both pricing and 'other' trading conditions. To date, most contributions have focused on the pricing aspect. In this regard, the *Facebook* case focusing on the privacy aspect is a true novelty.

Article 102 TFEU defines exploitative abuses as 'directly or indirectly imposing unfair purchase or selling prices or other unfair trading conditions', which is commonly interpreted as meaning that monopolies must not impose abusive contracting terms and charge 'excessive prices' that lead to direct loss of consumer welfare.[797] Assessing exploitative conduct in online markets centres around the earlier raised fact or reality that consumers may often use online services, such as web-messaging services or social networks, without providing monetary payment but, rather, by 'trading in' a bit of their privacy in the form of personal data. Botta describes it so that the consent they give to the processing of their personal data at least partially serves as payment.[798]

When looking at privacy in the context of exploitative conduct, Nicholas Economides and Ioannis Lianos present an insightful model of market failure focusing on the acquisition of personal information from users and restrictions on privacy as a form of exploitation.[799] There are typically informational asymmetries between the data controller and the data subject in these situations, where the latter is not aware of her data being harvested, in the first place, or that the data is processed by the data controller for a different purpose, shared or sold to third parties.[800]

Unfair contract terms. The existing case law on Article 102 TFEU has so far not provided a clear definition of when a contractual clause must be considered *unfair*. Even though the focus of the existing case law lies on industrial customers, there is no reason to a priori exclude unfair contractual terms imposed on final consumers from the scope of applicability of Article 102 TFEU.[801] In the *Facebook* case, the terms of

794. Bundeskartellamt case summary (n 18) 12.
795. French-German joint report (n 9) 25. *See also* Emil Paulis, 'Article 82 EC and Exploitative Conduct' in Claus-Dieter Ehlermann and Mel Marquis (eds), *European Competition Law Annual 2007: A Reformed Approach to Article 82 EC* (Hart Publishing 2007) 2–3.
796. *Europemballage Corporation and Continental Can Company, Inc. v Commission* (n 474) para. 26.
797. O'Donoghue and Padilla (n 398) 603–604; Whish and Bailey (n 300) 759–766.
798. Botta and Wiedemann (n 95) 59. *See also* Ariel Ezrachi and David Gilo, 'Are Excessive Prices Really Self-Correcting?' (2008) 5 Journal of Competition Law and Economics 249–268.
799. Nicholas Economides and Ioannis Lianos, 'Restrictions on Privacy and Exploitation in the Digital Economy: A Competition Law Perspective' (2019) 5 CLES Research Paper Series 4.
800. Economides and Lianos (n 799) 5.
801. Botta and Wiedemann (n 95) 59.

service, including the grant of consent to processing user data, were central to the competitive assessment and analysis.

In this regard, a key issue concerning Facebook's unlimited data collection is that mostly users are unaware of the company's extensive data gathering 'off Facebook'. According to the Bundeskartellamt, Facebook's terms of service in this respect are inappropriate and violate data protection provisions to the disadvantage of its users. In view of the company's dominant position, the authority holds that 'it cannot be assumed that users effectively consent to this broad form of data collection and processing'.[802] The reasons for this include the fact that considering Facebook's dominant position in the market, users consent to the terms and conditions for the sole purpose of concluding the contract, which cannot be assessed as their free consent within the meaning of the GDPR. Here, the German authority based its decision concerning effective consent – or the lack thereof – pursuant to Article 6(1a) of the GDPR.[803]

Illusory consent. According to the legal assessment, Facebook is in a dominant position and when operating its business model, as a dominant company, Facebook must consider that its users cannot switch to other social networks. Users can only agree to the 'whole package' and its illegal terms of service, or refrain from opening a Facebook account altogether.[804] This effectively constitutes a 'take it or leave it' situation for consumers. One can view this as a significant imbalance between users and Facebook that places the validity of consent under question, indeed making it doubtful whether users have effectively given their consent. The concept of consent becomes 'illusory' in the sense described above concerning situations of power asymmetries. The German authority accordingly notes that:

> we are not convinced that users have given their effective consent to Facebook's data tracking and the merging of data into their Facebook account. The extent and form of data collection violate mandatory European data protection principles.[805]

As such, violation of data protection law forms a key part of the decision irrespective of whether Facebook's conduct is abusive under Article 102 TFEU.[806]

One of the most striking aspects of the German precedent is that it is entirely based on an infringement of European data protection rules enshrined in the GDPR. No doubt this case severely blurs the line between data protection and competition law. But the finding is significant in many ways, one also being that, so far, competition authorities have not always been successful in their efforts and initiatives explaining why privacy is a competition issue. Here, the German authority makes it clear with its theory that Facebook's dominance is what allows it to impose contractual terms that require users to allow Facebook to track them extensively. Another way of looking at

802. Bundeskartellamt case summary (n 18); Bundeskartellamt background paper (n 790).
803. With regard to the requirements under the GDPR, according to the Bundeskartellamt, Facebook does not have to process data to fulfil its contract pursuant to Article 6(1b) GDPR and none of the stipulations of Article 6(1c-e) GDPR apply to justify data processing for special purposes.
804. Bundeskartellamt case summary (n 18) 10; Bundeskartellamt background paper (n 790) 1.
805. Bundeskartellamt background paper (n 790) 10.
806. Botta and Wiedemann (n 95) 59.

it is that when there is a lack of competition, users accept terms of service that they perhaps would not in another situation, which is not truly consenting.

As noted by Inge Graef, the Bundeskartellamt's case can also be seen through the lens of fairness, so as to illustrate the complementarity of the competition and data protection regimes that is based on the unfairness of conditions as a form of exploitative abuse of dominance under Article 102 TFEU.[807] At the same time, the whole investigation seemed to be built on the premise that data protection law principles can be used as benchmarks for assessing whether certain exploitative behaviour of a dominant company should be considered anticompetitive. This development can also be seen as boosting competition enforcement by incorporating data protection principles, according to Graef, who holds that the use of principles from data protection law as benchmarks for analysing whether abuse of dominance under competition law exists can bolster the enforcement capabilities of competition authorities.[808] Currently, competition authorities rarely challenge behaviour that directly harms individual consumers and instead focus on addressing the conduct of dominant companies leading to the foreclosure of competitors.

The decision leads to an interesting outcome where the competition authority concludes that Facebook has breached the GDPR and prohibits the infringing activity also on the basis of competition law. Not only does the decision raise issues on the interface between competition and data protection law but it also brings into question the general demarcation between competition and DPAs. According to the Bundeskartellamt, the GDPR does not rule out that 'substantive data protection law can also be applied by authorities other than the national data protection authorities'.[809] The German authority has stated that during the proceeding it maintained regular contact with DPAs. Indeed, this decision comes at a time when it is encouraged that cooperation should take place between the relevant authorities in responding to the challenges of digital markets and competition law and data protection policies should have more dialogue and interaction in the context of the data economy. As mentioned, the EDPS has been particularly vocal in calling for regulatory collaboration and its founding of a Digital Clearinghouse to bring regulators together is but one example of these calls for action. Recently also the Finnish competition authority has emphasized that collaboration between competition and consumer authorities and DPAs is essential in ensuring the functionality of the digital market.[810]

Real consumer harm or paternalism? One may ask, as critics and sceptics of the *Facebook* case have done,[811] where is the harm to consumer welfare in this? Competition law becomes relevant only if conduct, albeit in breach of data protection law,

807. Inge Graef, Damian Clifford and Peggy Valcke, 'Fairness and Enforcement: Bridging Competition, Data Protection, and Consumer Law' (2018) 8 International Data Privacy Law 210.
808. *Ibid.*
809. Bundeskartellamt case summary (n 18) 9.
810. FCCA report (n 15) 34.
811. *See e.g.* Alfonso Lamadrid de Pablo, 'Facebook, Privacy and Article 102 – A First Comment on the Bundeskartellamt's Investigation' (Chilling Competition blog, 2 March 2016), https://chillingcompetition.com/2016/03/02/facebook-privacy-and-article-102-a-first-comment-on-the-bundeskartellamts-investigation/, accessed 19 April 2020.

gives rise to harm - to competitive harm and, in this case, harm to consumers. As Facebook offers its service for free (zero money), it is true that users do not suffer any direct economic loss from exploitative business terms. This means that the damage for users and alleged consumer harm lies not in financial harm, but in *loss of control*, as users are not able to determine how their personal data is used. Facebook users are oblivious as to what data from which sources are being merged to develop a detailed profile of them and their online activities. According to the Bundeskartellamt, Facebook's merging of data also constitutes a violation of users' constitutionally protected right to informational self-determination.[812]

Some of the criticism against the *Facebook* case may fail to fully consider the case-specific facts and market reality. Arguably, the case concerning Facebook involves some kind of market failure, which relates to consumers' freedom to choose, and asymmetries of information and power imbalance.[813] These are relevant concerns under both data protection and competition laws. This kind of market failure in the form of exploitation of consumers can be addressed by competition law, contrary to what some argue, because competition law is concerned with power asymmetries. Data protection law, for its part, is concerned with information asymmetries. Together, the competition and privacy regimes can address this type of market failure. However, it is true that this kind of expansion of competition law powers should be approached with some caution. It should be done only when a close link exists between the dominance of the company, its data collection processes and competition on the relevant markets.[814] In other words, data processing has to have an effect on competition, which justifies that it is being considered as part of the competitive assessment.

In this regard, it is perhaps not that surprising that the Bundeskartellamt looks at the legality of Facebook's conduct under data protection law as part of its competitive assessment and making it an integral part of its dominance case, considering the report published by the authority jointly with the Autorité de la Concurrence in 2016. The view expressed in the authorities' joint paper is that the use of privacy policies and the corresponding processing of personal data can be taken into consideration when they affect competition, especially if the aforementioned close link between market power, data collection processes and competition is there.[815] In line with this, the President of the Bundeskartellamt explains that the *Facebook* case is about 'shaping privacy issues in the area of platforms and networks' and represents a 'genuine' competition issue since it deals with consumer choice and the treatment of data as a good.[816] This statement points to the central role of consumer choice in the case, a competition value tracing its origins back to ordoliberal traditions and perhaps now gaining renewed attention, as this book suggests.

812. Bundeskartellamt background paper (n 790).
813. *See e.g.* Economides and Lianos (n 799) 5.
814. Cf French-German joint report (n 9) 23–24.
815. *Ibid.*
816. Speech by Andreas Mundt, 'Innovation Economics for Antitrust Lawyers' (Concurrences Review and King's College, London, 3 February 2017).

Network effects and switching costs. The German Facebook case also illustrates and underlines the understanding of market power based on network effects. According to the Bundeskartellamt, the social network's market dominance comes from the platform's powerful network effects, the consequence of which is that users have no choice but are practically locked in to Facebook and find it extremely difficult to switch to one of Facebook's competitors.[817]

As to its market position, the Bundeskartellamt holds that Facebook is dominant in the German market for social networks with some 30 million users per month in Germany of which 23 million use Facebook on a daily basis. Competitors in the area of social networks have been experiencing a continuous decrease in user-based market shares in recent years; some of them have already left the market. For example, Google+ announced in the spring of 2018 that it would discontinue its service for private users.[818] The Bundeskartellamt notes that while there are some smaller German competitors, the substitutability of their products with Facebook is perceived as limited on account of network effects. This is a question of so-called identity-based network effects because, from the users' perspective, decisive criteria for the choice of a social network are its size and the possibility to find the persons they want to be in contact with on the network. Moreover, existing functionalities and interfaces do not alleviate the consequences of Facebook's incompatibility with other social networks.[819]

As explained in Chapter 3, §3.02 when looking at key concepts and notions in competition theory, network effects are particularly strong in digital markets. There are several examples of network effects in the technology industry, such as Google's Search engine, or Amazon's e-commerce service. Network effects occur when the value of a product or service for a customer increases when the number of other customers also using it increases. This can of course positively affect competition, since consumers are better off as the popularity of a product or service increases. On the other side of the coin, network effects also give rise to the possibility of one or only a few companies dominating a market, especially in view of the likelihood of 'tipping effects', where all users in a particular market decide to opt for the product of one company or for one particular technology. The concern that arises is that while competition may exist in principle, it is chilled by the strong network effects and high switching costs.

Facebook's social network illustrates these network effects. For a consumer, it may be difficult trying to break away from a Facebook profile with hundreds of friends. The same is true for a Twitter account with thousands of followers or the Microsoft Office suite with its familiar keyboard shortcuts. Not to mention trying to use the Internet without the Google search engine. What this means is that a market failure seems to occur as shown by lack of consumer choice. The question that arises is whether competition law should correct this kind of market failure. In this regard, the probe against Facebook and the collision between competition and privacy that arises

817. Bundeskartellamt Background paper (n 790). *See also* Matthew Newman, 'Facebook's German Antitrust Probe Hinges on Market Power of Network Effects' MLex Market Insight (8 January 2018).
818. Bundeskartellamt case summary (n 18) 6.
819. *Ibid.*

has been criticized for expressing a wrongly paternalistic competition law, and it is maintained that Facebook does not constitute an unavoidable trading partner; if consumers do not think it is worth giving data in exchange for the service, they can choose not to join.[820] The case is also seen by some as reinforcing a tendency in EU competition law towards the evergrowing responsibility of the dominant company, extending its special responsibility in order to comply with the law, not limiting this to competition law.[821]

On the other hand, competition law is there to protect consumer choice, and here, so the argument goes, there is no real choice for consumers because of Facebook's market position based on user data, its powerful network effect and the significant imbalance between users and Facebook. Moreover, some argue that part of the reason for lack of choice and alternatives for consumers is that Facebook bought its most obvious competitors, Instagram and WhatsApp, and continues to acquire upstart companies before they can reach that point.[822] So, arguably, there are no effective alternatives to Facebook for consumers, as the following example perhaps illustrates to some extent. At a hearing in connection with the Facebook/Cambridge Analytica scandal, one of the questioning senators told the chief executive of Facebook, Mark Zuckerberg, 'If I buy a Ford and it doesn't work well and I don't like it, I can buy a Chevy. If I'm upset with Facebook, what's the equivalent product that I can go sign up for?' Zuckerberg did not have a good answer, except to say that he did not "feel like" he has a monopoly.[823] He may have been the only one that saw it that way.

Time will tell what the final outcome of the *Facebook* case will look like. At the time of finalizing this book, Facebook has just successfully appealed the competition authority's decision to the Düsseldorf Court, which ordered a suspension based on doubts concerning the Bundeskartellamt's opinion.[824] While the court may not have stated that privacy is the wrong parameter, it seems the court differed from the German competition authority on whether consumers have a choice about whether to use

820. Lamadrid de Pablo (n 811).

821. And indeed, upon launching the investigation against Facebook, the President of the Bundeskartellamt stated that '[d]ominant companies are subject to special obligations. They are not allowed to abuse their market power. They are also obliged to use adequate terms of service as far as these are relevant to the market'. *See* Interview with Andreas Mundt: President of the Bundeskartellamt, Competition Policy International (17 July 2016).

822. *See* Richard Blumenthal and Tim Wu, What the Microsoft Antitrust Case Taught Us' New York Times (18 May 2018) https://www.nytimes.com/2018/05/18/opinion/microsoft-antitrust-case.html, accessed 19 April 2020.

823. Sarah Jeong, Zuckerberg struggles to name a single Facebook competitor, The Verge (10 April 2018), https://www.theverge.com/2018/4/10/17220934/facebook-monopoly-competitor-mark-zuckerberg-senate-hearing-lindsey-graham, accessed 19 April 2020.

824. Higher Regional Court of Düsseldorf press release, 'Facebook: Anordnungen des Bundeskartellamts möglicherweise rechtswidrig und deshalb einstweilen außer Vollzug' (26 August 2019); Beschluss Facebook gegen Bundeskartellamt VI-Kart 1/19 (V) (26 August 2019). Despite the court order, the President of the Bundeskartellamt has defended the German competition authority's decision in the case and will be appealing the order, holding that '[t]his is about giving back some sovereignty to consumers ... In the words of competition people, to give back choice, and competition is always about choice'. *See* Pallavi Guniganti, 'FCO Officials Defend Tech Decisions' Global Competition Review (10 September 2019) https://globalcompetitionreview.com/article/1197424/fco-officials-defend-tech-decisions, accessed 19 April 2020.

Facebook. However, this book does not allow for further elaboration on this development and the court order. It suffices to say here that the case will go on to a higher court,[825] perhaps even a referral to the Court of Justice. Despite the preliminary character of the Düsseldorf Court's decision, this could represent a significant setback for the Bundeskartellamt and of course have some degree of signalling effect beyond the German borders. For the time being, however, what this essentially means is that there will be a delay in the application of the German competition authority's decision against Facebook, who may continue to harvest data until further decisions are made. There could be years of appeals ahead with little near-term prospects of changes in Facebook's business practices related to data.

In any event, the German competition authority's novel approach is of utmost interest to both the competition and privacy communities, sparking further debate on the competition/privacy intersection, and the implications may be far-reaching, touching also upon societal, political and even democratic perspectives. It may well be that in the end the Bundeskartellamt's opinion will ultimately hold and the social network will be forced to change its data policies and how it collects data from users in Germany, the objective being that consumers will be better off considering their privacy protection and freedom to choose. Facebook may also be required to execute the ordered implementation plan for an internal divestiture, where user data from Instagram and WhatsApp would not be allowed to be integrated with the Facebook user profile without explicit and adequate consent.[826]

Interestingly, regarding WhatsApp, an internal divestiture would almost seem like a partial unbundling of or imposition of some sort of post-clearance remedies in the European Commission's *Facebook/WhatsApp* merger. As mentioned, the case was approved unconditionally at the time, and the European Commission excluded data protection considerations from the application of competition law, stating that any privacy-related concerns do not fall within the scope of EU competition law (*see* discussion on traditionally separate regimes in §4.02). What also remains to be seen going forward is whether this novel approach by the Bundeskartellamt will be extended to other companies under investigation by the German authority, something its President has hinted would be a possibility. For example, an abuse probe into Amazon is already ongoing, focusing on terms and conditions for traders selling via the Amazon marketplace.[827] Not surprisingly, the EDPS is supportive of the bold approach of the Bundeskartellamt, holding that: '[t]his case is the tip of the iceberg – all companies in the digital information ecosystem that rely on tracking, profiling and targeting should be on notice'.[828]

825. The Bundeskartellamt has confirmed that it will appeal the order. A decision of the Federal Court of Justice is expected in 2020.
826. Bundeskartellamt case summary (n 18) 12. *See also* Facebook's blog post, Why We Disagree with the Bundeskartellamt (7 February 2019) https://newsroom.fb.com/news/2019/02/bundeskartellamt-order/, accessed 19 April 2020.
827. *See* Rupprecht Podszun, 'After Facebook: What to Expect from Germany' (February 2019) 10 Journal of European Competition Law & Practice 69–70.
828. Giovanni Buttarelli, 'Big Step Towards Coherent Enforcement in the Digital Economy' (EDPS blog, 7 February 2019) https://edps.europa.eu/press-publications/press-news/blog/big-step-towards-coherent-enforcement-digital-economy_fr, accessed 19 April 2020.

[C] Implications Beyond National Law

Reliance on national law but implications beyond. One of the interesting aspects of the Bundeskartellamt's opinion is that Facebook's practices are tackled under national German competition law and its general prohibition of abuse of a dominant position, leaving Article 102 TFEU aside, which is usually relied on in parallel to national law. Speculation has been aired about the underlying reasons, one possible reason for this being that national German law on unilateral conduct may be stricter than EU law.[829] The reliance on national law in the case might also be the result of discussions within the European Competition Network (ECN) and trying to avoid having the German authority setting a controversial precedent based on EU law.[830] However, the outcome – controversial as it may be – still has implications that go beyond national jurisdiction in the sense that the competition community is watching closely, there will likely be a ripple effect on competition policy more widely, and the case has the potential to broaden considerably the scope of competition law enforcement. What the competition authority's novel approach clearly signals is that some competition authorities are willing to exercise their powers beyond the conventional bounds, perhaps even to embrace enforcement of data protection rights.

With regard to relying on national law, the Bundeskartellamt has elaborated on its theory of harm, noting that '[i]f a dominant company makes using its service conditional upon the user granting the company extensive permission to use their personal data, this can be taken up by the competition authority as a case of "exploitative business terms"'.[831] Indeed, under German competition law, the use of exploitative business terms is a type of exploitative abuse. With its provision on exploitative abuses, national law essentially aims to protect a contracting party in an imbalanced or asymmetrical negotiating position from being exploited by a dominant company. Exploitation can take the form of excessive prices and unfair business terms. According to the case law of the German Federal Court of Justice, civil law principles can also be applied to determine whether business terms are exploitative.[832] Often, such principles stem from legislation on unfair contract terms or the German Constitution.[833] Following the Federal Court of Justice's approach, the Bundeskartellamt applied data protection principles in its assessment of Facebook's terms and conditions. It is noteworthy that the recently revised Section 18(3a) of the German Act against Restraints of Competition directly refers to personal data as a criterion relevant when establishing market power, especially in the case of online platforms.[834] In this regard, data protection law has the objective of protecting individuals from having their

829. *See* Section 19(1) of the German Competition Act GWB; cf. Article 3(2) Reg. 1/2003.
830. *See* Silke Heinz, 'Bundeskartellamt Sends Preliminary Assessment to Facebook' (Kluwer Competition Law Blog, 9 January 2018) http://competitionlawblog.kluwercompetitionlaw.com/2018/01/09/bundeskartellamt-sends-preliminary-assessment-facebook/, accessed 19 April 2020. For further commentary, *see e.g.* McLeod (n 45); Graef and Van Alsenoy (n 45).
831. Bundeskartellamt background paper (n 790) 4; Bundeskartellamt case summary (n 18) 7.
832. Ezrachi (n 369) 19 fn 116; Bundeskartellamt background paper (n 790) 6.
833. Bundeskartellamt background paper (n 790) 6.
834. Competition Act – GWB Bundesgesetzblatt I 2013, 1750, 3245.

personal data exploited by the counterparty, allowing individuals to decide freely and without coercion how their personal information is used.

Despite being a national decision and currently suspended under an appeals process in German court, the potential impact of the Bundeskartellamt's Facebook ruling goes beyond the case at hand; it has the potential to considerably widen the scope of competition law enforcement and become a landmark case at the intersection of data protection and competition law. While the Bundeskartellamt has emphasized that not every infringement of data protection law by a dominant company automatically violates competition law, it also indicates a general willingness to protect parties in an imbalanced and potentially disadvantageous negotiating position.[835] No doubt the case also represents another abuse case in the Internet economy regarding the increasingly visible 'fairness' dimension of EU competition law.[836] Beyond highlighting the importance of fairness, the *Facebook* case also stresses the significance of consumers' freedom to choose as a theory of harm and core competition objective.

Another sign that the impact of the German Facebook investigation is not limited to the case at hand is that the Commission as the leading European competition regulator explicitly expressed its support for opening the German pioneering case, noting that it should not only be the EU regulator 'doing things that are new in terms of developing competition law'.[837] This may be interpreted as a sort of endorsement of the potential widening of the scope of competition law enforcement by means of the interplay between competition and data protection law.

[D] Growing International Divergence or Convergence

On the whole, the *Facebook* case can be viewed as signalling an intellectual shift and that there is scope - and some competition authorities are willing - to exercise competition law powers beyond the conventional bounds, to embrace enforcement of data protection and privacy rights. No doubt some view the case as too far-reaching and controversial, as it is testing the traditional boundary between competition and data protection law: since its opening it has stirred much debate and discussion.[838] Indeed, the German Facebook case reflects growing calls for incorporating privacy considerations into the realm of competition law[839] and the Bundeskartellamt is in

835. Since early 2017, the Bundeskartellamt, in addition to its classic competition law enforcement tools, has had enhanced consumer law powers (and is currently conducting sector enquiries related to price comparison websites and smart TVs).
836. Heinz (n 830). *See also* the discussion on fairness in Chapter 4.
837. Foo Yun Chee (n 44).
838. Lamadrid de Pablo (n 811); Jörg Hladjk, Philipp Werner and Lucia Stoican, 'The German Facebook Case - Towards an Increasing Symbiosis Between Competition and Data Protection Laws?' (25 February 2019) Competition Policy International; Peter Stauber, 'Facebook's Abuse Investigation in Germany and Some Thoughts on Cooperation Between Antitrust and Data Protection Authorities' (25 February 2019) Competition Policy International; Justus Haucapv, 'Data Protection and Antitrust: New Types of Abuse Cases? An Economist's View in Light of the German Facebook Decision' (25 February 2019) Competition Policy International.
839. EDPS Opinion 8/2016 (n 777); EDPS (n 10). *See also* Alec J Burnside, 'Antitrust, Privacy & Big Data - Setting the Scene' Address at Concurrences and Cadwalader, Wickersham & Taft LLP

many ways acting as a pioneer for pursuing a breach of data protection law under competition enforcement. Thereby, the probe is exploring new territory by falling into a grey zone between competition and privacy.[840] The case looks at the relationship between data and market power and reflects many of the shared current concerns by competition and data protection law, most notably power asymmetries.

The *Facebook* case also exemplifies an issue lying in a bedrock component of current competition law thinking that respects success on the merits, sometimes perhaps taking the concept too far? The theory goes that winners in a fair fight should deserve to exist without being turned upon, reflecting Judge Learned Hand's remarks about the successful competitor.[841] Of course, competition enforcers should not punish big technology companies, like Facebook or Google, for being successful. Consumers clearly want what these companies have to offer. And why should they not; big technology companies have delivered an extraordinary amount of consumer value and benefits through, for example, improved products and services.[842]

However, while respecting that success on the merits is a core element of competition law, especially US antitrust law, the importance of this principle should not be exaggerated or overemphasized so that companies behaving unfairly are out of reach of the scope of competition enforcement. As a matter of fact, competition law is not equipped to create competitors out of thin air, so when the need arises for more choices for consumers in digital markets, such as the market for social networking, what competition law can do, though, is to protect a market that allows a fair fight. So, if Facebook is behaving unfairly by using its dominant position to force users to allow unlimited data collection, competition law needs to find a way to address that kind of behaviour. This may include relying on data protection law to build a case. In the face of privacy-related concerns, authorities should make sure consumers are in a position to make informed choices. Competition law is there to preserve choices, and here consumers do not have those choices. So, in this regard, the German investigation has found the solution of combining data privacy and competition rules to address the unfair conduct of Facebook.

The *Facebook* case has not been without international criticism, especially in the USA, where the American antitrust authorities have expressed scepticism concerning the Bundeskartellamt's position that data is the equivalent of price. The analogy between data and price has been questioned, in particular whether it can really be assumed that 'a firm that is providing a service and acquiring data in exchange is effectively charging a price'. It is argued that one cannot assume that 'a firm acquiring more data from customers is imposing the equivalent of a price increase or quality

Antitrust, Privacy & Big Data seminar (3 February 2015) https://www.concurrences.com/en/archives-seminaires/antitrust-privacy-big-data-brussels-3-february-2015/, accessed 19 April 2020; Burnside (n 170).

840. *See e.g.* McLeod (n 45); Graef and Van Alsenoy (n 45); Jakob Kucharczyk, 'The German FCO's Facebook Case: Blurring the Line Between Competition and Data Protection Enforcement' (Disruptive Competition Project, 8 February 2019) http://www.project-disco.org/european-union/020819-german-fcos-facebook-case-competition-and-data-protection-enforcement/#.XQc6AfZuJPZ, accessed 19 April 2020.

841. *See* above Chapter 3, §3.02.

842. *See* similar discussion in the French-German joint report (n 9) 10.

decrease'.[843] This reads in stark contrast not only to the German case but also to the EU Competition Commissioner's various statements and speeches drawing a direct analogy between personal data and price. What impact will this EU/US rift or controversy have?

Some suggest that the German Facebook case and the various national competition authorities' reports and enquiries reflecting a sort of European pro-privacy approach are likely to influence governments elsewhere in the world.[844] On the other hand, it is not unthinkable that the German Facebook case and its American criticism may also lead to increasing divergence between EU and US antitrust policies regarding the approach to privacy and data protection as potential competition dimensions. If developments take this direction, that would raise the risk of a transatlantic divide in terms of merging competition and privacy. Distinct EU and US competition policy goals with regard to privacy protection could translate into more divergent outcomes of competition enforcement across the Atlantic in data-driven markets.

Divergent competition policy objectives across competition systems may lead even to identical business conduct being treated differently depending on the authority and the jurisdiction. This leads to disparate outcomes, with one jurisdiction finding illegal behaviour that the other does not – and may even view the exact same business practices as pro-competitive. Examples of this can be found in the recent past.

To date, the most illustrative examples of this phenomenon are perhaps the cases against Google (*Google Search* and *Android*). During the Obama administration, the FTC conducted a nineteen-month investigation into allegations that Google biased its search results in favour of its own products. The FTC ultimately closed the probe in 2013 unanimously voting to close its investigation after concluding the company's behaviour was not anticompetitive and without taking action against Google.[845] Conversely, the European Commission found Google guilty of breaching competition law on the same issue and levied a record fine of EUR 2.42 billion on Google in 2016.[846] In Europe, Google was also charged and penalized with another record fine of EUR 4.34 billion for abuse of dominance in a separate but related case concerning its Android operating system.[847]

843. Lewis Crofts, Joshua Sisco and Leah Nylen, 'Data Acquisition Doesn't Equate to Price Hikes, FTC's Hoffman Says' MLex market insight (12 April 2018), reporting that senior US antitrust officials are claiming that 'companies that gather more data from their customers aren't imposing the equivalent of higher prices or lesser quality service'. *See* MLex Market Insight, 'Data Acquisition Doesn't Equate to Price Hikes' Report from the 66th ABA Antitrust Law Spring Meeting (Washington DC, 11–13 April 2018) 37, https://mlexmarketinsight.com/db_images/special-reports-pdf/MLex-ABA-Antitrust-2018.pdf?utm_source = MLex + Email + Updates&utm_campaign = ebbc3cc2f8-Email + Campaign-2018-ABAReport-EMEA_Sub&utm_medium = email&utm_term = 0_f30f64c91d-ebbc3cc2f8-63791953, accessed 19 April 2020.

844. McConnell (n 785).

845. Statement of the FTC, *Google's Search Practices*, Google Inc., FTC File No. 111-0163 (FTC 3 January 2013) 3–4.

846. Certainly, factors specific to the EU case were also decisive to the outcome, such as larger European market shares and issues relating to market power and dominance.

847. Commission press release, 'Antitrust: Commission sends statement of objections to Google on comparison shopping services; Opens separate formal investigation on Android' (15 April 2015) IP/15/4780 (articulating the European Commission's first statement of objections);

The *Google* cases are but one example of how competition law enforcement can differ in the EU and the USA, and how a policy divide can exist across the Atlantic. The issue is that divergent competition policy across legal systems may not only lead to business conduct being treated differently depending on the jurisdiction but also it brings with it risks concerning legal certainty, not to mention that it is costly, too.

The German case has already been followed by the Italian competition authority running an almost identical proceeding against WhatsApp messaging service and Facebook in Italy, including the imposition of a EUR 3 million fine on WhatsApp over data sharing with its parent company.[848] Coincidentally (or not), this happened at roughly the same time as the European Commission decision on the aftermath of *Facebook/WhatsApp* and privacy policy changes.[849]

The important difference in the Italian case compared to the German one is that the Autorità Garante della Concorrenza e del Mercato (AGCM) went after Facebook by relying on *unfair use of commercial practices* and basing its theory and decision entirely on consumer protection law. During the proceedings, WhatsApp invoked the defence that its conduct was in compliance with data protection law, and thus could not be sanctioned as an infringement of the Italian Consumer Code. However, this defence was not accepted by the authority.[850] Although the Italian competition authority relied solely on consumer protection considerations, it might be argued that WhatsApp's conduct – that is, urging users to consent to data sharing between Facebook and WhatsApp by 'tricking' them into agreeing even though the grant of consent was not necessary for further use of the service – could also be pursued as a unilateral imposition of unfair contractual terms under Article 102 TFEU.[851] In this regard, it does not matter that WhatsApp's behaviour was deemed to be in compliance with data protection law. As already seen in *Astra Zeneca*, 'the illegality of abusive conduct under [Article 102 TFEU] is unrelated to its compliance or non-compliance with other legal rules and, in the majority of cases, abuses of dominant positions consist of behaviour which is otherwise lawful under branches of law other than competition law'.[852]

Finally, in this chapter, it is important to underline that the suggestion that the historical hard line between competition and privacy is softening, or that the conventional boundary is at least being increasingly tested, is made especially with regard to Europe, where data privacy is becoming more and more visible in EU competition law with the growing attention from national competition authorities and academia. This

---

Commission press release, 'Antitrust: Commission fines Google €4.34 billion for illegal practices regarding Android mobile devices to strengthen dominance of Google's search engine' (Brussels, 18 July 2018) IP/18/4581.

848. *See* discussion in Chapter 2, §2.03[B] and the decision and press release of the *Autorità Garante della Concorrenza e il Mercato* (n 251).
849. European Commission press release, Mergers: Commission fines Facebook €110 million for providing misleading information about WhatsApp takeover (Brussels, 18 May 2017). *See* discussion in §4.02.
850. *Ibid.*
851. *See* Botta and Wiedemann (n 95) 61.
852. Case C-457/10, *AstraZeneca AB and AstraZeneca plc v European Commission* (2012) ECLI: EU:C:2012:770, para. 132.

development culminated in the German Facebook dominance case, where the Bundeskartellamt acted as a pioneer in merging competition and data protection law in a bold precedent. One should be mindful, however, that this evolution seems to be happening mainly in Europe, at least to date, where European national regulators are focusing on the potential competition issues arising from data and privacy. In this regard, US antitrust law is lagging behind.

The reason for this is probably twofold. First, as described in Chapter 2, the American approach to privacy protection is very different from the European understanding of data privacy as a fundamental right. This means that privacy in itself has a much more prominent role in the EU, also because of the recent entry into force of the GDPR, strengthening the role of data protection even further.

Second, as described in Chapter 3, EU competition law is multidimensional and capable of advancing various policy goals, whereas US antitrust law is heavily price-centred, leaving less room for the potential inclusion of non-price competitive parameters, such as data privacy, in its policy goals. Therefore, the observations made with regard to the increasing interplay between the competition and privacy regimes are based on the current situation in Europe. This does not mean that US antitrust law will not accommodate data privacy concerns or that the American competition authorities are ignorant as to the importance of digital privacy in online markets. Rather, what this book suggests is that to date, it seems Europe is taking the lead in addressing the challenges of the data economy with the broader aim of protecting consumers from abuse of market power related to personal data, power asymmetries and lack of consumer choice.

§4.05 SUMMARY

This chapter has discussed how the two fields of competition and data protection law coexist and interact with each other. It started by exploring the traditional viewpoint and conventional treatment of the regimes as completely separate areas with distinct aims. As shown, this view reflects in the assessment by the competition authorities in cases such as *Google/DoubleClick* and *Facebook/WhatsApp*. However, the European Commission's 2016 decision in *Microsoft/LinkedIn* presents a more evolved perspective. In this case, privacy was explicitly mentioned as an important competitive parameter and an important driver of consumer choice. Indeed, it is possible to identify a gradual change in the approach to a potential privacy dimension in competition law when looking, for example, at the European Commission's analysis in *Google/DoubleClick* and *Facebook/WhatsApp*, compared to its later analysis in *Microsoft/LinkedIn* and *Apple/Shazam*. The approach has become more favourable, and there are some indications that the historical hard line between competition and data privacy is softening.

This chapter also examined the similarities and commonalities between the fields of competition and data protection. By focusing on the shared concerns or interests of the two regimes, potential does appear to exist for convergence and synergies. It is the common objectives of the competition and data protection regimes that enable an increasing interplay between the two areas that the German competition authority's *Facebook* case exemplifies. Indeed, one of the aims of this book is to challenge the fairly common assumption that the two worlds of privacy and competition are apart. This book strives to contribute to the intellectual shift that is on the rise, which promotes the integration of privacy considerations within the scope of competition law and thereby encourages increasing testing of traditional boundaries between the regimes to better protect consumer welfare. Here, consumer welfare is understood in a broad sense, or, as will be discussed in the following, as consumer *well-being*.

In the next chapter, the potential incorporation of a privacy dimension in competition law will be explored further. This is done by addressing, first, the shortcomings of the current competition approach in accounting for the value of data and privacy protection in digital markets and identifying the limitations of the existing static price-focused perspective in competition law. Second, the practical challenge of measuring privacy as an element in competition is explored by analysing the issue of how competition law should best deal with addressing the intangible harm of privacy protection. In its simplest form, this is also an issue whether the consumer welfare standard pursued by data protection laws overlaps with the consumer interests which competition policy aims to protect. In other words, does competition law have a role to play or is it irrelevant? Does data protection confer sufficient protection or is there a gap? Moreover, this leads to the following question: what is a desirable balance between the two legal frameworks of data protection and competition in order to achieve maximum protection for the welfare of consumers? Is a holistic conjoined approach between competition and data protection the solution and best way forward?

Addressing these complex questions involves operating at the intersection of privacy and competition, an interlinkage that culminates in tackling the issue of consumer welfare, and what it means in today's data economy. As in Chapter 4, the analysis in Chapter 5 focuses on EU competition law, as its multidimensional character and variety of policy goals allow envisioning inclusion of data privacy as a potential competition objective, and a holistic conjoined approach to data protection and competition.

CHAPTER 5

Rethinking Competition Policy for the Digital Age

Through the multidimensional character and variety of policy goals of EU competition law, it is possible to envision an inclusion of privacy as a competition objective and develop a holistic conjoined approach to data protection and competition. The intersection of privacy and competition culminates in the definition and understanding of consumer welfare, and how the concept should be interpreted as a competition goal in the data economy. The chapter explores incorporating a privacy dimension in competition law by addressing certain shortcomings in the current competition approach. There are limitations in the static price-focused perspective in competition law and challenges in measuring the intangible harm of privacy protection and privacy as a competition parameter. This is also an issue whether the consumer welfare standard pursued by data protection laws overlaps with the consumer interests which competition policy aims to protect. In other words, does competition law have a role to play, does data protection confer sufficient protection or is there a gap? In addition to addressing these questions, the chapter seeks to identify a desirable balance between the two legal frameworks in order to achieve maximum protection for the welfare of consumers. A holistic conjoined approach between competition and data protection is presented as an alternative solution and possible way forward.

§5.01 INTRODUCTION

Digital information is unlike any previous resource; it is extracted, refined, valued, bought and sold in different ways. It changes the rules for markets and it demands new approaches from regulators.

In the previous chapter, the interplay and commonalities between competition law and privacy were examined. In this chapter, the aim is to build on the previous chapters and rethink competition policy goals for the digital age in light of the growing importance of privacy and data protection. As reflected in the above quote from *The Economist* in May 2017, data has changed the dynamics of the markets and demands a new approach from regulators. Indeed, this book is part of a larger public debate over the need to update competition policy for the modern age of digitalization and big data. Rapid technological development, including the introduction of artificial intelligence, the IoT, big data and big analytics, have all contributed to the economy – and the world around us – going digital. These developments are not without effect on competition law, giving rise to many new challenges.

These challenges for competition law caused by the changing economic landscape and the evolution of the data economy are raised mainly on two levels.[853] First, on the more practical level, competition authorities are being confronted with added complexity and uncertainty when conducting investigations and assessing cases in a dynamic environment where the ability of markets to self-correct and the nature of consumer harm can be different from what it used to be. Second, on the policy level, the data economy's new dynamics raises issues concerning the normative scope of competition law. New market realities and forms of interaction between businesses and consumers raise questions as to the scope of competition law, its effectiveness, and more broadly, its optimal goals. This book looks more at the latter challenge, addressing issues at the policy level, and articulating the need for a conceptual and policy change in competition law and outlining the optimal objectives and values to be advanced by competition law in the data economy.

As articulated at the outset, the question whether the current approach to competition policy is fit for the data economy stands at the heart of this book. This is a very timely topic.[854] The broad question translates into a narrower one, namely whether the existing consumer welfare standard that currently guides competition policy and enforcement is capable of addressing harmful conduct in digital markets. Is current competition policy too price-centred in its objectives? If so, the objectives should perhaps be revisited with the aim of giving more weight to 'non-economic' or social goals. How should consumer data protection and privacy be considered in competition policy? As discussed in previous chapters, data protection and privacy are

853. This categorization of two levels is presented in Ezrachi (n 369).

854. Noteworthy in this respect is that in March 2018, the EU Competition Commissioner set up a special team of advisers to focus on how competition policy should adapt to future challenges of digitization. This culminated in the report published in early 2019 in connection with the public consultation and conference by the European Commission on the topic of shaping competition policy in the era of digitization. *See* European Commission Call for contributions and Crémer, de Montjoye and Schweitzer (n 656); European Commission News, 'Commission appoints Professors Heike Schweitzer, Jacques Crémer and Assistant Professor Yves-Alexandre de Montjoye as Special Advisers to Commissioner Vestager on future challenges of digitalization for competition policy' (28 March 2018) https://ec.europa.eu/commission/commissioners/2014-2019/vestager/announcements/commission-appoints-professors-heike-schweitzer-jacques-cremer-and-assistant-professor-yves_en, accessed 19 April 2020.

increasingly important rights and values in our digital world, where online products and services are exchanged for users' personal data.

This chapter envisions what a sound competition policy for the digital age might look like. This is done by exploring how competition law could consider privacy protection in its policy objectives with the aim of providing welfare or – as will be elaborated – 'well-being' for consumers. In today's digital economy, do competition law's policy goals meet the challenges of data-driven business models and markets, where non-price elements, such as privacy, are often of utmost significance? This is of fundamental importance, as these policy goals shape and steer how law and policy are implemented and enforced. This issue is addressed by relying on the discussion in Chapter 3 concerning the underlying objectives of competition policy.

As will be explored further in §5.02[A], one of the shortcomings and challenges with existing competition policy is that it is too price-centred. Digitalization has given rise to a new economy where market power is no longer tied to price. This situation requires a critical look at the current price-focused approach to competition policy, especially in the technology sector. The concern is that competition policy and enforcement may be stuck in an outdated view of the world, a view that fails to see that dominance in online markets is all about users and views. It is the businesses with most users and page views that can dominate, and accumulating those users is crucial and something only a small number of companies are able to do. Because of this specific feature of the technology markets, the need arises to rethink competition policy in order to avoid ending up in monopolistic and oligopolistic markets where just a few companies dominate the industries and swallow any potential disrupters at birth. Another specific feature of technology markets is the importance of network effects, as explored in connection with the German Facebook case.

In addition to, or as part of, being overly focused on price, a limitation of current competition policy is that it has relegated one of the most important values in our time, which is free choice, to the margins. This book holds that one way to an optimal competition policy in the digital age is to bring back consumer choice, in the ordoliberal sense of the concept, as a guiding policy goal. As explained in Chapter 3, the initial goals of European competition law were multiple and included non-price elements such as fairness and consumer choice. Somewhere along the way competition law became too focused on prices. This is especially true for US antitrust law, where the influences of the Chicago school were enormous. But now, with the rise of big data and the transition to a data-driven economy, it is time to consider where competition policy perhaps took a wrong turn and understand how it can find the right way back on track.

Competition policy should respond to the problems of our time, as the law exists to correct market problems and failures. This entails that competition policy goals should reflect the values we need to protect in today's digital age, such as data privacy. This leads to a central question of the book, which is how to incorporate data privacy into competition law. One of the key characteristics of privacy is that it is an intangible concept, which makes it difficult to measure. The challenge of measuring privacy as a dimension in competition law will be explored in §5.03[B]. As an element of examining the introduction of a data privacy dimension into competition policy, it is also considered whether the fundamental right to data protection can be used as a normative benchmark for the application of competition law to advance privacy protection. This is done in §5.02[C].

Bringing a privacy dimension to competition law and thereby merging competition and privacy may face policy objections. Some may say that competition law should not be mixed with politics. This invites the more philosophical question of what is purely legal, and whether competition law, or any legal discipline, can exist that is not influenced by politics, not to mention history and societal values? This more philosophical discussion is touched upon at the end of §5.03[C] when expanding horizons beyond price.

§5.02 CURRENT SHORTCOMINGS

> *Antitrust efforts have become too fixated on the idea that the only real harm consists of raising of prices for consumers. Yet in the Microsoft case, Internet Explorer was 'free', even though Microsoft was bent on destroying competition with it. Today, both Google and Facebook offer products that are free. Society has grown to rely on them, but because they have no dollar price, antitrust regulators have been hesitant to take action.*
>
> *Any American can tell you that there is no free lunch. Everything has a price. We pay for these products and services with our time and our data. And like Microsoft, these firms have come to exert too much control over our shared technological future.*

The above citation, from a recent *New York Times* opinion,[855] is a representative example of rising public concern about the shortcomings of the existing competition paradigm and its suitability for the data economy. The problem is that current competition law is overly centred on price competition. Some competition scholars and theorists steeped in price theory still think that without prices there can be no markets, and consequently no exercise of market power.[856] One of the great risks with this kind of approach is that it overlooks significant welfare harms relating to non-price dimensions of competition, such as consumer privacy, and that competition efforts are too fixated on the idea that the only real harm consists of raising prices for consumers. However, as has already been mentioned several times throughout this book, price is not optimal for measuring the value of digital products and services, which are often paid for by users giving access to personal data.[857] Relying only on price effects and economics will steer the focus too little on what people really care about. Economists often assume that prices are all anyone needs to know. This biases many of their conclusions and limits their relevance to some serious human issues and values.[858]

855. Blumenthal and Wu (n 822).
856. *See* Newman (n 421).
857. *See* discussion in Chapter 2, §2.02.
858. The Economist, 'Economists Focus Too Little on What People Really Care About' (3 May 2018) https://www.economist.com/news/finance-and-economics/21741563-fourth-our-series-professions-shortcomings-economists-focus-too, accessed 19 April 2020.

More broadly, this raises concerns that digitalization and technological progress may create ever more situations in which ethical considerations conflict with narrowly material ones. In this context, the question of how, in such a world, to increase not only consumer welfare but also well-being deserves greater attention.

As so eloquently articulated by Friedrich Hayek in his speech on accepting the Nobel Prize for Economics, value is not limited to those things that are tangible and easily measured:

> Unlike the position that exists in the physical sciences, in economics and other disciplines that deal with essentially complex phenomena, the aspects of the events to be accounted for about which we can get quantitative data are necessarily limited and may not include the important ones. While in the physical sciences it is generally assumed, probably with good reason, that any important factor which determines the observed events will itself be directly observable and measurable, in the study of such complex phenomena as the market, which depend on the actions of many individuals, all the circumstances which will determine the outcome of a process, for reasons which I shall explain later, will hardly ever be fully known or measurable. And while in the physical sciences the investigator will be able to measure what, on the basis of a prima facie theory, he thinks important, in the social sciences often that is treated as important which happens to be accessible to measurement. This is sometimes carried to the point where it is demanded that our theories must be formulated in such terms that they refer only to measurable magnitudes. [...] And because the effects of these facts in any particular instance cannot be confirmed by quantitative evidence, they are simply disregarded by those sworn to admit only what they regard as scientific evidence: they thereupon happily proceed on the fiction that the factors which they can measure are the only ones that are relevant.[859]

In line with the above quotation, we know from the real world that value and relevance are not limited to tangible and easily measured factors. In this context, when many products and services seem free in today's online economy, with our data privacy as the invisible cost, looking only at price effects is misleading. An overly price-centred approach to competition policy risks overlooking significant welfare harms relating to non-price dimensions of competition, especially data privacy, endangering our *well-being*.

The term 'well-being' embodies somewhat abstract normative properties. At times, the notion has been used by the CJEU as a substitute for the narrower prism of consumer welfare.[860] As noted by the General Court:[861]

> [T]he ultimate purpose of the rules that seek to ensure that competition is not distorted in the internal market is to increase the *well-being* of consumers.

859. The famous speech by Friedrich A Hayek on accepting the Nobel Prize for Economics 'The Pretence of Knowledge' (11 December 1974).
860. Ezrachi (n 369) 7, citing Case C-209/10 *Post Danmark* (n 527) electronic Reports of Cases, para. 42.
861. Joined Cases T-213/01 and T 214/01 *Österreichische Postsparkasse and Bank für Arbeit und Wirtschaft v Commission* [2006] ECR II-1601, para. 115.

When discussing the concepts of consumer welfare and well-being, Ezrachi notes how the former 'hints toward a clearer economic benchmark'.[862] Support for this statement is found, for example, in *Raiffeisen Zentralbank Österreich* and *GSK Spain*, where the General Court appeared to signal a narrow understanding, suggesting that welfare refers to the 'specific economic interests of end-purchasers',[863] in particular those purchasing 'the products in question'.[864] However, as Ezrachi underlines, the concept of consumer welfare does not embody universally agreed properties, and, as discussed in Chapter 3, different views exist, as to its scope, measurement and the means to promote it.[865] As commented by Werden: 'Every favoured policy is said to promote "consumer welfare" [...] [b]ut the superficial consensus on this point masks a deep disagreement about what "consumer welfare" means and especially about what policies best to promote it.'[866] In the debate over competition policy objectives, even among those who support an economic welfare objective, there is disagreement whether welfare reflects consumer welfare or total welfare, and what those concepts really mean.[867]

In an attempt to transform the consumer welfare standard into workable benchmarks, competition authorities have often approximated it through the use of the consumer surplus benchmark.[868] In the context of the data economy, this benchmark has some limitations, however. A potential discrepancy exists between the concept of consumer welfare and the narrower economic benchmark of consumer surplus. Consumer surplus is static in nature and thus may only partially reflect the original goal. This could ignore the full spectrum of effects in the digital economy.[869] The discrepancy also exists with regard to the more abstract goal of well-being. The concepts of consumer *welfare* versus *well-being* and how these two should be understood are addressed further in §5.03.

Often in competition analysis, review of market practices resorts to the consumer welfare standard that places its emphasis on price, whereby authorities focus on factors that are easily measurable, such as short-term pricing effects and short-term productive efficiencies (especially in mergers).[870] This perspective is not optimal in data-driven markets, where online offerings are offered for 'free' and consumers are used to 'not paying' for products and services – other than with their data.[871]

So what this book asserts is that the real value of users' personal data needs to be better accounted for considering the new market realities and forms of interaction between businesses and consumers brought about by the data economy. Data-focused

862. Ezrachi (n 369) 7; Ezrachi (n 334) 1.
863. *Österreichische Postsparkasse* (n 861) para. 99.
864. Case T-168/01 *GlaxoSmithKline* (n 443) para. 118.
865. Ezrachi (n 369) 7.
866. Gregory J Werden, 'Consumer Welfare and Competition Policy' in Josef Drexl, Wolfgang Kerber and Rupprecht Podszun (eds), *Competition Policy and the Economic Approach: Foundations and Limitations* (Edward Elgar Publishing 2011) 15.
867. *See e.g.* Blair and Sokol (n 549) 2497, 2499.
868. Ezrachi (n 369) 8; Orbach (n 369) 133. *See also* Chapter 3, §3.02.
869. Ezrachi (n 369) 8.
870. Stucke and Grunes (n 146).
871. *Ibid.*, 107. *See also* Gal and Rubinfeld (n 411).

business practices can differ from other more conventional practices, raising new kinds of concern about degrading consumers' privacy interests. In these cases, the potential harms are more difficult to quantify. However, this does not make them less significant. The challenge is to consider the intangible harm that comes from invasions of privacy interests; to measure privacy as a competitive harm. The practical implications of this challenge are addressed in §5.03.

[A] Static Price-Centric Perspective

One general challenge and limitation concerning competition law, as any law, is that its interpretation, enforcement and application bring with it an attempt try to fit the financial life and operations of the markets in a frame of rigid rules and paragraphs. In truth, business life is dynamic and unexpected, but the law relies on overly static methods and definitions that are beside the reality or include too many definitions.[872] Views vary as to whether reliance on sophisticated economics, including economic tests and models, has gained appropriate traction and is always good for competition policy.[873] Ezrachi notes the limited amount of practical price-centric tools that can be used to approximate the effects on consumer welfare.[874] This shortcoming is even more apparent in digital markets, where products and services are offered for no monetary payment, leading the price-centric approach to produce a distorted picture of effects.[875]

One may argue that Chicago school dictates and the EU's more economic approach that made consumer welfare the dominant standard of competition policy were a misleading assumption[876] and that narrowing the goal of competition law to a price-centred consumer welfare notion set competition policy on the wrong track. With digitalization of the modern economy and society, where privacy and freedom to choose are perhaps more important rights than ever, a price-centred approach to

872. Fredrik Neumeyer describes this well in his book (in Swedish) on US antitrust law, *see* Neumeyer, *Monopol kontroll i USA* (Kooperativa Förbundets Bokförlag 1951) 206: 'antitrustlagarna försöka stänga in det ekonomiska livet i en ram av stela paragrafer. Affärslivet är dynamiskt och uppfinningsrik, lagen är däremot helt byggd på statiska undersökningsmetoder och fasta begrepp (konkurrens, konkurrensbegränsning, monopol osv), som mest ligga vid sidan om verkligheten eller definieras på alltför många olika sätt.'

873. *See e.g.* Simon Bishop, 'Snake-Oil with Mathematics Is Still Snakeoil: Why Recent Trends in the Application of So-Called "Sophisticated" Economics Is Hindering Good Competition Policy Enforcement' (2013) 9 European Competition Journal 67–77 (expressing concerns that the pendulum has swung too far in the use of economics as a guide for enforcement with the introduction of new economic tests, such as upward pricing pressure and increasing reliance on theoretical possibilities). Similarly, *see* Michael R Baye and Joshua D Wright, 'Is Antitrust Too Complicated for Generalist Judges? The Impact of Economic Complexity and Judicial Training on Appeals' (2011) 54 Journal of Law & Economics 1.

874. Ezrachi (n 369) 8.

875. *Ibid.*

876. Ryan R Stones, 'The Chicago School of Antitrust and the "More Economic Approach" to EU Competition Law: A Mistaken Inspiration', Presentation at CLaSF workshop (Graz 19 April 2018).

competition needs rethinking. Scholars are already discussing whether the EU's 'more economics approach' should be revisited.[877]

In this regard, it should be recalled that at its origins, competition – or antitrust – law is a *political creation*.[878] In the USA, antitrust was created as an instrument designed to break up powerful corporations and prevent the consolidation of economic power that could threaten the political arm.[879] The political origins of antitrust law, its roots and goals, were only later constrained and rationalized by economic thinking.[880] Stucke notes that the 'US antitrust community never agreed that antitrust's goals were only economic or that antitrust only had one goal – to promote economic welfare'[881] and 'despite the push for a single economic antitrust goal, there is no consensus in the US or worldwide on any well-defined goal'.[882]

In EU competition law, the introduction of the more economic approach and the narrowing of competition law's objective solely to consumer welfare were undertaken by the European Commission, with few holdings in case law or court practice.[883] The Commission, under the leadership of former Competition Commissioners Mario Monti followed by Neelie Kroes, put consumer welfare on a pedestal as the primary competition goal but with little explanation or reasoning.[884] Commentators maintain that the underlying reason for the introduction in Europe of the consumer welfare standard has been, at least in part, to limit populistic use of competition provisions.[885]

In a speech, Mario Monti commented on how the USA has credited the EU 'for having brought explicitly the consumer welfare standard into our system'. He reflected on two meta-economic reasons that supported the adoption of the consumer welfare benchmark: 'One was to fight the emerging economic nationalism in the European Single Market which was coming up in those years.' The consumer welfare benchmark provided an anchor:

> to resist more strongly, more fiercely, political pressure that would derail the competition enforcement ... If you adopt a consumer welfare principle ... then you have an imperfect but rather objective reference and you can use that in order to limit the intrusion of economic nationalism.

The second reason, noted by Monti, was geopolitical: the desire to increase convergence and harmonious cooperation with the USA.[886]

877. The author participated in a workshop organized by The Competition Law Scholars Forum (CLaSF) called 'EU's more economic approach to antitrust revisited', XXXth CLaSF Workshop on Antitrust at the intersection of law and economics, CLaSF and the Graz Institute of Corporate and International Commercial Law (19 April 2018). Research conducted for this book was presented by the author at the workshop.
878. Ezrachi (n 334).
879. *See* Chapter 3, §3.04.
880. *Ibid.*
881. Stucke (n 613) 564.
882. Maurice E Stucke, 'The Implications of Behavioral Antitrust' (2012) University of Tennessee Legal Studies Research Paper No 192, 35.
883. *See* Chapter 3, §3.03.
884. *Ibid.*
885. Ezrachi (n 369) 7–8.
886. The full speech by Mario Monti is available at: www.competition-law.ox.ac.uk.

So, it is clear that, when the competition laws in the EU and USA were drafted, economic efficiency was not the exclusive objective.[887] The Chicago school's rise in the 1970s and Posner's influential ideologies, although obviously less in the EU than in the USA, played a decisive role in pushing competition law's non-price related goals to the margin. This development into a narrow price-centred consumer welfare objective is not optimal and, according to many, seems to be failing, in the sense that, today, several industries and sectors are growing in terms of concentration but with little competition. Some studies even show that the actual effect of the consumer welfare objective has been increased prices in many markets.[888]

Commentators argue that the Chicago school introduced a per se legality to anticompetitive market practices and simply gave the judiciary an excuse not to do their job.[889] A multidimensional competition law with multiple objectives can be understood as highlighting the judiciary's very role of balancing multiple competing values, otherwise known as exercising judgment.[890] Indeed, reformers, such as the progressive, antimonopoly New Brandeis movement, are now calling for change, as the mythical ability of the markets to self-correct has become doubtful in the modern economy. As argued by Ezrachi and Stucke, the invisible hand is being replaced by the digital hand.[891]

Opponents try to calm things down and defend free-market capitalism, suggesting that, provided the economy grows, the invisible hand of the market will take care of everything else. So the field of competition law now finds itself torn between aggressive interventionism and a laissez-faire attitude. Increasingly, voices in competition circles are challenging the obsession with price as the prime concern for competition enforcement, pointing to the fact that when times are changing, competition law should evolve and address the issues of the moment, which include values that matter to citizens and to the social fabric, indeed democracy itself.[892] As a way to bridge differences, there are arguments for an adjusted role for economic reasoning in antitrust enforcement, where convergence requires rethinking where and how to apply economics.[893]

Moreover, competition law is not only a political creation but also deeply rooted in ideology; indeed, it is 'a subcategory of ideology'.[894] Competition law is dynamic, which enables it to address a wide range of market and social realities. As explained by Ezrachi, this dynamism 'safeguards competition law from turning into a closed system, detached from domestic needs. It provides a reflection of the changing political landscape and forms part of the democratic process'.[895]

887. Frank Maier-Rigaud, 'On the Normative Foundations of Competition Law: Efficiency, Political Freedom and the Freedom to Compete' in Zimmer (n 441) 132.
888. Khan (n 753) 960.
889. Wu (n 606) 5.
890. *Ibid.*
891. Ezrachi and Stucke (n 146).
892. *See e.g.* Alec J Burnside, 'Bob Dylan and Consumer Welfare' (7 August 2017) Lexology.
893. Maria Lancieri (n 183) 1-27.
894. Ezrachi (n 369) 5. *See also* Bork (n 529) 408.
895. Ezrachi (n 334).

[B] Accounting for the Value of Data

The digitalization of personal data has led to an exponential increase in the scale of personal data processing and the ease with which this processing can occur. Almost every online transaction requires disclosure of personal information, which can then be aggregated, analysed and sold for further use. The growing role of data and privacy in increasingly steering and shaping the markets in itself supports their being taken into consideration as important parameters in competition assessment.

But how should competition law account for the value of personal data? To start with, it should be acknowledged that the overly price-centred approach to competition policy seems to overlook that the process and theory of competition includes both price and non-price parameters. For example, consumer choice, quality and innovation are key non-price aspects of competition. Quality is a fundamental consideration – in addition to price – determining whether consumers will buy a product or service.[896] As argued by Wouter Wils, an assumption that customers only value price, and not also quality and variety, has no sound economic basis.[897]

In today's online markets, where products and services are commonly offered to consumers at zero price, competition is increasingly conducted over non-price elements, such as quality. This has been recognized in the practice of some competition authorities. For example, in *Microsoft/Skype*, the European Commission noted that '[s]ince consumer communications services are mainly provided for free, consumers pay more attention to other features' and '[q]uality is therefore a significant parameter of competition'.[898] In this regard, then, how should quality be understood? And how does a potential data privacy dimension fit into this?

As a broad notion, quality includes privacy protection. By the same token, privacy is viewed as a parameter of non-price quality competition.[899] As the impact on non-price parameters, such as quality, has generally been given less attention than price in competition analysis, privacy as a competition concern has often been set aside as a non-economic interest standing outside competition law's policy goals.[900] However, as discussed in Chapter 4, recent developments point to an emerging intellectual shift by policymakers and academics in the perception of the role of data and privacy. Even the head of DG Competition has suggested a more dynamic approach to EU competition analysis that would look beyond a price-centric perspective and give more weight to longer-term effects in terms of new technologies and the digital economy.[901]

896. OECD, 'The Role and Measurement of Quality in Competition Analysis' (28 October 2013) 5.
897. Wouter PJ Wils, 'The Judgment of the EU General Court in Intel and the So-Called "More Economic Approach" to Abuse of Dominance' (2014) 37 World Competition: Law and Economics Review 405–434.
898. Case COMP/M.6281 *Microsoft/Skype* C(2011) 7279, 81. Similarly, *Microsoft/Yahoo* (n 524).
899. For example, the search engine DuckDuckGo, which does not track users or customize results, is one example of non-price quality competition, where differentiation from competitors in the marketplace is achieved on a privacy basis.
900. *See e.g. Google/DoubleClick* (n 673); *Facebook/WhatsApp* (n 133).
901. Speech by Laitenberger (n 526).

Moreover, by now, the notion that privacy is also a competition concern has been explicitly recognized in several major reports, such as the Furman report, the Commission expert report, the Stigler report and multiple others, displayed in Figure 4.1.[902] At least the numerous competition authority reports and other similarly timed initiatives seem to share a common goal of suggesting that there is consensus about the special risks posed by digital markets and the need to act. Public opinion (as well as many individual opinions too) seem to have shifted[903] and, in the words of Alfonso Lamadrid de Pablo, generated 'something of a natural snowball effect',[904] and the similarly timed publication of these reports may suggest some kind of consensus among experts and the broader competition community. In particular, the work of Yves-Alexandre de Montjoye, one of the co-authors of the Commission expert report, and the Computational Privacy Group at Imperial College London supports that there should be no tension between the pursuit of privacy and competition and that privacy and competition can actually reinforce one another.[905]

It follows that one way for competition law to better account for the value of personal data is by giving more room for non-price interests, such as choice, quality and privacy as a subcategory of quality, in the current standard of consumer welfare (as the principal aim of competition policy). As stated, consumer welfare is not only about economic efficiency or prices but also very much about non-economic or so-called 'social' values.[906] The current standard of consumer welfare that centres too much on price is out of touch with the operations of online markets, where consumers pay for Internet services through disclosure of their personal information - often unknowingly - with no monetary price that competition economists could measure with their traditional tools of economic analysis.[907]

This is not to say that the increasing use and commercialization of data consistently leads to competition issues. Most of the time these free online-based services provide real benefits to consumers and are clearly pro-competitive. Accordingly, in their joint report on data and competition, the French and German competition authorities note that the technological changes to the digital economy have revolutionized possibilities to collect, process and commercially use data in almost every business sector, thus in turn improving services and increasing economic efficiency. But, at the same time, the authorities warn that the collection and use of greater volumes of data can raise competition issues.[908]

902. *See* Chapter 4, §4.02.
903. *See e.g.* statement by Fiona Scott Morton to *The New Republic*: 'I actually have had the same opinion about antitrust enforcement I think for quite a while [...] I was just not as willing to say it as publicly because so few other people seemed to share it.' David Dayen, 'The Radicalization of Fiona Scott Morton' The New Republic (23 May 2019) https://newrepublic.com/article/153785/radicalization-fiona-scott-morton, accessed 19 April 2020.
904. 'Shortcuts and Courts in the Era of Digitization' Competition Policy International (October 2019).
905. Caffarra and Valletti (n 701).
906. *See also* Wasastjerna (n 645).
907. Gal and Rubinfeld (n 411) 530.
908. French-German joint report (n 9) 9.

Not only the role but also the value of data is increasing. Personal data has become so valuable that companies are willing to forego monetary payment for their digital products or services to gain access to data. Recognizing this new market reality, Article 3(1) of the proposed Directive on digital contracts applies when 'a price is to be paid or the consumer actively provides counter-performance other than money in the form of personal data or other data'.[909] While technology companies such as Facebook and Google initially may have used the data they collected from users to target advertising more effectively, in recent years data can be turned into any number of artificial intelligence or 'cognitive' services (such as translation, visual recognition), which may generate new sources of revenue when sold to other companies for use in their own products.[910]

Another way of saying that the value of data is growing is to recognize that data has become an asset: '[t]here's no such thing as a free search or anything like that, so obviously you pay, and your payment then becomes an asset'.[911] This means that valuable information concerning user behaviour and purchasing habits received by technology companies in return for their products amounts to an asset, which should be protected. One suggestion is to give data similar protection to property rights. This would give people more control over their information:

> Just as America drew up sophisticated rules about intellectual property in the 19th century, so it needs a new set of laws to govern the ownership and exchange of data, with the aim of giving solid rights to individuals.[912]

In this regard, the situation in Europe with its strong data protection legal framework is many steps ahead of the USA, as discussed in Chapter 2.

Data as a currency. Data is also likened to a new digital currency. However, some controversy exists among competition authorities as to the analogy between data and price, and different views are presented, especially between Europe and the USA. While European competition officials increasingly acknowledge the value of data and treat it as the price paid by consumers for accessing online offerings,[913] American antitrust officials are taking a more cautious and conservative approach, questioning whether privacy can be measured in the same terms as money.[914] Whereas Europeans, spearheaded by the German competition authority, are venturing into new territory by

909. Proposal for a Directive of the European Parliament and of the Council on certain aspects concerning contracts on the supply of digital content, COM(2015)634 Final.
910. The Economist 'Fuel of the Future' (n 5).
911. Xan Rice, 'Margrethe Vestager: The EU Commissioner Who's Taming the Tech Giants' NewStatesman (15 January 2018) https://www.newstatesman.com/science-tech/2018/01/margrethe-vestager-eu-commissioner-who-s-taming-tech-giants, accessed 19 April 2020.
912. The Economist, 'Competition in the Digital Age: How to Tame the Tech Titans' (18 January 2018) https://www.economist.com/news/leaders/21735021-dominance-google-facebook-and-amazon-bad-consumers-and-competition-how-tame?fsrc=scn/tw/te/bl/ed/howtotamethetechtitanscompetitioninthedigitalage&lipi=urn%3Ali%3Apage%3Ad_flagship3_feed%3Bwp7s8sQmSpqnAQjYKAS8fg%3D%3D, accessed 19 April 2020.
913. *Google Search (Shopping)* (n 46) and the German Facebook case (n 18) serve as illustrative examples of this development in Europe.
914. *See* Chapter 4, §4.04[D] speculating whether this may give rise to a growing transatlantic divergence.

testing the conventional boundaries between competition and data protection, Americans are raising concerns about the confluence of privacy and antitrust.[915]

Nevertheless, public concern is growing about personal data in the hands of a few powerful technology companies. This has led to increasing pressure from the media, journalists and leading newspapers as to the need for authorities and policymakers to think afresh about how technology markets work and to acknowledge that personal data is the currency in which customers actually buy services. As proclaimed by the *Harvard Business Review*:[916]

> [t]he coming battle in antitrust will not be about controlling markets in the traditional sense. It will be about the battle for control over consumers' information. The tech titans are currently in a race to see which of them can build a better digital replica of their consumers, which means finding a way to not just collect user data but also make it harder for competitors to do so. Tomorrow's monopolies won't be able to be measured just by how much they sell us. They'll be based on how much they know about us and how much better they can predict our behaviour than competitors.

Data as an asset. Essentially, two main ways are available to competition law to address some of the risks of data, especially when analysing abuse of dominance cases and assessing mergers. Data can be treated as a *qualitative parameter*. Competition law can incorporate into its analysis the impact of data on alternative dimensions of competition, such as quality.[917] This approach of looking at data privacy as a quality component captures some of the privacy-related concerns of data and will be explored further in its own §5.03[A].

The value of data is accounted for by treating it as an input or asset, which companies may use to enhance their market power and engage in abusive practices.[918] In markets where data can be an important input for business success, a concern may arise that the massive accumulation of personal information and intensive use of data analytics may enhance market power, lock in consumers and raise barriers to entry.[919] This may create incentives for companies to engage in anticompetitive practices, such as pre-emptive mergers,[920] exclusionary conduct and even to collude in novel ways.

---

915. As discussed in Chapter 4, §4.04[C], highly ranked American antitrust officials have even gone as far as to criticize the German competition authority's probe into Facebook that focuses on whether the social network is abusing its market power by extracting data from users that it can then monetize through selling ads. *See* speech by US Assistant Attorney General for Antitrust Makan Delrahim, 'Digital Platforms and Concentration' Stigler Center for Study of Economy and the State at the University of Chicago Booth School of Business (Chicago, 19–20 April 2018), reported in Leah Nylen, 'DOJ's Delrahim Says Antitrust Enforcers Shouldn't Intervene in Consumer Privacy Markets Absent Barriers to Entry' MLex Market Insight (19 April 2018).
916. Iyer, Subramaniam and Rangan (n 23).
917. *Ibid.*
918. *See* OECD Big Data (n 22) 3–4.
919. *Ibid.*
920. The concept of pre-emptive or defensive mergers refers to the aim of removing the threat of potential competition by buying the most threatening (potential) data rival while it is still small, which may be an effective foreclosure strategy in digital markets. *See* European Parliament (n 692) 60.

However, traditional competition tools can be applied to tackle such data-related anticompetitive practices, by treating data as any other input.[921] For instance, in merger control and exclusionary abuse cases, competition authorities may consider foreclosure risks and design remedies accordingly. Remedies such as requirements to share inputs – in this case data – could be used when no less intrusive alternatives are available. *Microsoft/LinkedIn* exemplifies the use of this kind of remedy concerning provision of data access to rivals. In 2018, the European Commission caused headlines by intervening in the proposed acquisition by Apple of song-recognition service Shazam.[922] Concern centred on access to data, because not only would the deal combine two significant and well-known players in the digital music industry but, more importantly, also Shazam possessed important and commercially sensitive data about Apple's rivals, potentially allowing the company to 'directly target its competitors' customers and encourage them to switch' to Apple's own streaming service.[923]

Data access is especially important in online advertising, where data is needed as an input for placing targeted ads. There, the potential concern with data as an asset is that the large platforms have paramount advantages as they can combine their reach and data access. This has led to the concept of 'walled gardens', referring to advertising platforms by Google or Facebook being closed systems with user restrictions.[924] This kind of data concentration in online advertising may have negative foreclosure effects on competition, in particular in the case of exclusive access to particularly relevant data volumes and network effects. Competition authorities in Europe are conducting sector enquiries into online advertising markets to better understand the competitive conditions and potential problems in this field.[925]

When looking at data as an asset or input in digital markets, before competition intervention is considered, competition authorities should carry out '[a] case-specific assessment of the reality and extent of the "data advantage"', meaning that they need to examine on a case-by-case basis to what extent business performance depends on data control and data analytics; in particular, the following considerations are relevant in the assessment: whether data is replicable in the relevant market, whether it can be

921. *See e.g. TomTom/Tele Atlas* (n 725) 1859.

922. *Apple/Shazam* (n 657). *See also* European Commission press release, 'Mergers: Commission opens in-depth investigation into Apple's proposed acquisition of Shazam' (Brussels, 23 April 2018) IP/18/3505; Adam Satariano, Apple's Deal for Shazam Is Delayed in Europe over Data Concerns' The New York Times (3 April 2018) https://www.nytimes.com/2018/04/23/business/apple-shazam-eu-data.html, accessed 19 April 2020.

923. *Ibid.*

924. Silke Heinz, 'Bundeskartellamt Launches Sector Inquiry into Online Advertising' (Kluwer Competition Law Blog, 9 March 2018) http://competitionlawblog.kluwercompetitionlaw.com/2018/03/09/bundeskartellamt-launches-sector-inquiry-online-advertising/, accessed 19 April 2020.

925. In February 2018, the German competition authority launched a sector enquiry into online advertising, press release (n 654). In parallel, the authority published a paper on online advertising, which sheds more light on the scope of the enquiry: 'Competition and Consumer Protection in the Digital Economy: Online advertising' (February 2018) http://www.bundeskartellamt.de/SharedDocs/Publikation/EN/Schriftenreihe_Digitales_III.pdf?__blob=publicationFile&v=5, accessed 19 April 2020. The German competition authority follows the French competition authority that made an online advertising sector enquiry in 2016 and published its results two years later, *see* Autorité de la concurrence, Avis n°18-A-03 (n 654).

collected from other sources, the degree of substitutability between different datasets, how quickly data becomes outdated, and how much data a potential entrant needs to compete.[926]

Data and trust. In the future, it is possible that consumers' views on the value of personal data as an asset will undergo changes and user preferences will shift due to loss of trust in online markets and service providers. As technology evolves and more personal data is collected, consumers become increasingly aware of how their personal information is used[927] sometimes in questionable ways. Think only of the Facebook-Cambridge Analytica scandal in which data from 87 million Facebook users was illegally accessed from the platform. If more data privacy scandals of this kind and magnitude come to light, it is not unthinkable that this may have the consequence of initiating a fundamental alteration in the marketplace, whereby users of digital platforms become better informed about the implications of sharing their private data. Perhaps in the future the world will be one in which a substantial number of consumers view their data as an asset they will not part with for free.[928] A feeling of insufficient control over use of their information and lack of understanding about its use may lead some consumers to choose not 'to share their data, to limit their data sharing with companies, or even to lie when providing information', as the UK's Competition and Markets Authority put it.[929]

This has significant consequences, as market economies rely on trust. For online markets to deliver their benefits, people must trust businesses and their use of personal data. When companies degrade privacy protections, consumers may forego online offerings, which they otherwise would have used if privacy protection were robust. This loss would amount to what economists call a deadweight welfare loss.[930] In other words, as distrust increases, society overall becomes worse off.[931]

The importance of trust is closely linked to freedom of choice. As Competition Commissioner Vestager explains:[932]

> Most people don't think about politics all the time. But they do have to buy things in the market every day. And if they get treated unfairly in the market, it affects how they relate to the whole world around them. If consumers don't have the chance to make their own choices, to walk away from businesses that don't serve them well, that undermines the trust that makes our society work.

At the same time, growing awareness among consumers about the value of their user data and personal information will increasingly make privacy a competitive advantage for technology companies. In a world in which companies have more personal information about citizens or consumers than ever before and holding data

926. French-German joint report (n 9) 53.
927. CMA Report (n 168).
928. *See also* speech by US Assistant Attorney General for Antitrust Makan Delrahim (n 889).
929. CMA Report (n 168) para. 4.165.
930. Stucke (n 407).
931. *Ibid.*
932. Speech by Margrethe Vestager, 'Competition in Changing Times' FIW Symposium (Innsbruck, 16 February 2018).

that can be used in myriad nefarious ways, privacy is a serious competitive advantage.[933]

[C] Fundamental Rights Aspect

> *The right to decide what happens with our personal information is one of our most fundamental rights as individuals. And we can't just leave it to the market to protect those rights.*[934]

As part of examining the introduction of a data privacy dimension into competition policy, it is justified to consider whether the fundamental right to data protection can be used as a normative benchmark for the application of competition law to advance privacy protection. This chapter looks at this fundamental rights aspect.

It is clear that, beyond having monetary value and being regarded as an asset,[935] personal data is closely linked to the dignity, autonomy and personality of individuals. EU data protection law aims to safeguard this dual nature of personal data by seeking to ensure the free flow of personal information while respecting the fundamental rights to privacy and data protection.[936] The EU data protection framework and the GDPR aim to ensure individuals' control over their personal data through mechanisms such as consent, rights to information, and rights to access, rectify and delete data.[937] This individual control may, however, be frustrated by asymmetries in information and power. This means that while individuals become increasingly 'transparent' or 'legible' to those processing personal information, data processing practices can be ambiguous and online services are often offered on a 'take it or leave it' basis, which leaves little scope for choice.[938]

So, in effect, the data protection framework may not in real life give the protection it sets out to do on paper. Critics argue that the EU data protection framework is not capable of addressing the challenges of current personal data processing practices in the Internet age. For example, some say that the continued belief in consent as a major legitimating ground also in online contexts denies the reality of 21st-century data processing.[939] Bert-Jaap Koops argues that EU data protection is inadequate in many ways and contends that the framework's main objectives are all based on fallacies.[940]

---

933. *See also* Rana Foroohar, 'Digital Economy – Privacy Is a Competitive Advantage' Financial Times (15 October 2017) https://amp.ft.com/content/0247b8f2-b012-11e7-beba-5521c713abf4?_twitter_impression=true, accessed 19 April 2020.
934. Speech by Vestager (n 684).
935. *See* Chapter 4, §4.02[A].
936. *See* Lynskey (n 137) 46–47.
937. Costa-Cabral and Lynskey (n 128) 12.
938. *See* Cate and Mayer-Schönberger (n 783) 67.
939. Bert-Jaap Koops, 'The Trouble with European Data Protection Law' (2014) 4 International Data Privacy Law 250.
940. *Ibid.*, in the words of Koops: 'The trouble with Harry, in Alfred Hitchcock's 1955 movie, is that he's dead, and everyone seems to have a different idea of what needs to be done with his body. The trouble with European data protection law is the same. In several crucial respects, data

Accordingly, the first fallacy is the delusion that data protection law can give individuals control over their data, which, arguably, it cannot.[941] The second is the misconception that reform through the GDPR simplifies the law, whereas in fact it may lead to even more complex compliance efforts.[942] The third is the assumption that data protection law should be comprehensive, which stretches data protection to breaking point and makes it 'meaningless law in the books'.[943]

Against this background and criticism against EU data protection law on the basis that it is insufficient to protect data privacy in the digital age, calls have been heard pressing for a broader approach to personal data protection by promoting closer integration with other EU law policies that shape markets, especially competition law. As mentioned, the EDPS has been particularly vocal in advocating that competition law enforcement should consider data protection and privacy.[944] To align competition law with data protection and to facilitate privacy-related goals, competition rules could be applied through the mechanism of the Charter of Fundamental Rights, which recognizes protection of personal data as a specific right.[945] The right protects not only against intrusion by the state but also against any interference that does not meet the required safeguards, that is, processing 'for specified purposes and on the basis of the consent of the person concerned or some other legitimate basis laid down by law'.[946]

Striving towards this superior hierarchy stipulation and aligning with more specific directives adopted to give effect to it, not least the GDPR, EU competition law can be applied so as to facilitate privacy protection generally. For example, in its competitive assessment in the case of *Google/Sanofi*, where post-merger concentration of patient data was a central issue, the European Commission relied on data protection rules in terms of data portability and of restrictions in the use of data by a joint venture between the parties.[947]

The European Commission has recognized the importance of data privacy as a fundamental right in the context of recent competition enforcement. For example, when commenting on its conditional clearance of Microsoft's merger with LinkedIn, the EU Competition Commissioner stressed that '[t]he right to decide what happens with our personal information is one of our most fundamental rights as individuals. And we can't just leave it to the market to protect those rights'.[948]

Insightful scholarship in this area by Francisco Costa-Cabral and Lynskey explores the fundamental right to data protection as a normative benchmark for the application of competition law.[949] To open the door for privacy-related goals, competition policy can reflect the fundamental right to data protection as a normative

protection law is currently a dead letter. The current legal reform will fail to revive it, since its three main objectives are based on fallacies [...].'

941. *Ibid.*
942. *Ibid.*
943. *Ibid.*
944. *See* Chapter 4, §4.04.
945. EU Charter of Fundamental Rights (n 188) 8.
946. EDPS Opinion (n 10) 16.
947. Case COMP/M.7813 *Sanofi/Google/DMI JV*, C(2016) 1223.
948. Speech by Vestager (n 684).
949. Costa-Cabral and Lynskey (n 96); Costa-Cabral and Lynskey (n 128) 11.

benchmark. One may ask why data privacy should deserve such special attention and protection. One justification is that data protection enjoys privileged status in EU law and can be distinguished from other public policy objectives due to its inclusion in the EU Charter of Fundamental Rights.[950] Further, the important role played by data and privacy in shaping online markets and the whole digital economy supports their need for increased protection as rights. Costa-Cabral and Lynskey have called for the EU Charter to exercise a more extensive influence by data protection on other policies, including competition law.[951] It is also suggested that the Commission should be under a positive obligation to respect and promote the EU Charter.[952]

The obligation to respect and promote the EU Charter stems from the wording of the EU Charter itself and the case law of the EU courts.[953] Article 51(1) of the EU Charter sets out an obligation for EU institutions and bodies to respect Charter rights and for Member States to respect these rights when 'implementing EU law'.[954] It follows that all EU institutions and bodies, including the Commission, can be challenged if they fail to respect Charter rights when enacting legally binding acts.[955] Non-legislative measures adopted by the Commission, such as decisions (for example legally binding competition law decisions), are also subject to checks, during drafting, on their compatibility with the Charter.[956] The obligation to promote the EU Charter comes not only from the wording of the EU Charter itself but also from the case law of the EU courts. For example, in the *Digital Rights Ireland* judgment, the CJEU declared the entire Data Retention Directive invalid due to its failure to comply with EU Charter rights to data protection and privacy.[957]

In the light of this legal context, the European Commission's approach in *Google/DoubleClick* and *Facebook/WhatsApp* is questionable for having dismissed data protection concerns as non-economic, beyond the scope of review and subject to a separate data protection assessment.[958]

However, although it seems clear that the European Commission has an obligation *not to infringe* the Charter rights of data protection and privacy when adopting legally binding competition law decisions, the extent of the obligation to *respect* and *promote* the EU Charter rights is ambiguous. Costa-Cabral and Lynskey argue for an extensive approach that would require the Commission to take affirmative action to

950. Costa-Cabral and Lynskey (n 96) 14.
951. *Ibid.*, 39.
952. *Ibid.*
953. *Ibid.*, 40.
954. According to Article 51(1) of the Charter, '[t]he provisions of this Charter are addressed to the institutions and bodies of the Union with due regard for the principle of subsidiarity and to the Member States only when they are implementing Union law. They shall therefore respect the rights, observe the principles and promote the application thereof in accordance with their respective powers'.
955. Such failure can be challenged via Article 263 TFEU or 267 TFEU and may result in a declaration that the act is unlawful.
956. Strategy for the effective implementation of the Charter of Fundamental Rights by the European Union, COM(2010)573 Final, 6.
957. *Digital Rights Ireland* (n 221) I-238.
958. Costa-Cabral and Lynskey (n 128) 43.

ensure that all areas of EU policy making, including competition policy, are compliant with data protection and other EU Charter rights.[959]

Based on the EU Charter of Fundamental Rights, it seems reasonable that at least the European Commission should not use its competition law competences in a manner that breaches the right to data protection, or jeopardizes its effectiveness.[960] But it is arguable whether sufficient basis exists for the Commission to take much of a proactive role and start vigorously enforcing data protection law through its competition law competences. At least, this would surely be faced with opposition on the ground that competition law is being 'hijacked to achieve data protection aims'[961] and critics would argue that it runs contrary to the principle of legality, which limits the application of competition law.[962] At the same time, this is effectively what the Bundeskartellamt has done in Germany.

Equally, it could be argued that 'once everything is relevant, nothing is dispositive'.[963] Requiring the European Commission to factor fundamental rights considerations into its competition analysis could be argued as leading it down a slippery slope.[964] One of the reasons why the Commission and other competition authorities alike have sometimes rejected the inclusion of public policy and social concerns into their analysis is the fear that this would open the door to political influence and incommensurable analysis. At the same time, history shows that competition authorities and courts have taken stances in questions on competition law due to political, social or strategic reasons, for example to smooth social tensions. In the USA, the antitrust laws were implemented more leniently in the Great Depression.[965]

However, it should be recalled that, in its origins, competition law is a *political creation*.[966] It would be naïve to think that competition law is immune to political influence and pure from social values; competition policy is a political construct and inherently susceptible to a wide range of societal variants. Therefore, these objections against incorporating fundamental data protection rights into competition analysis are hardly convincing. It is a matter of value choices and preferences for which policy goals deserve protection.

In this regard, it is noteworthy that the Commission has advanced cultural diversity as an important value or policy goal when enforcing competition law. Cultural diversity was explicitly taken into account in the field of merger control in the *Universal/EMI* decision.[967] Indeed, Article 167(4) TFEU provides that '[t]he Union shall take cultural aspects into account *in its action under other provisions* of the Treaties, in

959. *Ibid.*, 45.
960. *Ibid.*, 47-48.
961. *Ibid.*, 47.
962. According to the CJEU, the principle of legality 'implies that legislation must define clearly offences and the penalties which they attract'. *See* Case C-303/05 *Advocaten voor de Wereld* [2007] para. 49.
963. Frank H Easterbrook, 'Limits of Antitrust' (1984) 63 Texas Law Review 12.
964. *See*, by analogy, Odudu (n 439) 599.
965. Motta (n 322) 26-27. *See also* Theodore Voorhees Jr, 'The Political Hand in American Antitrust - Invisible, Inspirational or Imaginary?' (2014) 79 Antitrust Law Journal.
966. *See* discussion in §5.02[A]. *See also* Ezrachi (n 334).
967. Case COMP/M.6458 *Universal Music Group/EMI Music*.

particular in order to respect and to promote the diversity of its cultures'.[968] Here, one can draw a comparison with Article 16 TFEU affirming that 'Everyone has the right to the protection of [their] personal data.'[969] While not explicitly mandating that data protection aspects be considered in all actions conducted by the Union under the Treaties, Article 16 TFEU grants the Commission a basis for advancing data protection as a preferred policy goal when enforcing competition law. This was done with cultural diversity. It is an open question whether these provisions carry specific obligations for competition authorities.[970] However, in their joint report, the German and French competition authorities note this possibility and make specific reference to cases that may arise 'in which consumer welfare and data protection concerns appear to be at stake'.[971] This is closely connected to what the EDPS has advocated (since 2014) regarding a shift in policy, an introduction of a more holistic approach to competition law and data protection and more systematic dialogue between the regulators. Considering the criticism mentioned at the start of this chapter concerning the inadequacy of EU data protection law in actually protecting data privacy in the digital age, a holistic approach would be a sensible development forward. This holistic or conjoined approach is discussed in more detail in Chapter 6.

§5.03 BRINGING A PRIVACY DIMENSION TO COMPETITION POLICY

Having in the previous chapters discussed the shortcomings or limitations of the existing competition paradigm in a world transforming from price-centricity to data and privacy centricity, this chapter looks to the future and envisions what a sound competition policy for the digital age should look like. This is done by exploring how competition law can consider privacy protection in its policy objectives with the aim of providing welfare, or rather well-being, for consumers.

The guiding question steering the discourse in this chapter is how to incorporate data privacy into competition law and make such an approach fully operational. Section §5.03[A] looks at the treatment of privacy in competition policy as a quality component. One of the key characteristics of privacy is that it is an intangible concept, making it difficult to measure, as opposed to price. The challenge of measuring privacy as a non-price dimension in competition law is explored further in §5.03[B].

These issues are addressed by building on the previous discussions in Chapter 2 on privacy and data protection, as well as Chapter 3 concerning the underlying objectives in European and American competition law. A historical look at EU and US antitrust policy[972] demonstrates that antitrust and competition laws are influenced by social and historical factors and can respond to quite a wide range of distinct objectives.[973] Enforcement of competition policy has at different times been influenced

968. Emphasis added.
969. French-German joint report (n 9) 24.
970. *Ibid.*
971. *Ibid.*, referring to the EDPS Opinion (n 10).
972. *See* Chapter 4, §4.03 and §4.04.
973. *See also* Motta (n 322) 17.

by different political views and public policy considerations. Different policy objectives have been indicated in different circumstances and in different jurisdictions, meaning that a number of goals have inspired competition policies, especially in Europe.[974] The following analysis of another policy objective to inspire competition law, namely that of protecting consumer data and privacy, is a reflection of current-day concerns and priorities in the data economy. The interlinkage and increasing interplay between competition and data privacy, explored in Chapter 4, provides the necessary basis for exploring a shift or change in competition law's policy goals to include non-price elements such as privacy, which is of utmost importance in today's data-driven markets. This intellectual shift or conceptual change, or even transformation of competition policy, however one prefers to phrase the necessary policy discourse, is of fundamental significance, as the policy goals shape and steer how law and policy are implemented and enforced in digital markets.

As analysed in Chapter 3, although competition policy was originally enacted to address multiple goals - especially so in Europe - over time it transitioned away from political and non-economic goals to promoting more efficient allocation of resources, with primary focus on the price effects of competition. This development meant that factors that were easily measurable, such as price, became disproportionately important for enforcers.[975] This is true for the competition systems in both the EU and the USA, although US antitrust policy is far more dominated by price than EU competition policy, as described above, much due to the influence of the Chicago school.

However, we know from the real world that it is not only what is easily measurable that counts, as captured by Nobel prizewinner Hayek.[976] When many products and services today are seemingly free, and where our data and privacy are the cost, it is misleading to look only at price effects. The effects on non-economic and intangible elements of competition are as important for consumer welfare and the well-being of individuals. This means that privacy as a competition goal can be just as important as price-related goals. The issue is not whether, but *how* something that is hard to quantify can be included in competition analysis.

Of course, some would disagree. Some go as far as to argue that it is only a matter of time and proper institutional and case law development until political and non-economic competition goals will be pushed to the margin and become inconsequential.[977] However, considering that privacy is emerging as an increasingly major concern in the public discourse on big data and the digital economy, and national competition authorities in Europe are devoting more and more attention to the relationship between competition and privacy, it seems unlikely that non-economic competition goals, such as privacy, are becoming inconsequential. Quite the contrary, as this book asserts, it seems Europe is already engaging on a path which may lead to the transformation of its competition policy.

974. *See* Chapter 3, §3.03 discussing the multidimensional character of EU competition law and its various policy objectives.
975. Stucke and Grunes (n 146) 113.
976. *See* §5.02.
977. *See e.g.* Blair and Sokol (n 549) 2506.

When commenting on the *Google/DoubleClick* decision, former EU Competition Commissioner Almunia predicted that, while the Commission had not yet at that time encountered a merger where it suspected that personal data could be used to breach EU competition law, this did not mean that it could not happen: '[i]n time, personal data may well become a competition issue'.[978] Indeed, looking at where we are today, this prediction seems to have come true, at least conceptually.

Considering the differences in history, traditions and culture concerning privacy protection and competition policy between the EU and the USA, Europe's competition regime is more apt to incorporate privacy among its policy goals. This is mainly because of the focus on economic efficiency and the functional approach reflected in US antitrust law. In Europe, it is easier, at least on a theoretical level, to combine privacy and competition, as data protection and privacy enjoy special status in the shape of fundamental Charter rights. Non-economic goals are also more significantly embedded in EU competition law than US antitrust law. EU competition law generally focuses on *harm to competition*, and it is not excluded that other goals beyond economic efficiency play a part. This is especially so, as the original mission of competition law in the European Community had as its purpose the politics of market integration, among others. The position has since changed substantially with the European Commission's efforts to narrow EU competition goals and adopt a price-focused concept of consumer welfare as the main guiding principle, much as in US antitrust law. However, as discussed, academics and policymakers are increasingly abuzz exploring the topic of incorporating non-price aspects and societal concerns into competition analysis, including privacy and data protection issues.[979]

Some practical challenges exist, however, to integrating privacy considerations into competition law. These will be explored in the following chapters. It suffices to say here that this is partly because the competition regime has over time formed into a price-centric system, but even more so due to the fact that the subjectivity of privacy as an element creates inherent difficulties. There are also policy objections, and those who argue against letting privacy considerations affect competition analysis often contend that competition law enforcement objectives should only, or at least primarily, focus on economic efficiency.[980] This is especially common among voices expressed in the American debate.[981] But, under a purely economic approach to competition enforcement, the danger lies in the long-term consequences for the welfare, or well-being, of consumers not being immediately apparent. In recent years, with the rise of big data and digitalization, the European competition landscape has become more attentive to privacy harms in competition, reflecting an emerging intellectual shift, and

978. Almunia (n 678).
979. *See* discussion and references in Chapter 4, §4.04.
980. *See e.g.* James Cooper, 'Privacy and Antitrust: Underpants, Gnomes, the First Amendment, and Subjectivity' (2013) 20 George Mason Law Review 1129–1146; Tucker and Wellford (n 680) 3–4; Sokol and Comerford (n 680) in Blair and Sokol (n 41).
981. *See e.g.* Ohlhausen and Okuliar (n 667) 143.

although this trend can be debated,[982] it can, nevertheless, be viewed as a positive development in the sense that it fosters open dialogue about competition law's objectives.

The issue of incorporating privacy into competition law should be approached by recalling that the data protection and competition regimes have complementary goals in that competition law strives to ensure that consumers have a range of choices, while data protection aims to ensure that consumers are in possession of truthful and accurate information when making those choices. The joint study on competition and data by the German and French competition authorities notes that even though competition and data protection laws (also) serve different goals, privacy issues cannot be excluded from consideration under competition law simply by virtue of their nature.[983]

In the debate about competition and data resulting from the emergence of the big data phenomenon, arguments have been heard that competition law has no role to play in big data and that competition rules would somehow be set aside by the fact that big data comprises information about individuals that may be subject to data protection or privacy requirements.[984] Although it is easy to agree with the generalization that competition enforcement should be concerned with competition law, while data protection regulators should be concerned with data protection compliance, this does not mean there is no overlap. That would be a naïve assumption to make and an oversimplification of the situation. The fact is that in some cases market conduct by a dominant company may infringe both competition and data protection laws. This can occur, for example, by services enhancing privacy or choice being excluded in the marketplace. For example, concerns regarding privacy as a form of non-price competition would arise, for example, if Google were to acquire DuckDuckGo, which offers consumers greater privacy protection for their search queries.[985]

Of course, an overlap in applicable rules is nothing unique in itself. This is a question about the scope of application in the data economy of EU competition law and about identifying market failures in the data economy and the limits of data protection law that justify the applicability of EU competition law and the inclusion of privacy protection as a competition policy goal. The limits of data protection law in the context of the data economy are particularly evident in the so-called privacy paradox and its corresponding implications, and the (common) lack of transparency of data protection terms, as exemplified by the German Facebook case. As mentioned, a privacy paradox means that although many users are concerned about their privacy, few actually act on those concerns, and there is a situation of dysfunctional equilibrium when users become cynical and fail to read privacy policies, which in turn leads to companies having vague policies, as they expect few consumers read policies and demand would

982. *See e.g.* Alfonso Lamadrid de Pablo and Sam Villiers, 'Big Data, Privacy and Competition Law: Do Competition Authorities Know How To Do It?' (Winter 2017) 1 Competition Policy International Antitrust Chronicle.

983. French-German joint report (n 9) 23.

984. Tucker and Wellford (n 680) 3–4; Sokol and Comerford (n 680) in Blair and Sokol (n 41).

985. Grunes and Stucke (n 667) 5.

not shift significantly.[986] These limits of data protection law can be considered potential market failures and situations that justify the applicability of EU competition law as a sort of 'gap filler'.[987]

Moreover, these issues reflect a sort of regulatory gap and support that EU competition law should protect data privacy in the digital economy. This also answers the question posed earlier, namely whether EU competition law should play a part in protecting the personal data of consumers after the new EU data privacy rules. The answer is affirmative, though with certain disclaimers. While EU competition law should play a part in protecting the personal data of consumers, this should be done in carefully selected cases, where competition law has the role of a gap filler and is resorted to when no other law or policy is available to ensure consumers' right to privacy.[988]

As noted in the French-German joint report, the fact that some specific legal instruments serve to resolve issues on personal data does not mean that competition law is irrelevant to personal data.[989] Privacy issues cannot be excluded from consideration under competition law simply by virtue of their nature.[990] Moreover, when conducting a legal assessment under competition law, statutory requirements stemming from other bodies of law can generally be taken into account.[991] Arguments that competition law should not be extended so far into another policy area can be rebutted by noting that this would not be the first time when active enforcement of EU competition law has been used to support a related policy area.[992]

The question whether and to what extent privacy considerations can be considered within a competitive assessment recalls older debates concerning the application of competition policy to promote environmental objectives.[993] While citizens have an interest in clean air, competition law has never taken promoting environmental policy as its key enforcement task. However, this does not keep it from giving weight to environmental goals. So, for example, the Commission has used its powers to approve an otherwise restrictive agreement because it protected environmental objectives as defined in the directive on packaging waste.[994] This approach embraced the Treaty objective specifying integration of environmental protection requirements into EU policies and actions.[995] Guidance from DG Competition on exemption under Article

986. Farrell (n 96) 251; Costa-Cabral and Lynskey (n 128) 28.
987. Botta and Wiedemann (n 95) 20. *See also* Petri Kuoppamäki, 'Määräävän aseman väärinkäyttö digitaalisilla markkinoilla – mikä muuttuu?' (2018) Lakimies 996–1023.
988. Grunes and Stucke (n 126). For criticism of this view, *see* Sokol and Comerford (n 680) in Blair and Sokol (n 41) 17 ('Antitrust's role is not to fill gaps in the privacy laws').
989. French-German joint report (n 9) 23.
990. *Ibid.*
991. *Ibid.*
992. For example, this has reportedly been the case where legislative reform has failed to advance, such as the delayed legislation for liberalization of the EU energy market. Competition law also helped launch the liberalization of telecommunications. *See* Faull and Nikpay (n 314) 12.09.
993. Burnside (n 170).
994. *See* Commission Decision EC/837 DSD [2001] OJ L391/1.
995. *See* TFEU [2008] OJ C 115/53, 11.

101(3) recognizes that 'goals purposed by other treaty provisions can be taken into account ...'.[996]

The CJEU has relied on other areas of law when enforcing competition law. For example, in *Allianz Hungaria*, the court recognized that an infringement of one area of law could be a factor in deciding whether an infringement of competition law has occurred as well.[997] Similarly, a breach of data protection law can constitute a competition infringement.[998] This is what the German competition authority argued in the *Facebook* case, discussed in Chapter 4.

[A] Treating Privacy as a Quality Component

In this chapter privacy will be examined as a quality component. Quality is one central element or parameter of competition. As explained in the discussion on competition theory, at its simplest, the benefits of competition are lower prices, better products and services, wider choice and greater efficiency.[999] The main parameters of competition include price, quality, quantity, choice and innovation.[1000] In other words, competition includes both price and non-price parameters, and one key non-price aspect of competition is quality. Quality is a fundamental consideration - in addition to price - for consumers when determining whether to buy a product or service.[1001] Quality also fosters innovation and economic growth.[1002] As a broad notion, the concept of quality includes privacy protection and thus privacy can be viewed as a parameter of non-price competition.[1003] As noted by Ohlhausen and Okuliar, 'privacy protection has emerged as a small, but rapidly expanding, dimension of competition'.[1004]

Although this book has explored how price competition dominates competition analysis in the EU and the USA, it is important to recognize that the applicable legal framework and guidelines do not limit the competition authorities to consider only price effects in their competition analysis. For example, the EU Horizontal Merger Guidelines expressly state that one of the effects to be analysed in merger control is the effect on quality:[1005]

> Effective competition brings benefits to consumers, such as low prices, *high quality products*, a wide selection of goods and services, and innovation. Through its control of mergers, the Commission prevents mergers that would be likely to

996. Commission Guidelines on the application of Article [101(3) TFEU] 2004 OJ C 101797, 42.
997. Case C-32/11 *Allianz Hungaria* [2013] 39–47.
998. EDPS, 'Report of Workshop on Privacy, Consumers, Competition and Big Data' (11 July 2014) 3.
999. *See* Chapter 3, §3.02, p. 60.
1000. *See e.g.* C-413/06 P *Bertelsmann*, para. 121, T-168/01 *GlaxoSmithKline* (n 443), para. 106, and many other judgments, including C-413/14 *Intel*, para. 134.
1001. OECD Quality Report (n 896) 5.
1002. *Ibid.*
1003. EDPS Opinion (n 10) 17.
1004. *See* Ohlhausen and Okuliar (n 667) 133.
1005. Guidelines on the assessment of horizontal mergers (n 538), 8. *See also* Commission, Guidelines on the Assessment of Non-Horizontal Mergers under the Council Regulation on the Control of Concentrations Between Undertakings [2008] OJ C 265/07, 10.

> deprive customers of these benefits by significantly increasing the market power of firms.[1006]

According to the European Commission, an 'increase in market power' in this context 'refers to the ability of one or more firms to profitably increase prices, reduce output, choice or quality of goods and services, diminish innovation, or otherwise negatively influence parameters of competition'.[1007] The Commission further explains in its guidance that the expression 'increased prices' is 'often used as shorthand for these various ways in which a merger may result in competitive harm'.[1008] This effectively places the competitive harm caused by a reduction in quality on a par with an increase in prices.[1009]

Similar to the above-mentioned merger guidance, guidance from the European Commission on the assessment of agreements and unilateral conduct also includes the notion of quality as a factor in competitive analysis. The Horizontal Guidelines set out how various kinds of cooperation agreements between actual or potential competitors can have negative or positive effects on product quality.[1010] The Vertical Guidelines contain similar guidance regarding distribution agreements.[1011] Besides, the General Guidelines concerning agreements contain guidance on how to assess quality improvements in analysing efficiencies,[1012] and the Market Definition Notice provides information on how quality considerations can be relevant for defining the relevant product market.[1013] Thus, the wording in the Commission's various guidance documents shows that competition analysis can look beyond price-related harms and take into account the element of quality, which, as a broad notion, includes a privacy dimension.

Quality considerations can play a role in determining the boundaries within which rivals compete against each other, and how close competitors they are.[1014] Quality degradation has been assessed as a factor in anticompetitive harm, and the extent of possible quality improvements of a merger or agreement has been analysed in the context of efficiencies. However, dynamic efficiencies[1015] tend not to be considered fully by competition authorities. Although the legal framework does not limit the authorities to considering only price effects in their analysis, the Horizontal Merger Guidelines, for example, contain elements that are difficult to reconcile with dynamic efficiencies.[1016] One of them is that efficiencies have to be 'verifiable', 'precise' and 'convincing' according to the guidelines. So, even though dynamic competition can be

1006. Emphasis added.
1007. OECD Quality Report (n 896) 83.
1008. *Ibid.*
1009. *Ibid.*
1010. Guidelines on the application of Article 101 of the TFEU 1.
1011. Guidelines on Vertical Restraints (n 538), 1.
1012. European Commission, Guidelines on the application of Article 81(3) of the Treaty (n 345), 97.
1013. Notice on definition of relevant market for the purpose of Community competition law [1997] OJ C372, 5.
1014. Inge Graef et al., 'How Google and Others Upset Competition Analysis: Disruptive Innovation and European Competition Law' 25th European Regional Conference of the International Telecommunications Society (Brussels, 22-25 June 2014).
1015. *See* Chapter 3, §3.02.
1016. *Ibid.*

argued as being more important, antitrust agencies and courts often avoid dynamic efficiency analysis and focus instead on static price competition and productive efficiencies.[1017] As Tim Wu notes, 'the emphasis on measurable harms to consumers still tends to bias the law toward a focus on static harms and, especially, on prices. Such "price fixation" inevitably tends to marginalize parts of the antitrust law concerned with dynamic harms'.[1018]

However, in its decisional practice, the European Commission has adopted decisions which take quality into account in competitive assessment in the field of both antitrust and mergers.[1019] The importance of quality has been noted as a competitive feature by competition authorities, especially when the product or service is offered for free; in instances where price is constrained, quality becomes more important. For example, in *Microsoft/Skype* it was noted that '[s]ince consumer communications services are mainly provided for free, consumers pay more attention to other features', and in *Microsoft/Yahoo* it was held that '[q]uality is therefore a significant parameter of competition'.[1020]

It seems conceptually clear that the concept of quality includes privacy protection, and – as discussed above in the context of *Microsoft/LinkedIn* – one may say that an intellectual shift has occurred in the European Commission's approach to privacy and factoring in privacy as a quality element. For example, in *TomTom/Tele Atlas*, privacy was considered as a quality component in the European Commission's competitive assessment of the merger. The Commission looked at the dimension of privacy and held that 'confidentiality concerns can be considered as similar to product degradation in that the perceived value of the map for [PND] manufacturers would be lower if they feared that their confidential information could be revealed to TomTom'.[1021] According to the Commission, confidentiality concerns as to the customer information in question could lead to reputational damage and customers considering switching products.[1022]

In *Microsoft/LinkedIn*, the European Commission considered privacy an element of quality-based competition and specifically acknowledged it as a driver of consumer choice.[1023] This emphasis on quality places the competitive harm caused by a reduction in quality, for example, as a privacy degradation in a service such as LinkedIn, on a par with an increase in prices.[1024] Alternatively one can think of it as privacy being equivalent to price and consumers paying more – as in giving away more personal data – for the product. Privacy can be categorized both as quality competition and as equivalent to price. However, privacy is also a right on its own as a fundamental right, as discussed in §5.02[C].

1017. OECD, 'Policy Brief: What Is Competition on the Merits?' 1 (2006) 4.
1018. Wu (n 606) 5.
1019. OECD Quality Report (n 896) 78.
1020. *Microsoft/Skype* (n 898); *Microsoft/Yahoo* (n 524).
1021. *TomTom/Tele Atlas* (n 725) 274–276.
1022. *Ibid.*, 274–275.
1023. *Microsoft/LinkedIn* (n 413) paras 350, n.33.
1024. *See e.g.* OECD Quality Report (n 896) 83.

Nevertheless, while it may be conceptually clear that privacy can be an element in quality-based competition, the challenge lies in making this approach fully operational, something that will be examined further in §5.03[B] when exploring how to measure privacy. The issue is that consumers attach widely different values to privacy, which confounds rigorous analysis. Even if most consumers would probably agree that a reduction in product quality is undesirable (at least at constant prices), consumers will differ greatly in the value that they attach to privacy protection exceeding the legal standard that all service providers are obliged to respect.[1025] For example, receiving exploitative ads that are delivered when the user is exhausted, hungry or stressed constitutes a reduction in the quality of the service, but users may have very different views as to what is the degree of intrusiveness or undesirability of such quality decrease. This challenge with measuring quality and privacy as a subset of quality will be looked into in more detail in the following.

Another challenge with privacy as a quality dimension is that despite the importance of quality being recognized as an important competitive element and the legal framework allowing for non-economic considerations in competition analysis, competition policy today is often still driven predominantly by how competition affects price. Although some recent decisional practice reflects the start of an intellectual shift within the European Commission and activities by national competition authorities signal increasing attention towards privacy harms, the focus is still often on price impact in competitive assessment.[1026] This is particularly evident in merger control, where price is the common denominator. When assessing a merger, the competition authorities enquire whether the transaction will likely give the parties the power to raise the price of the product or service above competitive levels. The so-called Small, but Significant, Non-transitory Increase in Price (SSNIP) test is used to assess customer reactions to a price increase in the range of 5% to 10% by the hypothetical monopolist (also known as the hypothetical monopolist test).[1027]

The point is that when digital products or services are offered for free to users, the SSNIP test cannot be applied. This was noted by Commission officials in the context of the *Facebook/WhatsApp merger*.[1028] The test fails because the practical implication of a price of zero is that some of the standard tools of market definition and market power analysis break down as a pure mathematical matter: '5 percent of nothing is nothing, and because the nature of the product may be such that the hypothetical monopolist would still find it profit-maximizing to price at zero.'[1029] Similarly in connection with the more recent case concerning *Google Android*, the EU Competition Commissioner held that 'we had to deal with the fact that Android is accessible for free – so there's no

1025. *See* Ohlhausen and Okuliar (n 667) 133.
1026. Stucke and Grunes (n 146) 108–113.
1027. *Ibid.*, 117.
1028. Eleonora Ocello, Cristina Sjödin and Anatoly Subočs, 'What's up with Merger Control in the Digital Sector? Lessons from the Facebook/WhatsApp EU Merger Case' (February 2015) 1 Competition Merger Brief 3.
1029. Stucke and Grunes (n 146) 117, citing David S Evans, 'The Antitrust Economics of Free' (Spring 2011) Competition Policy International 22.

price that we could use for a SSNIP test. So instead, we asked ourselves what would happen if Google reduced the quality of Android a bit'.[1030]

In two-sided markets, where products are offered to users for free and monetized through targeted advertising, while personal data is critical to both sides, data is mostly seen as a means for targeted advertising. This has led competition analysis to focus on the advertising market but often to ignore the free side of the market.[1031] The presumption is that the viability of the company's business depends on such advertising, and the revenue from the advertising is assumed, in turn, to subsidize the free services provided.[1032] For example, in the *Google/DoubleClick* merger discussed above, the Commission did not examine the impact of the concentration on competition for free services, which meant that the role of data protection on the side of the free service was largely ignored.[1033]

Even in the situation where competition in the market for free services is considered, it has been done only with regard to its consequences for the advertising side. For example, in *Facebook/WhatsApp*, despite acknowledging that competition on privacy exists for free services, the Commission did not examine the effects of the merger on competition but considered only the effects of the merger on advertising. When noting that competition on data protection can exist, the Commission stated that 'apps compete for customers by attempting to offer the best communication experience', including 'privacy and security, the importance of which varies from user to user but which are becoming increasingly valued, as shown by the introduction of consumer communications apps specifically addressing privacy and security issues'.[1034] While the Commission did recognize privacy as one of many parameters of competition between consumer communications apps, it concluded that most consumer communications apps on the market do not compete mainly on privacy features.[1035]

Consequently, in *Facebook/WhatsApp*, no review was performed into whether personal data from end users could be collected to a greater extent due to the combination.[1036] Despite the merging companies reflecting two different data use approaches - where WhatsApp scanned entire address books but did not market the user information, in contrast to Facebook's approach - the Commission held that there was no basis in the EU Merger Regulation to require Facebook as the acquiring entity to respect the privacy agreement signed up to by WhatsApp customers. The European Commission considered the data concentration only on the advertising side of the market and did not analyse whether consumers might be harmed if Facebook were to start collecting and using data from WhatsApp users or alter WhatsApp's data protection conditions. Even though the Commission did observe that following the

1030. Speech by Margrethe Vestager, 'Defining Markets in a New Age' Chilling Competition Conference (Brussels, 9 December 2019).
1031. EDPS Opinion 8/2016 (n 777) 6.
1032. Stucke and Ezrachi (n 409) 70.
1033. *See* Chapter 4, §4.02. *See also* EDPS Opinion (n 10) 27.
1034. *Facebook/WhatsApp* (n 133) 7239, 87.
1035. *Ibid.*, 174.
1036. *Ibid.*, 164: 'For the purposes of this decision, the Commission has analysed potential data concentration only to the extent that it is likely to strengthen Facebook's position in the online advertising market or in any sub-segments thereof.'

announcement of Facebook's acquisition of WhatsApp, many users switched services due to privacy concerns,[1037] concerns with Facebook holding a significant amount of data were dismissed as strictly a privacy issue, outside the scope of competition law.[1038] Because the European Commission declared 'privacy-related concerns' outside the scope of its review,[1039] it could not subject approval of the merger to conditions in this regard.[1040]

When investigating the *Facebook/WhatsApp* concentration in the USA, the FTC took another approach and imposed on the merging parties a requirement to give customers notice and choice if they departed from the privacy conditions. The FTC sent a letter to the merging parties urging them to continue to honour the promises made to consumers with respect to WhatsApp's privacy policies as well as public statements made about privacy when the transaction was announced.[1041] Failure to honour these promises could constitute deceptive or unfair practices in violation of the FTC Act, Section 5.

Each regulator approach, in both Europe and the USA, implies that users of the messaging services were required to choose between accepting the new privacy conditions or simply being barred from using the service.[1042] The European Commission's reasoning in *Facebook/WhatsApp* – namely that the merging parties' activities did not overlap in the relevant market and that the data protection concerns that the merger raised fell outside the scope of review – is unsatisfactory. The reasoning is also unsatisfactory from the viewpoint of protecting consumer welfare or well-being. As maintained by Costa-Cabral and Lynskey:[1043]

> [t]he data protection concerns that the merger raised, dismissed as non-economic, hinted at the true competitive problem: both Facebook and WhatsApp actively acquired personal data, and not only did Facebook acquire a competitively relevant acquisition, but it may have also effectively neutralized WhatsApp's innovation on better data protection conditions.

The competitive assessment conducted in *Facebook/WhatsApp* is illustrative of the challenges in reviewing the impact of a merger in two-sided or multisided digital markets, where competition authorities are tempted to consider the effects of the concentration only on the advertising side, ignoring impacts on the free side. Google/Fitbit bears some resemblance to *Facebook/WhatsApp*. It will be an important case in shaping the development of the competition/privacy interface and the role of privacy in competition enforcement, at least in mergers, especially as it concerns data is perhaps the most sensitive of all areas, biometric information on individuals' daily health and even emotions. This is data that reveals the most intimate aspects of a person's health and lifestyle, and under the GDPR (as well as probably most data

1037. *Facebook/WhatsApp* (n 133) fns 79 and 174.
1038. *Facebook/WhatsApp* (n 133) para. 164. *See also* Commission press release (n 675).
1039. *Ibid.*
1040. Reg. 1/2003 on the implementation of the rules on competition laid down in Articles 81 and 82 of the Treaty, O.J. 2003, L 1/1, Article 9(1).
1041. *See* Letter from Rich (n 702); EDPS Opinion 8/2016 (n 777) 9.
1042. EDPS Opinion 8/2016 (n 777) 10.
1043. Costa-Cabral and Lynskey (n 93) 38.

privacy laws around the world) processing of such data requires that individuals have given an explicit, specific, and informed consent. The case bears similarities to the *Facebook/WhatsApp* saga, and there are concerns that just as Facebook at the time swore blind they would not exploit WhatsApp data, Google today promises that Fitbit health and wellness personal data will not be used for Google ads. According to Cristina Caffarra and Tommaso Valletti, 'a promise not to use personal information for advertising purposes is a statement that is, at best, empty and, at worse, misleading and obfuscating'.[1044] Caffarra and Valletti argue that it is now time to get the analysis right.[1045] 'Six years down the road, where are we? Surely, we cannot be saying that "privacy issues" are extraneous to merger assessment in a case of this kind today; and only a "conventional" theory of harm ... can justify a competition concern.'

Little is actually known about the consequences of this kind of competition analysis, which does not include non-economic privacy considerations in its assessment. The long-term consequences of such arguably narrow-minded competition analysis, focusing on price effects, can make consumers worse off, or at least there is no assurance that this will not happen. Reason for concern indeed exists, as the effects on the free (user) side might be just as important and significant for consumer welfare as the effects on the paid (advertising) side. Arguably, a decrease in quality can be as harmful to consumers as a price increase, and therefore protecting and advancing quality should also form important objectives of competition policy. What this may require is that there is general acceptance that in many transactions and deals in digital markets, data is actually the key driver. When assessing data-driven deals, competition authorities should avoid getting caught in the weeds of market definition and product overlaps, missing the wood for the trees and missing the issue because there is no immediately obvious antitrust overlap. As articulated by Caffarra and Tommaso, 'we need to slow down and avoid mistakes that are irreversible' (a merger prohibition, on the other hand, is not irreversible), and we want innovation to happen in ways that are sustainable and do not undermine society's goals.[1046]

[B] Addressing Challenges of Measuring Privacy

After discussing privacy as a quality component on a conceptual and theoretical level, the focus in this chapter shifts to identifying and examining the challenges and practical limitations of incorporating privacy as a dimension of competition law and policy. This is done by looking at the practical possibilities of measuring privacy as a quality harm, such as through considering the usability of the SSNDQ test, assessing methodologies and estimation techniques for assigning monetary value to personal data, and considering using behavioural economics in addition – or as an alternative – to traditional law and economics.

Measuring privacy as a quality component of competition is tricky because measuring quality is tricky. Making a precise definition of quality for a given product

1044. Caffarra and Valletti (n 701).
1045. *Ibid.*
1046. *Ibid.*

is a complex task in competition assessments for many reasons: the subjective features that contribute to a perception of quality by customers, as well as the multidimensional nature of quality and competition that is increasingly focusing on non-price elements.[1047] And even if some quality-related features are measurable, the overall perception of product quality is often based on a combination of several features. To take cars as an example: the number of measurable variables that customers may take into account when assessing quality is huge and quite complex, ranging from speed, emissions, acceleration and consumption to precise parameters of individual components.[1048] Therefore, assessing quality is often a complex and imprecise exercise in itself that involves weighing evidence, which is often of a subjective nature, such as different customer perceptions. Many acknowledge that the importance of quality-based competition in digital markets cannot be underestimated, but note that an assessment of quality is challenging.[1049] However, this should not keep competition law and policy from evolving by trying to factor into the assessment the competitive elements of quality, and privacy as its subset.

As quality is often difficult to measure and define, in practice quality considerations are commonly assessed by means of customers' and competitors' views collected during market research or as documentary evidence, such as internal analysis or surveys conducted by firms. The possibility to use more exact quantitative tools is – in contrast to a price-centred assessment – more limited.[1050]

In some cases (perceived) quality correlates with the price positioning of a given product or service. In other words, consumers at times assess quality using price as a proxy, namely you get what you pay for; a decrease in quality for a given lower price.[1051] The more customers perceive a product or service as being highly qualitative – by way of its own characteristics or by marketing – the more they are willing to pay for it and the more the observed prices of the given products differ.[1052] For example, price levels can be indicative of the (perceived) quality positioning of brands, such as watches, where luxury watches are several – even many – times more expensive than technically comparable 'regular' watch brands.[1053]

Of course, this heuristic has some problems in digital markets with zero-price products and services.[1054] In these instances, personal information is exchanged for products or services that are free, or do not reflect the value of the information. This makes it challenging to identify at what point the requirement for consumers' disclosure of personal data for online transactions in goods or services – without improving them or lowering their price – is commensurate with the value of the data, and therefore is anticompetitive. When does 'the price become too high', so to speak?

1047. OECD Quality Report (n 896) 78–79.
1048. *Ibid.*
1049. *See e.g.* Mäihäniemi (n 521) 10.
1050. Ariel Ezrachi and Maurice E Stucke, 'The Curious Case of Competition and Quality' (2015) 3 Journal of Antitrust Enforcement 227–257.
1051. *Ibid.*
1052. OECD Quality Report (n 896) 79.
1053. *Ibid.*
1054. Ezrachi and Stucke (n 1050).

The EU Competition Commissioner has stated that consuming free services against disclosure of one's data 'doesn't have to be a problem, as long as people are happy that the data they share is a fair price to pay for the services they get in return'.[1055] This is not really helpful, though, as what constitutes a 'fair' price, just like the concept of 'fairness', is highly subjective and open to interpretation. If the agreement to disclose and permit personal data processing had a price tag, it would fit more easily within the competition law framework. Consumer decisions and preferences reflect whether competition in the marketplace exists, but they cannot determine whether certain behaviour is anticompetitive. For example, if consumers are charged high prices as a result of abuse, collusion or a merger, they would still pay what they believe a product or a service is worth to them.[1056]

This also makes the question of competition authority intervention very difficult. Although this book focuses on the normative scope of competition law and addresses the challenges in the data economy concerning competition law more on the policy level rather than the practical level, it should be noted here that degradation in quality can sometimes be balanced by improvements in other competitive parameters, which calls into question whether competition authorities should look into that practice. Moreover, the specific point at which a quality degradation should trigger authority intervention is difficult to determine. Similarly, how should one consider a situation where, despite a degradation in privacy, a company still offers consumers a superior quality product overall?[1057]

Competition authorities generally do not want to assume the role of price regulators, so they probably do not want to become privacy regulators either. Sceptics fear that there are no limiting principles if privacy harms are pursued in competition law[1058] and point to the lack of concrete benchmarks on which to base a decision whether to intervene or not. However, this may also lead to a kind of 'paralysis'.[1059] Nevertheless, uncertainty is no reason for not condemning abusive behaviour or anticompetitive practices. It is common in legal practice to make decisions under some uncertainty and on the basis of predictions,[1060] especially in the face of novel kinds of abusive behaviour.

Another challenge is that although the significance of quality and privacy as non-price parameters of competition might be recognized, the authorities implementing and enforcing competition laws may not currently have the tools and analytical schemes for assessing these non-price dimensions. Consequently, considerations regarding quality and privacy have not been sufficiently present in current competition analysis. This is something now also recognized by the Commission and one notable development after her re-election was the EU Competition Commissioner announcing

1055. *See* speech by Vestager (n 484).
1056. This is shown in demand curves by competition economists for any market.
1057. Ezrachi and Stucke (n 1050) 108.
1058. *See e.g.* Ohlhausen and Okuliar (n 667) 40.
1059. Costa-Cabral and Lynskey (n 96) 30.
1060. Joseph Drexl, 'Real Knowledge Is to Know the Extent of One's Own Ignorance: On the Consumer Harm Approach in Innovation-Related Competition Cases' (2009) Max Planck Institute for Intellectual Property, Competition & Tax Law Research Paper No 09-15.

the revision of the Commission's notice on market definition in light of the digital economy and increasingly data-driven markets:[1061]

> One thing about being competition commissioner for five years is that you pick up some handy pieces of jargon. One of my favourites is the 'SSNIP test' – this idea that you can see where the boundaries of a market lie, by seeing which products people would switch to if the price for the one they're using goes up a little. The trouble is that a test like this, which is linked to changing prices, can't be used with a product that consumers use for free.

Due to the unfamiliarity and difficulty in measuring and appraising quality, little attempt has traditionally been made to quantify, for example, how mergers may lessen quality. To address this gap, it has been suggested that competition authorities would use the SSNDQ test, which stands for a Small, but Significant, Non-transitory Decline in Quality.[1062]

However, as mentioned, for many products and services, quality attributes are of a subjective nature, complex and difficult to measure. Therefore, the test is in practice difficult, if not impossible, to apply, because of the lack of a single parameter that defines quality. For example, for the SSNDQ test to work, the quality component would have to be measurable, objective, transparent and well accepted.[1063] The SSNDQ test may work in industries with well-accepted metrics of quality, such as healthcare. For example, Ezrachi and Stucke discuss the use of the SSNDQ test by the UK competition authority in its review of hospital mergers.[1064]

Just like the difficulty with applying the SSNDQ test to assess a merger's implications on quality, the test has limitations in terms of privacy. Just like quality, privacy is subjective and lacks quantifiable metrics. Due to the subjectivity of consumer preferences about privacy, the SSNDQ test is not practical for measuring a potential privacy degradation or the degree of privacy protection generally. The element of subjectivity makes privacy – like quality more generally – harder to define and measure than price, which mirrors the lack of a commonly accepted analytical framework and consequent superficial treatment by the competition authorities.[1065] Generally, the economic analysis of privacy has evolved over time, but characterizing a single unifying economic theory of privacy has proven hard. This is partly also due to privacy issues of economic relevance arising in widely diverse contexts.[1066]

As mentioned, applying the SSNDQ test to assess privacy involves inherent difficulties, due to the subjectivity of consumer preferences about privacy and the lack of quantifiable metrics. However, despite the unavailability of a commonly accepted analytical framework for privacy, some studies on the value of personal data look at different methodologies to measure and estimate the monetary value of personal

1061. Speech by Vestager (n 1030).
1062. OECD Quality Report (n 896) 164.
1063. Ezrachi and Stucke (n 1050).
1064. *Ibid.*
1065. Stucke and Grunes (n 146) 266.
1066. For further reading on the economics of privacy, *see* Alessandro Acquisti, Curtis R Taylor and Liad Wagman, 'The Economics of Privacy' (8 March 2016) 52 Journal of Economic Literature.

data.[1067] Many of these studies acknowledge that while personal data is creating economic and social value at an increasing pace, estimating the value being generated is difficult. This is because not only is a huge amount of data being generated, but personal data is used in so many different situations for numerous purposes.[1068] In the following, some relevant methodologies and estimation techniques for assigning monetary values attached to personal data are looked at in more detail. These methodologies for valuing personal data could be used to further develop the economic and legal analysis of privacy and to provide a measuring tool for competition authorities to use in their assessment of privacy as a competition dimension.

Market prices for data. As noted, consumers at times assess quality using price as a proxy.[1069] The same logic applies to assessing the value of personal information. The most direct way to approach the value of personal data is probably to evaluate the market prices at which personal data are legitimately offered and sold. The values are imprecise as they only represent the price of data sold in a specific context to one participant and do not show the total 'earnings' of the data over time. They do, however, offer a market-based measurement based on the intersection of supply and demand. Examples of prices for personal data in the USA can range from USD 0.50 for a street address, USD 2 for a date of birth, USD 8 for a social security number, USD 3 for a driver's licence number and USD 35 for a military record.[1070] These are only estimates but give some insight into the relative market values of different pieces of personal data.

Financial results per data record. Financial results are another principal way of assigning monetary value to personal data according to the OECD study on the economics of personal data.[1071] Financial results include market capitalizations, revenues or net income per individual record. Market capitalization as an approach is suitable for companies whose business models are based primarily on personal data. However, market capitalization data leads to valuations that can fluctuate considerably. For example, the implied market capitalization (or valuation) per Facebook user fluctuated between USD 40 and USD 300 (per user) at different times between 2006 and 2012.[1072] The fluctuations are influenced to a large extent by other economic factors and not solely by the monetary value of the underlying data.[1073]

Revenue or net income per record/user is another and arguably a more stable measure of the annual market value of personal data. For example, Facebook and Experian, two companies whose business models are based on personal data, have

---

1067. *See* in particular OECD Economics of Personal Data (n 167). The author discusses this study and the various methodologies to measure and estimate monetary value of personal data in an article that relates to this book, *see* 'The Implications of Big Data and Privacy on Competition Analysis in Merger Control and the Controversial Competition-Data Protection Interface' (2019) 30 European Business Law Review 337–366.
1068. *Ibid.*, 2.
1069. *See* n 163.
1070. OECD Economics of Personal Data (n 167) 25–27. The examples are taken from the OECD study at the time of writing the report (2013).
1071. *Ibid.*
1072. *Ibid.*, 20–25.
1073. *Ibid.*

annual revenues per record/user of roughly USD 4–7 per year. While imprecise, the data can serve as a useful point of reference. It should be noted, however, that only at the level of net profit per record is added economic value actually measured.[1074]

Costs of data breach. Another approach to considering the monetary value of personal data is through an assessment of the economic costs of a data breach. This methodology includes measures of the cost to individuals who have their identities stolen or the costs to companies when a data breach occurs. The costs associated with the loss and misuse of personal data can give some indication of its value. A drawback to this approach is that reported figures vary widely.[1075] Moreover, it does not measure the value of the underlying data but rather the monetary cost of a breach on a per-record basis. For example, the data or data security breach concerning the Sony PlayStation Network and Sony Online Entertainment in 2011 resulted in the exposure of 103 million records. According to Sony executives, the data breach would cost the company at least USD 171 million (USD 1.7 per record).[1076] It does not, however, cover loss in company reputation, brand impact and other indirect and opportunity costs.

Payment for data protection insurance. Another way to put an economic value on personal data is to understand how much someone would be willing to pay to protect that data in the form of insurance. This can also be seen in markets in the form of insurance policies to protect against identity theft. For example, the data broker Experian sells an identity-theft protection service called ProtectMyID for USD 155 per annum in the USA. It is interesting to compare this figure with the mentioned examples of average revenue per record (USD 6.42) and market capitalization per record (USD 19.24) for some perspective on the difference between measures.[1077]

Economic experiments and surveys. Another way to assign economic value to personal data is to conduct economic experiments and surveys that extract the price that companies would have to pay individuals for them to give up some of their personal information. Several experimental studies have attempted to quantify individual valuations of personal data in diverse contexts.[1078] Research in this area is still developing, as the notion of individual valuation of privacy is complex and extremely

1074. *Ibid.*

1075. *Ibid.*

1076. *Ibid.*

1077. It is, however, questioned whether services that offer to protect and rectify theft of personal data are actually effective and thus can be viewed as a valid instrument of measurement. OECD Economics of Personal Data (n 167) 33.

1078. Numerous empirical studies focus on both the valuation of personal data and the valuation of privacy.

Examples include Kai-Lung Hui, Hock-Hai Teo, Sang-Yong Tom Lee, 'The Value of Privacy Assurance: An Exploratory Field Experiment' (2007) 31 MIS Quarterly 19–33; Ramnath K Chellapa and Raymond G Sin, 'Personalization Versus Privacy: An Empirical Examination of the Online Consumers' Dilemma' (2005) 6 Information Technology and Management 181–202; Luc Wathieu and Allan Friedman, 'An Empirical Approach to Understanding Privacy Valuation' (2005) Proceedings of the Fourth Workshop on the Economics of Information Security (WEIS 05); Dan Cvrcek et al., 'A Study on the Value of Location Privacy' (2006) Proceedings of Workshop on Privacy in the Electronic Society (WPES 06) 109–118; Sarah Spiekerman, Jens Grossklags and Bettina Berendt, 'E-Privacy in 2nd Generation E-Commerce' (2002) ACM Conference on Electronic Commerce (EC'01) 38–47.

context dependent, which makes it challenging to analyse in a laboratory setting.[1079] As will be discussed below, the notion of individual valuation of privacy can also be irrational, which brings even more complexity to the issue and requires an understanding based on behavioural economics.[1080]

It is important to note on these methodologies and measurements that research results show that there is a difference between individual valuation of personal data and individual valuation of privacy in the sense that people tend to differ with respect to their individual valuation of personal data (the amount of money sufficient for them to give away personal data) and their individual valuation of privacy (the amount of money they are ready to spend to protect their personal data from disclosure). Generally, the proportion of consumers who will reject an offer to obtain money in exchange for reduced privacy is larger than the proportion of consumers who will accept an economically equivalent offer to pay money in exchange for protection of privacy.[1081] According to Hui and Png, the difference between the individual valuation of personal data and the valuation of privacy could help explain some of the disparate findings from empirical studies.[1082]

Empirical studies also show that both the valuation of privacy and the valuation of personal data are sensitive to contextual effects. Studies suggest that even supposedly privacy-conscious individuals are likely to share their personal sensitive information with strangers.[1083] A strict application of the economics principle of 'revealed preferences' would invite the conclusion that people do not care about their privacy or their personal data.[1084] Efforts to explain this inconsistency involve using techniques developed by behavioural economics that weigh in and take into account relevant context, psychological and individual motives in economic settings. Studies based on behavioural economics reveal how significantly the valuation of privacy and the valuation of personal data can be affected by contextual effects that arguably should play a limited role in decision-making.[1085] These studies also demonstrate the complexity of individual privacy preferences by examining the underlying privacy and personal data valuations, finding that these are not normally or uniformly distributed, but clustered around extremes and focal points.[1086]

It should be acknowledged that these different approaches for assigning monetary values to personal data and the economics of personal data and privacy have some caveats or limitations. Importantly, the methodologies reflect a purely monetary

1079. However, economic experiments and procedures are well described in the literature, *see e.g.* John H Kagel and Alvin E Roth, *The Handbook of Experimental Economics* (Princeton University Press 1997).
1080. *See* §5.03[B].
1081. Acquisti, John and Loewenstein (n 6) 249–274.
1082. Kai-Lung Hui and Ivan PL Png, 'The Economics of Privacy' in T Hendershott (ed.) *Handbook on Economics and Information Systems* (Elsevier Publishing 2006) 471–498.
1083. Spiekerman, Grossklags and Berendt (n 1078) 38–47.
1084. *See e.g.* Paul Rubin and Thomas Lenard, *Privacy and the Commercial Use of Personal Information* (Springer 2002).
1085. OECD Economics of Personal Data (n 167) 30, citing studies by Norbert Schwarz, 'Self-Reports: How the Questions Shape the Answers' (1999) 54 American Psychologist; Acquisti, John and Loewenstein (n 6) 249–274.
1086. Acquisti, John and Loewenstein (n 6) 249–274.

perspective in that they do not take into account the indirect impact of use of personal data on the economy or society. Further, they produce monetary estimates of values that are context-dependent, and they may lead to biased results if relying solely on one specific approach. In addition, challenges arise with concepts and definitions, due to inherent difficulties in determining precisely what amounts to personal data, and in comparing different proxies for personal data such as 'records' or 'users'.[1087]

Markets are likely to evolve in which individuals control and sell their own data. As mentioned, online users and consumers generally are more and more waking up to how technology companies with data-driven businesses are using and monetizing online user data in ways that which may raise privacy risks. New developments are on the horizon that could produce novel valuations of personal data and shed further light on their market valuations. For example, some firms are now offering 'data lockers'. These allow users to contribute and edit the data they are willing to share with third parties in exchange for a portion of the proceeds when their data is sold.[1088] These data lockers could potentially improve transparency about how data is collected, sold and used. Users may be willing to share more personal data if they feel they have more control over how it is used and receive a clear economic or social benefit in exchange for sharing. Consequently, sales prices through 'data lockers' might become a key method for valuing personal information and privacy.[1089] This is a new area and although it is unclear if data lockers will emerge with viable business models, this is an area worth following up in the privacy context.

Digital taxation as comparison? It is interesting to note that the EU's initiative on digital taxation reflects elements that bear similarities to the discussion on measuring privacy harm by looking at the number of users. In the EU tax reform proposal, the Commission suggests new measures to ensure that digital business activities are taxed fairly in the EU.[1090] The initiative aims to reform corporate tax rules so that profits are registered and taxed where businesses have significant interaction with users through digital channels. Consequently, one of the criteria for considering a digital platform as having a taxable 'digital presence' or a virtual permanent establishment in an EU Member State is that it has more than 100,000 users in a Member State in a taxable year. Another alternative criterion is that a digital platform has more than 3,000 business contracts for digital services created between the company and business users in a taxable year.

Further to the question of valuation of personal data, it should be noted that related issues often arise in the context of two-sided advertising-supported markets, which brings about challenges in terms of how to balance possible benefits on the 'paid' advertising side of the market against harms on the 'free' consumer side of the market, as seen in *Facebook/WhatsApp* and *Google/DoubleClick*. What makes it even more difficult is that situations arise in the digital economy where protection of privacy

1087. *Ibid.*, 4–5.
1088. *Ibid.*, 5.
1089. *Ibid.*
1090. European Commission press release, 'Digital Taxation: Commission proposes new measures to ensure that all companies pay fair tax in the EU' (Brussels, 21 March 2018) IP/18/2041.

can both enhance and detract from individual and societal welfare.[1091] Another challenge is that consumers' ability to make informed decisions about their personal information and privacy may be hindered because they are often in a position of imperfect information about when their data is collected, for what purpose, and with what consequences.[1092] Further, consumers' concern for their data protection can also be distorted by other factors, such as the power of defaults[1093] and the 'free effect',[1094] of which more below.

The phenomena highlighted and discussed above may contribute to the existing privacy paradox, namely that while many users are concerned about privacy, few actually act on those concerns.[1095] Nevertheless, those few privacy-aware consumers that do value data protection may be enough to raise competitive concerns. As mentioned, privacy is subjective, meaning that not all consumers value the same things, and privacy might affect marginal consumers who are those to keep market power in check.[1096] In this context, it is noteworthy that consumers' views on the value of personal data may be shifting in the wake of the Facebook-Cambridge Analytica scandal and users will likely become more attentive to privacy, and the Cambridge Analytica affair may even be remembered as the beginning of a larger reckoning. Even Facebook's CEO Marc Zuckerberg has said that new regulation is 'inevitable'.[1097]

Further to the privacy paradox, which reflects irrational consumer behaviour, consumers can behave irrationally in other ways in the context of digital markets, often because they are lured by free services, the so-called free effect.[1098] For example, the power of default, an idea stemming from behavioural economics, makes consumers stick to the default option not only due to the practices of the dominant company but also because of an artificial lock-in effect. This means that consumers sometimes prefer to stick to the default option, even if faced with better or higher quality alternative options because they feel comfortable and do not want to experience additional learning costs.[1099] This phenomenon can also be referred to as consumers experiencing

1091. Acquisti, Taylor and Wagman (n 1066) 2.
1092. *Ibid.*
1093. Ezrachi and Stucke (n 146) 35.
1094. Gal and Rubinfeld (n 411) 530.
1095. Costa-Cabral and Lynskey (n 96) 28.
1096. *Ibid.*, 28.
1097. Aaron Pressman, 'Facebook Can't Fix This Problem Alone' Fortune (20 April 2018) http://fortune.com/2018/04/20/facebook-data-privacy-problem-fix/, accessed 19 April 2020.
1098. Gal and Rubinfeld (n 411) 530.
1099. For example, consider *Google Android* in the EU. Commission Decision of 18 July 2018 relating to proceedings under Article 102 TFEU and Article 54 Agreement on the European Economic Area AT.40099 – *Google Android*. When commenting on the case, the EU Competition Commissioner described that 'we asked ourselves what would happen if Google reduced the quality of Android a bit. And we found that this wouldn't make consumers switch to Apple. Without a certain expertise, they might not register the lower quality; and if they did, then the costs of switching to Apple would discourage them from switching – costs like buying a new smartphone, downloading new apps and transferring their data in situations where providers don't ensure portability'. Speech by Vestager (n 1030).

'high switching costs'.[1100] A key point with the power of the default option is that this notion from behavioural economics, which often stands in contrast to the approach of traditional law and economics, can help explain the market power of dominant companies in online markets and the presence of barriers to entry.[1101] Dan Ariely, an expert in applied behavioural economics, captures the problem with privacy and the irrational behaviour of consumers in the following question:

> Wouldn't economics make a lot more sense if it were based on how people actually behave, instead of how they should behave?[1102]

Behavioural economics. One way to address the challenges in measuring the value of personal data and privacy is by resorting more to the thinking expressed by behavioural economics. Therefore, the issue of how to make privacy practically operational as an element in competition law and policy can be examined with behavioural economics in mind, as it can help explain human behaviour with respect to data privacy in digital markets. An illustrative example of irrational human behaviour is the common feeling by many Internet users that they cannot stop sharing but feel concerned about how their data is used. In fact, a three-year study conducted in Germany showed that the more people disclosed about themselves on social media, the more privacy they said they desired.[1103] In short, what behavioural economics aims to solve is the issue that whatever economists have studied in the past couple of centuries involves humans, and sometimes in the pursuit of elegant models by traditional economics, they tend either to forget the human aspect or to overlook it. It is the study of human miscalculations and their effects on markets.[1104]

Traditional economics assumes that rational forces shape everything. Indeed, conventional traditional law and economics explain in economic terms the interaction of humans in the context of social and political institutions with the presupposition that humans behave rationally and predictably. As we know, and as noted in Chapter 3, §3.02 when discussing the limits of competition theory, this is not always the case. Thus, the notion of *homo economicus* as an individual who is a self-interested actor, competitive by nature and striving for rational maximization of a personal utility, is not an optimal concept for competition policy in digital markets, where humans often tend to behave less rationally (and, for example, share their personal information on social online media despite feeling concerned about its use). This tendency of irrational

1100. On switching costs, *see e.g.* Aaron S Edlin and Robert G Harris, 'The Role of Switching Costs in Antitrust Analysis: A Comparison of Microsoft and Google' (2013) 15 Yale Journal of Law and Technology 169–213.

1101. For discussion, *see* Mäihäniemi (n 521) 262–263.

1102. Dan Ariely, *Predictably Irrational: The Hidden Forces That Shape Our Decisions* (HarperCollins 2008).

1103. Sabine Trepte and Leonard Reinecke, *Privacy Online. Perspectives on Privacy and Self-Disclosure in the Social Web* (Springer 2011).

1104. Much has been written in the field of behavioural economics. Central scholarship includes work by economist and Nobel Laureate Herbert Simon, Daniel Kahneman (Nobel Laureate 2001), Amos Tversky and Richard H Thaler (Winner of the 2017 Nobel Prize in Economics) who helped establish the field of behavioural economics. Thaler played an important role in popularizing the application of this field to real-life problems, *see* especially his book *Misbehaving: The Making of Behavioural Economics* (Penguin 2017).

behaviour taking place in digital markets could be accounted for in competition law and policy by making better use of behavioural economic thinking and findings.

The relationship between behavioural economics and competition law is arguably not completely straightforward.[1105] While conventional economics enjoys a strong foothold in competition law, notably in recent years more competition policy discourse has been influenced by behavioural economic thinking.[1106] According to Stucke, behavioural economics can today be regarded even as part of 'mainstream' economics.[1107] This is because, over the past twenty years, economics has recognized and measured how willpower is imperfect, how people care about treating others and being treated fairly, and the biases and heuristics that affect decision-making.[1108] Further, economics has moved beyond neoclassical economic theory's assumptions of perfectly rational market participants who pursue their economic self-interest with willpower.[1109]

The benefits of considering behavioural economics in competition law and policy have been noted by a growing number of competition scholars. In the Nordic and Finnish discourse, Kalle Määttä has presented insightful considerations on this topic and contends that behavioural economics can produce undisputed benefits for competition policy and give cause for rethinking, or at least adjusting, some competition policy assumptions.[1110] Framed in a more economical way, this essentially means that psychological or behavioural costs need to be taken into account in addition to conventional transactional costs.[1111]

Behavioural economics goes beyond the assumptions about consumer behaviour of conventional economics, subjecting them to the tests of experiment and empirical observation.[1112] Behavioural economics examines the difference between the theory and reality of how humans behave. According to findings by behavioural economics, in many situations, consumers consistently depart from behaviour predicted by the assumptions of conventional economics. This means that consumer choices are directed away from those which would occur if their behaviour conformed to the economic assumption of 'rationality'. This irrational consumer conduct and biases can lead to market failures. Relevant from the competition policy standpoint are those consumer biases that lead to significant detriment, so-called 'costly biases', which refer to behavioural biases that lead to significant departure from optimal decisions.[1113]

Findings of behavioural economics have identified some costly biases. These include unstable preferences, a concern for fairness, choice and information overload,

1105. *See e.g.* Agustín Reyna, 'The Psychology of Privacy – What Role for BE in Antitrust Enforcement?' presentation at CLaSF and University of Graz workshop, Antitrust at the intersection of law and economics, 19 April 2018.
1106. Määttä (n 105) 38.
1107. Stucke (n 882).
1108. *Ibid.*
1109. *Ibid.*
1110. Määttä (n 105) 38, 42. *See also* the FCCA report (n 15).
1111. *Ibid.*, 38 fn 243.
1112. *Ibid.*, 39. *See also* OECD, 'Roundtable on Economics for Consumer Policy' (2007) Summary Report.
1113. *Ibid.*

endowment bias, overconfidence, misevaluation of future benefits and costs.[1114] When markets fail because of costly biases, remedies should be shaped accordingly. For example, a situation of choice or information overload will probably be aggravated by a requirement for more information disclosure. Instead, the appropriate intervention may involve reframing the information which is available to consumers in a way that makes choice easier, such as perhaps rewriting complicated privacy policies.[1115]

According to studies by Nicolas Petit and Norman Neyrinck, behavioural economic arguments play a role in the application of EU competition law in cases of abuse of a dominant position.[1116] Indeed, behavioural insights have been used by the European Commission and national authorities to identify consumer attitudes and biases. For example, in *Microsoft*, considerations were given to switching costs due to insufficient information and also the psychological effects of tying were examined.[1117] The national competition authority in the Netherlands used behavioural insights in *Chicken of Tomorrow*, where the price increase of sustainably produced poultry was taken into account.[1118]

In his scholarly work on behavioural antitrust, Stucke insightfully explores how competition law can consider the implications of behavioural economics on a policy level. Behavioural economics can be helpful in revisiting the fundamental questions, namely what the goals of competition law are and what should be the legal standards to promote those goals.[1119] This also makes behavioural economics relevant for the topic of this book. Behavioural economics can inform the debate concerning competition law policy goals, and address fundamental policy questions, such as why there has not been greater convergence on the basic issue of what competition is.

In this regard, Stucke notes that one reason is the divergence over the premises of any theory of competition. Competition, like any theory, depends on its premises, the validity of which may not hold true across industries, countries, and time.[1120] Although neoclassical economic theory has informed the basic theory of competition, no consensus exists worldwide on a theory of an effective competition process, that is what competition is.[1121] Whereas the Chicago and Post-Chicago schools rely on the premise that market participants are rational profit-maximizers with willpower, one can rely on a different premise: that many consumers are imperfectly rational, have limited willpower, are concerned about fairness, and are willing to punish unfair

1114. *Ibid.*, 11–12.
1115. *Ibid.*, 12.
1116. Nicolas Petit and Norman Neyrinck, 'Behavioral Economics and Abuse of Dominance: A Proposed Alternative Reading of the Article 102 TFEU Case-Law' (2010) 2 The Global Competition Law Centre (GCLC) Working Papers Series.
1117. Case T-201/04 *Microsoft v Commission* (n 65).
1118. Dutch Consumer and Market Authority (ACM), Analysis of the sustainability arrangements concerning the Chicken of Tomorrow (2015) ACM/DM/2014/206028.
1119. Stucke (n 882). For further reading on the implications of behavioural economics on antitrust by Stucke, *see* 'The Behavioral Antitrust Gambit' in Ariel Ezrachi (ed.), *International Research Handbook on Competition Law* (Edward Elgar 2012).
1120. *Ibid.*, 24–25.
1121. *Ibid.*

behaviour even when not in their economic self-interest. Accordingly, the theory of competition will look different.[1122]

As shown in this chapter, quantifying personal data and privacy is not an impossible task, as some methodologies are available to assign monetary value to personal data and privacy. By treating privacy as a quality component, privacy can be measured, just like quality. However, it should be noted that conventional economics may not always be the appropriate or optimal tool for measuring privacy. Behavioural economics can inform competition law and policy, bring about benefits for competition policy and accommodate the privacy paradox and other phenomena commonplace in the data economy, as well as help adjust some competition policy assumptions, such as consumers always behaving rationally. Besides, behavioural economics can inform policymakers on the goals of antitrust, help rethink competition objectives for the data economy and expand its horizons beyond price, as will be discussed in the next chapter.

[C] Expanding Horizons Beyond Price

> *Importantly, we are not just looking for short-term price effects – we are also interested in competition in the longer term, and not only on price. A merely static, short-term, price-centric perspective will fail to deliver the benefits of competition.*[1123]

During the course of conducting research for this book and throughout the writing process, the author has on many occasions presented and discussed the topic of the book at conferences, workshops and seminars as well as in more informal settings with peers and colleagues. Sometimes when mentioning privacy and data protection in the context of competition law, there are those who react with surprise and even scepticism: is not competition law only supposed to be concerned with price? Well, no, not really, as has been explored throughout this book.

This book asserts that competition is actually about consumer choice, which goes back to ordoliberal origins, and price is just one aspect of choice. The ultimate purpose of competition law and policy is to protect and help ensure that the free market will offer consumers everything they want from competition. This may start with competitive prices, but consumers also want an optimal level of variety, quality, and other forms of non-price competition,[1124] including privacy protection.[1125]

Although it may indeed seem obvious to many that privacy is one form of non-price competition, there is a need for a conceptual change and philosophical shift in the mindset of policymakers, academics and practitioners of competition law, so that in the data economy, where consumers access online offerings in exchange for their

1122. *Ibid.*, 24. *See also* Gary S Becker, *The Economic Approach to Human Behavior* (University of Chicago Press 1976).
1123. Speech by Laitenberger (n 526).
1124. Lande (n 277) 1.
1125. *Ibid.*

personal information, privacy and data protection are elevated to values that are also protected by competition policy.

If the sole function of competition law were maximization of consumer welfare by achieving the most efficient allocation of resources and by reducing costs as much as possible, then formulating and applying legal rules would be relatively simple. Such a policy would be essentially economic. But privacy can play a role in competition policy only if the understanding of the goals of competition policy includes more than economic efficiency. Privacy can be fitted into the scope of competition policy provided that one moves away from understanding the consumer welfare standard only in the narrow, static, price-centred sense. As discussed above, the competition rules are very broadly worded. Nowhere does it say that competition policy goals are just about prices and should ignore everything else. Thus, regulators are not restricted from considering non-price dimensions when enforcing competition law, including privacy.

Arguably, the more economic approach was a half-revolution in EU competition law.[1126] The EU never fully embraced Chicago school postulates and has a historical link to goals beyond consumer welfare, in contrast to US antitrust law. As examined in earlier parts of this book, the introduction of economics and the consumer welfare objective in the narrow economic sense did not fully establish itself in the EU judiciary. The EU courts have never articulated consumer welfare, understood as price competition, as the sole objective of competition law. Instead, the courts have emphasized the multidimensional nature of EU competition policy, which allows for various goals to be advocated. For example, in *TeliaSonera*, the court defined its understanding of the legal objective of competition law very broadly:

> The function of those rules is precisely to prevent competition from being distorted to the detriment of the public interest, individual undertakings and consumers, thereby ensuring the well-being of the European Union.[1127]

In this context, what is interesting is that recent empirical research led by Anu Bradford shows that the international influence of the Chicago school is more limited than what may appear. In other words, the Chicago school's antitrust revolution that promoted economic analysis of competition law has been limited, not only in Europe but also in antitrust regimes in other countries.[1128]

Through analysis of new datasets on antitrust laws and enforcement around the world, research shows that ideas embraced by the Chicago school have not spread internationally to any large degree. On the contrary, many ideas explicitly rejected by the Chicago school – such as using antitrust law to promote goals beyond efficiency or regulate unilateral conduct – are now common features of competition law regimes in jurisdictions around the world.[1129] What this essentially means is that the diffusion of economic analysis of competition law generally – as opposed to only the Chicago

1126. Stones (n 876).
1127. Case C-52/09 *Konkurrensverket v TeliaSonera Sverige AB*, para. 22.
1128. Anu Bradford, Adam S Chilton and Filippo Maria Lancieri,' The Chicago School's Limited Influence on International Antitrust' (December 2019) University of Chicago Law Review (Forthcoming)' https://ssrn.com/abstract=3435097, accessed 19 April 2020.
1129. *Ibid.*

school specifically – has had limited global influence on shaping competition law policies around the world. The Chicago learnings have actually gained limited traction in international antitrust thinking and philosophy generally than many would imagine.[1130]

Particularly interesting in this context is that the use of antitrust law for redistributive ends or the promotion of industrial policy, something strongly condemned by Chicago scholars, is in several countries an explicitly listed goal of antitrust laws, for example, when evaluating mergers based on whether the deal advances the 'public interest'.[1131] Further, among the most interesting findings, at least in the context of this book, is that contrary to the teachings of the Chicago school, half of all countries with antitrust regimes across the world have explicitly articulated and codified goals aimed at broader industrial or social policy – referred to as 'non-efficiency-related goals' by the research – in their antitrust laws by 2010.[1132]

It follows also from this insightful datapoint that there may actually be little basis – or less than one may have previously believed – to say that consumer welfare, understood as price competition, should be the sole objective of competition law. Rather, defining the goals of competition law in the digital age should build on the basis that competition law, just like other legal disciplines, is a social and political construct that has its origins in the local values and foundations of each jurisdiction.[1133] The objectives of competition laws vary widely from one jurisdiction to another, and the potential goals are numerous. In many competition systems, parallel objectives, possibly even conflicting with that of economic efficiency or consumer welfare, are present.[1134] Goals matter to competition law because the goals selected steer the execution of competition law. The underlying competition objectives are fundamentally important as these goals shape how law and policy are implemented and enforced.

Unlike in competition theory and conventional economics, in reality there is no single unifying policy, nor is there any simple premise from which decisions flow through the application of logic alone.[1135] Values and views shift with time, and different systems of competition law reflect different concerns. In this regard, it is worth noting that competition law has grown at a phenomenal rate in response to the changes in economic activities that have taken place around the world. Competition laws have been adopted in over 100 countries whose economies and economic development may be very different. It would be impossible to suppose that each system would have identical concerns.[1136]

1130. *Ibid.*, 28.
1131. *Ibid.*
1132. *Ibid.*, 22. Moreover, more than 40% of countries with antitrust regimes had adopted merger defences unrelated to efficiency reasons by 2010 – in opposition to the Chicago school's teachings.
1133. Ezrachi (n 334).
1134. *See* International Competition Network, Advocacy and competition policy report (2002) 32–33.
1135. Whish (n 366) 17.
1136. Eleanor M Fox, 'The Kaleidoscope of Antitrust and Its Significance in the World Economy: Respecting Differences' in Hawk B (ed.), *International Antitrust Law & Policy: Fordham Corporate Law* (Juris Publishing 2001) 597.

Dynamic nature. Competition policy is an expression of the current values of society and is capable of adjustment and modification.[1137] In the words of Richard Whish, one of Europe's foremost competition scholars and the author's professor of law at the College of Europe:

> competition policy does not exist in a vacuum: it is an expression of the current values and aims of society and is susceptible to change as political thinking generally.[1138]

In this sense, competition law is characterized by inherent dynamism. Dynamism enables competition law and policy to address a wide range of market and social realities, while still retaining its conceptual core. As such, its dynamic nature safeguards competition law from turning into a closed system, detached from domestic and timely societal needs. As framed by Ezrachi, competition law reflects the changing political landscape and forms part of the democratic process.[1139] This is key for understanding and defining competition policy for the data economy.

The dynamic nature of competition law not only affects the analytical framework but also impacts on enforcement policies. The way one understands competition law and its goals is naturally linked to one's approach to the selection of cases and remedies. Areas affected may include case selection and prioritization, budget allocations, investment in capacity building, advocacy or case investigation.[1140] Thus, the way one understands competition law objectives impacts prioritization of case enforcement. Including privacy goals in competition policy is possible by rethinking competition objectives, looking beyond price and importantly, in practice, by changing or altering one's prioritization of cases. Those where privacy risks are present should be considered together in collaboration with another regulator, if necessary. This kind of conjoined approach is discussed below.

The various EU competition goals and values were illustrated earlier in a figure from Ezrachi. In it, the values centre around the umbrella concept of consumer welfare.[1141] No hierarchy among the goals is implied. Considering the research question of this book – namely, whether privacy plays a role in competition law – one now needs to place privacy among those goals and values, to see where it fits best.

1137. Whish (n 366) 17.
1138. *Ibid.*; Whish and Bailey (n 300) 20.
1139. Ezrachi (n 334) 19.
1140. *Ibid.*, 20.
1141. *See* discussion on EU competition law's multitude of goals and related figure in Chapter 3, §3.03[A].

Figure 5.1 Privacy as Competition Goal

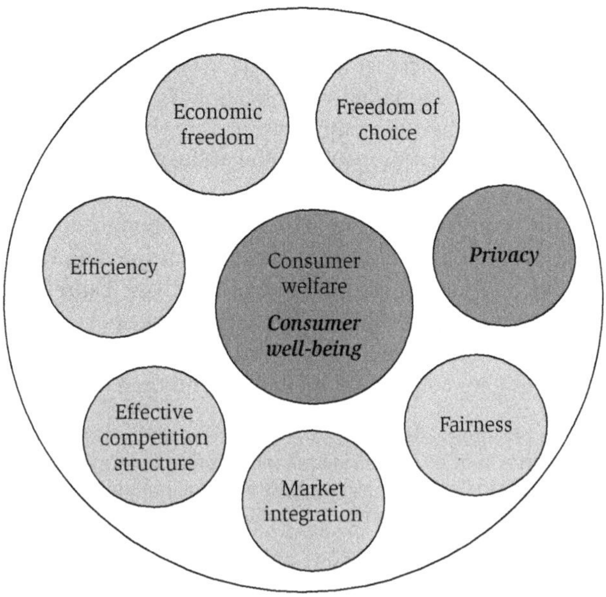

Source: created by the author.

As explored in §5.03[B], privacy is an element of the competitive parameter of quality. This makes privacy closely connected to quality, as these two are closely interlinked, or privacy can be viewed as an inherent part of quality. However, privacy can be understood not only as part of quality but also as a part of fairness, which is a wider notion, goal or principle, as discussed in Chapter 3, §3.03[A]. Consequently, privacy fits close to fairness in the image. Privacy is also regarded as a dimension of consumer choice, analysed in Chapter 3, §3.03[B] in relation to the ordoliberal traditions.

The argument could be taken one step further, if privacy is understood as a right on its own, considering that it is a fundamental right in the EU. In this case, one would place privacy even in its own box. This is illustrated in Figure 5.1, which is a replica of the figure presented in Chapter 3, §3.03[A] in the context of EU competition law's multitude of objectives. Here, according to what has been examined in this book, consumer welfare is understood more widely as consumer well-being, which invites wider concerns and moral values among competition law's policy goals, and the notion of privacy is placed between freedom of choice and fairness, as these values are closely related to one another.

Competition law's identity crisis. Today the objectives of competition policy are being debated and its traditional goals are being challenged.[1142] Competition law can be

1142. *See e.g.* Ezrachi (n 369).

said to be undergoing an identity crisis.[1143] In the last few years, rejection of technocratic competition policy and enforcement has increased, which some – especially in the USA – describe as 'populist' or even 'hipster' antitrust.[1144] In the USA, there have been signs of a more consumer-focused antitrust approach by policymakers and academics advocating a more activist antitrust policy, including calls for a tougher stance on large mergers and corporate consolidation as a response to the growing dominance of a small number of companies in the technology industry.[1145] For example, there have been calls for more interventionist enforcement against large companies acquiring innovative companies that are emerging as potential competitors in the sector.[1146] Some go as far as saying that any acquisition by dominant companies should be blocked.[1147] A 'big is bad' ideology seems to be gaining wider traction and becoming more visible and widespread in the public debate, expressing fear that the size and influence of technology companies in the digital age pose a danger for society and the global economy. Some warn that the 'Frightful Five' (Amazon, Google, Apple, Microsoft and Facebook) are collectively more powerful than many governments:[1148]

> Their growth has prompted calls for greater regulation and antitrust intervention. There's rising worry, too, over their softer, noneconomic influence over culture and information – for instance, fears over how Facebook might affect democracies – as well as the implicit threat they pose to the jurisdictions of world governments.

This recalls events in history. In the late 19th century, the term 'trust' came into use as a way to describe big businesses that controlled the majority of a particular market. President Theodore Roosevelt gained a reputation as the original 'trust buster'

1143. This thought has been elaborated by the author in academic articles and presentations, *see e.g.* Wasastjerna (n 645); Maria Wasastjerna 'Antitrust's Identity Crisis – Time for Less Economics?' Presentation at XXXth CLaSF Workshop on Antitrust at the Intersection of Law and Economics, Competition Law Scholars Forum (CLaSF) and the Graz Institute of Corporate and International Commercial Law (Graz 19 April 2018).
1144. The term 'hipster antitrust', popularized by Joshua Wright, law professor at George Mason University, basically aims to capture the recent trend and movement in the USA (and other parts of the world) to depart from conventional antitrust law due to concerns about how digital markets will look like in the future and the power of multinational corporations.
1145. For example, since 2017, US congressional democrats have called for changing US antitrust laws to become stricter towards big mergers and corporate consolidation.
1146. For example, law professor Steven Solomon at the University of Berkeley California has advocated more aggressive antitrust enforcement against big technology companies' acquiring innovative start-up companies, *see* 'Tech Giants Gobble Start-Ups in an Antitrust Blind Spot' New York Times (16 August 2016) https://www.nytimes.com/2016/08/17/business/dealbook/expect-little-antitrust-challenge-to-walmarts-bid-for-jet-com.html, accessed 19 April 2020. *See also* Matthew Newman, 'Facebook, Amazon Acquisitions Shouldn't Change Antitrust Policy, US Official Says' MLex ITC & Media (27 October 2017).
1147. For example, Amazon's purchase of organic food retailer Whole Foods Market and Facebook's acquisition of THB, a polling app targeted at teenagers, aroused much public criticism. Newman (n 1146). For further reading on these so-called killer acquisitions, *see e.g.* Mats Holmström, Jorge Padilla, Robin Stitzing and Pekka Sääskilahti, 'Killer Acquisitions? The Debate on Merger Control for Digital Markets' (2018) Finnish Competition Law Yearbook 35–54.
1148. Farhad Manjoo, 'Tech's Frightful Five: They've Got Us' The New York Times (10 May 2017) https://www.nytimes.com/2017/05/10/technology/techs-frightful-five-theyve-got-us.html, accessed 19 April 2020.

by breaking up the beef and railroad trusts and filing forty more antitrust suits during his presidency.[1149] Fast-forward some hundred years, and one finds US President Donald Trump announcing that his administration should not approve the *AT&T/Time Warner* merger 'because it's too much concentration of power in the hands of too few' and just a year later, the US Justice Department sued to block the merger.[1150]

However, despite concern about the 'Frightful Five', conservative politicians and critics of a 'hipster antitrust' movement contend that it would only lead to an 'incoherent' policy moving away from a structural view of the market based on presumptions.[1151] Innovation does carry risks, as a more interventionist antitrust policy against large technology companies and their transactions could harm the flow of venture capital to innovators by making acquisitions of start-ups more difficult. In other words, 'you would kill off the process that's creating business in the first place'.[1152] So far, the dominant view of the American antitrust agencies – the US DOJ and the FTC – seems to be that 'consumer welfare is the right standard for antitrust'[1153] expressing opposition to the potential widening of antitrust objectives to address political and public policy concerns.

Similarly, Carl Shapiro argues that:

> while antitrust enforcement has a vital role to play in keeping markets competitive, antitrust law and antitrust institutions are ill suited to directly address concerns associated with the political power of large corporations or other public policy goals such as income inequality or job creation. Campaign finance reform, tax policy, labour, education, and other policies are far better suited to address those critical public policy goals.[1154]

As discussed in this book, since competition laws were enacted, two different welfare goals have dominated the competition debate and modern academic and policy discourse: total welfare (the overall surplus from producers and consumers) and consumer welfare (the surplus only from consumers).[1155] Many articles suggest that maximizing consumer welfare brings antitrust closer to total welfare.[1156] However, there are also those who believe that antitrust analysis should be driven by total

1149. James F Rill and Stacy L Turner, 'Presidents Practicing Antitrust: Where to Draw the Line?' (2014) 79 Antitrust Law Journal 577, 599.
1150. Greg Ip, 'The Antitrust Case Against Facebook, Google and Amazon' The Wall Street Journal (16 January 2018) https://www.wsj.com/articles/the-antitrust-case-against-facebook-google-amazon-and-apple-1516121561, accessed 19 April 2020.
1151. Newman (n 1146).
1152. *Ibid.*
1153. *Ibid.*
1154. Carl Shapiro, 'Antitrust in a Time of Populism' (2018) International Journal of Industrial Organization, Forthcoming. *See* generally Pallavi Guniganti and Ron Knox, 'A Populist Now: What Can Antitrust Do for Inequality?' (2 March 2017) Global Competition Review; Jan Blockx, 'Technocracy and Populism in Antitrust in the US and the EU' (18 December 2017) https://ssrn.com/abstract=3089609, accessed 19 April 2020.
1155. *See* Chapter 3, §3.02.
1156. *See e.g.* Damien J Neven and Lars-Hendrik Röller, 'Consumer Surplus vs. Welfare Standard in a Political Economy Model of Merger Control' (2005) 23 International Journal of Industrial Organization 829; Sven-Olof Fridolfsson, 'A Consumer Surplus Defense in Merger Control' in Vivek Goshal and Johan Stennek (eds), *The Political Economy of Antitrust* (Emerald Group Publishing Limited 2007) 287.

welfare rather than consumer welfare.[1157] The battle over these welfare standards in competition law and policy could be characterized as overblown, as often the goals are indistinguishable in practice because conduct that violates antitrust law often reduces both consumer and total welfare.[1158] The situation is different if including non-price goals in the consumer welfare standard, as this may lead to a different outcome in practice, as discussed in the context of *Facebook/WhatsApp* and the Bundeskartellamt's Facebook case.[1159]

Ambiguity and inconsistency about the goals of competition policy can be costly. Divergences among standards across jurisdictions are costly.[1160] However, as mentioned, it may not be possible to strive for total harmonization in goals; the various competition law systems that have been adopted in jurisdictions around the world with different economies and economic developments do not reflect identical concerns.[1161] Indeed, competition law has evolved and varied over time. This reflects that it is a system that adapts to society's evolving norms of justice and fairness.[1162] For example, quite a few of the older European Commission decisions would possibly look different if decided today as a result of evolution and change in competition policy over the years.[1163]

This also means that competition law is infused with tension, as views and insights shift over a period of time. Different systems of competition law reflect different concerns, an important point in this book when comparing the competition laws of the EU and the USA. While competition regimes around the world share similar key principles and basic properties, they also reflect different societal interests and local policy considerations that influence competition enforcement.[1164] It is impossible to suppose that each system has identical values, goals and interests.[1165] For example, the debate at the time of the negotiations concerning the EU Lisbon Treaty of 2007 showed that some Member States are less enthusiastic about the process of competition than others.[1166]

Coming back to the welfare goals of competition and the notion of privacy, it is key to understand that just like any other non-economic goal of competition policy, privacy issues can form part of competition policy provided the understanding of the objectives of competition policy includes more than economic efficiency. Those who argue against this kind of policy development assert that privacy as a competition

---

1157. For an overview of this scholarship, *see e.g.* Bork (n 529) 50; Motta (n 322); Posner (n 559); Farrell and Katz (n 360) 3; Alan J Meese, 'Debunking the Purchaser Welfare Account of § 2 of the Sherman Act: How Harvard Brought Us a Total Welfare Standard and Why We Should Keep It' (2010) 85 New York University Law Review 659.
1158. Blair and Sokol (n 549) 2500 ('Most of the time, the welfare standard does not matter').
1159. *See* Chapter 4, §4.04.
1160. Blair and Sokol (n 549) 2506.
1161. Fox (n 1136) 597.
1162. Ezrachi (n 334) 3.
1163. Carl Wetter, Johan Karlsson and Marie Östman, *Konkurrensrätt – en kommentar* (4th edn, Thomson Reuters 2009) 18.
1164. In South Africa, e.g., public interest grounds, such as employment, play a role in the assessment of mergers. South Africa Competition Act (n 429).
1165. Fox (n 1136) 597.
1166. Whish and Bailey (n 300) 20.

concern could muddle the goal of competition enforcement.[1167] However, considering that the process of competition itself is intended to deliver benefits to consumers, and referring to what has been said with regard to the current shortcomings of competition policy in, among other issues, accounting for the value of data and being overly static and price-focused,[1168] it is possible to combine competition and privacy provided competition law's enforcement objective builds on a broader interpretation of the consumer welfare concept. This would also entail conferring on competition law a data protection function. But, this requires a change in the current approach to competition policy and the existing general understanding of consumer welfare tied to price.

Such a transition in competition policy and in the standard of consumer welfare from a price-centred notion to also embracing privacy as a non-economic goal cannot happen overnight. Institutional structures are a function of the time in which they were set up and institutional development is based upon that initial endowment.[1169] This creates path dependence to institutional development making integration of new learning and alternative approaches more difficult for some competition systems - especially authorities and courts - than others.[1170] A number of factors matter for competition policy development and explain why systems are shaped in a certain way. To a large extent, it is history and politics that explain divergent competition systems. Certainly, the application of economics to antitrust also plays a role.[1171] In the EU and USA comparison, many of the assumptions in the US antitrust system - with a history of limited government regulation and a dearth of state ownership - are not directly reflected in the European competition regime, which underwent more state intervention. EU competition law also has specific provisions on state aid[1172] and provisions specific to public undertakings.[1173]

In support of combining competition and privacy and broadening competition law's enforcement objectives beyond the price-focused consumer welfare standard, one may point to the fact that, ultimately, the process of competition and competition policy is there to serve its citizens. Thus, it should not blindly focus only on economic efficiency in the narrow Chicago school sense, but also look at values that go beyond price, including important social, political and even moral aspects.[1174] As argued by Stucke, '[a]ny competition policy that has the purpose of promoting well-being

1167. *See e.g.* Sokol and Comerford (n 680) in Blair and Sokol (n 41) 10–11; Cooper (n 980); Lamadrid de Pablo and Villiers (n 982).
1168. *See* §5.02.
1169. *See* generally William E Kovacic, 'Creating Competition Policy: Betty Bock and the Development of Antitrust Institutions' (1997) 66 Antitrust Law Journal 231, 244–245.
1170. D Daniel Sokol, 'Antitrust, Institutions, and Merger Control' (2010) 17 George Mason Law Review 1055 (describing institutional analysis within antitrust).
1171. *See* David J Gerber, *Global Competition: Law, Markets, and Globalization* (OUP 2010); Gerber (n 516).
1172. Article 107 TFEU (limiting 'any aid granted by a Member State ... in any form whatsoever which distorts or threatens to distort competition by favoring certain undertakings or the production of certain goods shall, insofar as it affects trade between Member States, be incompatible with the internal market'). For analysis, *see e.g.* Kelyn Bacon, *European Union Law of State Aid* (OUP 2013).
1173. Article 106 TFEU.
1174. Stucke (n 613) 551. *See also* Fox (n 624) 1153–54.

(consumer welfare in a wider sense), needs to balance multiple political, social, economic and moral objectives'.[1175] In the recent discourse on competition law's policy goals, some have proposed we add a moral compass to our antitrust toolkit.[1176] Others speak of restoring the competition ideal[1177] or fighting for the soul of antitrust.[1178]

These ideas are not actually that novel. Already decades ago there were concerns about restricting the goals of competition, as articulated insightfully by one of the leading American antitrust scholars, former US FTC Chairman Robert Pitofsky, and the author's professor at Georgetown Law School, who maintained that '[i]t is bad history, bad policy, and bad law to exclude certain political values in interpreting the antitrust laws'.[1179] He also warned that:

> [i]f the free-market sector of the economy is allowed to develop under antitrust rules that are blind to all but economic concerns, the likely result will be an economy so dominated by a few corporate giants that it will be impossible for the state not to play a more intrusive role in economic affairs.[1180]

This prediction may not have been that far off the mark, considering today's economic climate and growing concerns about market concentration.[1181] Robert Pitofsky's predictions made decades ago about the risks of ignoring non-economic concerns in competition policy are still valid today. Moreover, the risks are arguably even bigger in the data economy, where the most serious harm may be to non-price dimensions, such as privacy.

In 2008, Pitofsky argued that '[b]ecause extreme interpretations and misinterpretations of conservative economic theory (and constant disregard of facts) have come to dominate antitrust, there is reason to believe that the USA is headed in a profoundly wrong direction'.[1182] More and more individuals and institutions have come to agree with that assessment.[1183] Concerns about privacy harm, protecting personal data and the power of the so-called Frightful Five in increasingly concentrated markets have led to calls for breaking up powerful Internet companies[1184] and regulating online platforms:[1185]

1175. Stucke (n 613).
1176. Burnside (n 892).
1177. Stucke and Ezrachi (n 579).
1178. Ariel Ezrachi and Maurice E Stucke, 'The Fight over Antitrust's Soul' (2017) Journal of European Competition Law & Practice.
1179. Robert Pitofsky, 'Political Content of Antitrust' (1979) 127 University of Pennsylvania Law Review 1051.
1180. *Ibid.*
1181. *See e.g.* speech by Vestager (n 522): 'Digital technology is transforming every part of our lives [...]. And we're seeing signs that competition might not be working the way it should. There's evidence that some markets might be getting more concentrated, with more of the market in the hands of just a few companies.'
1182. Pitofsky (n 626) 1, 6.
1183. Wu (n 606) 2.
1184. Galloway (n 404).
1185. Jonathan Taplin, 'Is It Time to Break Up Google?' New York Times (22 April 2017) https://www.nytimes.com/2017/04/22/opinion/sunday/is-it-time-to-break-up-google.html ?smprod = nytcore-ipad&smid = nytcore-ipad-share&_r = 0, accessed 19 April 2020. *See also* Ip (n 1150); The Economist, 'How to Tame the Tech Titans' (n 912).

> We are going to have to decide fairly soon whether Google, Facebook and Amazon are the kinds of natural monopolies that need to be regulated, or whether we allow the status quo to continue, pretending that unfettered monoliths don't inflict damage on our privacy and democracy.

There are concerns that the acquisition of data could help a dominant company maintain its market power. This implies even greater societal, political and even ethical concerns when just a few companies are amassing a significant amount of personal data. Over the past decade, Amazon, Apple, Facebook, and Google – or, 'the Four', as referred to by Scott Galloway – have aggregated more economic value and influence than nearly any other commercial entity in history. Together, their market capitalization amounts to USD 2.8 trillion (equalling the GDP of France), a staggering 24% share of the S&P 500 Top 50, close to the value of every stock traded on the Nasdaq in 2001.[1186] Scott Galloway is part of the so-called tech lash movement in the USA, known for advocating the break-up of the technology giants:[1187]

> Why should we break up big tech? Not because the Four are evil and we're good. It's because we understand that the only way to ensure competition is to sometimes cut the tops off trees, just as we did with railroads and Ma Bell. [...] a key part of a healthy economic cycle is pruning firms when they become invasive, cause premature death, and won't let other firms emerge. The breakup of big tech should and will happen, because we're capitalists. It's time.[1188]

Indeed, one extreme alternative that lawmakers mentioned during the hearing of proceedings with Facebook in the midst of the Cambridge Analytica scandal included the possibility of breaking up the company and forcing it to divest Instagram and WhatsApp.[1189] Similarly, Google's market power has faced suggestions for breaking up the company. In 2014, the European Parliament voted for the breaking up of Google[1190] and again in 2018 the European Parliament advocated that competition enforcers should consider breaking up Google.[1191]

Experts have suggested breaking up digital or technology companies to avoid their being able to control the marketplace. The model would be the robust antitrust enforcement that led to the break-up of Standard Oil, in 1911, and AT&T, in 1984, in the USA. A less drastic alternative might draw inspiration from actions taken by regulators in the 1990s to force Microsoft to stop bundling a web browser with its operating system. What is being pondered essentially is whether 'Big Tech' is the new Standard Oil.

This is because one of the most concrete examples, especially in American history in terms of business monopoly, is the classic case of Standard Oil, the American oil company established by John D. Rockefeller in 1870. Standard Oil grew to become one

1186. *Ibid.*
1187. Galloway (n 404).
1188. *Ibid.*
1189. Pressman (n 1097).
1190. *See* European Parliament, Resolution of 27 November 2014 on supporting consumer rights in the digital single market (2014/29738RSP) 17.
1191. While a report by the European Parliament on this matter is non-binding, it does underscore political interest in Google's competition law cases.

of the world's largest multinational corporations by the early 1900s and controlled significant wealth. Standard Oil's dominance of the oil industry continued until 1911 when the US Supreme Court decided that the business trust operated in violation of the Sherman Act.[1192] The Supreme Court affirmed the dissolution of the trust and split Standard Oil into thirty-four business entities, some of which continue to exist today as ExxonMobil and ConocoPhillips.

Today it is suggested that Apple, Google, Facebook and Microsoft each easily have more than ten times the net income as did Standard Oil when it was broken up. These suggestions reflect that, in this regard, history is in a way repeating itself. One may think of it as a crossroads where competition policy is proposed to be rethought as it was back in 1890, as reflected in Figure 5.2. The antimonopoly cartoon 'The Menace of the Hour' from 1899 illustrates the public and populist view of monopolies, reflecting the Standard Oil and coal trusts, the electric transit railways ('The Traction Monster') and competition from the New York City subway supported by Theodore Roosevelt after citizens demanding improved transit and change monopolized the city's street railways.[1193]

Figure 5.2 The Menace of the Hour

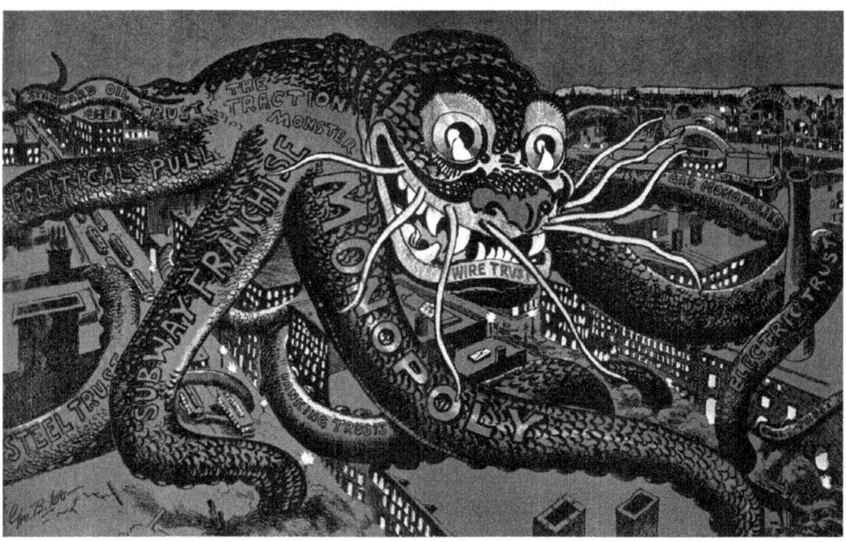

Source: The Menace of the Hour cartoon for the *Verdict* Magazine in 1899 by George Luks.

Figure 5.3 from 2018 of the technology octopus reflects the powers and influence of 'the Four', as referred to by Scott Galloway, that have broad economic, political

1192. *Standard Oil v United States*, 221 US 1 (1911).
1193. George Luks, 'The Menace of the Hour' cartoon for *Verdict* Magazine (1899). *See also* Nicolas Petit, 'Should the tech giants be broken up?' Presentation University of South Australia (Adelaide 16 February 2018).

(reaching to the White House) and societal implications, as well as legal risks and privacy intrusion (illustrated by the octopus getting into the minds of people on their phones).[1194]

Figure 5.3 The Tech Octopus

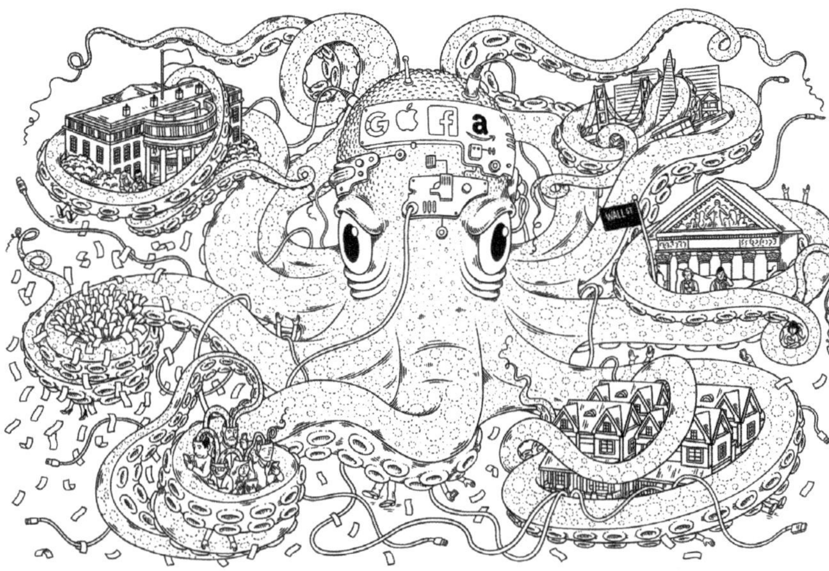

Source: Tech Octopus cartoon for *Esquire* magazine in 2018 by Andrew Rae.

Whether breaking up powerful technology companies is the right solution today is questionable. This way of tackling significant market power in the data economy relies on an overly simplistic assumption that break-ups will necessarily lead to more competition in the digital markets. There is no basis for such an assumption. Just because this is what was done with the American railroads back in the 19th century, when the markets were also overly concentrated and monopolies hindered competition, does not mean that the same remedy for addressing market failure would work for competition in data-driven markets, where access to data and network effects are exactly the reason for consumers being able to enjoy new and enhanced products and services.

As noted by Christine Lagarde, head of the International Monetary Fund, even though 'it used to be the right answer', breaking up some of the 'tech titans' in the USA and in other places in the world is unlikely to prove the way forward.[1195] Instead of

1194. Andrew Rae, 'Tech Octopus' (cartoon) for *Esquire* magazine (2018); *see also* Galloway (n 404). Similarly to n 1193, *see* Nicolas Petit, 'Should the tech giants be broken up?' Presentation University of South Australia (Adelaide 16 February 2018).

1195. Lewis Crofts, 'New Thinking on Tech Titans Needed, Not Break-Up, IMF's Lagarde Says' MLex Market Insight (19 April 2018).

breaking up technology companies, which may be counterproductive as regards productivity and innovation, new thinking is needed across fields. This includes not only competition but also tax and other fields, to ensure that 'market disruptors' can also compete. This is because the old solution of breaking up monopolies is not necessarily replicable in the digital age, where most of the assets of dominant technology companies have intangible value, such as data, and when the benefits from those assets are derived using particular mechanisms that are themselves intangible. How do you do the breaking up? How do you enable market disrupters to actually be able to operate? The tech lash movement and proponents of breaking up 'tech titans' often overlook these important questions and the surrounding complexities of the digital economy.

One of the important aspects often overlooked is that, as much as competition scholars would like to think the world economy revolves around antitrust, it does not. Much bigger forces are at play, such as the economy, globalization, and especially the rise of intangible assets, something that is particularly important.

In the world's most advanced economies, investment in intangible assets – meaning ideas – has outstripped investment in tangibles and is now far more important in the modern economy. The importance of intangible assets has played a role in some of the big economic changes of the last decade.[1196] The economic characteristics of intangible assets are creating a shift in favour of 'winner takes all' competition in the global marketplace. When important competitive assets are intangible, they can be copied and scaled rapidly, which can mean that the platforms through which new innovations can reach the market become more important than the ideas themselves. In the data-driven economy, the world's largest digital platforms are simultaneously key competitive bottlenecks and innovation accelerators, bringing new technologies to consumers in a fraction of the time that it might otherwise take. When Facebook acquired Instagram, the company had 30 million users and low revenues. Only five years later it had 600 million users and the prospect of being a multibillion dollar business in its own right.

So breaking up powerful technology companies is unlikely to be the way forward. Another solution that has been aired to level the playing field for fair competition is a progressive data-sharing mandate.[1197] This would leave technology companies intact but require them to share anonymized slices of the data they collect with other companies. Under such a system, a company above a certain size or share of the market that systematically collects and analyses data would have to let other companies in the same market access a subset of its data. The larger a firm's market share, the more of its data others would be allowed to see. The role of regulators would be limited to

1196. For further reading, *see e.g.* Jonathan Haskel and Stian Westlake, *Capitalism Without Capital: The Rise of the Intangible Economy* (Princeton University Press 2017). *See also* David Autor's empirical work showing how the economy has increasingly shifted in favour of a smaller number of 'superstar firms', 'The Fall of the Labor Share and the Rise of Superstar Firms' (May 2017) NBER Working Paper No 23396.

1197. Viktor Mayer-Schönberger and Thomas Ramge, 'A Big Choice for Big Tech – Share Data or Suffer the Consequences' Foreign Affairs comment (September/October 2018) https://www.foreignaffairs.com/articles/world/2018-08-13/big-choice-big-tech, accessed 19 April 2020.

assessing market share, and if necessary also enforcing access to data, but they would not necessarily actively organize or operate the sharing system.[1198]

Recent EU legislation on data portability has boosted the idea of data sharing. Thanks to new rules, consumers can now force companies to provide competitors with access to their banking data (as part of so-called open banking), as well as any other personal data as part of the GDPR. How is this different from the data-sharing mandate? The data-sharing mandate would differ from data portability in that the latter requires each consumer to act independently. But the legislative aim is similar: to break the stranglehold companies may maintain on data and create a competitive market with innovative data-driven services. As both the European Commission and members of the European Parliament are studying how to legislate progressive data-sharing mandates,[1199] this is an interesting theme to follow, in particular as to its potential reconciliation with the GDPR and interoperability considerations.

Whether the data economy, new technologies and evolving business practices require adjustments to or rethinking of competition law and policy is currently being explored by leading competition authorities in Europe and the USA, as discussed in Chapter 4, §4.01. Among significant initiatives are the public consultations and hearings conducted by the European and American authorities. In 2018 and 2019, the FTC held a series of public hearings on competition and consumer protection in the 21st century with the aim, among others, of analysing whether big technology companies have grown too big and wield too much power in the digital era.[1200] Citing then FTC Chairman Robert Pitofsky, who held hearings of a similar kind in 1995, the agency's focus is the state of American antitrust (and consumer protection) law and development in digital markets, considering technology networks, market power and entry barriers featuring online platforms, and a variety of issues concerning the use of big data.[1201] The European Commission conducted a similar exercise in the EU through its consultation on shaping competition policy for the digital age, and similarly in the United Kingdom, the government reviewed the impact and market influence of powerful digital technology companies and the possible need to adjust competition policy accordingly.[1202] In the UK, the competition implications of concentrations of data among a small number of companies were of special focus.[1203]

1198. *Ibid.* In this regard, the French competition authority's decision requiring GDF Suez to disclose part of its customer database to competing energy companies is interesting. In this case, the personal data was acquired by GDF when performing its (former) monopoly duties in French gas supply markets. *See Autorité de la Concurrence*, Avis n°18-A-03 portant sur l'exploitation des données dans le secteur de la publicité sur interne (6 March 2018).

1199. *Ibid.*

1200. The FTC invited public comments on the questions on its website, *see* US FTC Hearings on Competition and Consumer Protection in the 21st Century, Hearings on Competition & Consumer Protection, Public comment topics and process, available at https://www.ftc.gov/policy/advocacy/public-comment-topics-process#1. *See also* Gene Quinn, 'Has Big Tech Finally Become Too Big for the FTC to Ignore?' IPWatchdog (21 June 2018) http://www.ipwatchdog.com/2018/06/21/big-tech-finally-become-big-ftc/id=98598/, accessed 19 April 2020.

1201. *Ibid.*

1202. European Commission Call for contributions (n 656); HM Treasury, The economic value of data: discussion paper (August 2018) 17.

1203. *Ibid.*

Arguably, the debate about the soul – that is, the goals – of competition law concerns whether the discipline should be about the protection of consumer welfare or some other benchmark. According to Alfonso Lamadrid de Pablo, one way of framing the debate about the objectives of competition law is by identifying two fundamentally different views towards the discipline, namely the discretionalists and the legalists.[1204]

The discretionalists are those who believe that competition authorities and courts should be as unconstrained as possible in reaching the outcome considered to be correct in any given case. Getting it right, in other words, is more important than other factors (such as the consistency or predictability of enforcement). For example, following a precedent is not as relevant as reaching an outcome that is deemed appropriate.[1205] Conversely, the legalists downplay the importance of 'getting it right' in every given case. What is more, legalists accept that enforcement errors – both type I and type II, according to the so-called error-cost approach to law enforcement[1206] – are unavoidable in a legal discipline such as competition law. Legalists also place importance on placing restrictions on competition authorities and courts that would stem, among others, from the need to ensure that intervention is predictable and consistent. Thus, precedents should be followed unless truly compelling reasons suggest departing from them.

This approach stands on the premise that enforcement of competition law and policy is imperfect and inevitably includes decision errors. The error-cost analysis is generally considered as one of the most influential theories in competition law and economics. It assumes that false positives are more costly than false negatives. This is because false negatives are believed to be capable of being fixed by markets' self-correcting mechanisms, in contrast to false positives. Both kinds of error are inevitable, but the theory goes that the costs of over-enforcement can be viewed as higher than those of under-enforcement, especially in dynamic markets. However, little research has actually been undertaken about the costs of false negatives and what the possible long-term consequences may be if there is little competition activity. So one may question whether the time has now come to focus more on false positives. In this regard, Daniel Rubinfeld, while crediting the Chicago school for improving the general understanding of the economics of competition, voices the following critique:

> [C]onservative economics has overshot the mark in a number of ways. It has worried more about false positives (bringing the wrong case) than false negatives (failing to bring the right case). ... And, it has fostered a tendency to downplay enforcement in dynamic technological industries in which innovation issues play a significant role.[1207]

1204. Alfonso Lamadrid de Pablo, 'Discretionalists vs Legalists: The True Divide in the Competition Law Community?' (Chilling Competition blog, 28 May 2018) https://chillingcompetition.com/2018/05/28/discretionalists-vs-legalists-the-true-divide-in-the-competition-law-community/#comment-114483, accessed 19 April 2020.
1205. *Ibid.*
1206. *See e.g.* Howard Shelanski, 'Information, Innovation, and Competition Policy for the Internet' (2013) 161 University of Pennsylvania Law Review 1663, 1669.
1207. Daniel Rubinfeld, 'Conservative Economic Analysis and Its Effects' in Pitofsky (ed.) (n 626).

In a similar vein, Carl Shapiro suggests that sound competition policy would tolerate some false positives in order to avoid some false negatives.[1208]

The debate between the camp of the discretionalists on the one side and the legalists on the other side is perhaps older than competition law itself, as it effectively goes back to the battle between deontological and teleological ethics.[1209] Legal tradition likely owes most to the former, with its focus on rights and duties. Economics likely owes more to the latter, with its focus on outcomes and welfare. Competition law is a particularly intense collision or culmination point for these two opposing philosophies. Thus, the debate can be framed into a more philosophical question of whether one sides with Immanuel Kant or John Stuart Mill.

Moral aspects. It follows that the question as to competition law's policy goals can be elevated or transferred into a more philosophical and even moral environment. An essential feature of the legal discipline, including the field of competition law, is the existence of a close connection between law and morals. Law and morality are necessarily intertwined with each other. This connection can be summarized by Gustaf Radbruch's famous formula: extreme justice is not law. This notion reflects the dual nature of law: it is both real and ideal, and both are necessary elements of law.[1210] It goes beyond the scope of this book to address the wide and deep philosophical discussions on law and its link to morals, ethics and ethical values. However, let it suffice to say here that moral principles are immanent to the foundation of law, while morals and values are bound to legal argumentation, being part of the procedure of justification.[1211] This idea is close to what Aristotle presented. In the Nicomachean Ethics, Aristotle emphasizes that the just is lawful and fair, and the unjust is unlawful and thus unfair too. However, he later added that the unfair and the unlawful are not the same thing. Everything that is unfair is unlawful, but not everything unlawful is unfair.[1212]

While Aristotle's thoughts relate to his specific conception of the relationship between law and justice, they are insightful for this book. They can inform the discourse on fairness as a guiding principle for competition policy. Moreover, Aristotle's thinking is helpful in the debate about the competition law objectives between the discretionalists and the legalists, which represent two fundamentally different views about the discipline. It is easy to side with the discretionalists, which place importance on getting it right, even at the expense of following precedent. This is because, with the

1208. Shapiro, (n 1154); Lynskey (n 205), 11.
1209. Lamadrid de Pablo (n 1204).
1210. *See* Gustaf Radbruch, 'Statutory Lawlessness and Supra-Statutory Law' (2006) 26 OJLS 7; Robert Alexy, 'A Defense of Radbruch's Formula' in MA Freeman (ed.), *Lloyds Introduction to Jurisprudence* (7th edn, Sweet & Maxwell 2001) 374. For a discussion on law and morals from a Nordic perspective and considering the Scandinavian tradition, *see* Aarnio (n 28) 53. *See also* Lars D Eriksson, 'Värderingar, fakta och juridik' (1969) 5 Tidskrift utgiven av Juridiska Föreningen i Finland 414–430.
1211. *See* Aleksander Peczenik, who introduced the notion of deep justification of law, Peczenik (n 84) 158. Aarnio (n 29) 54. *See also* discussion in Chapter 1, §1.04.
1212. Aarnio (n 28) 54; Aristotle, *Nicomachean Ethics* (edited and translated by Roger Crisp, CUP 2000).

transfer to the data economy, following precedent does not always necessarily mean getting it right.

One may say that it was the appeal of simplicity that partly led competition law on to the wrong track. The attempt to implement a more economics-based approach to EU competition law disregards the inherent, multidimensional nature of EU competition law, under which various policy goals can be advocated. Ignoring the multiple objectives of EU competition law and resorting to a simplified and superficial adoption of economic efficiency as the single goal of EU competition policy ignores the underlying historical and cultural context in which competition law was created. As incisively noted by Lamadrid de Pablo:

> [Economic] efficiency is seen as an objective yardstick preferable to the complexity of alternative standards. And all too often the appeal of simplicity trumps complexity.[1213]

Looking only at consumer welfare as a price-centred concept may lead to losing social, political and moral concerns, something that is raised by the rising fairness evolution in the EU and the New Brandeis movement in the USA. This reflects that people feel disenfranchised from competition policy development, which culminates in a choice between technocratic or democratic law enforcement. Arguably, EU competition law is not a precise science. Competition law is far from agnostic or merely technocratic. Just like any other legal regime, it is ultimately underpinned by core political values.[1214]

This understanding of competition law as a value-driven policy is central to bringing in privacy as a dimension when envisioning a sound competition policy for the digital age. That no doubt is a complex exercise, as this book demonstrates. Focusing only on price competition is appealing in its simplicity because it arguably brings coherent parameters to competition policy and may enhance legal certainty. In contrast, expanding horizons beyond price may risk legal certainty. As framed by Justice Ginsburg, enforcement in the USA until the 1970s was 'close to random'. Robert Bork, one of the key proponents of the Chicago school, puts it even more boldly when holding that '[t]o abandon economic theory is to abandon the possibility of rational antitrust law'.[1215]

According to Frank H. Easterbrook's scholarship on 'workable' antitrust policy, one needs to consider the error costs of over-inclusion and under-inclusion plus enforcement costs to estimate a sound (workable) competition policy. The rules are imperfect and filters are presumptive. According to this approach, rules that do well on average are the best that courts and regulators can produce and apply. The pursuit of the perfect is the enemy of the good.[1216] So, looking only at price effects in competition law arguably avoids over-enforcement of the rules. Economics can bring considerable benefits to inform enforcement of competition law, but not everything has to be or

1213. Alfonso Lamadrid de Pablo, 'Competition Law as Fairness' (2017) 8 Journal of European Competition Law & Practice 147–148.
1214. Lamadrid de Pablo (n 123).
1215. Bork (n 529).
1216. Frank H Easterbrook, 'Workable Antitrust Policy' (1986) 84 Michigan Law Review 1696, 1704.

should be 'effects-based' or quantitative. Structured rules should be informed by economic theory and empirical evidence. One may ask whether the push for economic analysis in competition law has not gone so far as to sometimes forget the existence of some of the problems that competition rules were enacted to address.

Looking at competition law as a political construct and questioning its underlying policy objectives brings the discussion close to the discourse on law judged in the light of its social effects and the ideas around philosophical pragmatism promoted by Raimo Siltala.[1217] In his treatise *Law, Trust, and Reason*, he argues that meaning and truth are essentially instrumentalist notions that are inextricably interwoven with human action, social practices, and the successful attainment of various kinds of human endeavour. In other words, 'truth is what works'.[1218] Yet, in the context of law, the notion of what works may prove to be hard to determine, because of the inherently contested character of law and because usually no consensus exists as to the values to be pursued. This is precisely the situation in competition policy, where a lack of consensus remains about the ultimate goals of competition law and the precise meaning of consumer welfare, whether and to what extent the notion includes social concerns.

According to legal pragmatism, the merits and demerits of law are to be judged primarily, if not even exclusively, by the social consequences thereby brought into effect.[1219] This is based on the underlying belief that 'human laws are devices, tools which society uses as one of its methods to regulate human conduct and to promote those types of it which are regarded as desirable'.[1220] This reflects a consequentialist notion of law where its social consequences are the primary criterion in legal decision-making. The truth or, rather, the justifiability or usefulness of how to construct and read the law can thus be evaluated in the light of the economic, social or other consequences brought into effect by law in society.[1221] Legal argumentation should never take place in a social or ideological void, detached from the constitutive value premises operative in the various legal instruments.[1222] This is in contrast to legal formalism. Legal pragmatism is in essence anti-formalist, and whereas formalism is typical of legal rules, it is not typical of legal principles.

The fairness discussion in EU competition law and considerations around non-price aspects such as privacy in competition policy may mean a new ideology for EU competition law. This mirrors the so-called hipster or populist antitrust movement in the USA. Will the EU move towards factoring in social dimensions into competition policy? Some indications suggest this kind of emerging development in the light of the EU Competition Commissioner's speeches: 'That the market is not the society,' she

1217. On the lure of simplicity and pragmatism in relation to law from a philosophical perspective, *see* Raimo Siltala, *Law, Truth, and Reason: A Treatise on Legal Argumentation* (University of Turku, Springer 2011) 102.
1218. *Ibid.*, 97.
1219. *Ibid.*, 103–104.
1220. *Ibid.*, 104, citing Walter Wheeler Cook's reflection on the judge's method of interpretation: Walter Wheeler Cook, 'Scientific Method and the Law' (1927) 13 American Bar Association Journal 303.
1221. Siltala (n 1217) 104.
1222. *Ibid.*, 105.

says, simply. 'For a long time we have been told that is all it is. But the market is there to serve us as citizens. If the market becomes everything, you have this feeling that you are being cheated all the time, and that you are not in control. I think we have the power to change that.'[1223]

Further, if competition policy really is an expression of the current values of society, and has the ultimate objective of serving its citizens, then it is quite a compelling idea that competition policy should also consider other values beyond price, such as privacy protection. In today's modern economy, data protection and privacy are, after all, fundamental rights and reflect significant values that shape markets and their development. This book is by no means alone in arguing that competition policy ought to broaden its price-centred policy objective to incorporate other important values. Recalling the words of Robert Pitofsky, it would indeed be 'bad law' to exclude these values in interpreting competition law. Moreover, Ezrachi and Stucke explain in their excellent editorial 'The fight over antitrust's soul':

> The reality is that 'competition law' has never been, nor will it ever be, pure from normative political, social and economic values. Ultimately, it comes down to the values we want to promote and our belief in how competition works.[1224]

Indeed, values are creations of mankind; they are born and modified in society, tied to time and place. As argued in this book, the price-centred consumer welfare standard suffers from certain limitations in the digital economy and is not optimal for today's data-driven markets. To date, scholarly work and literature has failed to advance a substitute devoid of its defects. But it is increasingly acknowledged, beyond the legal disciplines, that equating euro or dollar costs with value can be misleading in many ways. For example, that economic statistics such as GDP are flawed is not news.[1225] Despite efforts to improve such statistics, these problems remain. Economists also generally ignore the value of non-market activity, such as unpaid work. Overall, it seems likely that economists today continue to treat things which cannot easily be measured as if they do not matter at all. They work on the basis that tangible costs and benefits outweigh subjective values. This is basically the whole problem with having an overly price-centred competition policy whose primary objective is an economic understanding of consumer welfare that centres around price competition. It is not completely misguided to argue that competition policy has undergone the same development as the evolution of philosophy and economics, where the narrow focus on immediate and easily measured aims became dominant.

The current understanding of consumer welfare in competition law centres on price and, as discussed, is arguably under-inclusive. Some voices suggesting to do

1223. Tim Adams, Interview: Margrethe Vestager: 'We Are Doing This Because People Are Angry' (17 September 2017) https://www.theguardian.com/world/2017/sep/17/margrethe-vestager-people-feel-angry-about-tax-avoidance-european-competition-commissioner, accessed 19 April 2020.

1224. Ezrachi and Stucke (n 1178). *See also* Fox (n 624) 1153–54; Stucke (n 613) 564.

1225. As a clear example, measures of output include spending on cigarette advertisements, napalm and the like, while they omit the quality of children's health and education. *See e.g.* The Economist, 'Economists Focus Too Little on What People Really Care About' (n 858).

away with the consumer welfare standard in antitrust policy go as far as to argue that consumer welfare was an instrument of class domination, invented by Robert Bork to eliminate constraints on plutocrats.[1226] The standard's focus on short-term price effects (and output) arguably leaves unchallenged other significant harms, both economic and perhaps even political ones.[1227]

When debating competition law's policy goals, one may argue: why stop at political and social values; why not consider even more important values that should be advanced by competition policy, such as happiness? For example, Stucke argues that instead of talking about consumer welfare as the guiding competition goal, one should focus on the well-being and especially the happiness of consumers.[1228] The question whether happiness could constitute a policy goal for competition law requires first that one agrees on the question whether competition policy should consider societal goals at all.[1229] Many would probably argue that happiness simply is not important enough and that it is misguided as a policy aim. It all depends on how one understands competition policy, either as strictly economic regulation or more broadly as social regulation, including political dimensions. This shift comes with profound consequences on the storytelling, as explained by Nicolas Petit.[1230] For indeed, one moves from one world to another, where, he argues, 'evidence gives way to rhetorical mastery' and 'reason is superseded by emotion'.[1231]

Happiness as a policy goal? Emotion and rhetorical mastery aside, questioning the consumer welfare standard in competition law is closely linked to the challenge of measuring well-being and value, and thus also happiness. As mentioned, economists often work with the assumption that prices are all anyone needs to know. In practice, this biases many of their conclusions and limits their relevance to some of the more serious issues concerning humans and important values that people really care about, even much more than money, such as happiness. One of Oscar Wilde's characters identifies a cynic as a man who knows the price of everything and the value of nothing. Is competition law cynical by being obsessed with price? Probably not. As philosophers have long known, assigning values to things or situations is fraught.

Equating money with value is no doubt in many cases a necessary expedient. People undertake transactions with money, of one form or another, rather than, for example, 'utility' or happiness. However, as acknowledged in this book, price is a poor measure of the value of digital products and services, which are often paid for by giving

1226. Especially the American New Brandeis movement has expressed vocal criticism against the consumer welfare standard in US antitrust policy. *See e.g.* Khan (n 564) 742.
1227. Nicolas Petit, 'Rule-Based Antitrust & the #DeleteConsumerWelfare Movement' (Symphony of Disruption blog, 5 April 2018) https://symphonyofdisruption.org/2018/04/05/rule-based-antitrust-the-deleteconsumerwelfare-movement/, accessed 19 April 2020.
1228. Maurice E Stucke, 'Should Competition Policy Promote Happiness?' (2013) 81 Fordham Law Review 2575.
1229. For example, Mäihäniemi discusses in her book whether societal goals should be considered in competition policy, *see* Mäihäniemi (n 521) 308.
1230. Nicolas Petit, 'Changing the Conversation Movement' (Symphony of Disruption blog, 13 February 2018) https://symphonyofdisruption.org/2018/02/13/changing-the-conversation/, accessed 19 April 2020.
1231. *Ibid.*

access to individuals' data. Technological progress is likely to create ever more situations in which ethical considerations conflict with narrowly material ones. Indeed, public concern suggests that the question of how to increase well-being in such a world needs greater attention.[1232]

This concern is not completely novel. The problem of value has existed ever since the origins of science. Throughout history numerous thinkers, prophets and ordinary people have struggled to define happiness. Some see it as the supreme good. In ancient Greece, the philosopher Epicurus explained that worshipping gods is a waste of time and that happiness is the sole purpose of life.[1233] Modern thinkers tend to see happiness as a collective project. In this sense, happiness could perhaps be pursued as a competition policy goal, for consumers as a collective?

At the end of the 18th century, British philosopher and legal reformer Jeremy Bentham declared that the supreme good is 'the greatest happiness of the greatest number' and concluded that the sole worthy aim of the state and the market is to increase global happiness. John Stuart Mill took many elements of his version of utilitarianism from Jeremy Bentham.[1234] Like Bentham, Mill believed that happiness (or pleasure, which both Bentham and Mill equated with happiness) was the only thing humans do and should desire for its own sake. Since happiness is the only intrinsic good, and since more happiness is preferable to less, the goal of the ethical life is to maximize happiness. This is what Bentham and Mill call 'the principle of utility' or 'the greatest-happiness principle'. Both Bentham and Mill thus endorse 'classic' or 'hedonistic' forms of utilitarianism. More recent utilitarians often deny that happiness is the sole intrinsic good, arguing that a variety of values and consequences should be considered in ethical decision-making.

During the 19th and 20th centuries, although many paid lip-service to Bentham's and Mill's vision, governments and corporations focused on more immediate and well-defined aims. At the time Bentham laid out the basis of this utilitarian approach, Adam Smith published his *Wealth of Nations*. It soon became the central book in economics, after which generations of economists built on his vision of defining economic activity in rational terms to provide models and equations that describe and predict behaviour. For example, Alfred Marshall declared the right focus of economics to be the 'attainment and ... use of material requisites of well-being'. Or, as his student, Arthur Pigou, framed it, 'that part of social welfare that can be brought directly or indirectly into relation with the measuring rod of money'.[1235]

Leaning more towards the view of the discretionalists in the debate on competition law's objectives, this book also contends that the findings of happiness literature could perhaps offer some useful insights on the debate over competition goals. A review of the literature, as conducted by Stucke, suggests that competition policy in a post-industrial wealthy country would get more 'bang' – in terms of increased

1232. The Economist, 'Economists Focus Too Little on What People Really Care About' (n 858).
1233. Yuval Noah Harari, *Homo Deus: A Brief History of Tomorrow* (Random House 2016) 34.
1234. Bentham (n 69) and Mill (n 347).
1235. Alfred Marshall, *Principles of Economics* (first published 1890, 8th edn, Macmillan 1920); Arthur C Pigou, *The Economics of Welfare* (first published 1920, Macmillan 2013).

well-being – in promoting economic, social and democratic values, rather than simply promoting a narrowly defined consumer welfare objective.[1236] To maintain the discussion here within reasonable limits, happiness as a competition policy goal will not be explored in any further depth, but some insights are worth mentioning below.

One key insight concerning happiness is that well-being is promoted along multiple dimensions. These include both *material* well-being, such as income and wealth, housing, and jobs and earnings, and *quality of life*, such as health status, work and life balance, education and skills, social connections, civic engagement and governance, environmental quality, and personal security.[1237] A competition policy that aims to increase only material well-being makes more sense in developing economies where most consumers have insufficient wealth to satisfy their most basic needs.[1238] After one's basic needs are met, increasing income does not significantly increase the experience of day-to-day happiness.[1239] As living standards increase and citizens' basic material needs, such as food, clothing and shelter, are met, then citizens will likely place greater importance on quality-of-life factors associated with well-being, such as work and life balance, social connections, safety, and environmental quality.[1240] Consequently, the goals of competition policies must evolve accordingly. The primary goal can no longer be maximizing consumer surplus at the expense – or instead – of other significant quality-of-life factors, such as individual freedoms, autonomy and democracy. Incremental gains in total well-being come not from more luxury products at lower prices, but in fostering markets and market relations that promote other-regarding civic virtues.[1241]

This is also where behavioural economics can help inform competition policy goals. As an initial premise, competition policy ultimately should improve consumers and citizens' well-being.[1242] So if, as a result of a jurisdiction's or country's competition policy, the physical and mental health of its citizens deteriorates, their isolation and distrust increase, and their freedom, self-determination and well-being decrease, then the policy is not worthwhile. So, one's theory of competition as defined largely by one's competition policy must promote – or at the very least not impede – overall well-being.[1243] The point is that competition law is not divorced from subjective well-being. It does not exist independently of legal and informal norms. Rather, competition is defined in part by prevailing legal and informal social, ethical, and moral norms.[1244]

So, where does this all leave us? This book asserts that competition policy is currently undergoing a welcome intellectual shift and the start of a transformation resulting from digitalization and the data-driven economy. We are witnessing the start

1236. Stucke (n 1228) 2575, 2602.
1237. *Ibid.*, 2626.
1238. *Ibid.*, referring to Daniel Kahneman et al., 'Would You Be Happier If You Were Richer? A Focusing Illusion' (2006) 312 Science 1908, 1909.
1239. *Ibid.* For further reading, *see* Carol Graham, *The Pursuit of Happiness: An Economy of Well-Being* (Brookings Institution Press 2011) 17.
1240. Kahneman et al. (n 1238).
1241. Stucke (n 1228) 2575, 2629.
1242. Stucke (n 882) 36–37.
1243. *Ibid.*
1244. *Ibid.*

of a larger trend or development in competition policy, whereby non-economic factors and moral values will gain more of a foothold and influence the development of policy objectives. After decades of trying to narrow competition policy objectives into price-based efficiency-enhancing aims, we are now at the stage where we see the result of this narrow approach, which looks like market failure, especially as regards adequate protection of consumers' data privacy.

Thus, we have reason to halt, start rethinking the scope and maybe change the course of competition policy. Bringing moral values into the discourse on competition policy objectives and consideration of data and privacy will advance a conceptual change and intellectual shift that will affect regulators and policymakers. The tide is turning and the extent to which privacy concerns may come to influence competition policy has perhaps not yet even reached a high, as more Facebook-like scandals may be rolling out, with citizens starting to clearly see the data economy's effects on privacy values and beyond, such as democracy and integrity.

With the rise of virtual competition and Internet gatekeepers benefiting from network effects and access to big data and big analytics, concerns arising from monopoly power and abusive practices will intensify, with concern for privacy becoming increasingly central.[1245] As noted by Ezrachi and Stucke:[1246]

> While monopolies of the past might subject us to higher prices and poorer quality products, abuses by today's super-platforms will affect not only our wallets. They can affect the news and entertainment we receive and ultimately, our privacy, well-being, and democracy.

Therefore, tomorrow's competition policy should not blindly focus only on prices or economic efficiency, but should also take into account important social, political and even moral aspects. The risks of ignoring these aspects can be highly significant in data-driven markets, where the biggest harm may be on non-price dimensions, especially privacy. It is also very much a question about consumer choice and freedom of expression – not just about dominant companies being able to exploit consumer user data or exclude data from rivals.

Thus, the need is to redefine competition objectives as the potential scope for competition policy is enormous in the modern economy with online platforms exercising a previously unseen scale of influence on not only the economy but also on society as a whole, including democracy, politics and freedom of speech. In some instances, this may also mean that competition regulators should not shy away from political considerations, where a certain form of conduct implicates important non-economic values, particularly political values.[1247] This kind of approach attempts to capture far more of the dynamics of the competitive process than does existing price-driven analysis.

1245. Ezrachi and Stucke (n 1178). *See also* Stucke and Ezrachi (n 579).
1246. Ezrachi and Stucke (n 1178).
1247. Wu (n 606) 8–9.

CHAPTER 6

Conclusions and Looking Ahead

After having explored the potential role of privacy in competition law, this concluding chapter looks at the way forward and builds on the idea of rethinking or optimizing the competition paradigm to the data economy by bringing a privacy dimension to the competition policy objectives. The chapter considers the findings that the current paradigms of competition law – price and economic efficiency – do not work well enough in today's digital economy and considers some implications. In particular, there is increasing pressure on competition policy to evolve from a static price-centric nature to embrace a more dynamic approach. This is likely to invite further discourse and research on including non-price aspects as part of competition's policy goals and as part of the consumer welfare standard. Competition law will continue to evolve and interact with other policy areas, such as data protection, but also beyond. There is already growing research looking into the link between competition and sustainability, in particular climate change – these may well prove to be the next important non-price parameters and social goals of modern-day competition policy.

§6.01 THE WAY FORWARD

In the *Master Switch*, a book that depicts the history of modern communications businesses and outlines a thought-provoking future of the digital Internet age, Tim Wu contends that to prevent power-abusing monopolies from controlling information, regulators need to adopt a broader definition of competition's goals and look beyond the typical emphasis on the effect on prices. The central idea of the book is that market competition brings significant benefits, but the market itself does not always ensure competition, or, more broadly, desirable outcomes. Wu aptly captures the essence of this:

> Antitrust, perhaps all law, is ultimately pliable by perceptions of right and wrong, good and evil.[1248]

As this quote by Wu goes to show, there is no absolute truth. Competition law is a political construct, created and interpreted by humans, who reflect different values and dimensions. Humans are not machines – at least, not yet. However, a universe modified by technological developments, where big data becomes a paradigm, suggests a possibility that humans are under threat of losing control in a data-driven world. Indeed, as posed by the rhetorical question in the bestselling book *Homo Deus*: 'What will happen to society, politics and daily life when non-conscious but highly intelligent algorithms know us better than we know ourselves?'[1249] This human factor, which still prevails today, means that competition policy reflects the values and concerns of its time and is influenced by moral underpinnings.

Of course, one may also argue, as does Raimo Siltala, that 'truth' is the outcome of the relationship that exists between a scientist and a set of empirical observations.[1250] By being open to public disposition and critique, scientific knowledge is self-corrective in the long run: any mistakes made in the course of scientific research will ultimately tend to become corrected by the scientific community, once more – and more accurate – empirical evidence is provided of the subject matter of research.[1251]

In this book, however, the discourse and research questions have been conducted at the policy level, looking at issues raised by the data economy concerning the normative scope of competition law, its effectiveness, and more broadly, its optimal goals. As Kuoppamäki describes it, the discourse on competition policy consists of two layers: the political level and the operative level.[1252] In that sense, this book addresses the political level rather than the operative level, as it looks at competition policy as a political construct, articulates the need for a conceptual change in competition policy and outlines a privacy dimension among the optimal objectives and values to be advanced by competition law in the data economy.

1248. Tim Wu, *Master Switch: The Rise and Fall of Information Empires* (Atlantic Books Ltd 2010) ch. 3. Wu argues that all communications businesses, starting from telephone, radio, television and film, ending with the Internet as the world's modern communications network, are prone to political effects far greater than in other industries. Once a company starts building a communications network or gaining control over one, it begins slouching towards monopoly. If the government is not already deeply involved in the business by then, it soon will be. The book's title comes from a line by Fred Friendly, the long-time CBS News executive, in which he distinguished between free-speech laws and 'exclusive custody of the master switch'. Wu holds that keeping government out of the business does not work, because the industry tends to form private monopolies if left alone, but having the government run the business, as England and other countries have tried, also presents its own problems. The government itself is a monopolist and often behaves like one. Wu instead calls for constraining 'all power that derives from the control of information'. He writes, 'If we believe in liberty, it must be freedom from both private and public coercion.'

1249. Harari (n 1233) 462.

1250. Siltala (n 1217) 100. Similarly, *see* Niiniluoto (n 51) 83–84.

1251. *Ibid.*

1252. Kuoppamäki (n 110) 28–29.

As discussed in the introduction to this book, competition policy can be viewed as consisting of three areas; the setting of objectives for competition policy (hypostasis), the detection of problems regarding functioning competition (diagnosis) and the selection of means to remedy competition issues identified (therapy).[1253] According to this view of competition policy, in this book the focus is on *diagnosis* and *therapy*. The book also covers hypostasis, that is the setting of objectives for competition policy, as this effectively forms part of the research question. The question whether the current approach to competition policy is fit for the data economy stands at the heart of this book, and translates into the narrower questions of competition policy's optimal objectives, and the role of privacy and data protection as a potential objective or concern for competition law.

In answering these questions, the current shortcomings of competition policy are identified. This is the diagnosis part of competition policy. Accordingly, Chapter 5, §5.02 can be regarded as the diagnosis as it detects the problems or limitations of functioning competition in the data economy. The problems identified in functioning competition law today are especially its price-centricity and static nature (Chapter 5, §5.02[A]), the need to better account for the value of data (Chapter 5, §5.02[B]), as well as considering the fundamental rights aspect in EU law (Chapter 5, §5.02[C]).

The diagnosis is followed by the therapy part, where means are proposed for remedying the shortcomings. Chapter 5, §5.03 can be viewed as constituting the therapy as it selects embracing privacy considerations and going beyond price as solutions for the way forward. Here, bringing a privacy dimension to competition policy is suggested, and the book proposes different ways of doing this: by treating data protection as a quality component (Chapter 5, §5.03[A]), exploring different ways of measuring privacy (Chapter 5, §5.03[B]), and considering a conceptual change by expanding horizons beyond price to consider social, moral and even ethical factors (Chapter 5, §5.03[C]). Moreover, Chapter 6 looks ahead and describes the way forward through a potential conjoined approach between policy areas, and as such contributes to the therapy.

In the introduction to this book, certain questions and sub-questions were articulated to guide the way through the book.[1254] From time to time throughout the book, the author has referred to or recalled those same questions. It is worth recalling those questions at this stage to confirm in this concluding chapter that they have been adequately addressed and answered. Indeed, the book set out to explore the impact of the digital economy and big data on competition law. This broad question has been tackled through addressing several narrower sub-questions, specifically, the role of personal data and privacy in competition law. It has been asserted that competition law in the data-driven economy should in certain circumstances protect privacy among its policy objectives. To some extent, competition policy even today considers privacy in its goals, for example as an element of quality competition, and there is a growing trend among national competition authorities of incorporating privacy considerations in their thinking on competition policy.

1253. *See* Chapter 3, §3.02 and Kuoppamäki (n 110) 98–99.
1254. Chapter 1, §1.02.

As shown, the impact of the digital economy and big data on competition law is undeniable. As the economy and the world goes digital, introducing various new technological developments, artificial intelligence, the IoT, big data and big analytics, all of these developments, some of which are happening at a mind-blowing pace, have an impact on competition law and policy. They necessitate calling into question whether the current narrow economic approach of competition law is optimal for addressing abusive conduct in online markets, where data often constitutes the new asset and currency, and where concerns related to non-price dimensions, such as privacy, can be of fundamental importance. This book has identified a concern that competition law's obsession with price may run the risk of ignoring socially, ethically and morally important aspects of the digital economy, which include privacy, democracy and the well-being of individuals.

When addressing the question concerning the potential role of personal data and privacy in competition law, this book has aimed to present perspectives on these issues and introduces the idea of rethinking and optimizing the competition paradigm to the data economy by bringing a privacy dimension to policy objectives. As shown, the current paradigms of competition law - price and economic efficiency - do not work well enough in today's digital economy. Accumulated experience has displayed their shortcomings, such as being hard to fully understand and not particularly transparent in their application.[1255]

Moreover, in a disturbingly large number of circumstances, current paradigms are unable to address the important issue of non-price competition. Accordingly, this book suggests replacing the older and demonstrably outdated price-driven competition paradigm with a somewhat broader approach to consumer welfare that would include a privacy dimension. This approach is influenced and guided by the important values of *consumer choice* and *fairness*. Privacy can be understood in many ways, and, as we know, lacks a single definition. Thus, privacy can be viewed as part of fairness and as a reflection of consumer choice. But, privacy is also a quality component. Adopting this broader approach to consumer welfare with a privacy dimension may mean going back to the origins of ordoliberal thinking and more strongly embracing *consumer choice* as a guiding policy principle or goal.[1256] As this book asserts, competition is really about consumer choice, and price is just one aspect of choice. Accordingly, a price-centred consumer welfare standard suffers from certain limitations in the digital economy and is not optimal for data-driven markets.

As much as some more conservative competition scholars might want to dismiss privacy and fairness as relevant in this age of sophisticated economic approaches to competition law and policy, the conceptual change or intellectual shift in competition's policy objectives - as argued in this book - is justified, because much has changed since the broad outlines of today's competition regime took shape. Today we live in a different time with different trends affecting markets, with different societal objectives and values part of the modern economy, some of which may not have played such a big role as they do now, such as data protection and privacy, for instance. With these

1255. Averitt and Lande (n 733) 176.
1256. *Ibid.*

changed circumstances, the expectations for competition law are also taking a new shape. The problems of today's increasingly digitalized, globalized - and, in some sectors, concentrated - economy are very different from those when the competition rules were enacted and that antitrust so far has been used to dealing with. When confronted with these new challenges, competition law is forced to recognize its shortcomings and adjust.

However, unless one is an idealist, it is difficult to believe that competition policy in any democracy with reasonable pluralism could actually be reduced to a single, precise goal. Lawyers like to simplify, but oversimplifying matters, which in the real world are complex does not solve the problem. As discussed, any competition policy that has the purpose of promoting well-being - consumer welfare in a wider sense - needs to balance multiple political, social, economic and moral objectives. Clearly, when looking at the USA, for example, the quest for a single economic goal for antitrust law has not been successful, considering current concerns covering concentrated technology markets, monopolistic profits, data privacy exploitation, and generally less consumer choice. One may say that the quest for a single economic goal in US antitrust law has failed, as it distanced antitrust policy from important policy issues.[1257] As noted by Wu, '[d]ecades of practice have shown that the promised scientific certainty of the Chicago method has not materialized, for economics does not yield answers, but arguments'.[1258]

Because of pluralism, differences in values, concerns and local preferences, together with cultural and historical differences in privacy protection and competition objectives, the outcomes of competition policy and enforcement between Europe and the USA have been and will likely continue to be divergent. The different approaches of the two regimes also lead to distinctive assumptions as to how data-driven markets work and how they should be regulated and monitored by governments, especially in terms of protecting consumers from potential privacy harms. The different approaches to privacy protection and the distinct underlying policy goals of EU and US competition law affect the outcome of the question of the role of privacy in competition policy. The distinct approaches lead to distinctive assumptions on how privacy as a non-price dimension can and should play a role in competition policy in digital markets.

As explored in Chapter 2, on the privacy side a stark contrast exists between the European view of privacy and data protection as an inalienable right, and the Americans treating it more as a freely tradable asset. On the competition side, which was analysed in Chapter 3, the main distinction is that American antitrust policy is strongly price-centred, whereas EU competition policy features multiple goals. These include non-economic dimensions such as fairness and freedom of choice, meaning that EU competition policy is already influenced by consumer choice and liberty considerations - although there is room for increased influence, as argued here - other than the economic efficiency-driven rationale prevalent in the USA. This puts EU competition policy in a unique position to (further) develop the interconnection between policies on competition and privacy.

1257. Stucke (n 613) 551.
1258. Wu (n 606).

What this book does is to invite and encourage further conceptual and normative discussion with regard to consumer welfare, the dominant term in current competition discourse, though without a clear consensus as to what it exactly means. The problem is that, to date, the notion of consumer welfare is still not underpinned by any single idea. Similarly, there is no one single idea of privacy – it is a concept open to multiple, possibly inconsistent, interpretations. Here, however, one should recognize that in some ways calls for rethinking the consumer welfare concept are not new. Legal opinions and academic writings abound with discussions of economic efficiency and the concept of consumer welfare, but while these terms are much used in competition writing, they are little analysed.[1259] Therefore, these concepts still require clarification and more precise definition. More clarity on the way forward may need to come through conflicts, antitrust probes and courts unless policymakers tackle the question on the role of privacy in competition policy in today's digital markets. The concept of consumer welfare needs an open and transparent discussion on its underlying values and moral underpinnings because ultimately competition authorities and courts will be called upon to supply clarity where policymakers will not.

Consumer welfare and efficiency are not identical, but have distinct meanings, with sometimes conflicting policy implications. Efficiency is not unitary but can be broken down into several differing types of efficiencies, some more important to competition law than others. Consumer welfare, in turn, is not identical to efficiency, but a distinct concept that refers to the welfare, or well-being, of consumers. Thus, one may say that consumer welfare adds a distributional thrust to competition law.[1260] Perhaps one solution would be that competition policy should concern itself only when market conduct occurs that is both unfair and inefficient. This could be a two-part cumulative test, starting with identifying situations that appeal to our instincts of justice and fairness, and then assessing whether they also endanger the efficient operation of competitive markets.[1261]

However, it should be stressed that this book does not contend that competition policy should do away with its prime goal of consumer welfare. Nor does this book suggest rewriting the rules of competition law in the digital economy or reinventing the whole competition toolkit. Nor, too, does this book generally promote more aggressive intervention in digital markets. What is suggested is to consider the meaning behind the concept of consumer welfare, and to revisit that concept, broadening or adjusting it to better encompass non-price dimensions, which seem to have been marginalized in the search for a more economics-based approach.

Believing that consumer welfare is the appropriate goal of competition policy does not mean being passive or taking the view that competition law in the pursuit of

---

1259. For discussion on the concepts of consumer welfare and efficiency as applied to antitrust law, *see* Harry First, Eleanor M Fox and Robert Pitofsky (eds), *Revitalizing Antitrust in Its Second Century. Essays on Legal, Economic and Political Policy* (Quorum Books 1991).

1260. Joseph F Brodley, 'Antitrust, Efficiency and Progress', in First et al. (n 1259).

1261. David Foster, 'Cry Me a River. The Concept of Fairness in Competition Law' (10 May 2018) https://www.linkedin.com/pulse/cry-me-river-concept-fairness-competition-law-david-foster/, accessed 19 April 2020.

consumer welfare cannot be improved. Competition law has changed as our understanding of market effects and dynamics has become more sophisticated, and competition policy should continue to evolve as the predictive tools are being refined. Digitalization and transferring from an offline economy to an online marketplace requires ongoing discussion on the right, or just, goals of competition policy. In a way, this discussion will be familiar to the antitrust community, which has already for a generation been debating whether competition law encompasses non-economic goals, or whether the law is limited to purely economic objectives.

Developing a privacy dimension in competition policy will require further work, thought and future practice to arrive at practicable standards. Indeed, this book does not represent final thoughts on the matter. Rather, what is described here is the beginning of what the author sees as an important – indeed essential – project for the future development of the law.

§6.02 CONJOINED POLICY APPROACH

So, where does this leave us? By rethinking competition policy for the digital age, this book questions whether we still want price to be the dominant metric for assessing competition in the data economy, or whether we want to reverse this trend by reconsidering the definition of consumer welfare with the aim of bringing competition policy into the 21st century. What this book argues is that, as circumstances change, competition law must evolve. Competition law should embrace an adjusted or revised approach due to inevitable changes in the economy and business environment brought about by the digital age.

Competition law is susceptible to change and has what it takes to bravely embrace more ambitious goals within the notion of consumer welfare than mere economic efficiency. While competition abuses of the past may have subjected consumers to higher prices and poorer quality products, abuses in digital markets may impact not only our wallets but also the news we read, the advertising we are subjected to, and ultimately our privacy, democracy and welfare. Today, competition policy should protect privacy and data among its objectives in carefully selected cases where fairness and consumer choice may work as guiding principles.

Competition law that was written for an offline world which did not know of the Internet is not optimal today. Thus the current approach to competition policy needs to be updated to meet the demands of the digitalized world we live in today and to protect the welfare of consumers, offline as well as online. Privacy is a value which should be promoted in competition policy. Therefore competition law should expand its scope to include a broader definition of consumer welfare.

The strong support given to data protection and privacy in Europe, together with EU competition policy's multiple goals that leave room for including non-price objectives, makes EU competition policy fitter and more flexible to incorporate privacy goals than US antitrust law. Generally, it can be said that while the USA represents a more functional approach to antitrust that focuses on economic efficiency in the sense of price competition, EU competition policy centres on harm to competition, and is also influenced by goals other than the efficiency-driven economic rationale typically present in the USA. Because privacy is given little protection in the USA, and because US antitrust law does not have the same multitude of goals but reflects a strictly price-centred approach, US antitrust policy is less receptive to integrating privacy concerns than EU competition policy.

With the modern economy and increasing concerns regarding digital privacy, this book holds that it is time to reconsider competition law's narrowly defined consumer welfare objective and bring back political, social and moral concerns that were pushed to the side by Chicago school dictates. Competition law can be more responsive and better serve citizens' concerns about promoting consumer well-being or welfare in a wider sense if it reconsiders competition policy goals as a means not only to achieve price competition but also to secure political, economic and individual freedoms. This book also invites considerations around morality and happiness as potential goals of competition policy when debating whether competition is about efficiency or some greater good.

Even though a consensus might not yet have been achieved on what should replace the EU's 'more economic approach' and the Chicago school, there is a growing acceptance, at least in Europe, of the fact that privacy harms can be just as significant as price effects. Competition policy cannot be interpreted as simply a question about prices and economic efficiency. Rather, competition policy should be interpreted flexibly in order to properly understand the dynamics, especially in digital markets. For the consumer welfare standard to work as an optimal welfare or well-being standard in competition law and policy, a shift should take place from static consumer harm (which is price-based) to dynamic consumer harm (focus on non-price dimensions, including privacy).

Competition law can play an important role in maximizing the benefits of the data-driven economy, while also taking the role of mitigating its risks. However, it is doubtful whether competition law, even modified from the current price-centric approach, can do this alone. This book puts forward that it is likely that what the digital economy and society at large needs is a multi-regime response, which in turn entails that privacy and competition laws need to work together. Stucke argues that global competition laws alone are not sufficient to deter harms to consumer welfare and well-being in the data economy: 'Antitrust enforcers must coordinate with privacy [and consumer protection] officials to ensure that the conditions for effective privacy competition and an inclusive economy are in place.'[1262]

When exploring the interplay between competition law and data protection rules, it comes naturally to engage with the idea of increased collaboration between the competition and DPAs. Indeed, the traditionally perceived incompatibility between the two systems is reflected in the past lack of cooperation between competition and DPAs. As observed by the EDPS in 2016, 'overall there is a quite fragmented scenario in enforcing EU rules, with competent authorities not necessarily talking to each other whilst dealing with cases featured by considerable overlaps in terms of substance'.[1263]

1262. Stucke (n 407); Grunes and Stucke (n 126); Stucke and Grunes (n 146).
1263. EDPS Opinion 8/2016 (n 777) 9.

Today, there is increasingly 'enforcement actions [that] demonstrate clear interactions between different legal fields that are traditionally applied and enforced in isolation'.[1264] At the same time:

> there is room to apply the different regimes in a more coherent way to achieve a better protection of consumers.[1265]

Echoing these ideas, this book engages with the notion that more collaboration should take place between the competition and DPAs to protect consumers from privacy risks. As explored in this book, competition and data protection policies can be applied in a holistic manner by acknowledging that the two areas of law share several concerns and have common objectives, most notably, market integration, welfare of the individual, and power asymmetries. In this context, the EDPS has called for competition law intervention to address privacy-related concerns and perceived regulatory gaps.[1266] According to the agency, against the fast-evolving backdrop of big data, more interaction should be occurring in policies on competition and data protection in order to minimize the potential for consumer harm and to incentivize the development of privacy-enhancing services.[1267] It is predicted in this book that calls for more cooperation between regulators will likely continue to grow.

The EDPS has encouraged more cooperation between authorities to respond to the challenges of privacy and competitiveness in digital markets. In its opinion on enforcement of fundamental rights in the age of big data, the EDPS initiated a Digital Clearinghouse to bring together regulators to protect consumers from privacy risks.[1268]

The Digital Clearinghouse is the first network of its kind to bring together all regulators responsible for the enforcement of laws in the digital ecosystem. At present, it includes competition, data protection, consumer protection and electoral regulators and authorities from Europe and beyond. Discussions in the forum are meant to support a convergence in the understanding of the complex world.[1269] The Clearinghouse met for the first time in Brussels in May 2017 and discussion began on identifying principles for cooperation.[1270] Since then, the Clearinghouse has met a handful of times with attendance from some twenty to twenty-five authorities 'from the EU and across the globe' with discussions around important issues at the intersection of data protection, competition and consumer law, including liabilities and general fairness of online service providers, unfair price discrimination, the relevance of personal data in merger control and developing best practices for DPAs to support competition authorities in digital sector mergers.[1271] The network expects more meetings in the future and

1264. Graef, Clifford and Valcke (n 807) 200.
1265. *Ibid.*, 210.
1266. EDPS Opinion (n 10) 30.
1267. *Ibid.*, 37–38.
1268. EDPS Opinion 8/2016 (n 777) 15.
1269. Giovanni Buttarelli, 'This Is Not an Article on Data Protection and Competition Law' (25 February 2019) Competition Policy International.
1270. Digital Clearinghouse, Statement from first meeting (29 May 2017).
1271. Digital Clearinghouse, Statement from second meeting (27 November 2017); Digital Clearinghouse, Statement from third meeting (21 June 2018).

it is not unlikely that this establishment reflects such a forward-thinking move that it will be replicated at national level in the EU and in other jurisdictions.[1272]

One interesting aspect of the *Facebook* case examined in Chapter 4 is that the German competition authority's investigation exemplifies the conjoined approach promoted by the EDPS and its Clearinghouse initiative. According to public information about the case, the German authority conducted the proceedings in close connection with data protection officers, consumer protection associations, and the European Commission.[1273] As regards the data protection aspects of the case, the German competition authority consulted with DPAs and cooperated with consumer protection associations.[1274] This kind of joined-up approach by competition and data protection regulators reflects the proposition envisioned in the EDPS opinions and the Digital Clearinghouse.[1275] As noted by the Bundeskartellamt:[1276]

> Data protection, consumer protection and the protection of competition interlink where data, as in Facebook's case, are a crucial factor for the economic dominance of a company.

Even as the precise role that privacy should play in developing competition policy remains open to debate, calls for a shift in policy are merited, as is a more holistic approach to policy and enforcement, in which a more systematic dialogue is maintained between competition and DPAs 'wherever a specific case arises in which consumer welfare and data protection concerns appear to be at stake'.[1277] While critics proclaim that antitrust's role is not to fill gaps in privacy laws, EU competition law can play a part in protecting the personal data of consumers in some specific and carefully selected cases, where competition law embraces a sort of role as 'gap filler' and is resorted to when no other law or policy is available to ensure consumers' right to privacy.

Beyond increased regulatory collaboration, plans and ideas have been aired to put in place stricter regulation on digital platforms through digital agencies.

Some European Member States, such as Germany and Denmark, have suggested enacting stricter regulation on digital platforms through digital agencies that would wield extensive antitrust powers.[1278] The German Federal Ministry for Economic Affairs and Energy in its White Paper 'Digital Platforms' proposes establishing a new

---

1272. Lynskey (n 137) 179–180; Buttarelli (n 1269).
1273. Bundeskartellamt press release (n 18); Bundeskartellamt case summary (n 18).
1274. *Ibid.*
1275. EDPS Opinion 8/2016 (n 777) 8.
1276. Bundeskartellamt press release (n 20).
1277. EDPS Opinion (n 10) 37.
1278. Adam Taylor, 'Denmark Is Naming an Ambassador Who Will Just Deal with Increasingly Powerful Tech Companies' The Washington Post (4 February 2017) https://www.washingtonpost.com/news/worldviews/wp/2017/02/04/denmark-is-naming-an-ambassador-who-will-just-deal-with-increasingly-powerful-tech-companies/?utm_term=.6745cbb270b5, accessed 19 April 2020; Christian Ritz, 'Germany Suggests Ramping up Regulation of Digital Platforms by Establishing a "Digital Agency" with a Robust Antitrust Mandate' Kluwer Competition Law Blog (6 April 2017) http://competitionlawblog.kluwercompetitionlaw.com/2017/04/06/germany-suggests-ramping-regulation-digital-platforms-establishing-digital-agency-robust-antitrust-mandate/, accessed 19 April 2020.

Digital Agency for Europe.[1279] At the time of writing this book, the European Commission is about to introduce online platform regulation as an additional layer to competition rules in order to address concerns relating to technology companies misbehaving in the digital markets.[1280] The long-awaited proposal published in May 2018 went through the European Parliament and the Council and several Member States are pushing for its swift adoption in support of the objective of more closely regulating online platforms and search engines. The EU proposal would set certain limits on dominant platforms operated by the likes of Google, Amazon, Facebook or Apple, but by and large, however, the limits offer a relatively light-touch approach to force platforms to be more transparent and to improve their redress systems when things go wrong.

Further, suggestions have been put forward to establish a single European regulator for the digital economy. Such an agency would gather competition and privacy concerns under one unified authority as a way of tackling powerful online and technology companies. This notion of a unified digital regulator has been advocated – in connection with the entry into force of the GDPR – by different parties, such as the EDPS, predicting that in the next decade calls will be growing for a single EU digital watchdog to ensure companies fulfil their obligations across sectors, including data protection, privacy, competition, as well as consumer protection and various rules on product safety.[1281] Parallels can be drawn with the EU banking sector, where patchy oversight was widely blamed for some of the failures that allowed the 2009 financial crisis to lead to such damage, whereas now powerful EU bodies are in place responsible for ensuring the sustainability of the banking Union.[1282] Noteworthy in this regard is also Emanuel Macron's proposal for a European Agency for Digital Trust, *Agence Européenne pour la Confiance Numérique*, a body that would be responsible for regulating big digital platforms to safeguard both competition and individuals' rights. Further, when visioning the future, the EDPS holds that '[t]he potential of a unique, digital regulator, responsible for a coherent and linear monitoring of our markets and societies in the digital age is [also] tempting in terms of resources efficiencies and likely linearity of results'.[1283]

However, in practice, bringing together all digital-related regulatory functions under the roof of one EU-wide body is likely too difficult to put in place, however promising it may sound on paper. Most likely the EU will keep its current patchwork of national and supranational authorities into the 2020s.

Institutional implications. With a growing role of privacy in competition law and policy, certainly cooperation between competition and DPAs is on the rise. Such collaboration, envisaged as part of the conjoined policy approach discussed in this

1279. German Federal Ministry for Economic Affairs and Energy, White Paper (n 459).
1280. *See* European Commission, 'Proposal for a regulation on promoting fairness and transparency for business users of online intermediation services' (26 April 2018).
1281. Blog by EDPS Giovanni Buttarelli, 'It's Not the End of the World as We Know It' (7 December 2017) https://edps.europa.eu/press-publications/press-news/blog/it%E2%80%99s-not-end-world-we-know-it_en, accessed 19 April 2020.
1282. *Ibid.*
1283. Buttarelli (n 1269).

book, raises some very concrete follow-up issues on the relationship between data protection and antitrust authorities and possible institutional implications.

One of the most important issues concerns the *ne bis in idem* principle. If infringements of data protection rules qualify as market abuse within the meaning of Article 102 TFEU, or the relevant provision under national competition laws, one important question that this leads to is whether companies are protected from parallel investigations and penalties by the *ne bis in idem* principle, i.e. a fine decision by one authority prevents the other authority from also imposing a fine. This possibility of parallel investigations and fines by competition and DPAs will need to be seriously considered and addressed by regulators to ensure legal and procedural certainty.

One may argue that to the extent that the two areas of law serve different legal interests, parallel sanctions by a competition authority and a DPA may not violate the *ne bis in idem* principle. However, both fine decisions would still have the infringement of data protection laws as their (sole) substantive basis.[1284]

According to Lynskey, when considering cooperation between competition and DPAs, '[t]urf wars are inevitable unless a clear division of labour between these authorities is planned'.[1285] One of the initial questions to be considered is the proper allocation of cases at the intersection of competition and data protection law between respective authorities, or how cooperation should function in practice. Addressing these issues concerning case allocation, authority cooperation in practice and institutional interplay would be necessary, for example, to make sure that companies do not receive conflicting guidance regarding the lawfulness of particular practices from different authorities. *Google/Fitbit* not only demonstrates the difficulties in assessing mergers in the digital sector but also shows the institutional implications when the competition/privacy interface grows broader. To avoid stifling progress on the conjoined approach and enable institutional collaboration, the development of clear guidance at the crossroads of competition and privacy is one of the next challenges for interested parties.

In terms of enforcement overlaps, it is instructive to note that the GDPR seems to have taken competition law's enforcement mechanisms as inspiration to improve some procedural elements of EU data protection law. Despite certain new procedural strengths through the GDPR, one of the main differences with the enforcement of EU competition law persists under the GDPR, namely that there is no EU-level body that has the competence to take action and adopt measures under EU data protection law.[1286] This also explains the calls to consider data protection interests in devising competition law remedies as a way to improve compliance with data protection law throughout the EU.

International outlook. What is important to underline when envisioning the creation and development of a conjoined approach is that, currently, Europe is more

1284. For example, German law solves such situations by a 'first come first served' general rule which determines the authority that shall be competent for conducting administrative fine proceedings, if the subject matter could be investigated and sanctioned by several authorities. For further reading, *see* Stauber, (n 838).

1285. Lynskey (n 161) 179–180.

1286. Graef, Clifford and Valcke (n 807) 218.

likely than the USA to be able to advance a conjoined approach between competition and privacy in a timely manner. This is because EU competition policy is in a unique position to (further) develop the interconnection between its policies on competition and privacy and promote a holistic view of competition and privacy enforcement in digital markets.

What will be the impact of this development? At its simplest, the more privacy protection and competition are merged in EU competition policy, and privacy takes on the role of an important non-price dimension in competition analysis, EU competition policy may diverge (further) from US antitrust policy. This may give rise to international tensions and create a transatlantic divide. In the past, there has already been potential signs of this direction with the recent European Commission decisions in *Google Search* and *Google Android* imposing record fines.

One potential risk connected with the conjoined approach is that the divide between the EU and the USA in approaches to competition policy and privacy may grow. For example, antitrust scholars have noted that 'the attention paid by European antitrust enforcers to dominant firms that collect and aggregate data diverges from the US approach'.[1287] In some ways, it seems that developments are at an inflection point when the great wave of optimism about technology is giving way to growing alarm and public concern about whether current competition policy is failing. This is the moment when Europeans are likely to turn to the state for protection and answers and are less likely than Americans to rely on the market to sort out imbalances. In this sense, the final outcome of the German case against Facebook combining antitrust and privacy, where at the time of finalizing this book, the Bundeskartellamt's decision is suspended and an appeal process is awaited, will be telling. To date, the most illustrative example of a divide in approaches is *Google Search*. In the future, it might be that the attitude towards data privacy in competition policy will be a question where the transatlantic difference is at its biggest. Perhaps the German Facebook case may inspire other competition authorities to take on cases at the intersection of competition and data protection law.

The effect in Europe of having decentralized enforcement of EU competition law may of course be that there will be national variation and local flavours when the rules are applied by local authorities and courts. As noted by Inge Graef, while the national competition authorities' awareness of the growing interaction between competition and data protection issues is a welcome development, it raises the question of how to create coherence in enforcement between Member States: '[d]ifferences in the degree of enforcement create risks for the internal market for companies that have to comply with distinct requirements throughout the EU and for consumers who rely on the success of their national agencies to act'.[1288] Moreover, as the conduct of companies in data-driven markets is blurring the boundaries between legal regimes, Graef also

1287. Giuseppe Colangelo and Mariateresa Maggiolino, 'Data Accumulation and the Privacy – Antitrust Interface: Insights from the Facebook Case' (2018) 8 International Data Privacy Law 237.

1288. Graef, Clifford and Valcke (n 807) 201.

argues that 'a better coordination between enforcement authorities is necessary to adequately protect consumers'.[1289]

With regard to the transatlantic divergence, as an alternative course, there may also be convergence. Perhaps the USA will end up following Europe. Indeed, the potential and need for a conjoined approach is recognized not only in Europe but also among some American antitrust scholars and policymakers. For example, the 2020 presidential campaigns will likely cement antitrust law as a platform issue (especially US Senator Elisabeth Warren has been vocal on antitrust concerns related to technology companies that should be broken up); the recent Stigler report advocates progressive changes to US antitrust law, such as creating a new specialist digital authority to better regulate digital platform markets; and leading American antitrust scholar Stucke urges that 'antitrust enforcers must coordinate with privacy and consumer protection officials to ensure that the conditions for effective privacy competition and an inclusive economy are in place'.[1290]

One may spontaneously think that it is in Europe's and everyone's best interest to promote assimilation of thought and values across jurisdictions. However, different legal provisions and especially goals, as well as institutional design, inevitably limit that endeavour. In his visit to Europe, US Attorney General Makan Delrahim noted the good collaboration between the EU and the USA and, indeed, the benefits of close transatlantic cooperation cannot be overstated; it helps prevent fragmentation of global markets, reduces system friction and limits populism in decision-making, for example.[1291] The Attorney General noted that '[t]oday, we stand together in upholding the political consensus regarding the proper use of antitrust law, and we continue to work together to promote consumer welfare in our own jurisdictions and worldwide'.[1292] While this statement may be true in many ways, it can only be desirable to the extent that it does not eradicate the EU's norms and values, however.

Similarly, statements about the desire that the EU and USA will close 'the gap in the area of unilateral conduct' or that they have aligned their intervention benchmarks[1293] should only be understood within the different legal and normative structures. As contended by Ezrachi, any other assumption implies a worldwide monolithic enforcement standard designed with the American vision at its heart.[1294] One should remember that arguments for the 'purity' of competition law, while appealing, propagate 'a mirage of objectivity, clarity and analytical superiority – traits that are not always present'.[1295] As argued in this book, competition law cannot be pure in the

1289. *Ibid.*
1290. Elizabeth Warren, 'Here's How We Can Break up Big Tech' Medium (8 March 2019) https://medium.com/@teamwarren/heres-how-we-can-break-up-big-tech-9ad9e0da324c, accessed 19 April 2020; Stigler report (n 662); Stucke (n 407).
1291. Ezrachi (n 369) 25.
1292. Speech by Makan Delrahim, 'Good Times, Bad Times, Trust Will Take Us Far: Competition Enforcement and the Relationship Between Washington and Brussels' Remarks at the College of Europe (Brussels, 21 February 2018).
1293. *Ibid.*
1294. Ezrachi (n 369) 26.
1295. Ezrachi (n 334) 1, 3.

meaning of the adjective, as competition law will always be intrinsically predisposed to a wide range of considerations and values.

These comments should not be seen as suggesting that one cannot challenge the use of EU competition law in different market settings. Such arguments may often have merit and contribute to the development of European jurisprudence. But the key issue lies in recognizing that these arguments must be understood within the framework of goals and values and institutional structures. One may indeed argue for different weighing of goals and values, challenge the choice of cases, theories of harm or challenge the possible utilization of other instruments to achieve similar goals. One may, moreover, question whether economic analysis provides the ultimate prism through which enforcement of competition law is assessed.[1296]

This leads us to a key policy question and the theme pondered upon in this book in the light of the data economy and digitalization of markets: what role should privacy play in competition policy and how proactive should competition enforcers be in this regard? As this book has aimed to show, this question may invite different answers across Europe and the USA, and within individual national competition agencies. The answer should be considered while taking stock of the multitude of goals and values of EU competition law.

§6.03 EMERGING PHILOSOPHICAL SHIFT AND RISE OF NON-PRICE CONSIDERATIONS

In the context of the ongoing transitions towards a more data-driven as well as green economy, modern competition policy will increasingly face non-price considerations as part of its objectives and there seems to be the beginning of a philosophical shift towards softer and more social values. This chapter considers in brief the potential implications for modern competition policy of the growing focus on sustainability and climate change – topics which may well prove to be the next important non-price parameters and social goals of future competition policy.

> Europe today needs to find the right way forward. We are in the middle of not one, but two great transitions – to an economy that is both digital and green. And that is changing the world we know in fundamental ways.

As the above quote by EU Competition Commissioner Vestager[1297] goes to illustrate, the debate around data privacy and the digital economy shares some characteristics and similarities with another key theme in modern-day competition law and policy, namely sustainability. The shared characteristics between digital and sustainability include, in particular, that non-price factors lie at the heart of the issue and long-term impact should be assessed to ensure that dynamic efficiencies are considered. Moreover, stakeholders all over are clamouring for change; government,

1296. Ezrachi (n 369) 26.
1297. Speech by Margrethe Vestager 'Keeping the EU competitive in a green and digital world' (Bruges, 2 March 2020).

activists, shareholders and consumers alike.[1298] Similar to the debate concerning the interlinkage between privacy and competition explored in this book, the discourse on the relationship between sustainability and competition law involves a strong political dimension and the conduct under examination has effects beyond borders. This also has the practical implications that companies may be exposed to multiple and even incoherent laws and regulations on the matter - much similar to the fragmented privacy regulations and approaches existing around the world.

The EU Competition Commissioner has talked about the role of competition policy in a changing world where environment and tackling climate change are issues coming to the fore.[1299] Moreover, the new Commission, led by President Ursula von der Leyen, has clearly identified climate change as one of two major priorities - the other being creating a 'Europe fit for the digital age'.[1300] In its communication 'Shaping Europe's digital future', the European Commission unveiled a series of proposals laying out EU's approach to data, artificial intelligence and platform regulation over the next five years and beyond. What the Commission also stressed in its communication on Europe's digital future was the close relationship between digital and environment in the need for Europe to lead the transition to a healthy planet and a new digital world:

> This twin challenge of a green and digital transformation has to go hand-in-hand. It requires, as set out in the European Green Deal, an immediate change of direction towards more sustainable solutions which are resource-efficient, circular and climate-neutral. It requires that every citizen, every employee, every business person has a fair chance, wherever they live, to reap the benefits of our increasingly digitised society.

It is worth exploring this so-called twin challenge and the relationship between sustainability and competition law in light of the previously analysed relationship between digitalization and competition. It is clear that going back to the Treaty-based competition rules, owing to their constitutional nature, competition rules need to be interpreted in light of the European-wider normative values.[1301] In this context, the TFEU mandates that the EU must ensure consistency between its policies and activities, taking all of its objectives into account.[1302] It follows that, at least at the abstract level, EU policies may be implemented by taking into account, among other things, environmental concerns.[1303]

If environmental concerns are to be implemented in EU competition policy, the issue that arises is the tension that lies in measuring how non-economic interests, such as social-environmental aims measure up against conventional competition objectives, namely price effects. These tensions related to sustainability aims are similar to the

1298. Also competition lawyers are actively contributing to the sustainability discussion, *see e.g.* speech by Maurits Dolmans, 'Sustainable Competition Policy' Chilling Competition Conference (Brussels, 11 December 2019), for some insightful viewpoints on competition law and climate change.
1299. *Ibid.*
1300. European Commission Communication (n 1).
1301. Ezrachi (n 369) 4.
1302. Article 7 TFEU.
1303. Article 11 TFEU; Article 37 EU Charter of Fundamental Rights (n 188).

tensions concerning the role of data protection in competition policy that have been explored in previous chapters. It is a broader question of attempting to bring about non-economic goals within the scope of competition law. The EU's twin challenge of a green and digital transformation invites the rise of non-price goals and more social considerations in competition law and policy. If future competition policy will strive to accommodate not only the digital but also the green transformation, incorporating also environmental or sustainability goals, this will undoubtedly grow the importance of non-economic goals in competition law more generally.

Despite the apparent friction between sustainability initiatives and competition law, recent EU developments suggest a strong interest and growing focus towards this area. For example, the EU Competition Commissioner has hinted at a more worldly application of the EU competition rules by emphasizing that 'businesses should take responsibility, not just for the quality of their products, but for their effect on the world around them'.[1304] This would, however, require that competition authorities explore ways to translate non-economic benefits into economic terms, such as the economic effects of avoided emissions of harmful gases. This is important to ensure a complete cost-benefit analysis can be undertaken. In more complex cases, it may be worth considering whether it would be possible for wider government to balance the economic benefits against the competitive effects. Such balancing exercise may require some assessment of negative externalities, meaning environmental costs which are not reflected in the prevailing price (which may be what Commissioner Vestager is getting at when talking about the need for firms to take responsibility for the effects of their products).[1305]

The tensions related to the possible integration of environmental concerns into competition policy are in many ways similar to the tensions in incorporating privacy issues into competition policy. Both situations have a culmination point in their shared attempt to bring in non-price considerations within the scope of competition law. Another point of culmination or similarity becomes apparent when comparing the ecoparadox and the privacy paradox.

As discussed in previous chapters,[1306] the privacy paradox refers to a situation where users feel concerned about their privacy, but very few actually act on those concerns (demonstrating irrational consumer behaviour), and thereby markets fail to cater for users' privacy preferences.[1307] The privacy paradox leads to a situation of dysfunctional equilibrium where users become cynical and fail to read privacy policies, and companies are left with less incentives to implement fair and competitive privacy policies.[1308] One challenge in the digital economy is whether and to what extent traditional competition law tools and principles can be transferred from the offline to

1304. Grant Murray, 'Antitrust and Sustainability: Globally Warming up to Be a Hot Topic?' Kluwer Competition Law Blog (October 18, 2019) http://competitionlawblog.kluwercompetitionlaw.com/2019/10/18/antitrust-and-sustainability-globally-warming-up-to-be-a-hot-topic/, accessed 19 April 2020.
1305. *Ibid.*
1306. *See e.g.* discussion in Chapter 5, §5.03[B].
1307. Botta and Wiedemann (n 95) 4.
1308. Farrell (n 96) 251; Costa-Cabral and Lynskey (n 96) 28.

the online economy to remedy these situations or market failures. Similar to privacy economics, environmental economics can also be described as 'riddled with market failures'.[1309] The production of goods involves costs that are not reflected in the price of those goods, such as the harm of pollution created during manufacturing being borne by society as a whole, not just by the manufacturer or consumer of the goods produced. Companies that invest in environmentally friendly production methods or consumers who pay more for 'green' products receive no clear, short-term monetary benefit.[1310]

Similar to the privacy paradox, one can talk about there being an ecoparadox in sustainability when users feel concerned about the environment, but very few actually act on those concerns. As phrased by Maurits Dolmans, 'we claim to care about the environment until we destroy it first for small gain'.[1311] Just like the privacy paradox, the ecoparadox also demonstrates consumer behaviour that is irrational and leads to market outcomes that are not in the consumers' long-term interest or good for consumer well-being. It also relates to something called hyperbolic discounting - the tendency to choose a smaller benefit today over a larger one in the future - and moral licensing, excusing bad behaviour in one situation by referring to good behaviour in another.[1312] Both hyperbolic discounting and moral licensing account for competition policy's failure to integrate non-price environmental concerns and take action to address climate change.

However, just as this book argues that competition and data protection can work together through a conjoined policy approach, environmentalism and competition policy are not inherently opposed either. Dolmans refers to a 'philosophical shift' - not much different than the conceptual change and intellectual shift advocated in this book - and argues that competition authorities need to rethink the consumer welfare test to include environmental considerations, by adding an 'environmental impact accounting for cost externalities' and integrating the 'costs of climate change' into every competition decision.[1313] Moreover, enforcers should also consider if more or less competition in a market leads to a greater or lesser environmental burden.

These calls for integrating environmental concerns into competition law by rethinking the consumer welfare test are not so different from what this book illustrates in its circle of various EU competition goals and values that centre around the umbrella concept of consumer welfare.[1314] After considering the research question of this book - whether privacy plays a role in competition law - privacy is placed among the various competition policy goals in the circle. It would not be so hard to see a place there also for sustainability or environmental goals. It could also be argued that it is actually

1309. *See e.g.* Dolmans (n 1298).

1310. Dolmans refers to this issue as the 'tragedy of the commons'. Charley Connor, 'Include Environmental Costs in Competition Analysis, Dolmans Urges' GCR (9 December 2019).

1311. *Ibid.*

1312. *Ibid.*

1313. *Ibid.*

1314. *See* discussion on EU competition law's multitude of goals and related image in Chapter 5, §5.03[C] and earlier in Chapter 3, §3.03[A].

economically rational to integrate environmental concerns into the competitive assessment; according to neoclassic economic theory, competition gives rise to 'external effects' that must be internalized if society's resources are to be efficiently allocated.

By and large, as becomes clear when looking at sustainability initiatives and competition law, there are obvious similarities to the interplay between data protection issues and competition law. Similar to both is the challenge that they contribute to raising when adding to the multitude of possible competition policy objectives. Ezrachi describes this well:[1315]

> The multitude of competition goals, and their position within the wider normative EU values, is undoubtedly challenging, in particular when considered alongside the desire to engage in economic based analysis.

Further, the incorporation of both privacy concerns and sustainability concerns into competition law requires to some extent that moral and philosophical questions are brought into the discussion. Dolmans notes that competition policy should 'sacrifice philosophical purity' and start defining what options may harm consumers, regardless of price.[1316] Moral goals play in both when it comes to the relationship between sustainability and competition law, as well as that of data protection and competition law. Companies can pursue initiatives concerning sustainability completely independently, but their incentives to do so may not be there, for reasons relating to a first-mover disadvantage or free-rider concerns. Moreover, the law and lack of certainty may stand in the way of sustainability initiatives.

To date, EU competition law does not generally provide clear answers for companies contemplating sustainable goals, and in this context, how non-economic interests, such as social-environmental aims, should measure up against price effects. Sometimes, as a result, the law or a perception of the law may stand in the way of sustainability initiatives and lack of certainty can be invoked as a reason for opposing calls for change or for challenging legitimate conduct. However, case law, by its nature, is designed to evolve.

While sustainability efforts and agreements may increase price (since more expensive methods may need to be used), they are not on their face aimed at increasing companies' revenues. Instead they pursue moral goals and enjoy widespread popular and even government support.[1317] There can be a variety of reasons for companies to seek to achieve more sustainable outcomes, including responding to consumer or shareholder preferences, or even government pressure. There are multiple sustainability initiatives that arise in all sectors. Some common examples include arrangements to only bring to market products that are sustainable, arrangements or collective plans regarding an ancillary service, such as collective waste removal systems, or standardization for the purpose of logistics, distribution or packaging. But initiatives are more

1315. Ezrachi (n 369) 4.
1316. Connor (n 1310).
1317. Grant Murray, Antitrust and Sustainability: Globally Warming up to Be a Hot Topic? Kluwer Competition Law Blog (October 18, 2019) http://competitionlawblog.kluwercompetitionlaw.com/2019/10/18/antitrust-and-sustainability-globally-warming-up-to-be-a-hot-topic/, accessed 19 April 2020.

likely to be effective when taken on by a large part of the market. Pursuing non-economic goals may improve product quality but may sometimes also reduce product choice (for example, if non-sustainably produced products are removed from the supply chain), and how to balance and measure these various interests is not in any way a straightforward exercise.

The key question is how to measure the value that consumers place on those qualitative environmental factors. This broad question brings us back to this book's previous analysis and discussions in the context of data protection, for example in Chapter 5, §5.02 on the shortcomings in current competition policy and in particular to Chapter 5, §5.03[A] on treating privacy as a quality component, as well as Chapter 5, §5.03[B] addressing challenges of measuring privacy. Some apparent analogies could be made when trying to answer the question of measuring the value that consumers place in certain qualitative environmental factors.

It goes beyond the scope of this book to address the interplay between sustainability and competition law in further detail, but the aforementioned similarities to the interlink between privacy and competition are worth considering and will most likely be elaborated in a separate research. Relevant for both is that the notion defended by vested interests that market forces alone can ensure the best outcomes for consumers is starting to lose its once held credibility.

Moreover, the case law of the EU courts, as well as the decisional practice of the Commission, does not fully support the Commission's more economic approach and price-driven competition analysis. The Treaties demand that the EU strives towards a sustainable development and a high level of environmental protection. Traditionally, the EU courts have used a teleological interpretation method when analysing the provisions in the Treaties. It can be argued that the founding Treaties should be viewed as forming a coherent system and when the wording of Treaty statutes is vague enough to be open to interpretation, they should be interpreted as to help EU's overarching policy objectives and the multiple goals of EU competition law.

As noted by Johannes Laitenberger, competition law cannot solve all issues in our society but it has an important role to play vis-à-vis broader societal concerns:[1318]

> [C]ompetition law has always contributed and will continue to contribute to solutions beyond the mere enhancement of 'efficiencies'. [...] There is no reason to be shy about the overall impact of competition law – and even less reason to pretend that positive effects on big picture concerns are in themselves a sign of over-enforcement. [...] I think we should move beyond a way of thinking in terms of inevitable tension, polarisation, dichotomies, and trade-offs.
>
> Let's be ambitious instead.

Indeed, through this book, there is a strive for ambition and to contribute to the important debates that are shaping the future of competition policy in our economy and society in the digital era. It should be further explored in which ways EU competition law could apply in both digital and green economies as a tool to maximize the well-being of consumers. By helping to ensure that consumers can benefit from free

1318. Speech, Accuracy and administrability go hand in hand, CRA Conference (Brussels, 12 December 2017).

and open markets, in which companies compete on their merits, competition law and policy is an important method of improving consumer choice and satisfaction, more broadly well-being. It is really a matter of exploring means to better utilize and enforce EU competition law in the future.

§6.04 IMPLICATIONS FOR BUSINESS PRACTICE

This chapter considers in brief the potential implications for business practice from the growing role of privacy in competition law and the developments concerning data-driven markets. Thus, the outlook here goes beyond a policy discourse and reflects a more practical viewpoint than the conceptual change and intellectual shift that this book has so far focused on.

When considering the effects of the data economy and the increasing role of privacy in competition law and potential enforcement actions by authorities, companies should expect potential closer scrutiny ahead of commercial deals and practices.[1319] Despite views by critics that non-price dimensions such as data protection and privacy aspects play little role in competition investigations, the ongoing debate about data and what it all really means for consumers and competition will continue to attract the attention of officials, practitioners and academics alike. This means that businesses need to be alert. Latest developments prove that at least the European competition authorities are sensitive to the importance of privacy harms in online markets and will likely continue their focus on challenges posed by corporate ownership and use of data: in this respect, we need to think only of the German Facebook case.

Although some oppose merging competition and data protection policy issues, calls to incorporate privacy considerations within competition analysis will become more common as the prevalence of companies relying on consumer data grows. Therefore, looking ahead, businesses operating especially in Europe, with its history and culture of giving strong protection to privacy, should anticipate regulators also weighing in consumers' data protection interests in future antitrust cases, given that EU competition policy is multidimensional and apt also to protect non-price related objectives, such as data protection. The *Facebook* case in Germany is the prime example of this development. This bold approach by the Bundeskartellamt may well extend to other authorities and companies to be investigated. According to the EDPS at least, the case is just the tip of the iceberg and all companies in the digital information ecosystem that rely on user data should be on notice.[1320]

There may also be increased scrutiny of data-driven mergers, with a focus on whether transactions may lead to one company gaining an unmatchable competitive advantage based on combined data sets. An example of this is the *Microsoft/LinkedIn* transaction, which was only approved after commitments were given concerning data access. In this context, the European Commission explicitly stressed the significance of privacy as a competitive parameter and the right to data protection as a fundamental

1319. This is elaborated by the author in an article relating to this book, *see* Maria Wasastjerna, 'Competition Law, Big Data and Privacy' (2017) 39 International In-House Counsel Journal.
1320. Buttarelli (n 828).

right. This is illustrative of the growing intellectual shift in Europe concerning the interlinkage between data, privacy and competition. The in-depth investigation by the European Commission in Apple's acquisition of Shazam is another current example illustrating the increasing focus on the role of data in digital markets.

Further, businesses can expect tougher enforcement of data protection rules in the future. Irrespective of whether a more joined-up approach to data protection and competition will materialize in the future, tougher enforcement of data protection rules is nevertheless expected with the entry into force of the GDPR. Companies with business activities in Europe should continue to focus on compliance in their use of personal data, not least in the light of the heavy sanctions available with the reform of the EU data protection framework under the GDPR. Over recent decades, some businesses might have thought that EU data protection law was unlikely to be a major compliance risk because the average fines were comparatively low, and the likelihood of being fined was also rather small. Conversely, the cost of compliance has been relatively high. It is likely that businesses therefore considered that these costs were simply not worth it. However, with the GDPR introducing maximum fines of the greater of EUR 20 million or 4% of worldwide turnover, European DPAs now have the power to shock businesses into action, if needed, and it is therefore advisable for businesses to be well prepared.

As elaborated throughout this book, the implications for competition policy from the increasing use of data are multifold. All of these developments require businesses and their counsel to be aware of the potential antitrust risks connected to corporate ownership of data and the enforcement actions that could follow. These will test the traditional divide between competition law and data protection rules. In terms of competition, privacy and data protection, the next few years have the potential to be turbulent. Keeping an eye on developments, and watching where regulators are focusing, will be key to developing and maintaining a successful business and compliance strategy.

Even though the final outcome in the pioneering German Facebook case is still to come in light of the pending appeal process and suspensory court order, the practical implication for businesses of the Bundeskartellamt's controversial decision is that companies with data-driven business models now, more than ever, need to be familiar with competition law restrictions and how they may be applied to personal data. That is in addition to the impact that the GDPR will have on all businesses with activities in Europe. With the increase of data-driven products and services, such as social networks, there will likely be more of these cases testing the conventional boundaries between competition and privacy. In the words of the German competition authority:

> where access to the personal data of users is essential for the market position of a company, the question of how that company handles the personal data of its users is no longer only relevant for data protection authorities. It becomes a relevant question for the competition authorities, too.[1321]

1321. Bundeskartellamt background paper (n 790) 1–2.

§6.05 SUGGESTIONS FOR FUTURE RESEARCH

Competition, data and democracy. The current competition law debate does not just end with privacy and data protection. What needs further consideration - and in the author's view merits more research - is whether the focus should be on consumer welfare in the broadest sense, as the state of the economy and the rise of powerful technology companies have brought about casualties such as job losses, misinformation campaigns, and inability for young companies to compete. Some argue, perhaps rightfully so, that competition law cannot solve all societal problems, and just because academics are abuzz does not mean this should ever translate into stricter rules and more stringent enforcement. However, the relationship between competition policy and democracy is a question where more research is needed.

After all, competition enforcement in both Europe and the USA grew out of the notion that companies should never become so powerful as to threaten democracy.[1322] Competition has traditionally been considered as supportive of democracy, for example by dispersing economic power through efforts that guard against concentrations. Economic power is shared across a wide range of economic actors rather than in the hands of a selected few who could potentially exercise undue influence over government and political decision-making processes.

To illustrate, the global controversy over how Cambridge Analytica acquired the personal data of 50 million Facebook users for exploitation in unlawful activities regarding the American elections is an issue where privacy, competition and democracy interlink. The case was not just a breach of private and personal data but much more serious, amounting to a threat to democracy, to democratic plurality.

The role of trust in the digital age. Another topic closely related to the functioning of markets that would also benefit from more research is that of digital trust. Trust is an element that is needed in the digital economy, but all too often it is about blind trust, because of lack of better information or existing alternatives (or, in competition law parlance, lack of consumer choice). The Facebook scandal with Cambridge Analytica was a serious case of data breach, where the implications go beyond the company itself and may affect trust. Besides focusing on the negative aspects of the case, which are many, one may also see the positive side as a necessary growing pain of the digital economy. Society needs a shock example that receives a lot of publicity so that citizens wake up to their data rights, and so that the will to build trust in the digital economy grows big enough. Another more recent shock example to society is the corona epidemic, which is a significant global crisis to humankind. The decisions people and governments take in efforts to fight the epidemic will shape the society, the economy and the world for years to come. This includes the role of trust in the digital age. Trust is essential to achieve the necessary level of compliance and cooperation to stop the pandemic, as people need to trust science, public authorities and the media.

1322. For further reading on the relationship between competition and democracy, *see e.g.* Eleanor M Fox, 'Competition and Democracy' OECD Global Forum on Competition (4 April 2018).

The digital age has some distinctive features, one of which is that often the solutions that are needed to build trust cross nation-state borders and require international cooperation. Some sort of a conjoined approach could also be the solution in that regard.

Bibliography

Books

Aarnio A, *On Legal Reasoning* (University of Turku 1977)

Aarnio A, *Legal Point of View: Six Essays on Legal Philosophy* (University of Helsinki 1978)

Aarnio A, *Oikeussäännösten tulkinnasta. Tutkimus lainopillisen perustelun rationaalisuudesta ja hyväksyttävyydestä* (Juridica 1982)

Aarnio A, *The Rational as Reasonable: A Treatise on Legal Justification* (D. Reidel Publishing Company 1987)

Aarnio A, *Essays on the Doctrinal Study of Law* (University of Tampere 2011)

Aarnio A *Luentoja lainopillisen tutkimuksen teoriasta* (Unigrafia Oy, University of Helsinki 2011)

Allen AL and Rotenberg M, *Privacy Law and Society* (2nd edn, American Casebook Series 2011)

Akman P, *The Concept of Abuse in EU Competition Law. Law and Economic Approaches* (Hart Publishing 2012)

Amato G, *Antitrust and the Bounds of Power: The Dilemma of Liberal Democracy in the History of the Market* (Hart 1997)

Areeda PE and Hovenkamp H, *Fundamentals of Antitrust Law* (4th edn, Aspen Law & Business 2011)

Areeda PE and Hovenkamp H, *Antitrust Law: An Analysis of Antitrust Principles and Their Application* (first published 1978, 4th edn, Wolters Kluwer 2015)

Ariely D, *Predictably Irrational: The Hidden Forces That Shape Our Decisions* (HarperCollins 2008)

Aristotle, *Nicomachean Ethics* (Edited and translated by Roger Crisp, CUP 2000)

Bacon K QC, *European Union Law of State Aid* (OUP 2013)

Banakar R (ed.), *Rights in Context. Law and Justice in Late Modern Society* (Ashgate 2010)

Baird DG, Gertner RH and Picker RC, *Game Theory and the Law* (4th edn Harvard University Press 1994 2000)

Becker GS, *The Economic Approach to Human Behavior* (University of Chicago Press 1976)

Bellamy C and Child G, *Common Market Law of Competition* (5th edn, Sweet & Maxwell, London 2001)

Bentham J, *An Introduction to the Principles of Morals and Legislation* (first published 1789, 3rd edn New York, Hafner Publishing Co. 1963)

Bernitz U, *Marknadsrätt. En komparativ studie av marknadslagstiftningens utveckling och huvudlinjer* (Jurist- och samhällsvetareförbundets Förlag AB, Stockholm 1969)

Bernitz U, *Konkurrens och priser i Norden. En komparativ studie av konkurrens- och prislagstiftningens syften och medel i de nordiska länderna* (Jurist- och samhällsvetareförbundets Förlag AB 1971)

Bernitz U, Tiili V and Pokela H, *Kansainvälinen Markkinaoikeus* (Lakimiesliiton Kustannus 1998)

Bertrand A, *Droit a la vie privée et droit a l'image* (Lexis Nexis/LITEC 1999)

Bishop S and Walker M, *The Economics of EC Competition Law* (first published 1999, 2nd edn, Sweet & Maxwell 2002)

Bork RH, *The Antitrust Paradox: A Policy at War with Itself* (New York Basic Books 1978)

Bouckaert B and De Geest G, (eds), *Encyclopaedia of Law and Economics I* (Edward Elgar 2000)

Bradford A, *The Brussels Effect: How the European Union Rules the World* (OUP 2020)

Brüggemeier G, Ciacchi AC and O'Callaghan P, *Personality Rights in European Tort Law* (CUP 2010)

Bräutigam T and Miettinen S, *Data Protection, Privacy and European Regulation in the Digital Age* (University of Helsinki 2017)

Bygrave L, *Data Protection Law. Approaching Its Rationale, Logic and Limits* (Kluwer Law International 2002)

Bärlund J, *Reklamation i konsumentavtal – En kontraktsrättslig studie av konsumenten reklamation som en förutsättning för att konsumenten skall kunna åberopa näringsidkarens avtalsbrott* (Kauppakaari Juristförbundets Förlag 2002)

Bärlund J, Nybergh F and Petrell K, *Finlands civil- och handelsrätt – En introduktion* (Talentum 2013)

Castrén M, *EU-Suomen markkinaoikeus* (Kauppakaari Oy 1997)

Cini M and McGovan L, *Competition Policy in the European Union* (MacMillan Press Ltd 1998)

Craig P and De Búrca G, *The Evolution of EU Law* (OUP 1999)

Craig P and De Búrca G, *EU Law: Text, Cases and Materials* (6th edn, OUP 2015)

Cseres KJ, *Competition Law and Consumer Protection* (Alphen aan den Rijn, Kluwer International 2005)

Dworkin R, *Taking Rights Seriously* (Harvard University Press 1978)

Eisner MA, *Antitrust and the Triumph of Economics: Institutions, Expertise, and Policy Change* (first published 1987, The University of North Carolina Press 1991)

Ezrachi A, *EU Competition Law – An Analytical Guide to the Leading Cases* (5th edn, Bloomsbury Publishing 2016)

Ezrachi A and Stucke ME, *Virtual Competition - The Promise and Perils of the Algorithm-driven Economy* (Harvard University Press 2016)

Faull J and Nikpay A (eds), *The EC Law of Competition* (first published 1999, 3rd edn, OUP 2014)

Habermas J, *Knowledge and Human Interests* (first published 1968, Heinemann 1981)

Fejø J, *Monopolret og marked. Studier i EF-konkurrenceretten med US-amerikansk antitrustret som sammenligningsgrundlag og med støtte i markedsøkonomisk grundteori* (Jurist- og økonomforbundets forlag 1985)

Fejø J, *Monopoly Law and Market. Studies of EC Competition Law with US American Antitrust Law as a Frame of Reference and Supported by Basic Market Economics* (Kluwer Law and Taxation Publishers 1990)

First H, Fox EM and Pitofsky R, (eds), *Revitalizing Antitrust in its Second Century. Essays on Legal, Economic and Political Policy* (Quorum Books, New York 1991)

Galbraith JK, *American Capitalism: The Concept of Countervailing Power* (Houghton Mifflin 1952)

Gavil AI, Kovacic WE and Baker JB, *Antitrust Law in Perspective: Cases, Concepts, and Problems in Competition Policy* (Thomson/West 2008)

Gerber DJ, *Law and Economics and Competition in the Twentieth Century Europe: Protecting Prometheus* (Clarendon Press 1998)

Gerber DJ, *Global Competition: Law, Markets, and Globalization* (OUP 2010)

Goyder J and Albors-Llorens A, *Goyder's EC Competition Law* (5th edn, OUP 2009)

Graham C, *The Pursuit of Happiness: An Economy of Well-Being* (Brookings Institution Press 2011)

Harari YN, *Homo Deus: A Brief History of Tomorrow* (Random House 2016)

Hart HLA, *The Concept of Law* (Clarendon Press 1961)

Hartley T, *The Foundations of European Community Law* (5th edn, OUP 2003)

Haskel J and Westlake S, *Capitalism without Capital: The Rise of the Intangible Economy* (Princeton University Press 2017)

Hayek FA, *Individualism and Economic Order* (University of Chicago Press 1963)

Hervey T, Cryer R, Sokhi-Bulley B and Bohm A, *Research Methodologies in EU and International Law* (Hart Publishing 2011)

Hildebrand D, *The Role of Economic Analysis in EU Competition Law: The European School* (Kluwer Law International 2009)

Hirvonen A, *Mitkä metodit? Opas oikeustieteen metodologiaan* (Yleisen Oikeustieteen Julkaisuja 2011)

Hofstede GH, *Culture's Consequences: Comparing Values, Behaviors, Institutions, and Organizations Across Nations* (2nd edn, Sage Publications 2001)

Hofstede GH, Hofstede GJ and Minkov M, *Cultures and Organizations: Software of the Mind. Intercultural Cooperation and Its (Importance for Survival* (3rd edn, HarperCollins 1994)

Hovenkamp H, *The Antitrust Enterprise: Principle and Execution* (Harvard University Press 2008)

Jacquemin A and Admiraal PH, *Merger & Competition Policy in the European Community* (Basil Blackwell 1990)

Joliet R, *Monopolization and Abuse of Dominant Position: A Comparative Study of American and European Approaches to the Control of Economic Power* (Université de Liège Faculté de Droit 1970)

Jones A and Sufrin B, *EU Competition Law. Texts, Cases and Materials* (5th edn, OUP 2014)

Joutsamo K, Aalto P, and Kaila H, *Eurooppaoikeus* (Alma Talent 1996)

Kagel JH and Roth AE, *The Handbook of Experimental Economics* (Princeton University Press 1997)

Kahneman D, Slovic P and Tversky A, *Judgment under Uncertainty: Heuristics and Biases* (CUP 1982)

Kanniainen V and Määttä K, *Taloustieteellinen näkökulma kilpailuoikeuteen* (Lakimiesliiton Kustannus 2001)

Kelsen H, *General Theory of Law and State* (Russell and Russell 1945)

Kerse CS and Khan N, *EC Antitrust Procedure* (5th edn, Sweet & Maxwell 2005)

Klami HT, *Methodological Problems in European and Comparative Law* (2nd edn, Yleisen oikeustieteen laitoksen julkaisuja, Helsinki 1997)

Kuoppamäki P, *Markkinavoiman sääntely EY:n ja Suomen kilpailuoikeudessa* (Doctoral dissertation, University of Helsinki 2003)

Kuoppamäki P, *Uusi kilpailuoikeus* (Sanoma Pro Oy 2006)

Leivo K, Leivo T, Huimala M and Huimala H, *EU:n ja Suomen kilpailuoikeus* (Alma Talent 2012)

Letto-Vanamo P, Tamm D and Mortensen BOG, *Nordic Law in European Context* (Springer 2018)

Lipsey R and Chrystal A, *Economics* (10th edn, OUP 2003)

Lynskey O, *The Foundations of EU Data Protection Law* (OUP 2015)

Marshall A, *Principles of Economics* (first published 1890, 8th edn, Macmillan 1920)

Mentula A, Pokela H and Saraste T, *Määräävän markkina-aseman väärinkäyttö kilpailuoikeudessa* (Kauppakaari Oy, Lakimiesliiton Kustannus 1998)

Mill JS, *Utilitarianism* (first published 1861, OUP 1998)

Monti G, *EC Competition Law* (CUP 2007)

Motta M, *Competition Policy: Theory and Practice* (CUP 2004)

Mäihäniemi B, *Imposing Access to Information in Digital Markets Based on Competition Law – In Search of the Possible Theory of Harm in the EU Google Search Investigations* (Academic dissertation, Faculty of Law, University of Helsinki 2017)

Määttä K, *Oikeustaloustieteen aakkoset* (Helsingin Yliopisto 1999)

Määttä K, *Uusi kilpailurajoituslaki* (Edita Publishing Oy 2004)

Neumeyer F, *Monopol kontroll I USA* (Kooperativa Förbundets Bokförlag 1951)

Neuvonen R, *Yksityisyyden suoja Suomessa* (Lakimiesliiton Kustannus 2014)

Nicholls AJ, *Freedom with Responsibility: The Social Market Economy in Germany 1918–1963* (Clarendon Press 1994)

Niiniluoto I, *Johdatus tieteenfilosofiaan. Käsitteen- ja teorianmuodostus* (Otava 1984)

O'Donoghue R and Padilla AJ, *The Law and Economics of Article 82 EC* (Hart 2006)

Peczenik A, *On Law and Reason* (Reidel 1989)

Peterson W (ed.), *Market Power and the Economy. Industrial, Corporate, Governmental and Political Aspects* (Kluwer Academic Publishers 1988)
Philips L, *Competition Policy: A Game-Theoretic Perspective* (CUP 1995)
Pigou AC, *The Economics of Welfare* (first published 1920, Macmillan 2013)
Pitofsky R (ed.), *How the Chicago School Overshot the Mark: The Effect of Conservative Economic Analysis on US Antitrust* (OUP 2008)
Posner RA, *Antitrust Law: An Economic Perspective* (The University of Chicago Press 1976)
Posner RA, *Economic Analysis of the Law* (Aspen Law and Business 1998)
Posner RA, *Antitrust Law* (2nd edn, The University of Chicago Press 2001)
Pöyhönen J, *Juridisista teorioista. Reports from the Project for the Study of Legal Research No 3* (Suomen akatemia, Helsinki 1981)
Pöyhönen J, *Sopimusoikeuden järjestelmä ja sopimusten sovittelu* (Suomalaisen Lakimiesyhdistyksen julkaisuja 1988)
Raitio J, *Eurooppaoikeuden tavoitteet ja johtavat periaatteet* (Tampereen yliopisto 1997)
Raitio J, *The Principle of Legal Certainty in EC Law* (Academic dissertation, Faculty of Law, University of Helsinki 2001)
Raitio J, *The Principle of Legal Certainty in EC Law* (Kluwer Academic Publishers 2003)
Raitio J, *Euroopan integraatio ja Euroopan unionin rakenteet* (Unigrafia Oy 2011)
Raitio J, *Euroopan unionin oikeuden periaatteet ja perusvapaudet* (Unigrafia Oy 2017)
Rasmussen A, *Pristeori eller parameterteori. Studier omkring virksomhedens afsætning* (2nd edn, Erhvervsøkonomisk Forlag, Nyt Nordisk Forlag 1977)
Rawls J, *A Theory of Justice* (Belknap 1971)
Resnik DB, *The Ethics of Science: An Introduction* (Routledge 1998)
Richards N, *Intellectual Privacy: Rethinking Civil Liberties in the Digital Age* (OUP 2015)
Rissanen K, Tiili V and Mäkinen P, *Markkinaoikeuden perusteet: elinkeino, kilpailu- ja kuluttujalainsäädäntö* (Lakimiesliiton kustannus 1990)
Ross A, *On Law and Justice* (University of California Press 1959)
Rosen J, *The Unwanted Gaze: The Destruction of Privacy in America* (Random House 2000)
Roth P and Rose V (eds), *Bellamy & Child, European Community Law of Competition* (6th edn, OUP 2008)
Rubin P and Lenard T, *Privacy and the Commercial Use of Personal Information* (Springer 2002)
Scherer FM, *Industrial Market Structure and Economic Performance* (first published 1970, 2nd edn, Houghton Mifflin 1994)
Schumpeter JA, *Capitalism, Socialism, and Democracy* (first published 1942, 3rd edn Harper & Brothers 1950)
Schwab K, *The Fourth Industrial Revolution* (Penguin 2016)
Siltala R, *A Theory of Precedent, From Analytical Positivism to a Post-Analytical Philosophy of Law* (Hart Publishing 1998)
Siltala R, *Oikeustieteen tieteenteoria* (Suomalainen Lakimiesyhditys 2003)
Siltala R, *Law, Truth, and Reason: A Treatise on Legal Argumentation* (University of Turku, Springer 2011)

Simon HA, *Administrative Behavior: A Study of Decision-Making Processes in Administrative Organization* (first published 1947, 4th edn, The Free Press 1997)
Smith A, *The Wealth of Nations* (W. Strahan and T. Cadell 1776)
Smith A, *The Wealth of Nations* (Cannan, University of Chicago 1977)
Smith A, *The Theory of Moral Sentiments* (first published 1759, CUP 2002)
Sokol DD and Blumenthal W, 'Merger Control: Key International Norms and Differences', in Ezrachi A (ed.), *Research Handbook on International Competition Law* (Edward Elgar 2012)
Solove D, *The Digital Person: Technology and Privacy in the Information Age* (NYU Press 2004)
Solove D, *Understanding Privacy* (Harvard University Press 2008)
Solove DJ and Rotenberg M, *Information Privacy Law* (Aspen Publishers 2003)
Stigler GJ, *The Organization of Industry* (University of Chicago Press Economic Books 1983)
Stucke ME and Grunes AP, *Big Data and Competition Policy* (OUP 2016)
Sundby NK, *Om normer* (Universitetsforlaget 1974)
Thaler RH, *Misbehaving: The Making of Behavioural Economics* (Penguin 2017)
Thorelli HB, *The Federal Antitrust Policy: Origination of an American Tradition* (Johns Hopkins Press 1955)
Timonen P, *Määräysvalta, hinta ja markkinavoima. Julkisesti noteeratun yrityksen määräysvallan siirtymisen oikeudellinen sääntely* (Lakimiesliiton Kustannus 1999)
Tirole J, *The Theory of Industrial Organization* (MIT Press 1988)
Trepte S and Reinecke L, *Privacy Online. Perspectives on Privacy and Self-Disclosure in the Social Web* (Springer 2011)
Tridimas T, *The General Principles of EU Law* (2nd edn, OUP 2006)
Tuori K, *Oikeus, valta ja demokratia* (Lakimiesliiton Kustannus 1990)
Tuori K, *Critical Legal Positivism* (Aldershot, Ashgate 2002)
Tuori K, *European Constitutionalism* (CUP 2015) 78
Twining W, *Law in Context. Enlarging a Discipline* (OUP 1997)
Russo F, Schinkel MP, Günster A, Carree M, *European Commission Decisions on Competition* (CUP 2010)
Vaughan D and Robertson A (eds), *The Law of the European Union* (OUP 2003 and supp)
von Neumann J and Morgenstern O, *Theory of Games and Economic Behaviour* (Princeton University Press 1944)
Warren SD and Brandeis LD, *The Right to Privacy* (Harvard Law Review 1890)
Wesseling R, *The Modernisation of EC Antitrust Law* (Hart 2000)
Wetter C, Karlsson J and Östman M, *Konkurrensrätt – en kommentar* (4th edn, Thomson Reuters 2009)
Westin A, *Privacy and Freedom* (Athenaeum 1967)
Whish R, *Competition Law* (5th edn, LexisNexis 2003)
Whish R and Bailey D, *Competition Law* (8th edn, OUP 2015)
Wikberg O, *Johdatus kilpailuoikeuteen* (Talentum 2011)

Wilhelmsson T, *Critical Studies in Private Law: A Treatise on Need-Rational Principles in Modern Law* (Springer 1992)

Wils WPJ, *Principles of European Antitrust Enforcement* (Hart Publishing 2005)

Wils WPJ, *Efficiency and Justice in European Antitrust Enforcement* (Hart Publishing 2008)

Witt AC, *The More Economic Approach to EU Antitrust Law* (1st edn, Hart Publishing 2016)

Wittgenstein L, *On Certainty* (Basil Blackwell 1969)

Wu T, *Master Switch: The Rise and Fall of Information Empires* (Atlantic Books Ltd 2010)

Zimmer D, *The Goals of Competition Law* (Edward Elgar 2012)

Book Chapters

Anderson DA, 'The Failure of American Privacy Law' in Markesinis BS (ed.), *Protecting Privacy* (OUP 1999)

Alexy R, 'A Defense of Radbruch's Formula' in Freeman MA (ed.), *Lloyds Introduction to Jurisprudence* (7th edn, Sweet & Maxwell 2001)

Austin J, 'The Province of Jurisprudence Determined' in Rumble WE (ed.), *Cambridge Texts* (CUP 1995)

Behrens P, 'The "Consumer Choice" Paradigm in German Ordoliberalism and Its Impact on EU Competition Law' in Nihoul P, Charbit N and Ramundo E (eds), *Choice – A New Standard for Competition Law Analysis* (Concurrences Review 2016)

Beignier B, 'La vie privée' in Cabrillac R et al. (eds), *Libertés et droits fondamentaux* (5th edn, Dalloz 1999)

Brodley JF, 'Antitrust, Efficiency and Progress' in First H, Fox EM and Pitofsky R (eds), *Revitalizing Antitrust in Its Second Century. Essays on Legal, Economic and Political Policy* (Quorum Books 1991)

Dworkin R, 'No Right Answer?' in Hacker PMS and Raz J (eds), *Law, Morality and Society. Essays in Honour of H.L.A. Hart* (Clarendon Press 1977)

Fox EM, 'The Kaleidoscope of Antitrust and Its Significance in the World Economy: Respecting Differences' in Hawk B (ed.), *International Antitrust Law & Policy: Fordham Corporate Law* (Juris Publishing 2001)

Blanco LO and Colomo PI, 'Evolving Priorities and Rising Standards: Spanish Law on Abuses of Market Power in the Light of the 2008 Guidance Paper on Article 82 EC' in Pace LF (ed.), *European Competition Law: The Impact of the Commission's Guidance on Article 102* (Edward Elgar 2011)

Gal M, 'The Social Contract at the Basis of Competition Law' in Lianos L and Gerard D (eds), *Competition Policy: Between Equity and Efficiency* (CUP 2017)

Harbour PJ, 'The Transatlantic Perspective: Data Protection and Competition Law', in Hijmans H and Kranenborg H (eds), *Data Protection Anno 2014: How To Restore Trust?* (Intersentia 2014) 225

Hofstadter R, 'What Happened to the Antitrust Movement' in Hofstadter R (ed.), *The Paranoid Style in American Politics, and Other Essays* (first published 1965, Vintage Books 2008)

Hui K-L and Png IPL, 'The Economics of Privacy' in Hendershott T (ed.), *Handbook on Economics and Information Systems* (Elsevier Publishing 2006)

Fridolfsson S-O, 'A Consumer Surplus Defense in Merger Control' in Goshal V and Stennek J (eds), *The Political Economy of Antitrust* (Emerald Group Publishing Limited 2007)

Kovacic WE, 'Public Choice and the Origins of Antitrust' in Fred S. McChesney and William F. Shughart II (eds), *The Causes and Consequences of Antitrust* (University of Chicago Press 1995)

Kühn K-U, 'Germany' in Graham EM and Richardson J (eds), *Global Competition Policy* (Washington DC, Institute for International Economics 1997)

Määttä K, 'Taloustieteen hyödyntäminen kilpailunrajoitusten sallittavuutta arvioitaessa' in Kanniainen V and Määttä K, (eds), *Taloustieteellinen näkökulma kilpailuoikeuteen* (Lakimiesliiton Kustannus 2001)

Nihoul P, 'Freedom of Choice: The Emergence of a Powerful Concept in European Competition Law' in Nihoul P, Charbit N and Ramundo E (eds), *Choice – A New Standard for Competition Law Analysis* (Concurrences Review 2016)

Paulis E, 'Article 82 EC and Exploitative Conduct', in Ehlermann C-D and Marquis M (eds), *European Competition Law Annual 2007: A Reformed Approach to Article 82 EC* (Hart Publishing, Oxford/Portland, Oregon 2007)

Peeperkorn L and Verouden V, 'The Economics of Competition' in Faull J and Nikpay A, (eds), *The EC Law of Competition* (first published 1999, 3rd edn, OUP 2014)

Reiman JH, 'Privacy, Intimacy, and Personhood', in Schoeman FD (ed.), *Philosophical Dimensions of Privacy: An Anthology* (CUP 1984)

Maier-Rigaud F, 'On the Normative Foundations of Competition Law: Efficiency, Political Freedom and the Freedom to Compete' in Zimmer D (ed.), *The Goals of Competition Law* (Edward Elgar 2012)

Rubinfeld DL, 'On the Foundations of Antitrust Law and Economics' in Pitofsky R (ed.), *How the Chicago School Overshot the Mark: The Effect of Conservative Economic Analysis on US Antitrust* (OUP 2008)

Rubinfeld DL, 'Conservative Economic Analysis and Its Effects', in Pitofsky R (ed.), *How the Chicago School Overshot the Mark: The Effect of Conservative Economic Analysis on US Antitrust* (OUP 2008)

Sokol DD and Blumenthal W, 'Merger Control: Key International Norms and Differences', in Ezrachi A (ed.), *Research Handbook On International Competition Law* (Edward Elgar 2012)

Sokol DD and Comerford R, 'Does Antitrust Have a Role to Play in Regulating Big Data?' in Blair R and Sokol D (eds), *Cambridge Handbook of Antitrust, Intellectual Property and High Tech* (CUP 2016)

Stiglitz JE, 'Government Failure vs. Market Failure: Principles of Regulation' in Balleisen EJ and. Moss DA (eds), *Governments and Markets: Towards a New Theory of Regulation* (CUP 2009)

Stucke ME, 'The Behavioral Antitrust Gambit' in Ezrachi A (ed.), *International Research Handbook on Competition Law* (Edward Elgar 2012)

Thomson JJ, 'The Right to Privacy' in Schoeman FD (ed.), *Philosophical Dimensions of Privacy: An Anthology* (CUP 1984)

Veljanovksi C, 'Economic Approaches to Regulation' in Baldwin R, Cave M and Lodge M (eds), *The Oxford Handbook of Regulation* (OUP 2010)

Werden GJ, 'Consumer Welfare and Competition Policy' in Drexl J, Kerber W and Podszun R (eds), *Competition Policy and the Economic Approach: Foundations and Limitations* (Edward Elgar Publishing 2011)

Zimmer D, 'On Fairness and Welfare: The Objectives of Competition Policy - Comment on David J. Gerber, Christian Ahlborn and A. Jorge Padilla' in Ehlermann C-D and Marquis M (eds) *European Competition Law Annual 2007 – A Reformed Approach to Article 82 EC* (Hart Publishing 2008)

Journal Articles

Acquisti A, John LK, and Loewenstein G, 'What Is Privacy Worth?' (2013) 42 The Journal of Legal Studies 249–274

Aarnio A, 'Ottakaamme oikeussäännöt vakavasti' (1989) Oikeus 112–122

Acquisti A, Taylor CR and Wagman L, 'The Economics of Privacy' (8 March 2016) 52 Journal of Economic Literature

Ahlborn C and Grave C, 'Walter Eucken and Ordoliberalism: An Introduction from a Consumer Welfare Perspective' (2006) CPI Antitrust Chronicle

Akman P, 'Searching for the Long-Lost Soul of Article 82 EC' (2009) 29 OJLS 267–303

Akman P, 'The Reform of the Application of Article 102 TFEU: Mission Accomplished' (2016) 81 Antitrust Law Journal

Albors-Llorens A, 'Competition and Consumer Law in the European Union: Evolution and Convergence' (2014) 33 Yearbook of European Law 163

Alexy R, 'On the Structure of Legal Principles' (2000) 13 Ratio Juris 294

Alexy R, 'On the Concept and Nature of Law' (2008) 21 Ratio Juris 281

Almunia J, 'Competition and Personal Data Protection', Privacy Platform event: Competition and Privacy in Markets of Data (Brussels, 26 November 2012)

Andriychuk O, 'Rediscovering the Spirit of Competition: On the Normative Value of the Competition Process' (2010) 6 European Competition Journal 575

Averitt NW and Lande RH, 'Using the "Consumer Choice" Approach to Antitrust Law' (2007) 74 Antitrust Law Journal 176

Bain J, 'Economies of Scale, Concentration, and the Condition of Entry in Twenty Manufacturing Industries' (1954) 44 The American Economic Review 15

Bain J, 'Relation of Profit Rate to Industry Concentration: American Manufacturing, 1936–1940' (1951) 65 The Quarterly Journal of Economics 293

Bain J, 'A Note on Pricing in Monopoly and Oligopoly' (1949) 39 The American Economic Review 448

Bartalevich D, 'The Influence of the Chicago School on the Commission's Guidelines, Notices and Block Exemption Regulations in EU Competition Policy' (2016) 54 Journal of Common Market Studies 267

Baye MR and Wright JD, 'Is Antitrust Too Complicated for Generalist Judges? The Impact of Economic Complexity and Judicial Training on Appeals (2011) 54 Journal of Law & Economics 1

Bernitz U, 'What Is Scandinavian Law? Concept, Characteristics, Future' (2007) 50 Scandinavian Studies in Law 13, 30

Bishop S, 'Snake-Oil with Mathematics Is Still Snake Oil: Why Recent Trends in the Application of So-Called "Sophisticated" Economics Is Hindering Good Competition Policy Enforcement' (2013) 9 European Competition Journal 67–77

Blair RD and Sokol DD, 'Welfare Standards in US and EU Antitrust Enforcement' (2013) 81 Fordham Law Review 2500

Blockx J, 'Technocracy and Populism in Antitrust in the US and the EU' (18 December 2017) https://ssrn.com/abstract=3089609, accessed 1 August 2019

Bradford A, Jackson RJ Jr. and Zytnick J, 'Is EU Merger Control Used for Protectionism? An Empirical Analysis' (2017) 15 Journal for Empirical Legal Studies 165–191

Bradford A, Chilton AS and Lancieri FM, 'The Chicago School's Limited Influence on International Antitrust (December 2019) University of Chicago Law Review (Forthcoming)'

Burnside A, 'No Such Thing as a Free Search: Antitrust and the Pursuit of Privacy Goals' (May 2015) CPI Antitrust Chronicle 4

Burnside A, 'Bob Dylan and Consumer Welfare' (7 August 2017) Lexology

Burnside A, 'Antitrust, Privacy & Big Data – Setting the Scene' (3 February 2015) Lexology

Buttarelli G, 'This Is Not an Article on Data Protection and Competition Law' (25 February 2019) Competition Policy International

Cate FH and Mayer-Schönberger V, 'Notice and Consent in a World of Big Data' (2013) 3 International Data Privacy Law 67

Charlesworth A, 'Clash of the Data Titans? US and EU Data Privacy Regulation' (2000) 6 European Public Law 253

Chellapa R and Sin RG, 'Personalization Versus Privacy: An Empirical Examination of the Online Consumers' Dilemma' (2005) 6 Information Technology and Management 181–202

Colangelo G and Maggiolino M, 'Data Accumulation and the Privacy – Antitrust Interface: Insights from the Facebook Case' (2018) 8 International Data Privacy Law 237

Coniglio JV, 'How the "New Brandeis Movement" Already Overshoots the Mark: Sketching an Alternative Theory for Understanding the Sherman Act as a Consumer Welfare Prescription' (2017) October Competition Policy International North America Column

Coniglio JV, 'Why the "New Brandeis Movement" Gets Antitrust Wrong' (2018) Law 360

Cook WW, 'Scientific Method and the Law' (1927) 13 American Bar Association Journal 303

Cooper J, 'Privacy and Antitrust: Underpants, Gnomes, the First Amendment, and Subjectivity' (2013) 20 George Mason Law Review 1129–1146

Costa-Cabral F and Lynskey O, 'Family Ties: The Intersection Between Data Protection and Competition in EU Law' (2017) 54 Common Market Law Review 20
Cvrcek D, Kumpost M, Matyas V and Danezis G, 'A Study on the Value of Location Privacy' (2006) Proceedings of Workshop on Privacy in the Electronic Society (WPES 06)
De Mauro A, Greco M and Grimaldi M, 'A Formal Definition of Big Data Based on Its Essential Features' (2016) 65 Library Review 122–135
Dolmans M and Lin W, 'Fairness and Competition Law: A Fairness Paradox' (November 2017) 4 Concurrences Review 1-20
Dworkin R, 'The Model of Rules' (1967) 35 University of Chicago Law Review 14
Easterbrook FH, 'Workable Antitrust Policy' (1986) 84 Michigan Law Review 1696
Easterbrook FH, 'Limits of Antitrust' (1984) 63 Texas Law Review 12
Eberle EJ, 'Dignity and Liberty: Constitutional Visions in Germany and the United States' (2002) 7 Law Faculty Scholarship 87
Eckhoff T, 'Guiding Standards in Legal Reasoning' (1976) 26 Current Legal Problems 205–219
Eckhoff T, 'Retningslinjer og "tumregler"' (1980) Tidskrift for retsvidenskab 146–163
Edlin AS and Harris RG, 'The Role of Switching Costs in Antitrust Analysis: A Comparison of Microsoft and Google' (2013) 15 Yale Journal of Law and Technology 169–213
Ehlermann C-D, 'The Contribution of EC Competition Policy to the Single Market' (1992) 29 CMLR 257
Elhauge E, 'Harvard, Not Chicago: Which Antitrust School Drives Recent U.S. Supreme Court Decisions?' (2007) 3 Competition Policy International 59
Elhauge E, 'Tying, Bundled Discounts, and the Death of the Single Monopoly Profit Theory' (2009) 123 Harvard Law Review 435–439
Eriksson LD, 'Värderingar, fakta och juridik' (1969) 5 Tidskrift utgiven av Juridiska Föreningen i Finland 414–430
Evans DS, 'The Online Advertising Industry: Economics, Evolution and Privacy' (April 2009) Journal of Economic Perspectives 37
Evans DS, 'The Antitrust Economics of Free' (Spring 2011) Competition Policy International 22
Evans DS and Schmalensee R, 'The Industrial Organization of Markets with Two-Sided Platforms' (2007) 3 Competition Policy International 151
Ezrachi A, 'Sponge' (2017) 5 Journal of Antitrust Enforcement 3
Ezrachi A and Gilo D, 'Are Excessive Prices Really Self-Correcting?' (2008) 5 Journal of Competition Law and Economics 249–268
Ezrachi A and Stucke ME, 'The Curious Case of Competition and Quality' (2015) 3 Journal of Antitrust Enforcement 227–257
Ezrachi A and Stucke ME, 'The Fight over Antitrust's Soul' (2017) 9 Journal of European Competition Law & Practice
Ezrachi A and Stucke ME, 'Emerging Antitrust Threats and Enforcement Actions in the Online World' (2017) 13 Competition Law International
Farrell J, 'Can Privacy Be Just Another Good?' (2012) 10 Journal on Telecommunications and High Technology Law 251

Farrell J and Katz ML, 'The Economics of Welfare Standards in Antitrust' (2006) 2 Competition Policy International 3

First H and Waller SW, 'Antitrust's Democracy Deficit' (2012) 81 Fordham Law Review 2543, 2544

Fox EM, 'The Modernization of Antitrust: A New Equilibrium' (1981) 66 Cornell Law Review 1153–54

Fox EM, 'Consumer Beware Chicago (1986) 84 Michigan Law Review 1714

Fox EM, 'The Politics of Law and Economics in Judicial Decision Making: Antitrust as a Window' (1986) 61 New York University Law Review 554, 585–588

Fox EM, 'The Battle for the Soul of Antitrust' (1987) 75 California Law Review 918

Fried C, 'Privacy' (1968) 77 Yale Law Journal 474, 477

Gal M, 'Monopoly Pricing as an Antitrust Offense in the US and the EC: Two Systems of Belief about Monopoly?' (2004) 49 Antitrust Bulletin 343–384

Gal MS and Rubinfeld DL, 'The Hidden Costs of Free Goods: Implications for Antitrust Enforcement' (2016) 80 Antitrust Law Journal 401

Geradin D and Kuschewsky M, 'Competition Law and Personal Data: Preliminary Thoughts on a Complex Issue' (2013) 2 Concurrences

Gerber DJ, 'Constitutionalizing the Economy: German Neo-Liberalism, Competition Law and the "New" Europe' (1994) 42 American Journal of Comparative Law 25

Gormley K, 'Long Live the Constitution (Subject to Change)' (2002) Pittsburgh Post-Gazette

Graef I, 'Market Definition and Market Power in Data: The Case of Online Platforms' (2015) 38 World Competition 473

Graef I, Clifford D and Valcke P, 'Fairness and Enforcement: Bridging Competition, Data Protection, and Consumer Law' (2018) 8 International Data Privacy Law 210

Grant J and Neven DJ, 'The Attempted Merger Between General Electric and Honeywell: A Case Study Of Transatlantic Conflict' (2005) 1 Journal of Competition Law and Economics 2

Guniganti P and Knox R, 'A Populist Now: What Can Antitrust Do for Inequality?' (2 March 2017) Global Competition Review

Harbour PJ and Koslov TI, 'Section 2 in a Web 2.0 World: An Expanded Vision of Relevant Product Markets' (2010) 76 Antitrust Law Journal 769

Haucapv J, 'Data Protection and Antitrust: New Types of Abuse Cases? An Economist's View in Light of the German Facebook Decision' (25 February 2019) Competition Policy International

Hladjk J, Werner P and Stoican L, 'The German Facebook Case – Towards an Increasing Symbiosis Between Competition and Data Protection Laws?' Competition Policy International (25 February 2019)

Holmes Jr, OW, 'The Path of the Law' (1897) 10 Harvard Law Review 457

Holmström M, Padilla J, Stitzing R and Sääskilahti P, 'Killer acquisitions? The Debate on Merger Control for Digital Markets' (2018) Finnish Competition Law Yearbook 35–54

Hui K-L, Teo H-H and Lee S-Y, 'The Value of Privacy Assurance: An Exploratory Field Experiment' (2007) 31 MIS Quarterly 19–33

Jareborg N, 'Regler og riktlinjer' (1979) Tidskrift for retsvidenskab 386–410

Kahn J, 'Privacy as a Legal Principle of Identity Maintenance' (2003) 33 Seton Hall Law Review 371

Kahneman D, Krueger A, Schkade D, Schwarz N and Stone A, 'Would You Be Happier If You Were Richer? A Focusing Illusion' (2006) 312 Science 1908, 1909

Kalimo H and Majcher K, 'The Concept of Fairness: Linking EU Competition and Data Protection Law in the Digital Marketplace' (2017) 42 EL Rev 210

Kaplow L and Shavell S, 'Fairness Versus Welfare' (2001) 114 Harvard Law Review 961, 969–970

Khan L, 'Amazon's Antitrust Paradox' (2017) 126 Yale Law Journal 564–907

Khan L, 'The New Brandeis Movement: America's Antimonopoly Debate' (2018) 9 Journal of European Competition Law & Practice 131–132

Khan L, 'The Ideological Roots of America's Market Power Problem' (2018) 127 Yale Law Journal 960

Kimmel L and Kestenbaum J, 'What's up with WhatsApp? A Transatlantic View on Privacy and Merger Enforcement in Digital Markets' (2014) Antitrust 48

Kirkwood JB, 'The Essence of Antitrust: Protecting Consumers and Small Suppliers from Anticompetitive Conduct' (2013) 81 Fordham Law Review 2425

Kobayashi BH and Muris TJ, 'Chicago, Post-Chicago, and Beyond: Time to Let Go of the 20th Century' (2012) 78 Antitrust Law Journal 147

Koops B-J, 'The Trouble with European Data Protection Law' (2014) 4 International Data Privacy Law 250

Kovacic WE, 'Transatlantic Turbulence: The Boeing-McDonnell Douglas Merger and International Competition Policy' (2001) 68 Antitrust Law Journal 805

Kovacic WE, 'Creating Competition Policy: Betty Bock and the Development of Antitrust Institutions' (1997) 66 Antitrust Law Journal 231, 244–245

Kuoppamäki P, 'Määräävän aseman väärinkäyttö digitaalisilla markkinoilla - mikä muuttuu?' (2018) Lakimies 996–1023

Lamadrid de Pablo A, 'Antitrust and The Political Center' (2013) CPI Antitrust Chronicle 3

Lamadrid de Pablo A, 'Competition Law as Fairness' (2017) 8 Journal of European Competition Law & Practice 147

Lamadrid de Pablo A and Villiers S, 'Big Data, Privacy and Competition Law: Do Competition Authorities Know How to Do It?' (Winter 2017) 1 Competition Policy International Antitrust Chronicle

Lancieri FM, 'Digital Protectionism? Antitrust, Data Protection, and the EU/US Transatlantic Rift' (2019) 7 Journal of Antitrust Enforcement 1–27

Lande RH, 'The Microsoft-Yahoo Merger: Yes, Privacy Is an Antitrust Concern' (2008) 714 FTC: Watch 1

Lindroos-Hovinheimo S, 'Henkilötietojen suoja EU-oikeudessa – yksityisyyttä yhteisön kustannuksella?' (2018) 1 Lakimies 52

Lindroos-Hovinheimo S, 'Legal Subjectivity and the "Right to Be Forgotten": A Rancièrean Analysis of Google' (2016) 27 Law & Critique 289

Lynskey O, 'Aligning Data Protection Rights with Competition Law Remedies? The GDPR Right to Data Portability' (2017) 42 European Law Journal

Lynskey O, 'At the Crossroads of Data Protection and Competition Law: Time to Take Stock' (2018) 8 International Data Privacy Law 179–180

Manne GA and Sperry B, 'The Problems and Perils of Bootstrapping Privacy and Data into an Antitrust Framework' (2015) CPI Antitrust Chronicle

Marx GT and Muschert GW, 'Personal Information, Borders, and the New Surveillance Studies' (2007) 3 Annual Review of Law and Social Science

McGowan L and Wilks S, 'The First Supranational Policy in the European Union: Competition Policy' (1995) 28 European Journal of Political Research 141

McLeod R, 'Novel but a Long Time Coming: The Bundeskartellamt Takes on Facebook' (2016) 7 Journal of European Competition Law & Practice 367

Meese AJ, 'Debunking the Purchaser Welfare Account of Section 2 of the Sherman Act: How Harvard Brought Us a Total Welfare Standard and Why We Should Keep It' (2010) 85 New York University Law Review 659

Meese AJ, 'Reframing the (False?) Choice Between Purchaser Welfare and Total Welfare' (2013) 81 Fordham Law Review 2197

Minda G, 'Antitrust at the Century's End' (1995) 48 SMU Law Rev 1749, 1762

Minkkinen P, 'Oikeus- ja yhteiskuntatieteellinen tutkimus – suuntaus, tarkastelutapa, menetelmä?' (2017) 7–8 Lakimies 908

Monti G, 'The Revision of the Consumer Acquis from a Competition Law Perspective' (2007) 3 European Review of Contract Law 295

Monti M, 'A Competition Policy for Today and Tomorrow' (2000) 23 World Competition 1

Moshell R, '... and Then There Was One: The Outlook for a Self-Regulatory United States Amidst a Global Trend Toward Comprehensive Data Protection' (2005) 37 Texas Technology Law Review 357, 383

Möschel W, 'The Proper Scope of Government Viewed from an Ordoliberal Perspective: The Example of Competition Policy' (2001) 157 Journal of Institutional and Theoretical Economics (JITE) 3, 4

Nehf JP, 'Recognizing the Societal Value in Information Privacy' (2003) 78 Washington Law Review 1, 58

Neven DJ and Röller L-H, 'Consumer Surplus vs. Welfare Standard in a Political Economy Model of Merger Control' (2005) 23 International Journal of Industrial Organization 829

Newman JM, 'Antitrust in Zero-Priced Markets' (2015) 164 University of Pennsylvania Law Review 149

Nissenbaum H, 'Privacy as Contextual Integrity' (2004) Washington Law Review

Ocello E, Sjödin C and Subočs A, 'What's up with Merger Control in the Digital Sector? Lessons from the Facebook/WhatsApp EU Merger Case' (February 2015) 1 Competition Merger Brief 3

Odudu O, 'The Wider Concerns of Competition Law' (2010) 30 OJLS 599–613

Ohlhausen MK and Okuliar AP, 'Competition, Consumer Protection, and the Right (Approach) to Privacy' (2015) 80 Antitrust Law Journal

Orbach BY, 'The Antitrust Consumer Welfare Paradox' (2010) 7 Journal of Competition Law & Economics 133

Orbach BY, 'How Antitrust Lost Its Goal' (2013) 81 Fordham Law Review 2253

Padilla J and Evans DS, 'Designing Antitrust Rules for Assessing Unilateral Practices: A Neo-Chicago Approach' (2005) 72 University of Chicago Law Review 76
Pitofsky R, 'Political Content of Antitrust' (1979) 127 University of Pennsylvania Law Review 1051
Posner RA, 'The Chicago School of Antitrust Analysis' (1979) 127 University of Pennsylvania Law Review 944–947
Podszun R, 'After Facebook: What to Expect from Germany' (February 2019) 10 Journal of European Competition Law & Practice 69–70
Pound R, 'The Scope and Purpose of Sociological Jurisprudence' (1911) 24 Harvard Law Review 591 (1911)
Pritts JI, 'Altered States: State Health Privacy Laws and the Impact of the Federal Health Privacy Rule' (2002) 2 Yale Journal of Health Policy, Law & Ethics 327, 330–48
Radbruch G, 'Statutory Lawlessness and Supra-Statutory Law' (2006) 26 OJLS 7
Rawls J, 'Justice as Fairness: Political Not Metaphysical' (1985) 14 Philosophy and Public Affairs
Reidenberg JR, 'Privacy Wrongs in Search of Remedies' (2003) 54 Hastings Law Journal 877, 887–88
Reyna A, 'The Psychology of Privacy – What Role for BE in Antitrust Enforcement?' presentation at CLaSF and University of Graz workshop, Antitrust at the intersection of law and economics, 19 April 2018
Rieter H and Schmolz M, 'The Ideas of German Ordoliberalism (1938–1945): Pointing the Way to a New Economic Order' (1993) 1 The European Journal of the History of Economic Thought 87–114
Rill JF and Stacy Turner SL, 'Presidents Practicing Antitrust: Where to Draw the Line?' (2014) 79 Antitrust Law Journal 577, 599
Rochet J-C and Tirole J, 'Platform Competition in Two-Sided Markets' (2003) 1 Journal of the European Economic Association 990
Rochet J-C and Tirole J, 'Two-Sided Markets: A Progress Report' (2006) 37 RAND Journal of Economics 645
Rosenfeld M, 'Dworkin and the One Law Principle: A Pluralist Critique' (2004) Revue Internationale de Philosophie
Rubinfeld DL and Gal M, 'Access Barriers to Big Data' (2017) 59 Arizona Law Review 339
Shapiro C, 'Antitrust in a Time of Populism' (2018) 61 International Journal of Industrial Organization 714–748
Shelanski H, 'Information, Innovation, and Competition Policy for the Internet' (2013) 161 University of Pennsylvania Law Review 1663, 1669
Schwartz PM, 'The EU-US Privacy Collision: A Turn to Institutions and Procedures' (2013) 126 Harvard Law Review 1966
Schwarz N, 'Self-Reports: How the Questions Shape the Answers' (1999) 54 American Psychologist
Solove DJ and Hartzog W, 'The FTC and the New Common Law of Privacy' (2014) 114 Columbia Law Review 583–587
Sokol DD, 'Antitrust, Institutions, and Merger Control' (2010) 17 George Mason Law Review 1055

Sokol DD and Ma J, 'Understanding Online Markets and Antitrust Analysis' (2017) 15 Northwestern Journal of Technology and Intellectual Property 43

Srinivasan D, 'The Antitrust Case Against Facebook' (10 September 2018) 16 Berkeley Business Law Journal 39)

Stauber P, 'Facebook's Abuse Investigation in Germany and Some Thoughts on Cooperation Between Antitrust and Data Protection Authorities' (25 February 2019) Competition Policy International

Stiles TJ, '"Robber Barons or Captains of Industry?" The Gilder Lehrman Institute of American History (June 2010) 24 History Now

Stucke ME, 'Reconsidering Antitrust's Goals' (2012) 53 Boston College Law Review 551

Stucke ME, 'Should Competition Policy Promote Happiness?' (2013) 81 Fordham Law Review 2575

Stucke ME, 'Should We Be Concerned About Data-Opolies?' (2018) 2 Georgetown Law Technology Review 275

Stucke ME and Ezrachi A, 'When Competition Fails to Optimize Quality: A Look at Search Engines' (2016) 18 Yale Journal of Law & Technology 70

Swire P, 'Protecting Consumers: Privacy Matters in Antitrust Analysis' Center for American Progress (19 October 2007)

Strahilevitz L, 'Towards a Positive Theory of Privacy Law' (2013) 113 Harvard Law Review 2036

Todino M and Schou ER, 'What Agenda for the Second Term of Commissioner Vestager?' (October 2019) Competition Policy International

Tucker DS, 'The Proper Role of Privacy in Merger Review' (2015) 2 Competition Policy International Antitrust Chronicle

Tucker DS and Wellford HB, 'Big Mistakes Regarding Big Data' (December 2014) Antitrust Source 3

Vickers J, 'Concepts of Competition' (1995) 47 Oxford Economic Papers 1

Voorhees Jr T, 'The Political Hand in American Antitrust – Invisible, Inspirational or Imaginary?' (2014) 79 Antitrust Law Journal

Waked DL, 'Antitrust Goals in Developing Countries: Policy Alternatives and Normative Choices' (2014) 38 Seattle University Law Review 945

Warma E and Nieminen J, 'Tietosuoja ja kilpailuoikeus – määräävässä markkina-asemassa olevan yrityksen toimitusvelvollisuudesta ja tietosuojalainsäädännöstä' (2016) 4 Defensor Legis 569

Wasastjerna M, 'EU Competition Policy for the Digital Economy' (2019) 24 Columbia Journal of European Law

Wasastjerna M, 'The Role of Data and Digital Privacy in Merger Review' (2019) 14 European Competition Journal 417–444

Wasastjerna M, 'Competition Law, Big Data and Privacy' (2017) 39 International In-House Counsel Journal

Wasastjerna M, 'European Union Competition Policy for the 21st Century Digital Economy' (2019) 24 Columbia Journal of European Law

Wasastjerna M, 'The Role of Data and Digital Privacy in Merger Review' (2019) 14 European Competition Journal 417–444

Wasastjerna M, 'The Implications of Big Data and Privacy on Competition Analysis in Merger Control and the Controversial Competition-Data Protection Interface' (2019) 30 European Business Law Review 337–366

Wasastjerna M, 'Blurred Lines: The German Facebook Case and the Interlink Between Competition Law and Data Protection' (2018) Finnish Competition Law Yearbook 23–34

Weiss LW, 'The Structure-Conduct-Performance Paradigm and Antitrust' (1979) 127 University of Pennsylvania Law Review 1105–1106

Whitman JQ, 'Consumerism Versus Producerism: A Study in Comparative Law' (2007) 117 Yale Law Journal 340, 361

Whitman JQ, 'The Two Western Cultures of Privacy: Dignity Versus Liberty' (2004) 113 Yale Law Journal 1151–1221

Wils WPJ, 'The Judgment of the EU General Court in Intel and the So-Called 'More Economic Approach' to Abuse of Dominance' (2014) 37 World Competition: Law and Economics Review 405–434

Winerman M, 'The Origins of the FTC: Concentration, Cooperation, Control, and Competition' (2003) 71 Antitrust Law Journal 1

Witt AC, 'Public Policy Goals under EU Competition Law – Now Is the Time to Set the House in Order' (2012) 8 European Competition Journal 443

Wu T, 'Blind Spot: The Attention Economy and the Law' (2018) 82 Antitrust Law Journal

Wu T, 'After Consumer Welfare, Now What? The "Protection of Competition" Standard in Practice' (April 2018) Competition Policy International Antitrust Chronicle

Zimmer D, 'Digital Markets: New Rule for Competition Law' (2015) 6 Journal of European Competition Law & Practice (Editorial)

Zingales N, 'Apple/Shazam: Data Is Power, But Not a Problem Here' (December 2018) Competition Policy International

Essays, Research and Working Papers

Alexy R, 'Rechtsregeln und Rechtsprinzipien' (1985) Archiv für Rechts- un Sozialphilosophie, Beiheft 25

Autor D, 'The Fall of the Labor Share and the Rise of Superstar Firms' (May 2017) NBER Working Paper No 23396

Botta M and Wiedemann K, 'EU Competition Law Enforcement Vis-à-Vis Exploitative Conduct in the Data Economy – Exploring the Terra Incognita' (2018) Max Planck Institute for Innovation and Competition Research Paper

Broulík J, 'Economics in Antitrust Enforcement and the Private Benefit of Scholarly Commentators' (13 January 2017) TILEC Discussion Paper No 2017-001

Caffarra C and Valletti T, 'Google/Fitbit Review: Privacy IS a Competition Issue' CEPR Policy Portal (4 March 2020)

Campaign for Accountability, 'Google Academics Inc Report' (11 July 2017) Google Transparency Project

Campbell PS, 'Democracy v. Concentrated Wealth – In Search of a Louis D. Brandeis Quote' (2013) University of Louisville School of Law Legal Studies Research Paper Series No. 2014

Costa-Cabral F and Lynskey O, 'The Internal and External Constraints of Data Protection on Competition Law in the EU' (2015) LSE Law, Society and Economy Working Papers

Drexl J, 'Real Knowledge Is to Know the Extent of One's Own Ignorance: On the Consumer Harm Approach in Innovation-Related Competition Cases' (2009) Max Planck Institute for Intellectual Property, Competition & Tax Law Research Paper No 09-15

Economides N and Lianos I, 'Restrictions on Privacy and Exploitation in the Digital Economy: A Competition Law Perspective' (2019) CLES Research Paper Series 5/2019

Evans DS, 'Multi-sided Platforms, Dynamic Competition, and the Assessment of Market Power for Internet-Based Firms' (2016) University of Chicago Coase-Sandor Institute for Law & Economics Research Paper No 753

Ezrachi A, 'EU Competition Law Goals and the Digital Economy' (6 June 2018) Working paper

Fox EM, 'Competition and Democracy' (4 April 2018) OECD Global Forum on Competition

Graef I et al., 'How Google and Others Upset Competition Analysis: Disruptive Innovation And European Competition Law' 25th European Regional Conference of the International Telecommunications Society (Brussels, 22–25 June 2014)

Grunes AP and Stucke M, 'No Mistake about It: The Important Role of Antitrust in the Era of Big Data' (2015) University of Tennessee Legal Studies Research Paper No 269

Grunes AP and Stucke M, 'Debunking the Myths Over Big Data and Antitrust' (2015) University of Tennessee Legal Studies Research Paper No 276

Lianos I, 'The Poverty of Competition Law' (2018) 2 CLES Research Paper Series

Lynskey O, 'Regulating "Platform Power"' (2017) LSE Law, Society and Economy Working Papers 1

Lynskey O, 'Non-price Effects of Mergers' (2018) Background note for 129th OECD Competition committee meeting 6-8 June 2018

Määttä K, 'Kilpailupolitiikan ja kuluttajapolitiikan yhtymäkohdat: onko niitä? Kilpailu- ja Kuluttajaviraston selvityksiä 4/2013' (Kopioniini Oy, Helsinki 2013)

Petit N and Neyrinck N, 'Behavioral Economics and Abuse of Dominance: A Proposed Alternative Reading of the Article 102 TFEU Case-Law' (2010) 2 The Global Competition Law Centre (GCLC) Working Papers Series

Ritter C, 'Bibliography of Materials Relevant to the Interaction of Competition Policy, Big Data and Personal Data' (29 September 2016)

Spiekerman S, Grossklags K and Berendt B, 'E-Privacy in 2nd Generation E-Commerce' (2002) ACM Conference on Electronic Commerce (EC'01) 38–47

Stucke ME, 'The Implications of Behavioral Antitrust' (2012) 192 University of Tennessee Legal Studies Research Paper

Vanberg VJ, 'The Freiburg School: Walter Eucken and Ordoliberalism' (2004) Freiburg Discussion Papers on Constitutional Economics No 04/11

Wathieu L and Friedman A, 'An Empirical Approach to Understanding Privacy Valuation' (2005) Proceedings of the Fourth Workshop on the Economics of Information Security (WEIS 05)

Institutional Papers, Opinions and Reports

International

OECD, 'Big Data: Bringing Competition Policy to the Digital Era' (29-30 November 2016)

OECD, 'Big Data: Bringing Competition Policy to the Digital Era, Executive Summary' (29-30 November 2016) 3–4

OECD, 'Data-Driven Innovation for Growth and Well-Being: Interim Synbook Report' (October 2014)

OECD, 'Exploring the Economics of Personal Data: A Survey of Methodologies for Measuring Monetary Value' (2013) OECD Digital Economy Paper No 220

OECD, 'Supporting Investment in Knowledge Capital, Growth and Innovation' (2013)

OECD, 'The Role and Measurement of Quality in Competition Analysis' (28 October 2013)

OECD, Roundtable on Economics for Consumer Policy (2007) Summary Report

OECD, 'Policy Brief: What Is Competition on the Merits?' 1 (2006)

World Economic Forum, 'Big Data, Big Impact: New Possibilities for International Development' (2012)

World Economic Forum, 'Personal Data: The Emergence of a New Asset Class' (January 2011)

EU

Crémer J, de Montjoye Y-A and Schweitzer H, 'Competition Policy for the Digital Era' (Report ordered by the European Commission, 2019)

Digital Clearinghouse, Statement from first meeting (29 May 2017)

Digital Clearinghouse, Statement from second meeting (27 November 2017)

Digital Clearinghouse, Statement from third meeting (21 June 2018)

EDPS, 'Privacy and competitiveness in the age of big data: The interplay between data protection, competition law and consumer protection in the digital economy' (Preliminary Opinion, March 2014)

EDPS, 'Opinion 8/2016 on coherent enforcement of fundamental rights in the age of big data' (23 September 2016)

EDPS 'Opinion on the Communication from the Commission to the European Parliament and the Council on the follow-up of the Work Programme for better implementation of the Data Protection Directive' [2007] C 255/01

EDPS, 'Towards a New Digital Ethics: Data, Dignity and Technology' (11 September 2015) Opinion 4/2015

European Commission, 'First Report on Competition Policy' (April 1972)

European Commission, 'Proposal for a regulation on promoting fairness and transparency for business users of online intermediation services' (26 April 2018)

European Commission, 'XXIInd Report on Competition Policy' (1992)

European Commission, 'Xth Report on Competition Policy' (2010)

European Commission, 'Report on Competition Policy 2016' (2016)

European Commission Directorate General for Communications Networks, Content & Technology, 'Flash Eurobarometer 443 – ePrivacy' (2017)

European Commission, White Paper on modernization of the rules implementing Articles 85 and 86 of the EC Treaty, Commission Programme No 99/027 (28 April 1999)

European Commission, White Paper on the future of Europe (January 2017)

European Commission Communication, 'Shaping Europe's digital future' COM(2020)67 (19 February 2020)

European Commission, Staff working document accompanying the Report on Competition Policy 2016, SWD (2017)

European Parliament, 'Challenges for Competition Policy in a Digitalized Economy' Study for the ECON Committee, Directorate-General for Internal Policies, Economic and Monetary Affairs (2015)

European Parliament, 'Resolution of 27 November 2014 on supporting consumer rights in the digital single market' (2014/29738RSP)

President Jean-Claude Juncker, 'European Commission, Exchanging and Protecting Personal Data in a Globalized World' COM(2017)

European Commission, 'Shaping competition policy in the era of digitisation' Call for contributions (12 July 2018)

US

FTC, 'Privacy Online: Fair Information Practices in the Electronic Marketplace – A Report to Congress (May 2000) https://www.ftc.gov/reports/privacy-online-fair-information-practices-electronic-marketplace-federal-trade-commission, accessed 1 August 2019

Letter from Jessica Rich, Director, Bureau of Consumer Protection, FTC, to Erin Egan, Chief Privacy Officer, Facebook, Inc, and Anne Hoge, General Counsel, WhatsApp Inc (20 April 2014)

Stigler Center for the Study of the Economy and the State, The University of Chicago Booth School of Business, Report by the Committee for the Study of Digital Platforms, Market Structure and Antitrust Subcommittee (15 May 2019)

National

Australian Competition and Consumer Commission, Digital Platforms Inquiry Final Report (26 July 2019) https://www.accc.gov.au/publications/digital-platforms-inquiry-final-report, accessed 1 August 2019

Autorité de la Concurrence, Avis n° 18-A-03 portant sur l'exploitation des données dans le secteur de la publicité sur interne (6 March 2018) http://www.mlex.com/

ITCMedia/DetailView.aspx?ppo = 7&cid = 968633&siteid = 145&rdir = 1, accessed 1 August 2019

Autorité de la Concurrence and Bundeskartellamt, Competition Law and Data (10 May 2016)

BEUC letter to Competition Commissioner Margrethe Vestager, 'A sector inquiry into online advertising practices '(13 March 2018) http://www.mlex.com/ITCMedia/DetailView.aspx?ppo = 7&cid = 971272&siteid = 145&rdir = 1, accessed 1 August 2019

Bundeskartellamt, Background information on the Facebook proceeding (19 December 2017)

Bundeskartellamt, Case summary: Facebook, Exploitative business terms pursuant to Section 19(1) GWB for inadequate data processing (15 February 2019)

Bundeskartellamt, Competition and Consumer Protection in the Digital Economy: Online advertising (February 2018) http://www.bundeskartellamt.de/SharedDocs/Publikation/EN/Schriftenreihe_Digitales_III.pdf?__blob = publicationFile&v = 5, accessed 1 August 2019

Dutch Consumer and Market Authority, 'Big platforms, big problems?' (September 2016) https://www.acm.nl/sites/default/files/old_publication/publicaties/16333_toezicht-online-platforms.pdf, accessed 1 August 2019

Dutch Consumer and Market Authority, ACM analysis of the sustainability arrangements concerning the Chicken of Tomorrow (2015) ACM/DM/2014/206028

Finnish Competition and Consumer Authority (FCCA), Questions related to competition and consumer protection in data economy (February 2019)

Furman J, Coyle D, Fletcher A, McAuley D and Marsden P, Unlocking digital competition, Report of the Digital Competition Expert Panel (March 2019)

German Federal Ministry for Economic Affairs and Energy, White Paper on Digital Platforms of the Economic Affairs Ministry (20 March 2017)

HM Treasury, The economic value of data: discussion paper (August 2018)

McKinsey Global Institute, Big Data: The Next Frontier for Innovation, Competition, and Productivity (June 2011)

McKinsey & Company, Digital globalization: The new era of global flows, McKinsey Global Institute Report (March 2016)

UK Competition and Markets Authority, The Commercial Use of Consumer Data: Report on the CMA's Call for Information (June 2015)

Encyclopaedias

Oxford English Dictionary

Merriam-Webster Collegiate Dictionary

Speeches and Presentations

Almunia J, 'Competition and Consumers: The Future of EU Competition Policy' European Competition Day (Madrid, 12 May 2010)

Almunia J, 'Competition – What's in It for Consumers?' (Poznan, 24 November 2011)

Burnside AJ, 'Antitrust, Privacy & Big Data – Setting the Scene' Address at Concurrences and Cadwalader, Wickersham & Taft LLP Antitrust, Privacy & Big Data seminar (3 February 2015)

Buttarelli G, 'Privacy and Competition: Big Issues for Big Data' IAPP Global Privacy Summit (Washington, DC, 27–28 March 2018)

Hayek FA, 'The Pretence of Knowledge' accepting the Nobel Prize for Economics (11 December 1974)

Hesse R, 'And Never the Twain Shall Meet? Connecting Popular and Professional Visions for Antitrust Enforcement' Presentation at the Global Antitrust Enforcement Symposium (Washington, DC, 20 September 2016)

Delrahim M, 'Assistant Attorney General for Antitrust, The 40th Anniversary of Robert Bork's The Antitrust Paradox' (Washington DC, 22 June 2018) Remarks at the College of Europe (Brussels, 21 February 2018)

Delrahim M, 'Good Times, Bad Times, Trust Will Take Us Far: Competition Enforcement and the Relationship Between Washington and Brussels' Remarks at the College of Europe (Brussels, 21 February 2018)

Delrahim M, 'Digital Platforms and Concentration' Stigler Center for Study of Economy and the State at the University of Chicago Booth School of Business (Chicago, 19–20 April 2018)

Delrahim M, 'Assistant Attorney General for Antitrust, Antitrust and the Digital Economy: New Challenges for International Cooperation?' Bocconi University Milan, reported by MLex Market Insight (25 May 2018)

Kroes N, 'European Competition Policy – Delivering Better Markets and Better Choices' European Consumer and Competition Day (London, 15 September 2005)

Laitenberger J, 'EU Competition Law in Innovation and Digital Markets: Fairness and the Consumer Welfare Perspective' MLex/Hogan Lovells event EU Competition Law Enforcement 2.0 (Brussels, 10 October 2017)

Ohlhausen M, 'Antitrust Enforcement in the Digital Age' Georgetown University (Washington, DC, 12 September 2017)

Mario M, 'The Future for Competition Policy in the European Union', Merchant Taylor's Hall (London, 9 July 2001)

Mario M, 'Festveranstaltung Präsidentenwechsel Bundeskartellamt' (Bonn, 13 January 2000)

Mundt A, 'Innovation Economics for Antitrust Lawyers' Concurrences Review and King's College (London, 3 February 2017)

Mundt A, 'Policy and Enforcement Choices' Online Markets and Offline Welfare Effects, Oxford Center for Competition Law and Policy Conference (22 May 2017)

Petit N, 'Should the Tech Giants Be Broken Up?' Presentation University of South Australia (Adelaide 16 February 2018)

Ramirez E, 'Privacy and Competition: Big Issues for Big Data' IAPP Global Privacy Summit (Washington, DC, 27–28 March 2018)

Reding V, 'The EU Data Protection Reform 2012: Making Europe the Standard Setter for Modern Data Protection Rules in the Digital Age' Innovation Conference Digital, Life, Design (Munich, 22 January 2012) SPEECH/12/26

Reyna A, 'The Psychology of Privacy – What Role for BE in Antitrust Enforcement?' presentation at XXXth CLaSF Workshop on Antitrust at the Intersection of Law and Economics, Competition Law Scholars Forum (CLaSF) and the Graz Institute of Corporate and International Commercial Law (Graz 19 April 2018)

Stones RR, 'The Chicago School of Antitrust and the "More Economic Approach" to EU Competition Law: A Mistaken Inspiration', XXXth CLaSF Workshop on Antitrust at the Intersection of Law and Economics, Competition Law Scholars Forum (CLaSF) and the Graz Institute of Corporate and International Commercial Law (Graz 19 April 2018)

Vestager M, 'The Values of Competition Policy' Speech at CEPS Corporate Breakfast (Brussels, 13 October 2015)

Vestager M, 'Competition in a Big Data World', DLD 16 (Munich, 17 January 2016) https://ec.europa.eu/commission/commissioners/2014-2019/vestager/announcements/competition-big-data-world_en, accessed 1 August 2019

Vestager M, 'Working Together to Support Fairer Competition Worldwide' UCL Jevons Institute Conference (London, 3 June 2016)

Vestager M, 'Making Data Work for Us', Data Ethics event on Data as Power (Copenhagen, 9 September 2016)

Vestager M, 'Competition for a Fairer Society' Speech at 10th Annual Global Antitrust Enforcement Symposium, Georgetown University (20 September 2016)

Vestager M, 'Big Data and Competition' EDPS-BEUC Conference on Big Data (Brussels, 29 September 2016) https://ec.europa.eu/commission/commissioners/2014-2019/vestager/announcements/big-data-and-competition_en, accessed 1 August 2019

Vestager M, 'Luther and the Modern World' Speech at 9th Luther Conference and the award ceremony of the Luther Rose 2016 (Copenhagen, 14 November 2016)

Vestager M, 'Protecting Consumers from Exploitation' Chilling Competition Conference (Brussels, 21 November 2016)

Vestager M, 'How Competition Can Build Trust in Our Societies' TED Talk (New York, 20 September 2017)

Vestager M, 'Competition in Changing Times' FIW Symposium (Innsbruck, 16 February 2018)

Vestager M, 'The Importance of Being Open – And Fair' European Conference (Harvard University, 2 March 2018)

Vestager M, 'Competition and a Fair Deal for Consumers Online' Netherlands Authority for Consumers and Markets Fifth Anniversary Conference (The Hague, 26 April 2018)

Vestager M, 'Defining Markets in a New Age' Chilling Competition Conference (Brussels, 9 December 2019)

Witt AC, 'The European Court of Justice and the More Economic Approach – Is the Tide Turning?' XXXth CLaSF Workshop on Antitrust at the Intersection of Law and Economics, Competition Law Scholars Forum (CLaSF) and the Graz Institute of Corporate and International Commercial Law (Graz 19 April 2018)

Wasastjerna M, 'Antitrust's Identity Crisis – Time for Less Economics?' presentation at XXXth CLaSF Workshop on Antitrust at the Intersection of Law and Economics,

Competition Law Scholars Forum (CLaSF) and the Graz Institute of Corporate and International Commercial Law (Graz 19 April 2018)

President Woodrow Wilson, Address to a Joint Session of Congress on Trusts and Monopolies (20 January 1914) http://www.presidency.ucsb.edu/ws/index.php?pid=65374, accessed 1 August 2019

Websites

European Commission, 'Shaping the Digital Single Market' https://ec.europa.eu/digital-single-market/en/policies/shaping-digital-single-market, accessed 1 August 2019

US FTC Hearings on Competition and Consumer Protection in the 21st Century, Hearings on Competition & Consumer Protection, Public comment topics and process https://www.ftc.gov/policy/advocacy/public-comment-topics-process#1, accessed 1 August 2019

www.agcm.it (the *Autorità Garante della Concorrenza e il Mercato)* accessed 1 August 2019

www.acm.nl/sites/default/files/old_publication/publicaties/16333_toezicht-online-platforms.pdf (the Dutch Authority for Consumers and Markets article) accessed 1 August 2019

Blogs and Online Journals

Adams T, Interview: Margrethe Vestager: 'We Are Doing This Because People Are Angry' (17 September 2017) https://www.theguardian.com/world/2017/sep/17/margrethe-vestager-people-feel-angry-about-tax-avoidance-european-competition-commissioner, accessed 1 August 2019

Buttarelli G, 'It's Not the End of the World as We Know It' (EDPS blog, 7 December 2017) https://edps.europa.eu/press-publications/press-news/blog/it%E2%80%99s-not-end-world-we-know-it_en, accessed 1 August 2019

Buttarelli G, 'Big Step Towards Coherent Enforcement in the Digital Economy' (EDPS blog, 7 February 2019) https://edps.europa.eu/press-publications/press-news/blog/big-step-towards-coherent-enforcement-digital-economy_fr, accessed 1 August 2019

Connor C, 'Include Environmental Costs in Competition Analysis, Dolmans Urges' GCR (9 December 2019)

Crofts L, 'New EU Data Rules to Help Competition, unlock Big Data Potential, Vestager says' MLex ITC & Media (13 April 2018)

Crofts L, 'New Thinking on Tech Titans Needed, Not Break-Up, IMF's Lagarde Says' MLex Market Insight (19 April 2018)

Crofts L, Joshua Sisco and Leah Nylen, 'Data Acquisition Doesn't Equate to Price Hikes, FTC's Hoffman Says' MLex market insight (12 April 2018)

Dayen D, 'This Budding Movement Wants to Smash Monopolies' The Nation (4 April 2017) https://www.thenation.com/article/this-budding-movement-wants-to-smash-monopolies/ accessed 19 April 2020

Dolmans M, 'Sustainable Competition Policy' Chilling Competition Conference (Brussels, 11 December 2019)

Facebook, Why We Disagree with the Bundeskartellamt (7 February 2019) https://newsroom.fb.com/news/2019/02/bundeskartellamt-order/, accessed 1 August 2019

Facebook, WhatsApp blog (19 February 2014) https://blog.whatsapp.com/499/Facebook, accessed 1 August 2019

Foster D, 'Cry Me a River. The Concept of Fairness in Competition Law' (10 May 2018) https://www.linkedin.com/pulse/cry-me-river-concept-fairness-competition-law-david-foster/, accessed 1 August 2019

Gladicheva V, 'EU Privacy Rules Key to Competition Analyses, Head of France's Antitrust Watchdog Says' (4 May 2018) GCR Live: 7th Annual Telecoms, Media & Technology)

Graef I and Van Alsenoy B, 'Data Protection Through the Lens of Competition Law: Will Germany Lead the Way?' (LSE Media Policy Project blog, 23 March 2016) http://blogs.lse.ac.uk/mediapolicyproject/2016/03/23/data-protection-through-the-lens-of-competition-law-will-germany-lead-the-way/, accessed 1 August 2019

Heinz S, 'Bundeskartellamt Sends Preliminary Assessment to Facebook' (Kluwer Competition Law Blog, 9 January 2018) http://competitionlawblog.kluwercompetitionlaw.com/2018/01/09/bundeskartellamt-sends-preliminary-assessment-facebook/, accessed 1 August 2019

Heinz S, 'Bundeskartellamt Launches Sector Inquiry into Online Advertising' (Kluwer Competition Law Blog, 9 March 2018) http://competitionlawblog.kluwercompetitionlaw.com/2018/03/09/bundeskartellamt-launches-sector-inquiry-online-advertising/, accessed 1 August 2019

Hickman T, White&Case, 'Everything Your Business Should Know about the Impending GDPR' (26 February 2018) https://www.whitecase.com/publications/article/everything-your-business-should-know-about-impending-gdpr?_lrsc=3a5faea8-5436-4765-999e-a2678e8d94b6&trk=&utm_source=LinkedInElevate&utm_source=LinkedIn&utm_content=LinkedInElevate, accessed 1 August 2019

Johnson F, 'Fair Play: The Facebook Conundrum' Bloomberg Blog (15 April 2018) https://www.bna.com/fair-play-facebook-b57982091103/, accessed 1 August 2019

Kahn J, Bodoni S and Nicola S, 'It'll Cost Billions for Companies to Comply with Europe's New Data Law' Bloomberg Businessweek (22 March 2018) https://www.bloomberg.com/news/articles/2018-03-22/it-ll-cost-billions-for-companies-to-comply-with-europe-s-new-data-law, accessed 1 August 2019

Kucharczyk J, 'The German FCO's Facebook Case: Blurring the Line Between Competition and Data Protection Enforcement the Disruptive Competition Project' (Disruptive Competition Project, 8 February 2019) http://www.project-disco.org/european-union/020819-german-fcos-facebook-case-competition-and-data-protection-enforcement/#.XQc6AfZuJPZ, accessed 1 August 2019

Lamadrid de Pablo A, 'Discretionalists vs Legalists: The True Divide in the Competition Law Community?' (Chilling Competition blog, 28 May 2018) https://

chillingcompetition.com/2018/05/28/discretionalists-vs-legalists-the-true-divide-in-the-competition-law-community/#comment-114483, accessed 1 August 2019

Lamadrid de Pablo A, 'Facebook, Privacy and Article 102 – A First Comment on the Bundeskartellamt's Investigation' (Chilling Competition blog, 2 March 2016) https://chillingcompetition.com/2016/03/02/facebook-privacy-and-article-102-a-first-comment-on-the-bundeskartellamts-investigation/, accessed 1 August 2019

Lomas N, 'Google Gobbling Fitbit Is a Major Privacy Risk, Warns EU Data Protection Advisor' Techcrunch (20 February 2020) https://techcrunch.com/2020/02/20/google-gobbling-fitbit-is-a-major-privacy-risk-warns-eu-data-protection-advisor/, accessed 19 April 2020

MLex Market Insight, 'Former Obama Antitrust Officials Urge Caution on Factoring Jobs into Merger Reviews' (17 March 2017)

MLex Market Insight, 'Canada's Competition Enforcers Pondering Big Data, Including in Mergers' (30 March 2017)

MLex Market Insight, 'Japanese Antitrust Chief Says Facebook Data-Collection Competition Issues on JFTC's Radar' (2 April 2018)

MLex Market Insight, 'Data Acquisition Doesn't Equate to Price Hikes' Report from the 66th ABA Antitrust Law Spring Meeting (Washington DC, 11–13 April 2018) https://mlexmarketinsight.com/db_images/special-reports-pdf/MLex-ABA-Antitrust-2018.pdf?utm_source = MLex + Email + Updates&utm_campaign = ebbc3cc2f8-Email + Campaign-2018-ABAReport-EMEA_Sub&utm_medium = email&utm_term = 0_f30f64c91d-ebbc3cc2f8-63791953, accessed 1 August 2019

Mayer-Schönberger V and Ramge T, 'A Big Choice for Big Tech – Share Data or Suffer the Consequences' Foreign Affairs comment (September / October 2018) https://www.foreignaffairs.com/articles/world/2018-08-13/big-choice-big-tech, accessed 1 August 2019

Menegus B, 'Amazon Japan Raided by Antitrust Agency' Gizmodo (15 March 2018) https://gizmodo.com/amazon-raided-in-japan-by-antitrust-agency-1823794268#, accessed 1 August 2019

Murray G, 'Antitrust and Sustainability: Globally Warming up to Be a Hot Topic?' Kluwer Competition Law Blog (October 18, 2019) http://competitionlawblog.kluwercompetitionlaw.com/2019/10/18/antitrust-and-sustainability-globally-warming-up-to-be-a-hot-topic/, accessed 19 April 2020

Newman M, 'Facebook, Amazon Acquisitions Shouldn't Change Antitrust policy, US official says' MLex ITC & Media (27 October 2017)

Newman M, 'Facebook's German Antitrust Probe Hinges on Market Power of Network Effects' MLex Market Insight (8 January 2018)

Nylen L, 'DOJ's Delrahim Says Antitrust Enforcers Shouldn't Intervene in Consumer Privacy Markets Absent Barriers to Entry' MLex Market Insight (19 April 2018)

Nylen L, 'US Hands-Off Approach Has Helped Google, Uber, Others Thrive, DOJ's Delrahim Says' Mlex ITC & Media (22 June 2018)

Petit N, 'A Quick and Dirty Note on FB, Competition and Individualism' Symphony of disruption (Symphony of Disruption blog, 29 March 2018) https://symphonyofdisruption.org/author/ieje/, accessed 1 August 2019

Petit N, 'Changing the Conversation Movement' (Symphony of Disruption blog, 13 February 2018) https://symphonyofdisruption.org/2018/02/13/changing-the-conversation/, accessed 1 August 2019

Petit N, 'Rule-Based Antitrust & the #DeleteConsumerWelfare Movement' (Symphony of Disruption blog, 5 April 2018) https://symphonyofdisruption.org/2018/04/05/rule-based-antitrust-the-deleteconsumerwelfare-movement/, accessed 1 August 2019

Quinn G, 'Has Big Tech Finally Become Too Big for the FTC to Ignore?' IPWatchdog (21 June 2018) http://www.ipwatchdog.com/2018/06/21/big-tech-finally-become-big-ftc/id=98598/, accessed 1 August 2019

Rating Legis blog, 'Merry Christmas, WhatsApp Users' (23 December 2016) http://ratinglegis.eu/en/eu-commission-looks-at-facebook-whatsapp-deal-again/, accessed 1 August 2019

Ritz C, 'Germany Suggests Ramping up Regulation of Digital Platforms by Establishing a "Digital Agency" with a Robust Antitrust Mandate' (Kluwer Competition Law Blog, 6 April 2017) http://competitionlawblog.kluwercompetitionlaw.com/2017/04/06/germany-suggests-ramping-regulation-digital-platforms-establishing-digital-agency-robust-antitrust-mandate/, accessed 1 August 2019

Solomon S, 'Tech Giants Gobble Start-Ups in an Antitrust Blind Spot' New York Times (16 August 2016), https://www.nytimes.com/2016/08/17/business/dealbook/expect-little-antitrust-challenge-to-walmarts-bid-for-jet-com.html, accessed 19 April 2020

Tene O, 'Privacy Is the New Antitrust' IAPP Privacy Perspectives (15 January 2015) https://iapp.org/news/a/privacy-is-the-new-antitrust-introducing-the-ftc-casebook/, accessed 1 August 2019

Warren E, 'Here's How We Can Break up Big Tech' Medium (8 March 2019) https://medium.com/@teamwarren/heres-how-we-can-break-up-big-tech-9ad9e0da324c, accessed 1 August 2019

WhatsApp blog, Why We Don't Sell Ads (18 June 2012) https://blog.whatsapp.com/245/Why-we-dont-sell-ads?, accessed 1 August 2019

White A and Ali H, 'Google-Fitbit Probe Isn't for Data Watchdogs, Vestager Says' Bloomberg (25 February 2020) https://www.bloomberg.com/news/articles/2020-02-25/google-fitbit-probe-is-for-me-not-data-watchdogs-vestager-says, accessed 19 April 2020

Newspaper Articles

Bittle J, 'A Mark Zuckerberg Presidency Isn't Ridiculous – It's Terrifying' The Nation (18 August 2017) https://www.thenation.com/article/a-mark-zuckerberg-presidency-isnt-ridiculous-its-terrifying/, accessed 1 August 2019

Blumenthal R and Wu T, 'What the Microsoft Antitrust Case Taught Us' New York Times (18 May 2018) https://www.nytimes.com/2018/05/18/opinion/microsoft-antitrust-case.html, accessed 1 August 2019

Bork RH, 'Antitrust and Google' Chicago Tribune (6 April 2012) http://articles.chicagotribune.com/2012-04-06/opinion/ct-perspec-0405-bork-20120406_1_unpaid-search-results-search-engines-search-algorithms, accessed 1 August 2019

Bray C, 'EU Fines Qualcomm $1.2 Billion Over Apple Deal' New York Times (24 January 2018) https://www.nytimes.com/2018/01/24/business/eu-qualcomm-fine-antitrust.html, accessed 1 August 2019

Chee FY, 'German Regulator Well Suited to Investigate Facebook: EU's Vestager' Reuters Technology News (7 March 2016) https://www.reuters.com/article/us-eu-facebook-antitrust/german-regulator-well-suited-to-investigate-facebook-eus-vestager-idUSKCN0W91OB, accessed 1 August 2019

Cobbe J, 'Reining in Big Data's Robber Barons' NYR Daily (12 April 2018) http://www.nybooks.com/daily/2018/04/12/reining-in-big-datas-robber-barons/, accessed 1 August 2019

Coghill K, Reuters, 'China to Bar People with Bad "Social Credit" from Planes, Trains' Reuters (16 March 2018) https://www.reuters.com/article/us-china-credit/china-to-bar-people-with-bad-social-credit-from-planes-trains-idUSKCN1GS10S, accessed 1 August 2019

Cukier K, 'Data, Data Everywhere' The Economist (London, 25 February 2010) https://www.economist.com/node/15557443, accessed 1 August 2019

The Economist, 'Fuel of the Future: Data Is Giving Rise to a New Economy' (6 May 2017) https://www.economist.com/news/briefing/21721634-how-it-shaping-up-data-giving-rise-new-economy, accessed 1 August 2019

The Economist, 'Competition in the Digital Age: How to Tame the Tech Titans' (18 January 2018)

The Economist, Schumpeter 'The University of Chicago worries about a lack of competition' (12 April 2017) https://www.economist.com/news/business/21720657-its-economists-used-champion-big-firms-mood-has-shifted-university-chicago, accessed 1 August 2019

The Economist, 'The Techlash Against Amazon, Facebook and Google – And What They Can Do' (20 January 2018) https://www.economist.com/news/briefing/21735026-which-antitrust-remedies-welcome-which-fight-techlash-against-amazon-facebook-and, accessed 19 April 2020

The Economist, 'America should borrow from Europe's data-privacy law' (5 April 2018) https://www.economist.com/news/leaders/21739961-gdprs-premise-consumers-should-be-charge-their-own-personal-data-right, accessed 1 August 2019

The Economist, 'Economists Focus Too Little on What People Really Care About' (3 May 2018) https://www.economist.com/news/finance-and-economics/21741563-fourth-our-series-professions-shortcomings-economists-focus-too, accessed 1 August 2019

Foroohar R, 'Digital Economy – Privacy Is a Competitive Advantage' Financial Times (15 October 2017) https://amp.ft.com/content/0247b8f2-b012-11e7-beba-5521c713abf4?__twitter_impression=true, accessed 21 August 2019

Foroohar R, 'Antitrust Policy Is Ripe for a Rethink' The Economist (24 June 2018) https://www.ft.com/content/b5ce2342-7624-11e8-b326-75a27d27ea5f, accessed 1 August 2019

Freshfields Bruckhaus Deringer, 'The Digitised Economy' (2019) https://www.freshfields.com/en-gb/our-thinking/campaigns/antitrust-10-key-themes/the-digitised-economy/, accessed 19 April 2020

Frost L, 'France to Sue Google, Apple over Developer Contracts' Reuters (14 March 2018) https://www.reuters.com/article/us-apple-google-france/france-to-sue-google-apple-over-developer-contracts-minister-idUSKCN1GQ0SP, accessed 1 August 2019

Galloway S, 'Opinion: The Case for Breaking up Amazon, Apple, Facebook and Google' (8 February 2018) http://www.stern.nyu.edu/experience-stern/faculty-research/case-breaking-amazon-apple-facebook-and-google, accessed 5 March 2018 (full article as published in Esquire https://www.esquire.com/news-politics/a15895746/bust-big-tech-silicon-valley/?src=nl&mag=esq&list=nl_enl_news&date=020818, accessed 1 August 2019

Guniganti P, 'FCO Officials Defend Tech Decisions' Global Competition Review (10 September 2019) https://globalcompetitionreview.com/article/1197424/fco-officials-defend-tech-decisions, accessed 1 August 2019

Harari YN, 'The World after Coronavirus' Financial Times (20 March 2020) https://www.ft.com/content/19d90308-6858-11ea-a3c9-1fe6fedcca75, accessed 19 April 2020

Hubbard S, 'Why Fake News Is an Antitrust Problem' Forbes (10 January 2017) https://www.forbes.com/sites/washingtonbytes/2017/01/10/why-fake-news-is-an-antitrust-problem/2/#4752b2263f0d, accessed 1 August 2019

Ip G, 'The Antitrust Case Against Facebook, Google and Amazon' The Wall Street Journal (16 January 2018) https://www.wsj.com/articles/the-antitrust-case-against-facebook-google-amazon-and-apple-1516121561, accessed 1 August 2019

Iyer B, Subramaniam M and Srinivasa Rangan U, 'The Next Battle in Antitrust Will Be about Whether One Company Knows Everything About You' Harvard Business Review (6 July 2017) https://hbr.org/2017/07/the-next-battle-in-antitrust-will-be-about-whether-one-company-knows-everything-about-you, accessed 1 August 2019

Kayali L, Heikkilä M and Delcker J, 'Europe's Digital Vision, Explained' Politico (19 February 2020) https://www.politico.eu/article/europes-digital-vision-explained/, accessed 19 April 2020

Lomas N, 'Handshake Is a Personal Data Marketplace Where Users Get Paid to Sell Their Own Data' Techcrunch (2 September 2013) https://techcrunch.com/2013/09/02/handshake/, accessed 1 August 2019

Lyall S, 'Who Strikes Fear into Silicon Valley? Margrethe Vestager, Europe's Antitrust Enforcer' The New York Times (5 May 2018) https://www.nytimes.com/2018/

05/05/world/europe/margrethe-vestager-silicon-valley-data-privacy.html, accessed 1 August 2019

Manjoo F, 'Tech's Frightful Five: They've Got Us' The New York Times (10 May 2017) https://www.nytimes.com/2017/05/10/technology/techs-frightful-five-theyve-got-us.html, accessed 1 August 2019

Manthorpe R, 'Europe vs Silicon Valley: Behind Enemy Lines with the Woman Deciding Google's Fate' Wired (27 June 2017) http://www.wired.co.uk/article/who-is-margrethe-vestager, accessed 1 August 2019

McConnell C, 'Stucke: US Should Follow Europe's Lead on Privacy' Global Competition Review (14 August 2017) https://globalcompetitionreview.com/article/usa/1145542/stucke-us-should-follow-europes-lead-on-privacy, accessed 1 August 2019

Pressman A, 'Facebook Can't Fix This Problem Alone' Fortune (20 April 2018) http://fortune.com/2018/04/20/facebook-data-privacy-problem-fix/, accessed 1 August 2019

Press G, '12 Big Data Definitions: What's Yours?' Forbes (3 September 2014) https://www.forbes.com/sites/gilpress/2014/09/03/12-big-data-definitions-whats-yours/#61a4e10513ae, accessed 1 August 2019

Rich J, 'Beyond Facebook: It's High Time for Stronger Privacy Laws' Wired (8 April 2018) https://www.wired.com/story/beyond-facebook-its-high-time-for-stronger-privacy-laws, accessed 1 August 2019

Rice X, 'Margrethe Vestager: The EU Commissioner Who's Taming the Tech Giants' New Statesman (15 January 2018) https://www.newstatesman.com/science-tech/2018/01/margrethe-vestager-eu-commissioner-who-s-taming-tech-giants, accessed 1 August 2019

Rogers C, 'What Your Car Knows about You' The Wall Street Journal (18 August 2018) https://www.wsj.com/articles/what-your-car-knows-about-you-1534564861, accessed 1 August 2019

Satariano A, 'Apple's Deal for Shazam Is Delayed in Europe over Data Concerns' The New York Times (3 April 2018) https://www.nytimes.com/2018/04/23/business/apple-shazam-eu-data.html, accessed 1 August 2019

Siegele L, 'New EU Data Rules Will Get Tough on Privacy' The Economist (The World in 2018 Special Issue, December 2017) http://www.theworldin.com/article/14563/edition2018new-eu-data-rules-will-get-tough-privacy, accessed 1 August 2019

Srinivasan D, 'Why Privacy Is an Antitrust Issue' The New York Times (28 May 2019) https://www.nytimes.com/2019/05/28/opinion/privacy-antitrust-facebook.html, accessed 1 August 2019

Stucke ME, 'Here Are All the Reasons It's a Bad Idea to Let a Few Tech Companies Monopolize Our Data' Harvard Business Review (27 March 2018 https://hbr.org/2018/03/here-are-all-the-reasons-its-a-bad-idea-to-let-a-few-tech-companies-monopolize-our-data, accessed 1 August 2019

Stucke ME and Ezrachi A, 'The Rise, Fall, and Rebirth of the U.S. Antitrust Movement' (15 December 2017) https://hbr.org/2017/12/the-rise-fall-and-rebirth-of-the-u-s-antitrust-movement, accessed 1 August 2019

Swisher K, 'White House. Red Chair. Obama Meets Swisher' Recode (15 February 2015) https://www.recode.net/2015/2/15/11559056/white-house-red-chair-obama-meets-swisher, accessed 1 August 2019

Taplin J, 'Is It Time to Break Up Google?' New York Times (22 April 2017) https://www.nytimes.com/2017/04/22/opinion/sunday/is-it-time-to-break-up-google.html?smprod=nytcore-ipad&smid=nytcore-ipad-share&_r=0, accessed 1 August 2019

Taylor A, 'Denmark Is Naming an Ambassador Who Will Just Deal with Increasingly Powerful Tech Companies' The Washington Post (4 February 2017) https://www.washingtonpost.com/news/worldviews/wp/2017/02/04/denmark-is-naming-an-ambassador-who-will-just-deal-with-increasingly-powerful-tech-companies/?utm_term=.6745cbb270b5, accessed 1 August 2019

Tiku N, 'Digital Privacy Is Making Antitrust Exciting Again' Wired (6 April 2017) https://www.wired.com/2017/06/ntitrust-watchdogs-eye-big-techs-monopoly-data/, accessed 1 August 2019

Tiku N, 'How to Curb Silicon Valley Power – Even with Weak Antitrust Laws' Wired (5 January 2018) https://www.wired.com/story/how-to-curb-silicon-valley-power-even-with-weak-antitrust-laws/, accessed 1 August 2019

Vestager M, 'Competition in a Big Data World', DLD 16 (Munich, 17 January 2016) https://ec.europa.eu/commission/commissioners/2014-2019/vestager/announcements/competition-big-data-world_en, accessed 19 April 2020

Ward JS and Barker A, 'The Big Data Conundrum: How to Define It?' MIT Technology Review (3 October 2013) https://www.technologyreview.com/s/519851/the-big-data-conundrum-how-to-define-it/, accessed 1 August 2019

Waters R, 'Data Mining: Microsoft-LinkedIn Deal Raises New Competition Concerns' Financial Times (3 November 2016) https://www.ft.com/content/d5ceda60-a1e1-11e6-82c3-4351ce86813f, accessed 1 August 2019

White A and Levring P, 'Facebook Grilled by EU's Vestager Over WhatsApp Merger U-Turn' Bloomberg Technology (9 September 2016) https://www.bloomberg.com/news/articles/2016-09-09/facebook-grilled-by-eu-s-vestager-over-whatsapp-merger-u-turn, accessed 1 August 2019

Wingfield N and Benner K, 'How LinkedIn Drove a Wedge Between Microsoft and Salesforce' New York Times (5 November 2016) https://www.nytimes.com/2016/11/06/technology/how-linkedin-drove-a-wedge-between-microsoft-and-salesforce.html, accessed 1 August 2019

Press Releases

EU

European Commission, 'Commission appoints Professors Heike Schweitzer, Jacques Crémer and Assistant Professor Yves-Alexandre de Montjoye as Special Advisers to Commissioner Vestager on future challenges of digitalization for competition policy' (28 March 2018) https://ec.europa.eu/commission/commissioners/2014

-2019/vestager/announcements/commission-appoints-professors-heike-schweitzer-jacques-cremer-and-assistant-professor-yves_en, accessed 1 August 2019

European Commission, 'Antitrust: Commission sends statement of objections to Google on comparison shopping services; Opens separate formal investigation on Android' (15 April 2015) IP/15/4780

European Commission, 'Mergers: Commission seeks feedback on certain aspects of EU merger control' (Brussels, 7 October 2016) IP/16/3337

European Commission, 'Commission fines Google €2.42 billion for abusing dominance as search engine by giving illegal advantage to own comparison shopping service' (27 June 2017) IP/17/1784

European Commission, 'Mergers: Commission approves acquisition of WhatsApp by Facebook' (Brussels, 3 October 2014) IP/14/1088

European Commission, 'EU Commission and United States agree on new framework for transatlantic data flows: EU-US Privacy Shield' (Strasbourg, 2 February 2016) IP/16/216

European Commission, 'Mergers: Commission approves acquisition of LinkedIn by Microsoft, subject to conditions' (Brussels, 6 December 2016) IP/16/4284

European Commission, 'Mergers: Commission alleges Facebook provided misleading information about WhatsApp takeover' (Brussels, 20 December 2016) IP/16/4473

European Commission, 'Mergers: Commission fines Facebook €110 million for providing misleading information about WhatsApp takeover' (Brussels, 18 May 2017) IP/17/1369

European Commission, 'Mergers: Commission opens in-depth investigation into Apple's proposed acquisition of Shazam' (Brussels, 23 April 2018) IP/18/3505

European Commission, 'Mergers: Commission clears Apple's acquisition of Shazam' (Brussels, 6 September 2018) IP/18/5662

European Commission, 'Antitrust: Commission fines Google €4.34 billion for illegal practices regarding Android mobile devices to strengthen dominance of Google's search engine' (Brussels, 18 July 2018) IP/18/4581

US

Dissenting Statement of Commissioner Pamela Jones Harbour, Google/DoubleClick, FTC File No. 071-0170 (20 December 2007), available at http://www.ftc.gov/sites/default/files/documents/public_statements/statementmatter-google/doubleclick/071220harbour_0.pdf

FTC press release, 'FTC Imposes $5 Billion Penalty and Sweeping New Privacy Restrictions on Facebook' (24 July 2019), available at https://www.ftc.gov/news-events/press-releases/2019/07/ftc-imposes-5-billion-penalty-sweeping-new-privacy-restrictions

Statement of Federal Trade Commission, Google/DoubleClick, FTC File No. 071-0170, 3 (20 December 2007), available at http://www.ftc.gov/system/files/documents/public_statements/418081/071220googledc-commstmt.pdf

National

Australian Competition and Consumer Commission, 'ACCC commences inquiry into digital platforms' (4 December 2017) https://www.accc.gov.au/media-release/accc-commences-inquiry-into-digital-platforms, accessed 1 August 2019

Autorità Garante della Concorrenza e del Mercato, 'WhatsApp fined for 3 million euro for having forced its users to share their personal data with Facebook' (Rome, 12 May 2017)

Autorité de la Concurrence, Avis n° 18-A-03 portant sur l'exploitation des données dans le secteur de la publicité sur interne (6 March 2018)

Bundeskartellamt, Bundeskartellamt prohibits Facebook from combining user data from different sources (7 February 2019)

Bundeskartellamt, 'Bundeskartellamt launches sector inquiry into market conditions in online advertising sector' (1 February 2018)

Bundeskartellamt, 'Bundeskartellamt initiates proceeding against Facebook on suspicion of having abused its market power by infringing data protection rules' (2 March 2016)

Bundeskartellamt, 'Preliminary assessment in Facebook proceeding: Facebook's collection and use of data from third-party sources is abusive' (19 December 2017)

Higher Regional Court of Düsseldorf, 'Facebook: Anordnungen des Bundeskartellamts möglicherweise rechtswidrig und deshalb einstweilen außer Vollzug' (26 August 2019)

Images

Luks G, 'The Menace of the Hour' cartoon for *Verdict* Magazine (1899)

Rae A, 'Tech Octopus' cartoon for *Esquire* Magazine (2018)

Table of Cases

EU

EU Courts

European Court of Human Rights

Commission Decisions

United States

Northern Pacific Co v. United States, 356 US 1 (1958), 103
Olmstead v. United States, 277 US 438 (1928), 55
Roe v. Wade, 410 US 113 (1973), 55
Standard Oil v. United States, 221 US 1 (1911), 214
United States v. Alcoa, 148 F.2d 416 (2nd Cir 1945), 77
United States v. Bazaarvoice, No 3:2013cv00133 (ND Cal 2014), 80
US Supreme Court, Verizon Communications Inc v. Trinko, 40 U.S. 398 (2004), 77, 108
Complaint 2-3, *The TJX Cos*, FTC Docket No C-4227 (1 August 2008), 58
Complaint, 2-4, *Snapchat Inc.*, FTC File No 132 3078 (8 May 2014), 58
Complaint, 7-9, *Facebook Inc.*, FTC Docket No C-4635 (27 July 2012), 58
Statement by the FTC, *Google's Search Practices*, Google Inc., FTC File No 111-0163 (3 January 2013), 157

National

Autorità Garante della Concorrenza e del Mercato of 11 May 2017 in the WhatsApp Inc case, para 36. The original text of the decision in Italian is available at: www.agcm.it (20 August 2018), 52
Bundeskartellamt proceeding against Facebook on suspicion of having abused its market power by infringing data protection rules (2 March 2016), 6, 145
Bundesverfassungsgericht, judgment of 15 December 1983, NJW 1984, 419, 52
Higher Regional Court of Düsseldorf, Beschluss Facebook gegen Bundeskartellamt, VI-Kart 1/19 (V) (26 August 2019), 152

Table of Legislation

International

The Universal Declaration of Human Rights (adopted 10 December 1948) UNGA Res 217 A(III), 49

EU

Charter of Fundamental Rights of the European Union [2000] OJ C364/01 and [2010] OJ C83/389, 43

Consolidated Version of the Treaty on the Functioning of the European Union [2010] OJ C83/47, 87

Consolidated version of the Treaty on the Functioning of the European Union [2012] OJ C326/47, 24

Directive (EC) 95/46 of the European Parliament and of the Council of 24 October 1995 on the protection of individuals with regard to the processing of personal data and on the free movement of such data [1995] OJ L 281, 291

Directive 2002/58/EC of the European Parliament and of the Council of 12 July 2002 concerning the processing of personal data and the protection of privacy in the electronic communications sector, 50

Directive 93/13/EEC of 5 April 1993 on unfair terms in consumer contracts [1993] OJ L95/29, 137

Directive 2005/29/EC of the European Parliament and of the Council of 11 May 2005 on unfair commercial practices, 137

Regulation (EC) 2016/679 on the protection of natural persons with regard to the processing of personal data and on the free movement of such data [2016] OJ L 119, 37

Regulation of the European Parliament and of the Council concerning the respect for private life and the protection of personal data in electronic communications

Treaty of Lisbon Amending the Treaty of on European Union and the Treaty establishing the European Community [2007] C 306/01, 47, 49, 210

Commission Guidance

Guidance on the Application of Article 81(3) of the Treaty [2004] OJ C101/08, 72
Guidelines on the assessment of horizontal mergers under the Council Regulation on the control of concentrations between undertakings [2004] OJ C 31/03, 100
Guidelines on the assessment of non-horizontal mergers under the Council Regulation on the control of concentrations between undertakings [2008] OJ C 265/07, 185
Guidelines on the application of Article 101 of the Treaty on the Functioning of the European Union to horizontal co-operation agreements [2011] OJ C11, 186
Guidelines on Vertical Restraints [2010] OJ C 130/01, 100, 186
Guidance on the Commission's enforcement priorities in applying Article 82 of the EC treaty to abusive exclusionary conduct by dominant undertakings [2009] OJ C45/02, 99
Notice on the definition of relevant market for the purpose of Community competition law [1997] OJ C372, 186

Other

Article 29 Data Protection Working Party, 'Guidelines on Consent under Regulation 2016/679' (2017), 51

US

Clayton Act, 15 U.S.C. §§ 12-27, 29 USC §§ 52–53, 65, 102, 113
Federal Trade Commission Act, 15 USC § 45(a) Ch 311 § 5, 58
Federal Trade Commission Act, 15 USC §§ 41–58, as amended, 108
Health Insurance Portability and Accountability Act (1996, Pub I, No. 104–191, 110 Stat 1936, 56
Sherman Act, 15 USC § 2, 24, 27, 65, 70, 103–105, 107, 108, 111–113, 123, 214

National

Finnish Constitution 731/1999, *Suomen perustuslaki*, 45
German Act against Restraints of Competition – *GWB Bundesgesetzblatt* I 2013, 1750, 3245, 154
South Africa Competition Act 1998 (Act No 89 of 1998) (SA) 16), s 2(f), 84

Index

This index aims merely to complement the table of contents. As the entire book is about competition law, the use of this term and related terms occurring constantly throughout as entry points, have been minimized. Only key locations are identified, such as where a term referenced is defined in a chapter and information is found under the corresponding detailed topics.

C

D

E

INTERNATIONAL COMPETITION LAW SERIES

1. Ignacio De Leon, *Latin American Competition Law and Policy: A Policy in Search of Identity*, 2001 (ISBN 90-411-1542-0).
2. Wim Dejonghe & Wouter Van de Voorde (eds), *M & A in Belgium*, 2001 (ISBN 90-411-1594-3).
3. Yang-Ching Chao, Gee San, Changfa Lo & Jiming Ho (eds), *International and Comparative Competition Law and Policies*, 2001 (ISBN 90-411-1643-5).
4. Martin Mendelsohn & Stephen Rose, *Guide to the EC Block Exemption for Vertical Agreements*, 2002 (ISBN 90-411-9813-X).
5. Clifford A. Jones & Mitsuo Matsushita (eds), *Competition Policy in the Global Trading System: Perspectives from the EU, Japan and the USA*, 2002 (ISBN 90-411-1758-X).
6. Christian Koenig, Andreas Bartosch, Jens-Daniel Braun & Marion Romes (eds), *EC Competition and Telecommunications Law*. Second Edition, 2009 (ISBN 978-90-411-2564-4).
7. Jürgen Basedow (ed.), *Limits and Control of Competition with a View to International Harmonization*, 2002 (ISBN 90-411-1967-1).
8. Maureen Brunt, Economic Essays on Australian and New Zealand Competition Law, 2003 (ISBN 90-411-1991-4).
9. Ky P. Ewing, Jr., *Competition Rules for the 21st Century: Principles from America's Experience*, Second Edition, 2006 (ISBN 90-411-2477-2).
10. Joseph Wilson, *Globalization and the Limits of National Merger Control Laws*, 2003 (ISBN 90-411-1996-5).
11. Peter Verloop & Valérie Landes (eds), *Merger Control in Europe: EU, Member States and Accession States*, Fourth Edition, 2003 (ISBN 90-411-2056-4).
12. Themistoklis K. Giannakopoulos, *Safeguarding Companies' Rights in Competition and Anti-dumping/Anti-subsidies Proceedings*, Second Edition, 2011 (ISBN 978-90-411-3404-2).
13. Marjorie Holmes & Lesley Davey (eds), *A Practical Guide to National Competition Rules across Europe*, Second Edition, 2007 (ISBN 978-90- 411-2607-8).
14. Sigrid Stroux, *US and EU Oligopoly Control*, 2004 (ISBN 90-411-2296-6).
15. Tzong-Leh Hwang and Chiyuan Chen (eds), *The Future Development of Competition Framework*, 2004 (ISBN 90-411-2305-9).

16. Phedon Nicolaides, Mihalis Kekelekis and Maria Kleis, *State Aid Policy in the European Community: Principles and Practice*, Second Edition, 2008 (ISBN 978-90-411-2754-9).
17. Doris Hildebrand, *Economic Analyses of Vertical Agreements: A Self- Assessment*, 2005 (ISBN 90-411-2328-8).
18. Frauke Henning-Bodewig, *Unfair Competition Law: European Union and Member States*, 2005 (ISBN 90-411-2329-6).
19. Duarte Brito & Margarida Catalão-Lopes, *Mergers and Acquisitions: The Industrial Organization Perspective*, 2006 (ISBN 90-411-2451-9).
20. Nikos Th. Nikolinakos, *EU Competition Law and Regulation in the Converging Telecommunications, Media and IT Sectors*, 2006 (ISBN 90-411- 2469-1).
21. Mihalis Kekelekis, *The EC Merger Control Regulation: Rights of Defence. A Critical Analysis of DG COMP Practice and Community Courts' Jurisprudence*, 2006 (ISBN 90-411-2553-1).
22. Mark R. Joelson, *An International Antitrust Primer: A Guide to the Operation of United States, European Union and Other Key Competition Laws in the Global Economy*, Third Edition, 2006 (ISBN 90-411-2468-3).
23. Themistoklis K. Giannakopoulos, *A Concise Guide to the EU Anti-dumping/ Anti-subsidies Procedures*, 2006 (ISBN 90-411-2464-0).
24. George Cumming, Brad Spitz & Ruth Janal, *Civil Procedure Used for Enforcement of EC Competition Law by the English, French and German Civil Courts*, 2007 (ISBN 978-90-411-2471-5).
25. Jürgen Basedow (ed.), *Private Enforcement of EC Competition Law*, 2007 (ISBN 978-90-411-2613-9).
26. Jung Wook Cho, *Innovation and Competition in the Digital Network Economy: A Legal and Economic Assessment on Multi-tying Practices and Network Effects*, 2007 (ISBN 978-90-411-2574-3).
27. Akira Inoue, *Japanese Antitrust Law Manual: Law, Cases and Interpretation of the Japanese Antimonopoly Act*, 2007 (ISBN 978-90-411-2627-6).
28. René Barents, *Directory of EC Case Law on Competition*, 2007 (ISBN 978-90-411-2656-6).
29. Paul F. Nemitz (ed.), *The Effective Application of EU State Aid Procedures: The Role of National Law and Practice*, 2007 (ISBN 978-90-411-2657-3).
30. Jurian Langer, *Tying and Bundling as a Leveraging Concern under EC Competition Law*, 2007 (ISBN 978-90-411-2575-0).
31. Abel M. Mateus & Teresa Moreira (eds), *Competition Law and Economics – Advances in Competition Policy and Antitrust Enforcement*, 2007 (ISBN 978-90-411-2632-0).
32. Alberto Santa Maria, *Competition and State Aid: An Analysis of the EC Practice*, 2007 (ISBN 978-90-411-2617-7).
33. Barry J. Rodger (ed.), *Article 234 and Competition Law: An Analysis*, 2007 (ISBN 978-90-411-2605-4).

34. Alla Pozdnakova, *Liner Shipping and EU Competition Law*, 2008 (ISBN 978-90-411-2717-4).
35. Milena Stoyanova, *Competition Problems in Liberalized Telecommunications: Regulatory Solutions to Promote Effective Competition*, 2008 (ISBN 978-90-411-2736-5).
36. *EC State Aid Law/Le Droit des Aides d'Etat dans la CE. Liber Amicorum Francisco Santaolalla Gadea*, 2008 (ISBN 978-90-411-2774-7).
37. René Barents, *Directory of EU Case Law on State Aids*, Third Edition, 2019 (ISBN 978-94-035-1101-6).
38. Ignacio De Leon, *An Institutional Assessment of Antitrust Policy: The Latin American Experience*, 2009 (ISBN 978-90-411-2478-4).
39. Doris Hildebrand, *The Role of Economic Analysis in EU Competition Law: The European School*, Fourth Edition, 2016 (ISBN 978-90-411-6245-8).
40. Eugène Buttigieg, *Competition Law: Safeguarding the Consumer Interest. A Comparative Analysis of US Antitrust Law and EC Competition Law*, 2009 (ISBN 978-90-411-3119-5).
41. Ioannis Lianos & Ioannis Kokkoris (eds), *The Reform of EC Competition Law: New Challenges*, 2010 (ISBN 978-90-411-2692-4).
42. George Cumming & Mirjam Freudenthal, *Civil Procedure in EU Competition Cases before the English and Dutch Courts*, 2010 (ISBN 978-90-411-3192-8).
43. A.E. Rodriguez & Ashok Menon, *The Limits of Competition Policy: The Shortcomings of Antitrust in Developing and Reforming Economies*, 2010 (ISBN 978-90-411-3177-5).
44. Mika Oinonen, *Does EU Merger Control Discriminate against Small Market Companies? Diagnosing the Argument with Conclusions*, 2010 (ISBN 978-90-411-3261-1).
45. Eirik Østerud, *Identifying Exclusionary Abuses by Dominant Undertakings under EU Competition Law: The Spectrum of Tests*, 2010 (ISBN 978-90-411-3271-0).
46. Marco Botta, *Merger Control Regimes in Emerging Economies: A Case Study on Brazil and Argentina*, 2011 (ISBN 978-90-411-3402-8).
47. Jürgen Basedow & Wolfgang Wurmnest (eds), *Structure and Effects in EU Competition Law: Studies on Exclusionary Conduct and State Aid*, 2011 (ISBN 978-90-411-3174-4).
48. George Cumming (ed.), *Merger Decisions and the Rules of Procedure of the European Community Courts*, 2012 (ISBN 978-90-411-3671-8).
49. Eduardo Molan Gaban & Juliana Oliveira Domingues (eds), *Antitrust Law in Brazil: Fighting Cartels*, 2012 (ISBN 978-90-411-3670-1).
50. Giandonato Caggiano, Gabriella Muscolo & Marina Tavassi (eds), *Competition Law and Intellectual Property: A European Perspective*, 2012 (ISBN 978-90-411-3447-9).
51. Ben Van Rompuy, *Economic Efficiency: The Sole Concern of Modern Antitrust Policy? Non-efficiency Considerations under Article 101 TFEU*, 2012 (ISBN 978-90-411-3870-5).

52. Liyang Hou, *Competition Law and Regulation of the EU Electronic Communications Sector: A Comparative Legal Approach*, 2012 (ISBN 978-90-411-4047-0).
53. Barry Rodger, *Landmark Cases in Competition Law: Around the World in Fourteen Stories*, 2012 (ISBN 978-90-411-3843-9).
54. Andreas Scordamaglia-Tousis, *EU Cartel Enforcement: Reconciling Effective Public Enforcement with Fundamental Rights*, 2013 (ISBN 978-90-411-4758-5).
55. Bernardo Cortese (ed.), *EU Competition Law: Between Public and Private Enforcement*, 2014 (ISBN 978-90-411-4677-9).
56. Barry Rodger (ed.), *Competition Law: Comparative Private Enforcement and Collective Redress across the EU*, 2014 (ISBN 978-90-411-4559-8).
57. Nada Ina Pauer, *The Single Economic Entity Doctrine and Corporate Group Responsibility in European Antitrust Law*, 2014 (ISBN 978-90-411-5262-6).
58. Urška Petrovčič, *Competition Law and Standard Essential Patents: A Transatlantic Perspective*, 2014 (ISBN 978-90-411-4960-2).
59. David Telyas, *The Interface between Competition Law, Patents and Technical Standards*, 2014 (ISBN 978-90-411-5418-7).
60. Katerina Maniadaki, *EU Competition Law, Regulation and the Internet: The Case of Net Neutrality*, 2014 (ISBN 978-90-411-4140-8).
61. Horacio Vedia Jerez, *Competition Law Enforcement and Compliance across the World: A Comparative Review*, 2015 (ISBN 978-90-411-5815-4).
62. Kadir Ba, *The Substantive Appraisal of Joint Ventures under the EU Merger Control Regime*, 2015 (ISBN 978-90-411-5816-1).
63. Alberto Santa Maria, *Competition and State Aid: An Analysis of the EU Practice*, Second Edition, 2015 (ISBN 978-90-411-5818-5).
64. Lúcio Tomé Feteira, *The Interplay between European and National Competition Law after Regulation 1/2003: "United (Should) We Stand?"*, 2016 (ISBN 978-90-411-5663-1).
65. Giovanni Pitruzzella & Gabriella Muscolo (eds), *Competition and Patent Law in the Pharmaceutical Sector: An International Perspective*, 2016 (ISBN 978-90-411-5927-4).
66. Małgorzata Cyndecka, *The Market Economy Investor Test in EU State Aid Law: Applicability and Application*, 2016 (ISBN 978-90-411-6102-4).
67. Damiano Canapa, *Trademarks and Brands in Merger Control: An Analysis of the European and Swiss Legal Orders*, 2016 (ISBN 978-90-411-6717-0).
68. Inge Graef, *EU Competition Law, Data Protection and Online Platforms: Data as Essential Facility*, 2016 (ISBN 978-90-411-8324-8).
69. Anders Jessen, *Exclusionary Abuse after the* Post Danmark I *Case: The Role of the Effects-Based Approach under Article 102 TFEU*, 2017 (ISBN 978-90-411-8996-7).
70. Baskaran Balasingham, *The EU Leniency Policy: Reconciling Effectiveness and Fairness*, 2017 (ISBN 978-90-411-8479-5).
71. Eugene Stuart & Iana Roginska-Green, *Sixty Years of EU State Aid Law and Policy: Analysis and Assessment*, 2018 (ISBN 978-90-411-8869-4).

72. Anna Renata Pisarkiewicz, *Margin Squeeze in the Electronic Communications Sector: Critical Analysis of the Decisional Practice and Case Law*, 2018 (ISBN 978-90-411-6246-5).
73. Ploykaew Porananond, *Competition Law in the ASEAN Countries: Regional Law and National Systems*, 2018 (ISBN 978-90-411-9102-1).
74. Corinne Ruechardt, *EU State Aid Control of Infrastructure Funding*, 2018 (ISBN 978-90-411-9099-4).
75. Amalia Athanasiadou, *Patent Settlements in the Pharmaceutical Industry under US Antitrust and EU Competition Law*, 2018 (ISBN 978-94-035-0113-0).
76. Miroslava Marinova, *Fidelity Rebates in Competition Law: Application of the 'As Efficient Competitor' Test*, 2018 (ISBN 978-94-035-0570-1).
77. Gabriella Muscolo & Marina Tavassi, *The Interplay Between Competition Law and Intellectual Property: An International Perspective*, 2019 (ISBN 978-90-411-8687-4).
78. Fevzi Toksoy, Bahadir Balki & Hanna Stakheyeva, *Merger Control in the EU and Turkey: A Comparative Guide*, 2019 (ISBN 978-94-035-0934-1).
79. Paulo Burnier da Silveira & William Evan Kovacic (eds), *Global Competition Enforcement: New Players, New Challenges*, 2019 (ISBN 978-94-035-0283-0).
80. Giovanna Massarotto, *Antitrust Settlements: How a Simple Agreement Can Drive the Economy*, 2019 (ISBN 978-94-035-1133-7).
81. Marc Veenbrink, *Criminal Law Principles and the Enforcement of EU and National Competition Law: A Silent Takeover?*, 2020 (ISBN 978-94-035-1434-5).
82. Ferdinand Wollenschläger, Wolfgang Wurmnest & Thomas M.J. Möllers (eds), *Private Enforcement of European Competition and State Aid Law: Current Challenges and the Way Forward*, 2020 (ISBN 978-94-035-0281-6).
83. Jorge Marcos Ramos, *Firm Dominance in EU Competition Law: The Competitive Process and the Origins of Market Power*, 2020 (ISBN 978-94-035-2030-8).
84. Ingrid Margrethe Halvorsen Barlund, *Leniency in EU Competition Law*, 2020 (ISBN 978-94-035-1722-3).
85. Jan Blockx, Mens Rea *in EU Antitrust Law: When Intentions Matter*, 2020 (ISBN 978-94-035-2353-8).
86. Maria Wasastjerna, *Competition, Data and Privacy in the Digital Economy: Towards a Privacy Dimension in Competition Policy?*, 2020 (ISBN 978-94-035-2220-3).